W9-BKJ-320

PHYSICAL
DISABILITY—
A PSYCHOLOGICAL
APPROACH

Under the Editorship of Gardner Murphy

PHYSICAL DISABILITY– A PSYCHOLOGICAL APPROACH

Beatrice A. Wright
Department of Psychology
University of Kansas

HARPER & ROW, PUBLISHERS
New York and Evanston

To My C.R.E.W.

Contents

Foreword

HUMAN PHYSIQUE HAS A CENTRAL PLACE IN NAIVE, COMMON-SENSE PSY-
chology. It is generally believed that a person's body influences his behavior by way of the many phenomenal properties it has for him and his
associates, and by way of its greater or lesser efficiency as the instrument
with which he attempts to carry out intended actions. Variations in physical size, beauty, and normality, for example, are widely presumed by
businessmen, artists, and athletes, by politicians, suitors, and doctors to
be important causal variables within the total context of factors which
determine behavior and personality. One common theory is expressed by
Shakespeare in *Richard III*, where the crippled Richard, Duke of
Gloucester, says:

> But I, that am not shaped for sportive tricks,
> Nor made to court an amorous looking-glass;
> I, that am rudely stamp'd and want love's majesty
> To strut before a wanton ambling nymph;
> I, that am curtail'd of this fair proportion,
> Cheated of feature by dissembling nature,
> Deform'd, unfinish'd, sent before my time
> Into this breathing world, scarce half made up,
> And that so lamely and unfashionable
> That dogs bark at me as I halt by them;
> . . . .
> . . . since I cannot prove a lover,
> To entertain these fair well-spoken days,
> I am determined to prove a villain
> And hate the idle pleasures of these days.
> Plots have I laid, ...

An opposed view is given by Robert Burton in his *Anatomy of Melan-
choly:*

Deformities and imperfections of our bodies, as lameness, crookedness, deafness, blindness, be they innate or accidental, torture many men: yet this may
comfort them that those imperfections of the body do not a whit blemish the
soul, or hinder the operations of it, but rather help and much increase it.

xiii

Scientific psychology has not in the past been much concerned with these kinds of relations between physique and behavior; it has emphasized other body-mind interdependencies; for example, those between the brain and behavior, emotions and ulcers, the cochlea and hearing, genes and intelligence, and hormones and personality characteristics. When the phenomenal and instrumental interconnections between the psyche and the soma have been considered by psychologists, they have usually been discussed in terms of rather unsystematic, recondite processes such as body image, organ inferiority, and cathexis to disabled parts; or they have been seen as mere technological problems for psychological practitioners who deal with the education, employment, or counseling of disabled persons.

Dr. Wright's book provides welcome evidence that a change is taking place in psychology with respect to these matters, and that the phenomenal and instrumental significance of physique is receiving a new and deserved emphasis. *Physical Disability—A Psychological Approach* is much more than a symptom of this change, however; it makes important contributions to the new development by carefully collating available data and relevant theories, by contributing new concepts and interpretations, and by integrating the whole problem within the context of persisting psychological issues. Altogether, Dr. Wright makes an impressive case for considering somatopsychology, as it has been called, a valid subdivision of the science of psychology, with a unique syndrome of facts, theories, and investigatory and therapeutic techniques. Every psychological theoretician would do well to confront his system with the facts of life and of psychological science to which Dr. Wright draws our attention.

As is proper in the early days of a new scientific development, Dr. Wright has a place in her book for diverse viewpoints and facts. She is not limited by a narrow theoretical partisanship. On the other hand, *Physical Disability—A Psychological Approach* is not merely eclectic; an organized conception of the somatopsychology of physique emerges.

Physical Disability—A Psychological Approach marks a milestone for the professions that deal in practical ways with the behavior and adjustment of physically deviant persons. It places the psychological side of disablement within a framework of sound concepts, and in doing so contributes in an important way to making rehabilitation psychology an applied science rather than, as heretofore, a welfare specialty based largely on experience and art. Her own extensive, practical experience with these matters saves Dr. Wright from leaving reality behind and soaring too soon into scientific outer space. The wealth of concrete examples she presents and her ability to deal with complicated issues without using an unduly technical language will make the *Physical Disability—A*

Psychological Approach of interest and value to a wide range of professional people.

ROGER G. BARKER
Professor of Psychology
University of Kansas

Preface

THROUGHOUT RECORDED HISTORY, AND PROBABLY BEFORE, MAN HAS BEEN intrigued by the possibility that the outward characteristics of physique might in some way be a guide to the inner nature of man, to his temperament, his character, his personality. It is not difficult to understand how such a deep-seated belief might become established.

In daily contacts there are many cues from physique, posture, clothing, and other aspects of outward appearance that serve to give information about a person's calling and habits. This identifying information readily breeds the impression that one "knows" more about the individual's personality than is actually the case. The philosophical tenet that holds man to be an essential unity, that the mind and the body are different aspects of the same individual, lends intellectual support to the belief in the intimate interdependence of physique and personality. Scientific investigations of psychosomatic medicine provide many indications of the effects of sustained emotional states upon the physical condition of man. Inversely, there are instances in which obvious physical stigmata, such as in cretinism, imply defects in mental functioning. Finally, it is only with sophisticated restraint that one guards against the jump from the incontrovertible fact that physique is an important determiner of behavior to the tempting conclusion that personality is manifested in physique.

There has been a sobering balance to the readiness to accept body-mind connections uncritically, however. Most of the inferences about personality based on physical signs have found no factual support in systematic investigation. Where relationships are revealed, the correlations are typically low. Ideologically speaking, the belief in free will has led some to look askance at physical constants that impose limitations on man's nature. If features of the face, or deformities of the body, or meanderings of body chemistry bespeak and determine personality, then man to some extent becomes a pawn of impersonal forces. The democratic viewpoint has also tended to find it more congenial to focus on environmental conditions, especially those controllable by man, rather than on immutable hereditary and physical factors under which man must bow. Particularly in American democracy, which upholds the value of man's rugged individualism and prefers the notion that man's future is determined by his own dogged will and ingenuity and not by coercive limitations on any front, did the emphasis tend to become the one of choice. Deeper analysis, of course, shows that there is no basic contradiction between these ideological viewpoints and the search for body-mind interrelationships, for the fact that man to some extent is influenced by impersonal factors does not keep him from influencing the course of events as well. He is as much a determining organism as one that is determined.

The present volume is concerned with one segment of the relation between man and his physique, namely, the somatopsychological problem as seen in disablement. The emphasis is on the kinds of social-psychological situations that confront a person with an atypical physique, and how he copes with them. Factors within the person and factors attributable to the environment are considered in terms of how they aid psychological adjustment or, on the negative side, how they create difficulties.

Many topics of importance to the problem of adjustment to disability do not appear within the pages of this volume, the reasons for exclusion being varied. First of all there is the matter of author limitations. The theoretical background and range of experience and competency naturally tend to prescribe certain questions and exclude others. Foreign references, unfortunately, are notable by their absence. Then there is the direction indicated by available research and the considered thinking of others. Moreover, the scope of a single book must perforce be limited, and the outlines become dictated in part by the substance initially worked through.

There is no doubt that to some extent the contents of this volume have been shaped by preconceived notions, but it should also be noted that they have been reshaped as the evidence of scientific investigation and considered opinion added to the perspective of the person as an active agent in meeting the impositions of a disability. Since fiction far more than fact characterizes many ideas about psychological aspects of disability, it is well to embark upon the reading of this book with an eye critical of those personal views that have long been cherished as well as of those that may here be proposed in their place. Certainly not all the assertions made have scientific validity. But it is hoped that many of them are supported by sound psychological thinking and by research evidence where possible. In any case all of them are advanced "until further notice."

I should like to say a few words about the personal documents as used herein. Because most of them are taken from literary productions written by the person himself, they sample predominantly the introspections of persons who are highly verbal, thoughtful, and who have a solid complement of psychological resources as well. But the purpose of these documents is not to prove the theoretical position advanced—rather the purpose is to illuminate it. Through the documents a vividness is achieved, a concreteness and exemplification of what might otherwise appear as too abstract and theoretical for the reality of psychological man. It is for this reason that the book was designed as a combination text and case book. Those readers who have a good deal of familiarity with problems of disability will easily be able to skim over the case material, but for others it illustrates the living situations in which the problems under discussion occur. It is also believed that many of the psychological events portrayed in the personal accounts are not unlike, in principle, those which touch the lives of the more drab, plodding, and unimaginative. Insofar as psychological principles are being expounded, the specification of causes and effects allows exemplification through the pertinent life history. At the same time, longitudinal records of the lives of persons among the less articulate and less successful with different disabling conditions would be valuable as a source of new insights as well as a check of old ones.

This volume was written for the practitioner in the field of rehabilitation, especially for the professional in training, though I would like to believe that the research worker will also find some leads for productive exploration. Because "the practitioner" covers a wide range of professions —medicine and nursing; occupational, physical, and speech therapy; social work, psychology, and psychiatry, to mention a few—and because in some instances the patient as well as his family may be interested in the material, an attempt was made to avoid technical language communicable only to "the trade." That some readers will find particular sections "too simple" or "too difficult" is foreseen, which situation can be used to advantage if the individual reader will select for more careful study those chapters that hold promise for him.

The recognition that one's own work is also in many ways the product of those from whom one has learned leads me to think about my psychological lineage. If I had to single out a handful of my teachers and colleagues who had the greatest impact on my thinking as a psychologist, the following would be high on the list: Solomon Asch, Roger Barker, Tamara Dembo, Fritz Heider, Kurt Lewin, Carl Rogers, and Erik Wright. Their mark is indelibly impressed in many of the ideas elaborated in this book and would be detectable even if no mention had been made of them.

I wish to express my thankfulness to those who have read all or parts of the manuscript: Roger Barker, Louise Barker, David Klein, June Kounin, Gardner Murphy, Stephen Richardson, Phil Schoggen, Anthony Smith, and Erik Wright. Their suggestions have led to wise clarification in the treatment of several of the problems discussed. The editorial acumen of David Klein was especially valuable in tightening the manuscript and detecting obscurities. It is also a pleasure to mention with gratitude the Association for the Aid of Crippled Children, who provided a grant and editorial assistance in support of this undertaking and patiently awaited its completion in spite of the vicissitudes that marked its course.

To the publishers who gave permission to use the material quoted, special thanks. The reference sources are generally indicated by author and date, referring to items in the bibliography.

I feel a special bond of friendship and indebtedness to those whose personal documents were used freely in the discussion. I only hope that reference to the details of their lives and innermost feelings, most of them from published sources, will be taken not as an intrusion into their privacy but as a contribution to the understanding of social-psychological factors important in adjustment to disability.

These remarks are strangely incomplete without the expression of my deepest feelings to my family—my husband, children, and parents—who did so much to make possible the completion of this book.

BEATRICE A. WRIGHT

November, 1959

PHYSICAL DISABILITY— A PSYCHOLOGICAL APPROACH

Circumscribing the Problem

AT CERTAIN TIMES AND PLACES, PARTICULAR FIELDS OF INVESTIGATION enjoy wide interest and prestige. In psychology, for example, the study of mental aberrations—the psychoses and severe neuroses—holds such a position today, whereas the study of adjustment to physical disability is only beginning to be regarded as a serious area of investigation by more than a few isolated psychologists.

That the place of the psychology of disability is secure, however, is guaranteed by several considerations of far-reaching importance. First of all, psychological knowledge gained from diverse fields can fruitfully be brought to bear on problems of physical disability, thereby reducing suffering and disablement and facilitating adjustment. Many concepts and findings "belonging" to the traditional areas of social psychology, perception psychology, and clinical and counseling psychology appear throughout the topics treated in this book, the title of which might appropriately have been *General Psychology Applied to Disability Problems.*

An equally exciting consideration is that direct study of the psychological aspects of disability is producing new knowledge that applies far beyond its immediate context. Just as probing into mental illness produced insights into many psychological phenomena that were later seen to be relevant to the mentally normal, so the examination of problems associated with physical illness and disability forces attention to important areas of general human behavior that otherwise tend to be neglected. The matter of accepting the loss of something valuable (Chap. 5) is one such area. The phenomena designated as the requirement of mourning (Chap. 9) are another. Problems arising from ordinary interrelationships, such as helping, sympathizing, pitying, staring, and questioning (Chap. 9), constitute a third. The idolizing of normal standards of behavior (Chap. 2) is still another. Even the sophisticated psychologist, we believe, will find several new signposts pointing toward the understanding of unexplored and vital areas of human nature.

The psychological aspects of disability as an area of investigation are also receiving higher priority with the recognition that most people are at some time forced, either directly or indirectly, to meet the challenge of disability. That the number of persons with physical disabilities is large is seen from the following brief sample (National Health Education Committee, 1955):[1]

Deaf and hard of hearing	4,560,000
Orthopedic impairments	3,168,000
Epilepsy	1,500,000
Blind and partially sighted	600,000
Cerebral palsy	550,000[2]

If family members and friends are legitimately included among those concerned, the number immediately affected becomes enormous. If we further consider the fact that adjustment to disability is made easier by wholesome preparation for this eventuality, especially when such preparation is facilitated by the attitudes and behavior of society, then nò one is excluded from having a vital stake in discoveries relating to psychological aspects of disability.

With the recognition that the psychological aspects of disability may be more handicapping than the physical aspects comes the realization that a psychological look at disability problems is imperative. Actually, in view of the democratic tenet that "all men are created equal," in the sense that the dignity and worthiness of the individual stand above differences in endowment, one does not have to seek additional justification for holding that the area of physical disability must command scientific attention.

THE SCOPE OF QUESTIONS CONSIDERED

Our broad concern will be with the way in which the person with a disability copes with its social and personal connotations, these being aroused by the fact that the disability imposes certain limitations and is felt as a loss or denial of something valuable. We shall explore some of the social-psychological conditions that hamper adjustment and those that facilitate constructive efforts. These matters are in the domain of what has been called the *somatopsychological* relation, a relation dealing with "those variations in physique that affect the psychological situation of a person by influencing the effectiveness of his body as a tool for actions or by serving as a stimulus to himself or others" (Barker *et al., 1953*:1). This is to be distinguished from the psychosomatic relation: that is, the

[1] Dates within parentheses refer to works listed in the bibliography, pp. 381–394.

[2] These figures are estimates for the U.S. based on information supplied by voluntary health groups and government agencies. More precise data can be expected from the continuing annual survey of the extent and nature of illness and disability in the U.S. inaugurated by federal legislation in 1956.

relationship between the mental and emotional characteristics of a person and his predisposition toward certain types of organic dysfunction. The psychosomatic problem is conceptually distinct from the somatopsychological and is not discussed in this volume.[3]

The somatopsychological relationship involves social-psychological factors: that is, conditions that depend upon the interaction between the person and others. Much of the psychology of the individual is, in fact, a social psychology, for the way in which one feels and behaves about many things depends in greater or smaller measure upon one's relationship to other persons. Problems that on first appraisal may seem to be purely personal often reveal, on more careful scrutiny, a social basis. Consider the person whose disability permits him to accomplish the basic routines of living, such as dressing or eating, only with great effort. One might feel that the difficulty resulting from the wide gap between his abilities and the task requirements has nothing to do with the social environment. Yet, when we recognize that some—and often an important part—of his difficulty stems from his expectations that he must eat in a certain way and wear certain clothes, *ways of behaving prescribed by society,* we realize that understanding the individual requires social-psychological understanding.

We are sure that there are far fewer psychological experiences peculiar to persons with physical disabilities than an offhand guess might indicate. Even in the case of sensory loss, as in blindness or deafness, the psychological significance of the deprivation has to do in large measure with such matters as the threat of social isolation, the struggle for independence, acceptance of a personal limitation, and so on—experiences with which many, if not all, human beings are conversant. Throughout this volume an effort is made to point out the generality of the concepts used as well as to apply generally used concepts to the disability-connected problem under discussion.

At the same time, certain kinds of psychological situation appear with such intensity in the lives of many persons with disabilities that these persons are forced to cope with them directly and to come to terms with themselves as human beings. The following scenes sample some of the great dramatic episodes experienced *in principle* by large segments of humanity, including the nondisabled, and, in their concrete manifestations, by many persons with disabilities.

Louise, a young woman who suffered the loss of one leg in childhood and is now on crutches, encounters prejudice in looking for a job:

[3] For a systematic statement differentiating several types of connection between a person and his disability see Barker *et al.* (*1953:*1–8). For an overall account of the psychosomatic problem and evidence bearing upon it, see Weiss and English (*1943*), Wittkower and Cleghorn (*1954*), and Dunbar (*1954*).

[I had] a letter in my purse which introduced me, with some flattering phrases, to the field secretary of a large national girls' organization. . . . I had operated for four summers on the Pacific Coast as a counselor in the camps of this organization. According to the Los Angeles executive, my work was highly satisfactory. She had used me in various capacities—camp craft, handcraft, swimming, hiking, etc. The children liked me and I had no discipline problems. . . .

In fact, the Los Angeles executive was sufficiently impressed to express the opinion that I had something of a talent for leading the young. She encouraged me to consider seriously the possibility of a career in her organization. With this in mind, she equipped me with the introduction and suggested that I . . . discuss the matter with the national executive. . . .

I was completely unprepared for the blasting brushoff I got. . . .

She [the field secretary] told me that with my horrible handicap I should never for a moment consider an active job that involved leadership of young people or contact with the public. Her implication was not only that I was halt, but that the very sight of me would warp a sensitive young mind.

In frantic haste to justify my mad entertainment of such ridiculous heresy, I tried to tell her how fast I could swim, how far I could hike, and all about my four summers in camp and the serenely happy and uncomplicated reactions of all the children I had shepherded.

I didn't talk very well because there was a sob suffocating its lonely self in my tight throat. I finally left and walked twenty-two blocks to my hotel rather than get in a taxi and let the driver see me cry [Baker, *1946:*128–131].[4]

Russell Criddle, an adolescent with sufficiently poor vision to be classified as blind, rejects pity and suffers the anguish of not being wanted as a dating partner:

I was further disturbed when I sensed that others were pitying me for my loneliness. I learned to pretend that I was not lonely, just as I pretended that I could see, but this pretense was far more difficult. A subtle advance, and a subtle rejection, one girl telling another, and it soon became general knowledge that I was an unwanted person. Had a girl felt attracted toward me it would have been humiliating indeed for her to have accepted me after ninety per cent of her associates had turned me down. I sensed all this, even then, and was ever alert for new girls, new faces, new circles of friends.

One night Bud arranged a party date for me with a cousin who was visiting his family. Bud neglected to tell her about my eyes, and she did not discover my handicap until the evening was well advanced. She had seemed to like me, and I had sensed her acceptance of me. But when she found me out she was so distraught that she left alone, without even waiting for the cake and ice cream [Criddle, *1953:*54–55].[5]

[4] Reprinted by permission from *Out on a Limb* by Louise Baker, published by McGraw-Hill Book Company, Copyright 1946 by Louise Baker.

[5] Reprinted from *Love Is Not Blind* by Russell Criddle by permission of W. W. Norton & Company, Inc. Copyright 1953 by Russell Criddle.

Wally, a 4-year-old boy seriously crippled from poliomyelitis, is angered and frustrated as he struggles to get his coaster wagon up a low incline between the road and sidewalk, a situation that would have been easily mastered by a nondisabled child:

9:44 a.m. Using the wagon as a prop and holding onto it with both hands, he pulled himself up off the ground from a sitting position. He put one knee in the wagon, and with the other knee began propelling himself up the short hill to the sidewalk. About halfway up, the weight seemed to be too much for him. He struggled hard. Then he rolled out of the wagon, sat down on the ground with a helpless air and held the wagon in place with both hands on the back end of the wagon. He sat behind the wagon with an expression of futility. He rolled over on his side till he was at the side of the wagon and held on. The wagon rolled back slightly.

9:45. With one hand he picked up a clod of dirt. He seemed to be angered at the difficulty he was now having with the wagon. He threw the clod into the ditch and shouted angrily, "Damned old mud!" He sat for a moment and glared at the muddy ditch [Barker and H. Wright, *1948–51*].

That there are triumphs in the lives of persons with disabilities, triumphs that arise in disability-connected situations, is just as important as the fact that there are suffering and failure.

In Wally's case, as he sat throwing the clod and casting imprecations at the mud, new ways to solve the problem began to dominate his attention, ending in victory.

9:45. Wally rolled over and, using the wagon as a prop, lifted himself up. With what seemed renewed determination, he put one knee in the wagon and with the other foot started to push the wagon up the hill. Since it was difficult for him to go directly up the hill, he tried to lessen the grade by taking a diagonal path up the hill. He turned the wagon to the left and pushed hard. He got caught in some weeds off the path along the side.

9:46. It was quite a struggle but he kept pushing strenuously. He rolled out of the wagon and tried to push the wagon with his hands. He pushed it up and tried to crawl up behind it but this was difficult because the wagon would not stay up; while he crawled, the wagon rolled back down. He had to block it with his body to prevent it from rolling all the way down the hill. Wally looked up at me [the observer]. He was getting quite annoyed at the whole procedure. He asked hopefully, "Will you pull me up?" I asked him kindly, "Well, what would you do if I weren't here?"

9:47. He smiled quizzically and coaxed, "Pull me up." I said, "Well, would you pull up yourself if I weren't here?" Again he smiled. He turned around with what seemed a little more determination. He put one knee in the wagon and, with a great effort, strenuously pushed the wagon up. The wagon moved up the hill. He looked at me and said determinedly, "I'm getting up," as though he were showing me that he could do it himself if I weren't there. After a good deal of struggling he finally pushed the wagon up onto the cement sidewalk. When he got it up onto the cement sidewalk, he gave one final hard push. *9:48.* The wagon suddenly moved forward on the sidewalk and he fell flat on his stomach. He accepted this matter-of-factly. He crawled up to the wagon and got in it. Then he turned around, looked at me and said with pride in his voice, "I made it" [Barker and H. Wright, *1948–51*].

So it was with the others. Russell Criddle, once rejected as a dating partner, eventually met the girl he was to marry. Louise, once denied a job because of her crippling, persisted until she found work to her liking. We do not wish to imply that all ends well in the lives of persons with disabilities, but we do wish to emphasize that satisfactions, and not sorrows only, are well represented.

Difficulties and triumphs, some having their source in the person himself, some primarily in the social environment—these will crop up at every turn of our exploration into the factors that serve man and those that hinder him in his efforts to live effectively and comfortably with a disability. Problems and solutions arising from the social and personal evaluation of a disability are discussed in the first half of the book (Chaps. 2–10). The more clinical chapters, those concerned with the way in which the person may be effectively encouraged in the rehabilitation setting to meet the challenges imposed by disability, come toward the end (Chaps. 11–14). The parent is the central figure in Chapter 12, the child in Chapter 13, and the adult client with a disability in Chapter 14. Throughout, attitudes and their origins are examined critically, for these are the springboards for a good deal of behavior as well as crucial leads to a person's inner life. Those sources of attitudes that did not naturally come into the discussion of specific problems are brought together and discussed in Chapter 10. The last chapter reviews the heritage of somatopsychology in the diverse efforts, past and present, to relate personality to physique and underscores the findings and conclusions that appear essential in the overall evaluation of the field.

We have not attempted to cover the literature; for this the reader may refer to such reviews as Garrett (*1952*), Barker *et al.* (*1953*), and Meyerson (*1957*).[6] The varying emphases and not infrequently divergent conclusions of the reviewers are worth more than a passing thought. At

---

[6] The following are fine bibliographic sources for somatopsychological literature: *Rehabilitation Literature* (National Society for Crippled Children and Adults, Chicage, Ill.), issued monthly, maintains the most comprehensive abstracting service of current literature; *Psychological Abstracts* (American Psychological Association, Washington, D.C.), issued bimonthly, has a section entitled "Physically Handicapped." An excellent source of information about on-going research is the Bio-Sciences Information Exchange at 1113 Dupont Circle Building, Washington 6, D.C.

several places in this book we have attempted to take divergencies into account as well as to account for them. Research findings and the considered opinions of others have generally been introduced as they bear upon the issues under discussion.

In the main, the problems and issues studied in this book have application to children and to older persons, and to persons with various disabilities. Most typically, the discussion draws its concrete demonstrations from different age levels; where it does not, its application across age levels is usually apparent. Sometimes it seemed more expedient to center the discussion on one or another age group, either because the problem seemed more directly relevant to a particular population segment or because the research and illustrative material dealt with subjects of certain ages. The same holds true for specific disabilities. The example may refer to a person with an amputation, paralysis, or a hearing impairment, but it is used only to make explicit a principle or point that has wider generality. The psychological problems surrounding mental retardation as such are not dealt with, although it should be noted that a good deal of the discussion has application to mental as well as physical shortcomings.

TERMINOLOGICAL ISSUES

Semantics has insistently pointed out that words and the ways in which they are put together play a large part in the continued misunderstandings of interpersonal relations and of psychological and physical facts (see Johnson, *1946;* Korzybski, *1951*). Several documents utilizing examples from diverse groups—primitive cultures and our own—show that language is not merely an instrument for voicing ideas but that it also plays a role in *shaping* ideas by guiding the experience of those who use it (see Whorf, *1947;* Lee, *1947;* Sapir, *1931;* Korzybski, *1951*). It behooves us, therefore, in studying the psychology of disability, to give serious attention to the problems and implications of word usage.

Dangers of Short Cuts

Is a physically disabled person one who is unable to do anything? Of course, this is an absurdity that calls forth the rebuttal that the designation is meant to refer to varying degrees of disability and not just to the extreme. More accurately, then, a physically disabled person is also a physically *abled* person. There are things that he *can* do as well as things that he *cannot* do. We may conclude that the designation "a physically disabled person" is a short cut to the more involved but psychologically sounder expression "a person with a physical disability." Such a reformulation is far reaching, for it connotes that a person with a disability is first a person with many unspecified characteristics in addition to a particular disability. A tolerant concurrence, combined with the feeling that this is much ado about nothing much, may greet this proposal; but, as we shall see in subsequent chapters, it is precisely the perception of a person with a physical disability as a *physically disabled person* that has reduced all his life to the disability aspects of his physique. The short cut distorts and undermines.

This is probably one major factor that gives to the words "disabled" and "handicapped" a derogatory connotation. It is reported that a woman, herself diabetic, who had been speaking energetically on discrimination in the employment of diabetics and their difficulty in obtaining insurance protested violently when National Employ the Physically Handicapped Week was mentioned, with the assertion, "I do not consider myself handicapped" (Rusk and Taylor, *1946*:111). She readily acknowledged her physical handicap, but she was reluctant—and rightfully so—to consider *all* of herself handicapped.

Titles of books and articles may well take into account the difference in connotation between the short cut such as "The Physically Handicapped" and the more careful reference, "Persons with a Physical Handicap." To be sure, the structure of our language makes it difficult to carry out this principle in all instances. Persons who are blind will still be referred to as "the Blind" as though in all significant matters this were the main identifying feature. As will be seen later, there is a tendency, where characteristics conveying status implications are involved, for inferiority on one scale to spread to total inferiority of the person. Since physique does stimulate value judgments, it is particularly important to use expressions insofar as feasible that separate physical attributes from the total person.

Disability vs. Handicap

We may now wonder wherein lies the distinction between the socalled physically disabled and the physically normal, since omnipotence is not a property of any creature on earth, and all of us must function within more or less defined limits. It might be suggested that the concept of physical disability implies deviation from a normal standard, deviation from a state that is natural or average. But here again there are difficulties. It could be asserted, for example, that the arthritic changes concomitant with aging represent a "natural" course of events; yet hardly a person would be ready to concede that the resulting extreme deformities are nondisabling.

Hamilton (*1950*) proposes a distinction between the terms "disability" and "handicap" that is helpful as a point of departure. "A disability is a condition of impairment, physical or mental, having an objective aspect that can usually be described by a physician. . . . A handicap is the cumulative result of the obstacles which disability interposes between the individual and his maximum functional level" (p. 17). A disability, then, is more particularly a medical condition, whereas a handicap more nearly refers to the somatopsychological relationship previously described.

It is important that the implications of this distinction be pursued further, for some clarity must be achieved amid the barrage of impressions emanating from the terminology used. To begin with, it must be recognized that not all conditions that may be described medically as disabilities are perceived as handicaps. The bound and diminutive feet of Chinese women were not felt to be handicapping among certain strata of the Orient, where this condition symbolized nobility. An important clue resides in the fact that the functional level of such a Chinese lady did not require efficient locomotion. In other words, the determination of maximum functional level, or what the person needs and is expected to do, itself partly depends upon the cultural setting in which the person lives.

It should be clear, then, that a handicap must be evaluated in terms of the demands of the situation in which the person finds himself. In general we do not consider children to be physically handicapped because their physical abilities are less than those of adults. And, to draw upon an even more pointed example, we do not consider all mankind handicapped because men are not as fleet as the deer, as strong as the lion, or able to soar into the air. Similarly, even severe disabilities need not represent major handicaps. For example, a blind person may not be handicapped in work that does not require visual orientation; a person whose job does not require rapid locomotion may find his wheel chair no more frustrating than a bus ride is to the person who takes it for granted that he has to ride a bus to work every morning.

Fielding (*1950*) investigated the attitudes of 40 women with moderate to severe orthopedic disabilities resulting from poliomyelitis. Although the disabilities were more than minor from the medical point of view, some 20 percent of the subjects affirmed that the disability at most annoyed them very little in physical activities. Although 98 percent of the subjects reported that they occasionally experienced the physical defect as a disadvantage, 70 percent also reported the defect to be a help in some phases of life. These results cannot be discounted as mere products of wishful thinking or subconscious rationalization. It is by now well corroborated by research and theoretical consideration that disability as the term is here used cannot automatically be equated with handicap.

Conversely, a person may feel physically handicapped even though from the medical point of view his physical limitations are not disabilities. A person who aspires to become a great singer although endowed with but an ordinary voice is handicapped in that his physical attributes impede his progress toward his goal. His maximum functional level is inadequate to the functional level required by his aspirations.

There are indications that in our society, irrespective of medical or "actual" disability, deep dissatisfaction with certain aspects of one's body is almost universal. Levy (1932), for example, in talking with children about matters pertaining to their bodies, found that 18 of 20 children exhibited sensitivity or a feeling of inferiority with respect to some aspect of their physiques. It was not a physical disability in the medical sense that proved handicapping to these children.

Finally, the obstacles that the disability interposes may be as much social in character as physical. With some disabilities, as in facial disfigurement, the handicapping factors reside almost entirely in negative social implications.

We are led to the interesting conclusion that a physical attribute is a physical handicap only when it is seen as a significant barrier to the accomplishment of particular goals. This means that, in the individual case, a physical disability may or may not be a physical handicap. This is also true of a physical attribute that is not a deviation. Moreover, a physical attribute may become handicapping not because it is physically limiting but because it adversely affects social relationships.

Physical Definitions and Psychological Understanding

One might suppose that the definition of the various disabilities would not involve such semantic complications. Are not deafness and blindness, for example, clear-cut disabilities? Actually, the problem of nomenclature regarding these disabilities continues to arouse controversy. Deafness is a case in point. One might suppose that all that is required is a reliable test of auditory acuity—for example, diminishing the intensity or amplitude of a sound until the subject no longer responds to it. Several issues, however, act against the uncritical application of this simple system. First, at what point of diminishing sound intensity shall it be said that a person is deaf, as opposed to hard of hearing? Shall the designation of deafness be reserved for those whose auditory acuity is functionally useless? A Conference of Executives of Schools for the Deaf (1938) did in fact adopt definitions in functional auditory terms:

The deaf: those in whom the sense of hearing is nonfunctional for the ordinary purposes of life. . . .

The hard of hearing: those in whom the sense of hearing, although defective, is functional with or without a hearing aid.

But then, of course, one has to set up criteria both for the evaluation of functional and nonfunctional hearing and for what constitutes "the ordinary purposes of life." To complicate the problem yet further, it has been shown that two individuals with the same degree and patterning of auditory acuity as measured by pure tone threshold may differ markedly in auditory functioning as measured by speech-hearing tests (Barker *et al.,* *1953:*191; Meyerson, *1956*). Likewise, two individuals with similar auditory functioning may display grossly divergent sensitivity to sound. These interesting results occur because *functional* hearing depends upon many factors other than sheer auditory capacity—e.g., motivation, age at loss of hearing with respect to language acquisition, etc.

A similar situation exists in the case of blindness. The definition of blindness varies from country to country, from state to state, and certainly from investigator to investigator. A person is legally blind in Norway, for example, if he cannot see to count his fingers in good illumination against a dark background at a distance of one meter (Holst, *1952*). Within the United States legal blindness is based on such diverse criteria as inability to perceive motion at a distance of one foot and Snellen Chart performance of 20/200, which is roughly equivalent to the ability to read 14-point type. Whatever the criteria, however, great caution must be used in inferring from them what the person can and cannot do simply because there is not a one-to-one relation between visual acuity and visual behavior. Thus, in one study, 8 percent of the children in special classes for the partially seeing had central visual acuity less than 20/200 Snellen, meaning that they could be classed as legally blind—yet these children could learn by visual methods (Kerby, *1952*).

The proposition that physique as defined medically in physical or physiological terms is not unequivocally related to behavior is an important one. Definitions of physical conditions are not psychological definitions. Like age or sex, they are of value in somatopsychological research chiefly as reference points that delimit gross characteristics of the individuals to be studied. They are the starting points for such crucial inquiries as: How does the person evaluate his disability? What are the physical limits it imposes? How does he feel that others see his disability and himself? How do society and those more immediately close to him view his deviation? These are somatopsychological questions that point to the underlying dynamics or genotypical variables that connect atypical physique, on the one hand, with attitudes and behavior, on the other.

Before embarking on the main discussions of this book, it is especially important for the "able-bodied" reader to realize that the topics are not of special moment to a different group but, rather, that they are of special moment to the totality of mankind, for each of us must at some time face the challenge of living with a disability. This is another way of saying that physical disability is a "natural" and "normal" part of life, that all of us experience illness, that time brings impairment. The next chapter initiates the exploration of social-psychological conditions affecting adjustment to disability by considering the powerful status implications of disability.

Chapter 2

Inferior Status Position

SOME INDIVIDUALS DENY THE FACT THAT PERSONS WITH DISABILITIES ARE looked down upon. This protest has come not only from those who have a disability but also from professional personnel, such as teachers and rehabilitation workers, actively engaged in disability matters. Perhaps it is felt that to assert the existence of inferiority as an attitude is to affirm it as a fact. Public attitudes are often positive, but negative, deprecating attitudes also exist, although these may be more covert. To recognize the existence of the negative is not to be defensive or to add to it but, rather, to be better able to effect countervailing changes.

If a person with a physical disability is unable to participate in some activities that are highly valued, his space of free movement is felt to be restricted. Part of the restriction may be due to the physical limitation itself. A person who is deaf will not enjoy a concert. A person with limb or heart impairments may avoid walking more than modest distances. But part of the restriction has its source in socially derogatory attitudes— attitudes which say, in effect, "You are (or I am) less good, less worthy because of the disability. It is something to be hidden and made up for."

Devaluation is expressed in various ways. It is seen in the patronizing attitude of the person who gives money to "help those poor little crippled children." It is seen in disparaging allusions to the physical particulars of an adversary. Jokes about disabled persons more often deprecate and ridicule than do jokes about other classes—e.g., farmers, salesmen, judges (Barker *et al.*, *1953:75*). The feeling "I am glad I am not like you," which not infrequently springs into consciousness as a reaction to a person with a disability, betrays devaluating attitudes. We do not entertain this feeling toward persons whom we accept on an equal or superior footing, even though we might not choose to exchange places. In an extreme form, devaluation is seen in aversion toward a person with a physical disability. The following is one incident among many variations on the same theme: disability leads to devaluation. Karen, a three-year-old child with cerebral palsy, journeyed far with her parents for medical consultation. They were seeking lodging for the night:

. . . The house was lovely—white clapboard, old and with lamplight at the windows, it looked warm and friendly. I rang the bell and the door was opened almost immediately. I stepped in out of the rain and turned to a sweet-looking middle-aged woman.

"We should like a room for the night," I said, "if you can put a cot in our room for Karen."

"I think I can accommodate you."

She led the way into a tastefully furnished living room and invited me to sit down. I relaxed comfortably, propping Karen on my arm. . . .

"Why don't you put the child down, she must be heavy," she inquired.

"That's all right," I said, "I'll hold her."

"Well, sit her in the chair next to you," she suggested, "I don't mind if she gets down and runs around. Traveling is hard on youngsters; she'd probably love to get down."

"Karen can't get down and run around," I explained. "As a matter of fact, she can't sit up alone. Even when I'm holding her you'll notice she has difficulty holding her head erect for any length of time. That's why we're here. We've come to see Dr. C. We hope he may be able to help her."

I suddenly realized that the woman was sitting in an attitude of frozen attention. Her face grew livid and she jumped to her feet. "Get out of my house!" she shouted. "Only bad, dirty people would have a child like that" [Killilea, *1952:64–65*].[1]

Self-devaluation as felt by the person with a disability is also manifested variously. Illustrations of its many ramifications appear in this and other chapters.

Physical limitations per se may produce suffering and frustration, but the limitations imposed by the evaluative attitudes toward physique cut far deeper and spread far wider; they affect the person's feelings about himself as a whole. One of man's basic strivings is for acceptance by the group, for being important in the lives of others, and for having others count positively in his life. As long as physical disability is linked with shame and inferiority, realistic acceptance of one's position and one's self is precluded. We might add and underscore that as long as a physically able person holds this linkage, he is ill prepared for the time when he too will be in the position of meeting disability. It behooves us, then, to give careful consideration to the sources of such feelings, ways of reacting to them, and ways of adjusting to them.

COMPARISON WITH MINORITY GROUPS

Underprivileged Status

The position of persons with a disability has been likened to that of

---

[1] Reprinted with permission of Prentice-Hall, Inc., and Staples Press, London, from *Karen* by Marie Killilea. Copyright 1952 by Marie Lyons Killilea.

underprivileged ethnic and religious minority groups (Barker, *1948*). For example, employment opportunities, particularly at the higher levels, are sharply limited. Many employers as a matter of policy establish physical-fitness standards for all employees irrespective of whether a particular job can be handled effectively by a person with a disability. Yet Henry Ford (*1926*) stated that "we are too ready to assume without investigation that the full possession of faculties is a condition requisite to the best performance of all jobs" (p. 107).

Likewise, the social and recreational activities in which persons with a disability are able to engage are frequently restricted. Even should the person be accepted as a participating member in many life areas, his disability is often seen as precluding marriage. In one study of 50 college students, 65 percent stated that they would not marry a person who had an amputated leg, and 50 percent stated that they would not date such a person; 85 percent stated that they would not marry and 72 percent that they would not date a deaf person (Rusk and Taylor, *1946:*219). This is social ostracism of the sort experienced by ethnic and religious minorities.

Moreover, many members of the favored majority wish and frequently insist that the minority-group member not only know his place but also *keep* his place—that is, that he feel and act like a less fortunate being. Certain of the driving forces behind this insistence have been coördinated under the concept "requirement of mourning," elaborated on pages 242–243. Here let it suffice to point out that the requirement of mourning stems from a need on the part of the majority-group member to maintain unchallenged those values which he cherishes, and which have given him elevated status. This dynamic is captured in the astute observations shared with Chevigny (*1946*), recently blinded, by a friend who said, "You're a blind man now, you'll be expected to act like one [p. 71]. People will be firmly convinced that you consider yourself a tragedy. They'll be disconcerted and even shocked to discover that you don't" (p. 74). Aren't some people disconcerted and even shocked when ethnic and religious minority-group members advocate equality or show in other ways that they feel as worthy as the next man?

A study dealing directly with the hypothesis that disability groups are viewed in certain ways as minority-group members (Cowen, Unterberg, & Verrillo, *1956*) analyzed correlates of attitudes toward blindness. The investigators found that negative attitudes toward blindness correlated significantly with antiminority, anti-Negro, and pro-authoritarian attitudes. These findings were essentially replicated in a cross-validating sample, thus confirming the underlying hypothesis.

Overlapping Situations

The person with a disability, like the members of other minority groups, may be represented in certain instances as subject to two different and often conflicting situations at the same time. On the one hand, being considered a disabled person by himself or others, he is subject to the behavioral mores and expectations of the disabled group (disabled determinants of behavior); on the other hand, his wish or the wish of others that he is "just like anyone else" predisposes him toward "normal" patterns of behavior.[2]

Illustrative of the problem is the situation of persons who are blind. As Chevigny (*1946*) has stressed, the world has an unusually fixed notion that a blind person is a tragic figure, utterly helpless and dependent. This is one situation in which the blind person finds himself. The other situation is more clearly that of a normal person, with its attendant values and expectations of independence and self-respect. A person who is blind may not only prefer to be in the latter psychological situation but may actually feel that he *is,* to some extent or fully, a part of it. He may, for example, consider his lot to be not at all tragic. He may have achieved an adequate degree of physical independence and his share of life's satisfactions. Instead of regressing into helplessness and self-pity, he strives to maintain a reasonable amount of independence from people and things and to carry out adult responsibilities. Yet he is subject to the behavior determinants of both the "disabled" and the "normal" situation. When he seeks a job, society may direct him to the sheltered workshop even though he may feel able, or at least wish to try, to compete in the world of normal persons (see Criddle, *1953:* Chaps. 21, 22). In ordinary relationships, people may insist that he act like a blind person and may be "disconcerted and even shocked when he doesn't."

The expectations and directives of others are not the only source of conflict in overlapping situations. The person himself may be torn between acting in terms of his disability and acting like a normal person. He may, for example, find it necessary to slacken his pace when ascending stairs while at the same time he may wish to hide his handicap and keep up with others. Of course, whether the conflicting situations are felt to be imposed by the outside or are felt to stem from internal conflicts makes a difference as to where the individual's resentments will be focused. In any case, a person with a disability—and, in fact, all members of minority groups—may frequently be placed in overlapping situations, both by

---

[2] A systematic discussion of the nature of overlapping situations and resulting behavior is given in Barker *et al.* (*1953:*27–46). Although the referents are to physical growth in adolescence, the points made have wide generality.

society's edict and by personal conflicts, in which the determinants of behavior are to some extent incompatible.

Group Stereotypes

The stereotype of a person with a disability typically describes one who has suffered a great misfortune and whose life is consequently disturbed, distorted, and damaged forever. Unlike the bereaved person, in whom the pain of loss formally ceases after a year and who is expected gradually to reap once again the fullness of life, the person with a disability is expected to be permanently enmeshed in the tragedy of his fate. Several factors contribute to this stereotype. In addition to the phenomenon of "spread" (p. 118), the "requirement of mourning" (p. 242), and the sources of attitudes examined in Chapter 10, popular misconceptions are perpetuated by the distortions of reality appearing in mass media.

Guilty of confirming pity stereotypes, popular culture finds ample use for them. Typical was the film *Moulin Rouge,* which depicted Toulouse-Lautrec as a piteous, embittered dwarf, morbidly obsessed by his deformity and tragic in his love relationships. How far this is from the truth can be seen in Gerstle Mack's biography, where the artist emerges as a witty, engaging personality who loved Paris night life and the sporting scene. The testimony of Lautrec's friends indicates that, with the exception of his last mentally aberrant years, he was amusing and well liked, highly regarded by the artistic and literary figures of his time. By falling into easy stereotype, the film distorted the facts of Lautrec's life to play up sentimental fancies and, unwittingly, to confirm popular notions of how the handicapped are handicapped [Maisel, *1953:*32].[3]

Where the social stereotypes of a group are stigmatizing, the individual often wishes to be judged in his own right and not "known" by his membership in the group. The reason for this is not hard to find, for the stereotyped evaluation of himself as a person and the stereotyped interpretation of his behavior often reflect underlying devaluating attitudes. Consider some common negative misinterpretations: A person with a disability is often considered to be compensating when he may merely be interested; he is assumed to be feeling inferior when he may merely be holding back because of realistic appreciation of his limitations; he is regarded as being suspicious when he may merely be wondering—all because he is seen as part of a larger group with certain presumed personality characteristics.

The dependence of a part on the whole does not always result in the part's taking over or assimilating the properties of the whole. Sometimes

[3] Edward Maisel, *Meet a Body,* by permission of the Institute for the Crippled and Disabled. Manuscript.

the influence is seen through the phenomenon of contrast. Suppose, for example, that a deaf person earns a living and is happily married. He may be judged by others as outstanding in his accomplishments and unusually well adjusted, simply because his behavior is perceived as contrasting with the stereotype about the deaf. The person himself may resent such accolades because he is aware that they actually depend upon devaluation of the group of which he is inextricably a part. Praise of him is merely a case of the exception proving the rule. "In the same way do we judge the personality traits and motivations of individual Jews, Republicans, Negroes, Catholics, Russians, etc. . . . Thus, many Americans, through the operation of the assimilation phenomenon, tend to overestimate the shrewdness of a particular Jew, or the inscrutability of a somewhat reticent Russian—because they believe Jews to be shrewd and Russians to be inscrutable. Because of contrast, they tend to overestimate the intelligence of a Negro who is normally intelligent and to underestimate the religious conservatism of a Catholic who is liberal in some of his religious views" (Krech and Crutchfield, *1948*:97).[4]

Assimilation appears when the difference between subparts of the whole is perceived as small, contrast when it is perceived as great (Heider, *1944*). It can be expected, therefore, that a person with a disability will have to cope with the phenomenon of assimilation more frequently when interacting with a stranger than with a close friend, for in the latter instance he is known as an *individual,* which makes him, though part of a group, different to some extent.

But the plea "Do not judge me by my brothers" cannot be followed in every respect because the individual *must* be apprehended in terms of the presumed characteristics of the group of which he is felt to be a part. This is not merely up to the whim of the perceiver, for experimentation has clearly shown that the perceived properties of a substructure are largely determined by the nature of the whole structure. But although we may never be able to avoid organizing individuals into groups, "there is no reason demanding that only certain defined personality traits should be perceived as 'belonging' to any specific grouping based on such differentia" (Krech and Crutchfield, *1948*:98).

Differences in Minority-Group Position

Although it is important to understand that a person with a disability

---

[4] The effect of the part-whole relationship on elementary perception and the perception of personal characteristics has been elaborated by Heider (*1944*), Krech and Crutchfield (*1948*), and others. Quotation from D. Krech and R. S. Crutchfield, *Theory and Problems of Social Psychology,* McGraw-Hill Book Company, copyright 1948, by permission of the publisher.

often shares problems in common with members of other minority groups, there are some marked differences. One of the most significant is that he rarely has the kind of group sanction and personal valuation that endorses behavior reflecting the disability. Rather, the typical advice is to appear as much like a nondisabled person as possible, and his adjustment is often measured in terms of his skill as an actor. Even where there is a high degree of acceptance of the disability, there is a resistance against behavior that unnecessarily spotlights the handicap. This is clearly seen in the following account by the mother of a blind child. On the basis of interviews, this mother was rated as showing good acceptance of the child and her handicap:

We helped Mildred to overcome some of her mannerisms which are some-times associated with blindness such as hanging her head. We explained to her that this habit was characteristic of the blind, and she earnestly tried to over-come it. We also discussed with her the frequently expressionless and vacant look on the faces of the blind, particularly when listening to speeches, etc. We tried to tell her that she must make an effort to show joy or sadness, surprise or disappointment. She seemed to appreciate and understand this when we explained that it would increase her personal attractiveness [Sommers, *1944:*52].

In contrast, a Jew or a Negro, for example, can take pride in many of the characteristics held to be uniquely Jewish or Negro, and such pride is looked upon as a sign of self-acceptance.

In addition, the minority position of the person with a disability is not likely to be closely shared with other individuals. Of primary importance is the fact that physical deviation does not generally continue from genera-tion to generation, as do other minority-group characteristics. Certain racial characteristics are genetically inherited; religious characteristics are socially inherited; but a person with a disability is often the only one in his family so affected, and hence he may lack the family identification that members of other minority groups usually have. As a child he may be unaware that there are other individuals with a disability like his and thus he may feel no affiliation with any minority group at all. Moreover, clubs and groups organized by and for persons with disabilities are rare in small communities. In the case of other minority groups, the psychological situation is often very different. A Jew or a Negro who lives in a com-munity in which he is the only member of his group may psychologically be a member of the larger group, sharing in its aspirations, accepting its values, and participating in its activities. But the person with a disability is often an isolated individual who must meet the limitations imposed by underprivileged status with but minimal support of group identification.

The underprivileged-minority position of persons with a disability creates difficulties of two kinds. There are the hardships and suffering resulting from the restrictions imposed by the dominant majority. There are also the person's devaluative feelings about himself and his handicap. Although not all persons with a disability have such feelings, many do, and probably all have at some time during the course of their adjustment. It is to the suffering and pain associated with shame and feelings of inferiority that we shall now turn our attention.

MANIFESTATIONS OF LOWER-STATUS POSITION

Shame, self-pity, and inferiority are difficult psychological states, and the person will muster varied and persistent efforts in order to overcome them. The effort to raise one's self-esteem may be directed toward one's own self-acceptance, or toward hiding or weakening one's identification with the devalued group. This problem has been explored by Dembo and her associates (1956), the main outlines of their analysis being reflected in the discussion below.

"As If" Behavior

In the effort to adjust, the person commonly tries to conceal his disability —and for understandable reasons. The person typically views his disability as does the normal majority. If it is taken for granted that a disability is something to be ashamed of, the obvious way to eliminate shame is to eliminate the fact of disability. Where this can be realistically accomplished through surgical and other therapeutic procedures, the person will feel relieved, and objectively he may effect a change from the handicapped to the nonhandicapped position. Where this cannot be accomplished, however, the person will attempt to hide, forget, or even deny what to him is a deficiency. The need to cover up in order to be acceptable as a person may be so strong that, even when the deviation is minor and temporary, the person may fumble his way through patent devices: thus 17-year-old Chip, who recently had an eye tooth extracted, "went about grinning with his tongue turned over to cover the almost unnoticeable gap" (Linduska, 1947:128). The person may even succeed in denying painful facts to himself. The psychoanalytic literature on repression leaves no doubt that the escape forces may be so strong as to alter one's memory and perception of the unacceptable.

We do not wish to imply that all efforts to cover up stem from personal depreciation. A person may fully accept a particular fact about himself and yet conceal it because of the belief that awareness on the part of others would contribute to disturbed social relations. This is one basis on which the cosmetic hand instead of the hook or no prothesis is recommended in casual relationships (Dembo and Tane-Baskin, *1955*). Realistically recognizing that the knowledge that one is a Jew, or an amputee, or hard of hearing may create social barriers to full acceptance by others; one may therefore not call attention to these facts even when it would be natural to do so.

In many such instances, however, the person does harbor depreciatory feelings about his minority-group status, for otherwise complete acceptance by the majority would not be crucial. In this case, concealment may draw its complete sustenance from the conviction that having a disability makes the person less wanted, less good. Consider the following autobiographical reminiscences. Frances was hard of hearing. As a small child she heard her aunts, who reared her, speak about a neighbor as "so stone-deaf he might as well be dead." In the value-atmosphere of the home, she began to see physical perfection as the royal road to success in all areas of life, including one of the most important, that of love and acceptance by others:

"Stop slipping your braces off," Aunt May said. "If you have crooked teeth you'll be sorry."

"Stop reading all the time and ruining your eyes," Aunt Harriet scolded. "If you have to wear glasses, you'll be sorry."

"Stop eating so much fudge; your complexion's bumpy, you're much too plump. Don't you want to be slender and beautiful and marry into a fine family like your oldest sister?"

"Stand up straight. Don't you want to be athletic like your second sister who is so popular and is invited everywhere?"

"Brush your hair a hundred strokes every night. Don't you want to have thick shiny braids like your sister Ann's?" [Warfield, *1948:*22].[5]

Frances, then, had no alternative but to conceal, however precariously, the fact that she couldn't hear well:

I mustn't let on I couldn't hear perfectly. People didn't like it. It made them scornful like Ann or exasperated like Aunt May and Aunt Harriet when they called and I didn't answer right away. . . .

I must listen hard. Sometimes, when I didn't hear at first, it would flash over me, a second later, what had been said. I must never look blank. No matter how much I wanted to, I must never say "What?" "What?" was perilous. "What?" would give away my secret and I'd be exposed to deadly danger [pp. 4–5].

[5] F. Warfield, *Cotton in My Ears*, New York, Viking Press, Inc. Copyright 1948 by Frances Warfield.

For Frances the deadly danger was being rejected because of her deafness, perhaps even sent away. And this rejection was expected by Frances and even supported by her because *she agreed that deafness made a person unworthy,* that a hearing loss was something to be ashamed of. Since a shameful fact cannot be accepted as long as it remains shameful, Frances tried to hide, deny, or at best compensate for her hearing loss. It was only later, after Frances discovered the futility of her pretense, that she began to reëvaluate the meaning of disability.

The effort to forget one's disability is supported by the presumption that relief from the intolerable state can be achieved by blotting it out or by acting as though it did not exist. If in some magical way one could only forget, one could then act like a normal person—and be, in fact, a normal person. This kind of magical thinking is displayed more clearly in devised rituals which, if followed exactly, will reward the performer. Frances, for example, "knew" that she would get her hearing back after her adenoidectomy at seven, but just to make sure she secretly pursued the rites of magic:

> . . . Crouched in my hideaway behind the lilac bushes in the yard, I closed my eyes and put my fingers in my ears and repeated, "wrinkelstiltskin" seven times every day. I even devised fancier magic, such as avoiding cracks in the pavement and touching every other railing of every fence I ever passed [Warfield, *1948*:12].

The fact that unrealistic and even fantastic attempts to overcome disability are clung to tenaciously may be due to a deep emotional need for their promised effects, but the choice of a particular mechanism emerges from a conscious or unconscious belief in the reasonableness of its action. All of us have at one time or another achieved solace in forgetting; all of us have sought relief in sleep, an escape from the immediate troubles that beset us, an interlude during which we consciously forget. All of us have attempted to conceal or deny some personal fact: the child refuses to admit that he took the candy; the young mother closes the door on the unmade beds. In so doing we may sometimes have successfully shielded the shameful fact from becoming a social reality. It is the social reality of an undesirable personal characteristic, awareness of it on the part of others, that threatens one's group status. To attempt to hide, to deny, to forget is common sense, although it does not make adjustive sense. It does not make adjustive sense because acceptance of a disability requires that the person absorb it within his psychological outlook in such a way that it is no longer a painful fact that must be concealed.

Even the more clearly magical ruse undoubtedly originates in some experience that makes it "logical." When Frances at the age of 7 realized that her operation did not produce clear hearing, she decided that when she started school she would have perfect hearing *because lightning would strike her kite and restore her hearing!* On the face of it, this seems truly magical. But to Frances, it was completely comprehensible because "Aunt Harriet had read a newspaper story aloud to Aunt May about a woman who had been sitting beside an open window during an electrical storm with a pair of scissors in her hand. Lightning had struck her scissors. According to the newspaper story, the woman had been somewhat deaf, but when her scissors were struck by lightning her hearing was restored" (Warfield, *1948*:15). Even Frances' choice of a kite was not accidental, for she had admired a life-size statue of Benjamin Franklin and dreamed of herself discovering electricity and being so acclaimed. It is the common-sense feel of these techniques as paths to the goal of full membership in the favored group that leads the person to persist in using them in the face of objective facts which negate them.

The attempt to conceal the disability, to act "as if," demands ingenuity and alertness, for the situations that require covering up are endless. Again let us share Frances' life (Warfield, *1948*):

. . . I had never even felt faint, really—just a sickish little ball of panic in the pit of my stomach sometimes when I wasn't hearing and was afraid someone was going to say, "What's the matter—cotton in your ears?" The dressmaker who made my wedding dress had kept mimbling and mumbling, down on the floor with her mouth full of pins. Several times during the fittings I'd pretended to feel faint to explain my not answering her. Feeling faint was a good alibi [p. 19].

I heard better when I could see people's faces; . . . In firelit rooms or on summer evenings on the porch, I would fall into reverie or pretend to go to sleep. I knew dozens of ways to get people to repeat what they had said without actually asking. For example:

Aunt May: "Will you remember to bring me some wrinkelawreedles on your way home?"

I (dreamily): "From the post office?"

Aunt May (tartly): "Since when does one buy darning needles at the post office?" [p. 21].

I tried hard to be as funny as possible all the time. I invented a sidesplitting story to explain why I took Aunt Harriet's crochet pattern to Mrs. Schlee instead of to Mrs. McGee. I was a daydreamer and a woolgatherer; I faked absent-mindedness, boredom, indifference [p. 21].

I had learned by experience to do all the talking when I walked along the street with a boy. Indoors I could keep voices raised by playing the victrola; outdoors I was in danger of missing what was said. I always walked fast, rattling on at random, trusting to luck that when a boy wanted to ask me to a dance he'd call me on the telephone [p. 24].

I didn't mind being teased about snoring, because I snored purposely. Stella [my roommate] was a great whisperer after lights were out and sleep was my alibi for not answering [pp. 29–30].

Musical shows were all right; there was plenty to see and the plot didn't matter. Plays dragged; I'd get bored imagining, and itch to know what the play was about. Naturally I never asked. During intermissions I might inquire offhand what Stella thought would happen next; with luck I'd get an inkling of what had already happened. That is, if I heard what Stella said [p. 34].

The price of trying above all to hide and forget is high. It is high because the effort is futile. A person cannot forget when reality requires him to take his disability into account time and again. The vigilance required for covering up leads to strain, not only physically but also in interpersonal relations, for one must maintain a certain distance in order to fend off the frightening topic of the disability.

There is ample evidence in autobiographical materials to support this thesis; yet objective observations are largely lacking. What little there is remains unclear. Landis and Bolles (*1942*) hold, on the basis of interviews with 100 handicapped women, that those using the "obliterative method" of adjustment (refusal to admit that they were incapacitated in any way, equivalent to our "as if" behavior) showed the best adjustment to handicap and general life adjustment. But the likelihood that these same subjects would also deny any other difficulties, thus leading interviewers to form a spuriously high impression of their adjustment, as well as other considerations, prevent our relying upon these observations (see pp. 135–136).

On the basis of our thesis, the following paradox becomes clear: Trying to forget is the best way of remembering. In trying, one must be ever aware of one's disability, for otherwise the disability might not be adequately concealed. Physical disability remains a *dominant* value for the person in *most* situations. On the other hand, to be able to submerge disability-connected matters in situations in which they are not relevant, the person must first recognize and accept the disability.

Idolizing Normal Standards

The efforts of the person to forget or cover up his disability in his fervent hope of being "normal" also have important consequences for the standards and values that guide his behavior and evaluations. It is understandable that, in the event of a disability, the person cannot simply revise his standards that determine his aspirations and the way he feels about things. He cannot simply decide, for example, that it is all right for him to limp, when he has always regarded the normal gait as the only really proper way to walk. If, with the injury to his body, his value system automatically underwent appropriate accommodations, he would be able, for example, to see beauty in the laboring locomotion of a person who is meeting the residuals of polio and to view the hand prosthesis as "working hands" rather than "claws." Although such perceptions reflect good adjustment to disability, they require major alterations within the value system of the person, alterations that are only gradually realized in the struggle for adjustment (see Chap. 5). An individual does not lightly toss over the basis for strivings and evaluations that he has taken for granted during the foregoing lifetime. By the same token, an immigrant does not leave his native customs behind when he comes to a new land.

The person with a disability clings to the standards of the normal majority for another, very different reason. We have seen that in the primitive effort to forget and conceal his disability, the person feels that he must act "as if" the disability did not exist. This means that with respect to his own behavior he must act as much like a person without the disability as possible; with respect to the behavior of others, he should be treated like anyone else. In other words, the standards of behavior relevant to the nondisabled are maintained or even enhanced as the ideal, the guide for the person's own behavior and relationships with others.

Arbitrarily holding up "normal" performance as the model of behavior unnecessarily commits many persons with a disability to repeated feelings of failure and inferiority. Careful experimental work has demonstrated that the experience of success and failure is largely independent of the person's performance per se but is determined by his goals, expectations, and aspirations (Lewin et al., 1944). Usually people set their aspirations near the top of their abilities. After success, goals are usually raised; after failure, they are usually lowered. In other words, the level of aspiration operates as a protective mechanism so that most persons, whatever their abilities, experience success much of the time. Where normal performance is unattainable, the person who idolizes this as the standard must suffer the ignominy of repeated failure. Performance that may represent genuine progress over past achievement may merit only dissatisfaction because it is still far from the elusive but imperious normal ideal. Moreover, even should the person with a disability achieve or surpass the standards of normal performance, this by no means guarantees a success experience, for as long as he views his disability as a stigma, he can have only the feeling that at best he is an imperfect facsimile of a "nondisabled person."

Let us share part of Raymond Goldman's (1947) life for exemplification. At the age of 4 he was stricken with polio. Laboriously he learned to sit up, to crawl. At the age of 8 he was fitted with long leg braces. By the time he was 12, he could walk straighter and faster and tripped less frequently. At about the age of 14 he was fitted with half-leg braces and could walk better than ever. Finally, he attempted the impossible and succeeded. Contrary to the prediction of his doctor, at the age of 17 he learned to walk without braces.

And yet, though he triumphed over severe difficulties, though his gait represented remarkable improvement over the years, his feeling of achievement in situations where the normal standards remained exemplary, as in contacts with girls, was abruptly replaced by the feeling of shame and dismay. At the beach he swam early in the morning to avoid people who would see his legs. "The very sight of my own uncovered legs stabbed me to the heart" (p. 86). In the afternoons he sat on the beach, in trousers and shoes. "I even made friends with a group of fellows and girls of my own age who came down every afternoon, my self-consciousness subsiding as I got to know them better; subsiding, that is, *to a certain point beyond which it could not go. When the girls were present I didn't walk*" (p. 89, italics added).[6] What had been true accomplishment in terms of progress was now seen as defeat and failure because in this situation the normal standards of walking were glorified into how one *should* walk.

Furthermore, idolizing normal standards serves to support not only inferiority feelings but also guilt feelings. (The emotional syllogism by which the *cause* of disability becomes associated with evil is discussed on pages 258–261.) To the extent that the person attributes the wrongdoing to himself, he will feel the uneasiness of guilt, though in a vague and uncomprehending way because its source is unclear. Since the idolizing of normal standards augments the severity of the disability by emphasizing the shortcomings of the person, in the syllogism of emotional sequences the wrongdoing responsible for the disability becomes correspondingly accentuated. Guilt prospers. Moreover, as Franz Alexander has pointed out (*1938*), guilt feelings and inferiority feelings tend to reinforce each other. The person tries to escape inferiority feelings by denial and by "as if" behavior, by ambitious competition, by resentment against an unjust world, all of which make him feel guilty because of new wrongdoings. He tries to free himself of guilt feelings by atoning or by inhibiting further aggressions. Sometimes these devices make him feel weak and dependent, providing a new cauldron for inferiority feelings. The vicious circle spirals upward. As Alexander (*1938*) puts it, using the criminal as subject: ". . . in order to escape inferiority feelings the criminal is driven to commit acts which give him the appearance of toughness, bravado, and aggressiveness.

[6] The selections from Raymond Goldman, *Even the Night*, copyright 1947, The Macmillan Company, are used with the permission of the publisher.

But this behavior which seeks to avoid the Scylla of inferiority feelings drives him into the Charybdis of guilt feelings" (p. 47).

In some way the normal standards of behavior themselves may become endowed with a quality very close to a moral imputation that it is right and proper for one to walk or talk in a certain way. At least under certain conditions, the shame of inferiority at being below standard is tainted with the shame of guilt at violating an ethical code. Raymond, the boy crippled through polio, in thinking of his youth poignantly compares his emotional reaction to that of a culprit: "It is hard to believe that I am describing the emotions of a youth who is guiltless of crime against society. His frantic fear of human eyes could not be more terrible if he had robbed a bank, committed murder, or escaped from a penitentiary. He is lame, that is all; and his soul is fevered with a burning shame" (Goldman, 1947:66).

Idolizing normal standards, then, relegates the person to an inferior position, not only objectively, in terms of a particular characteristic, but may also do so morally, as a total person. In turn, the feeling of shame and inferiority prompts "as if" behavior, which itself heightens the potency of normal standards, for in the frenzy of emotional logic, the success of forgetting, denying, and concealing requires that the person emulate the styles and standards of the nondisabled. Thus, the means of extricating oneself from more shame becomes the very means of submerging oneself further. (In Chap. 5 we shall consider value changes important to the acceptance of a disability that hold greater promise for the ultimate realization of the self as a worthy human being.)

The possible positive consequences of maintaining the standards of the "normal" majority must also be examined. It might be argued that the ideal of normal performance provides the necessary motivation for persistent effort to surpass one's existing condition, that without it the person would be satisfied with a more awkward gait or a less pleasant-sounding voice or a narrower range of activities than he could achieve. Almost any autobiography documents the fact that the feeling of inferiority, fed by the normal ideal, can serve, in a wide variety of situations, to prod the person to outdo himself. Some theorists even assert that all accomplishment primarily reflects compensation for inferiority.

It is revealing to examine several incidents in the life of Raymond Goldman (1947), the man who was both lame and hard of hearing, with the following questions in mind: Could Raymond's accomplishments have been brought about by driving forces other than the striving to be like a "normal" person? At what price were his accomplishments made? What were the positive implications for adjustment and what were the negative consequences?

When Raymond was fitted with full-length leg braces at the age of 8, the trying problem arose of motivating him to use them. Until then he had had little feeling of inferiority. He did not miss the companionship of other children his age, for they belonged to a world he knew nothing of. He was the center of his own world, where everyone loved him and took care of him. He not only had high self-esteem but did not think of himself as having misshapen legs (see pp. 144–145 for a vivid example of his lack of awareness of his deformity). When the braces were fitted, he hated them. They hurt, and only because of the prodding and solicitousness of his parents did he coöperate at all:

During that summer I wore my braces at least thirty minutes every day. I dreaded and hated them and made little effort to learn to walk. For a few weeks I would not attempt to walk at all, but sat down after they were put on and waited miserably for them to be removed. . . .

Quite naturally I preferred riding in the gocart to pedaling the velocipede, crawling to walking. But mother rose to the occasion. She tolerated my attitude for a while, then became annoyed with me.

"Get up and walk!" she commanded me, handing me my canes. "You'll never learn how to walk sitting in a chair."

I got up and practiced walking. Mother watched me, suffering, I am sure, even more than I. Propping myself up with the canes, I swung one weighted leg after the other, taking a step, resting, taking another step. The braces were half as heavy as I was. After getting across the room and back I was spent; I felt nauseated and dizzy with pain and weariness. Then Mother took off the braces, laid me on the bed, removed my stockings and rubbed me well with alcohol, gently patting the red bruises on my ankles and knees.

As the summer passed, the skin of my ankles became tougher and tougher, calluses began to appear. I wore my braces longer than half an hour a day; I wore them several hours. I got around the house—though I could not take the stairs—and I walked a little outside after I was carried down the front steps to the sidewalk. . . .

My happiness at entering school was all the greater when I learned that I was not to wear my braces there. Six hours in them was more than I was expected to endure. That torture would be reserved for late afternoons, after I returned from school. If I got along well at school, I thought, perhaps Mother would see the uselessness of wearing them and would throw them away. Mother was just being stubborn about it. Anyone could see that I got along much better without them. Without them I could crawl all over the house in the time it took me to walk across a room with them on [pp. 30–32].

Then occurred a momentous experience that was to usher in a totally new attitude toward himself and the world around him. At the age of 8½ Raymond entered school for the first time. The ridicule and torment to which he was subjected was overwhelming (see pp. 145–146 for the description of this nightmare). The hammer of comparison beat into him the barbs of shame. The standards of the "norm" began to have for him the character of a compelling ethic:

> . . . I knew now that legs *should* be stout and shapely and that mine were skinny and deformed. I knew that I *should* walk and could not. I learned indeed that I was a cripple, a pariah among the strong and straight, an object of pity to grown-ups and of scorn to children [p. 39, italics added].

Now that Raymond had suffered shame, his braces took on a new meaning. Before, they meant pain to him, and a way of locomotion that was less efficient than his tried and true method of crawling. Now they meant a way of becoming *like other children,* of meeting the standards of the normal majority, of escaping the pity due a disgusting, crippled boy. Small wonder that after school he asked for his braces:

> . . . Thereafter, day after day, week after week, month after month I struggled to walk. I put on my braces as soon as I got home from school and I kept them on until I went to bed. About forty pounds of boy, I dragged twenty pounds of steel across the room and back, across the room and back, holding myself upright with my canes. I must walk, I told myself, I must walk. I must get out of that shameful gocart, out of the arms of people who carried me. Of course I could do it! Hadn't I learned to crawl, even down the steps? [pp. 39–40].

An important question is whether Raymond would have learned to walk had he not been prodded by the horror of shame. Hadn't his parents tried to motivate him with reason, kindness, and command, but with limited success? And yet, we reply in the affirmative, relying on the emergence of new needs that develop in new situations and that may remain free of shame. Hadn't Raymond learned to crawl down the stairs when he was 6 in spite of great fear because he wanted to get there without being dependent on others? And shame did not crawl along with him!

> . . . I learned to climb up the stairs, but going down stumped me for a long time. In the upper hall I would venture to the head of the long carpeted stairway and look down. It was as forbidding as a bottomless pit and I would turn away only to return again and look down while I lashed my courage. If I wanted badly enough to go downstairs, I called someone to carry me; but there was no real satisfaction in that. . . . I was at the top of a long flight of steps, looking down, waiting to go down, held back by fear. Then, without conquering my fear but in spite of it, I started down, head first, and kept on going until I reached the bottom [pp. 12–13].

Likewise, it is highly probable that Raymond would have found it unsatisfactory to have to wait until someone could carry him or wheel him in school from room to room and sooner or later would have turned to his braces, in spite of the pain, as a way of achieving greater mastery over his environment. Walking might have been delayed, but, without the catalyst of shame, accomplishment represents the rewards of triumph over adversity unsullied by the sinking feeling that one is not yet up to par.

But, to press further, under such circumstances would Raymond have continued toward maximum improvement? Would he, nine years later, have defied the expert opinion of his doctor that he would never walk without braces and suffered the sweat and tears it took to accomplish the impossible? His doctor had said, "You ought to be satisfied" (p. 29). Would a Raymond free of shame have persisted, "But couldn't I try it? It couldn't do me any harm to try, could it?" We do not know. Perhaps the inconvenience of repeated broken braces, of heavy gear, would have led him to attempt discarding them. Perhaps not.

But even so, a challenging query is "So what?" Reducing the disability in no way assures a better adjustment. There is already sufficient research to establish as a fact that there is but little relationship between adjustment and degree of disability (see pp. 53–54). Was the gain of walking without braces worth the price of self-debasement? The feeling of inferiority is painful enough, but when the normal ideal not only spurs the person onward but also sparks deception and defeat, one wonders what it all adds up to. The consuming desire to be like other boys led Raymond, like a rat in a maze, to explore frantically first one blind alley, then another.

Sometimes the gateway was labeled "Lie, and you will be like other boys." For example, when Raymond was in the fifth grade, an idea came to him as he was watching a telephone repair man climb to the top of the pole by using the irons strapped to his legs. The next time Raymond was asked what he was wearing on his legs, he answered, "Tree-climbers."

Sometimes the gateway was labeled "Treat me like anybody else, no matter what!" This meant that he wanted not only to have the good things in life enjoyed by other boys but also to suffer the punishment that other boys received. One day he set out upon a deliberate campaign to change his teacher's attitude toward him from one of gentleness to that of the strict disciplinarian she was to all the other boys:

. . . In the silence of study period I clanked my steel braces against the iron stanchions of the desk.

"Raymond, will you please try not to make that noise?"

Not angrily, as she would have spoken to another boy. Not leaping up from her desk and striding down the aisle like a wrathful demon. What was the matter with her? I thought bitterly. Didn't she know I was doing it on purpose?

I came to school with a pocketful of marbles. I dropped one with a solid click and let it roll down the floor. I dropped another and another. Miss McIntyre left her desk and came to my seat.

"Let me have those marbles," she said, holding out her hands for them. "Give me every one of them."

I took them out of my pocket and poured them into her cupped palms.

"I want to talk to you after class," she said, so quietly I was afraid that the other children had not heard her.

I was triumphant. I had made her leave her desk and come after me. I was being kept in after school like the worst boys in the room. She had taken a knife away from one boy and several tops from another, and they had never gotten them back. She wouldn't give me back my marbles, either. Maybe, I thought, she'd whip me, though I had never heard of any boy actually getting a whipping.

I sat at my desk after the others marched out and Miss McIntyre squeezed sideways into the seat in front of me. She took one of my hands in hers and held it tenderly while she spoke to me. I was such a smart boy, she said, and she knew I was a very good boy. I just didn't understand that good, smart boys didn't do things to disturb the class. . . . While she spoke, tears came into my eyes. She thought, no doubt, that they were tears of repentance, but they weren't. They were tears of bitter disappointment and resentment. To make matters worse, she gave me back my marbles.

That was the time I boasted to the boys next day about Miss McIntyre's anger and the severity of her punishment [pp. 48–49].

Sometimes the very performance prompted by the normal ideal itself suffered. In high school, Raymond tried very hard to walk *as others did*. But the more he tried, the more awkward he became:

When I walked through the corridors from one class to another, my braces clanked loudly on the floor. *If I tried to walk less heavily, I became more noticeably lame.* I am sure that none of those girls I passed in the corridor paid any attention to me, that only a few of them gave me even a passing glance. But I imagined that every one of them looked at me—not at me but at my legs—with a shudder of revulsion or, even more terrible to contemplate, a wave of pity [p. 67, italics added].

Raymond tried to communicate *as others did*. But the more he tried, the more he felt like a dunce and a fool:

I am in a classroom. The class is at Latin recitation. We hold our books open at a certain page and one by one, as the teacher calls our names, we rise and translate the text, the bidden student taking up where his predecessor left off. I studied conscientiously the night before; I am thoroughly prepared. Yet, agony fills me. I am cold with terror, wretched with desperation, stricken by a sense of impending disaster.

I do what I can to avoid the horror of catastrophe. I try to save myself with my eyes. But I ask too much of my perceptive wits. My eyes must be on the teacher's lips whenever she happens to call my name. Even so, shall I know whether she says Goldman, or Goldsmith, or Gorham, or Bowman? I must be careful not to rise if it is one of the others whose name has been called.

And how shall I know where to begin, granting that I rise at the correct time? I know with what page we began; I made certain of it by looking over the shoulder of the student in front of me. I turn a page whenever the others turn theirs. But where, on two pages, are they? I watch the reciting student. If he is behind me, I turn and see his face, but I cannot read Latin from his lips. If he is in front of me, I watch the back of his head. I can tell whether we are on the left-hand or right-hand page. The head is turned slightly to the left; the chin slowly sinks; then suddenly the chin goes up and the head turns a little to the right. The right-hand page! But what paragraph? What sentence? My classmate sits down. Look at the teacher! Oh, God, why does she hold down her head that way, looking at the recitation cards! What did she say? Gorham, Goldman, Bowman . . . ?

In spite of my desperate efforts I wasn't always successful. There were times when I didn't rise when the teacher called my name, and sometimes I rose when she called on someone else. On one occasion I thought she spoke my name and I got up and began to recite. The class broke into laughter. Behind me, the boy whose name had been called, had risen and begun to recite before I got to my feet. When I got up and joined in, like a second alto coming into a musical round, the teacher had every right to look startled [pp. 67–68].

After his first year in high school, Raymond quit. The normal ideal, instead of encouraging him toward greater achievements, mocked him into despair. In grade school, he had achieved considerable success and much satisfaction in writing, but now his aspirations were destroyed, at least temporarily, because no matter how much he taxed his motor and perceptual potentialities, he did not fit the pattern of his normal ideal. He had to learn the hard way that a "crippled boy is essentially the same as any other boy; that man did not walk and run his way out of beastliness, but thought his way out; that man is not ashamed because his legs are relatively crippled as compared with the legs of a deer, and his arms relatively muscleless as compared with the strength of a gorilla" (p. 51).

Raymond stayed out of school for a year, during which time he worked in his father's furniture store. According to our interpretation, the normal ideal of being physically like other boys was *not* the source of the reawakening of his ambition. The source was, rather, his gradual recognition that life is more than physique and that other values are important and satisfying.

The experiences that contributed to this realization are enlightening:

1. Raymond's initial job assignment—addressing envelopes—was completely unsatisfying to him. It was boring and yielded little pay. He was also ashamed, but not of his lameness or of his impaired hearing, for when he was seated behind a desk where no one spoke to him these

characteristics were of little importance. He was ashamed at the thought of sitting there among women addressing envelopes. What had occurred here was the emergence of a *new* standard, a standard that did not define the necessary physical characteristics of a person but concerned the value "manliness" as determined by the kind of work he did.

2. Raymond's second job assignment was writing furniture descriptions for newspaper advertising. When he saw his work in print, something stirred within him. He dreamed again of authorship and after a while began to write. His revived ambition was stimulated at home by conversations about the success of other writers. Stories by a distant relative were beginning to appear in magazines, and his neighbor, Fannie Hurst, recently had had several stories published in the *Saturday Evening Post*. What had happened here? Again, Raymond became absorbed with new values. Physique, instead of being *the* determiner of all of life, began to recede into the background as he became attracted again to literary pursuits, an interest that dated from years before.

3. These value changes paved the way for the tremendous discovery that shame and strain are fed by concealment. Once he realized that physique was not *that* important, that other things were far more crucial, he could confess his deafness for the first time. This he did, to Fannie Hurst, and experienced a calmness and understanding which taught him that though he could never get away from deafness he could get along with it.

In this brief review, we have seen in process several of the value changes to be analyzed in more detail in Chapter 5. These are: enlarging the scope of values (*i.e.,* the disability is not the only thing that matters); subordinating physique (*i.e.,* other values are more important than physique) and containing disability effects (*i.e.,* the disability does not affect all situations).

Raymond was now able to return to school, a private high school for boys. During these years the ideal of normal physique remained relatively dormant. Because other values and ideas occupied him he found life, unsapped by shame, exciting and rewarding.

Yet the transformation of physique from a comparative value to an asset value (see pp. 128–133), the value change par excellence that would strip normal physique of its character as a standard for him, had not as yet taken place. Raymond was therefore still vulnerable to shame. Normal physique as an idol still could rear its terrifying head. At graduation from high school, the old shame returned to Raymond as he saw *the girls* in the crowded auditorium and faced the prospect of standing there on the stage, reciting his poem, with all eyes upon him. Once again he had to come to grips with his position in a world in which normal physique was an important criterion for personal evaluation.

And in coming to grips again and yet again, Raymond learned several important lessons: The thought that he could be accepted as he was, even by girls, began to come to him. During the summer following his graduation, young and beautiful Edna was willing to sit and talk with him at the beach even though, because he hadn't dared to walk in her presence, she thought he couldn't walk at all! With this revelation, the battle raged furiously within him. Could he, would he, allow others to see him as he was? The answer fought its way through:

Next afternoon I went down to the beach as usual. I took off my trousers and shoes and waited for the others to arrive. I let them see me as I was, I let them see my legs, the entire skinny, deformed length of them. Edna, too. I walked with her down to the sea, naked with a nakedness known only to a cripple [p. 91].

Raymond also began to realize that his disability could be of real advantage in some situations. In the college gym course he discovered that he could chin far more times than anyone else. His upper trunk had been well developed during the years of exercise in his own gym, and his legs had little weight to be lifted. The instructor was impressed with his achievement and called the other members of the class to watch (p. 94).

In thinking over this experience, Raymond achieved even greater insights. He realized that coping with a disability in itself merits recognition and that what he had sometimes taken as pity was in fact respect for his striving (see p. 165 for an account of this insight). He also learned that accomplishment and its reward in admiration depend upon what is expected of you, not merely upon doing something better than someone else.

These and other experiences and insights led Raymond by the time he was 30 to his mature formulations bearing upon the problem of normal standards:

[1.] I did not measure success by what others had accomplished, but by what it was possible for me to accomplish. Along with shame, I had put envy and self-pity out of my life forever [p. 101]. I walked anywhere without fear of being noticed, proud that I could walk at all. I was unconcerned about the skinniness of my legs. I said, "Pardon me, what did you say? I don't hear very well," as easily as I might have said, "Pardon me, will you tell me what time it is? I have no watch with me" [p. 102].

[2.] I can live a normal life *although* I am *not* the same as other men [p. 115]. . . . while I was not quite the same as other men, I was, nevertheless, not so very much different [p. 138].

In short, a normal physique ceased to be the standard by which Raymond measured and evaluated himself. This is not to say, of course, that he preferred his imperfect physique to a more adequate one. Rather, he could appreciate all the good things his body could do for him because he no longer compared himself with the normal ideal. Instead, the things he *could* do became proficiencies. He could walk without braces, and that was good. A hearing aid improved his hearing, and that was good. He notes:

. . . I derived happiness from the queerest sources, things that meant nothing to other people, mere trivialities such as walking—just walking—down the street, climbing or descending steps; for who else save a few, could remember . . . ? [p. 126].

In effect, normal physique had become an asset value for him—*i.e.*, a good thing to have when present, but not a disturbance when absent (see Chap. 5).

This value shift, the dethroning of the idol of normal physique, did not, as some might suppose, remove the source of motivation toward improvement. Raymond continued his four-days-a-week workout at the gym—not because the normal standard egged him on but because he treasured his own health and strength. He was able to get married—not because of a challenge to overcome his inferiority but because he wanted to share his life with the girl he loved. He applied himself diligently to writing, in which he achieved considerable success—not because the image of a deformed and degraded physique stalked behind him but because the satisfaction of writing enticed him onward.

And the value shift prepared him for the years of anguish that awaited him. Within a short time of each other, the two persons closest to him, his father and his wife, died, and the emptiness that followed was soon to be capped by a new disability, severe diabetes. But during those years of black despair the philosophy of life that was to carry him through the void remained dormant and not dead. He had learned life's lessons well. Could he not meet the onslaught of diabetes when he had already learned to get along with the best he had? Could he not meet the pain of bereavement when he had learned to look upon hardship and suffering as part of life, as meaningful and challenging and not as worthless and humiliating? The ideal of physical normality had nothing to do with the reawakening of his will to live, with his savoring again the glory of thinking and feeling and caring and writing. On the contrary, had it played a role, his despair might well have lasted even longer.

The role of misapplied standards has been explored in other contexts. To give a brief notion of its generality, the matter of neurosis and sexual deviation may be mentioned. Adolph Meyer (*1948*) has stressed unrealistic levels of aspiration and lack of self-acceptance as etiologically significant in the neuroses. He feels that many persons become emotionally disturbed because they are unable to "accept their own nature and the world as it is, and to shape their aims according to their assets" (p. 539). Newcomb (*1950*) has discussed sexual deviation, such as homosexuality, as a function of the degree of rigidity in the prescribed standards for male and female behavior. Margaret Mead (*1949*) has considered in similar terms other facts relating to sex roles. She points out that women who enter an occupation defined as masculine may do so in order to act as males or to prove they are as good as males. This drive, being compensatory and derivative rather than primary, "will blur their vision and make clumsy fingers that should be deft as they try to act out the behavior of the other sex deemed so desirable." Even should they enter such an occupation because of intrinsic interest "they will find themselves handicapped at every turn by the style that has been set by the other sex" (p. 377). The parallel case holds true for men.

The same applies to a person with a disability who attempts to abide immutably by the standards and styles of "normal" performance. Too often his own performance will suffer, not only because of the psychological strain of striving to be what he is not, but also because modifications appropriate to his individual characteristics are forestalled.

Even should the person achieve and surpass "normal" standards, this *in itself,* we hold, is no criterion for successful adjustment. Yet individuals with disabilities who have become outstanding sports figures are held up as models to be emulated, as examples of persons who have overcome their handicaps. Thus the statement about a young man who lost a leg in a railroad accident while still a child: "That he has found the loss no handicap is evidenced by the fact that he was a collegiate boxing and fencing champion, captured the men's badminton singles title in his home town . . ." (Shortley, *1948*:iv). We believe, on the contrary, that such a criterion for adjustment, especially when regarded as the main one, is psychologically unsound. Competing with normal persons in boxing, and on the basis of the regular boxing rules may mean precisely that the person has *not* adjusted to his disability but has instead been motivated to achieve in this particular area just to prove that his amputation does not matter. Actually it *does* matter, and matters a great deal.

What we are trying to point out is that "acting like a normal person" is not the same as "feeling like a normal person"—i.e., a worthy human being—and that emphasis on the former may militate against the latter. This is not to say, however, that persons with disabilities should never participate in sports designed for the nondisabled, but it is to say that the way of participation should fit the circumstances of the participants. It does not make sense to cling to the established rules of the game *just because* the physically able play that way. Such rigid adherence reminds us of the immaturity of the young child who in no circumstances can modify the rules of a game because "rules are rules," whereas older children are able to do so in agreement with the other participating members (Piaget, *1932*). All too often, one pays a price for the apparent success when the motivation is to prove that one is "as good as anybody else."

Though the overriding potency of "normal behavior" as such is to be decried, there are important considerations that support abiding by such standards under certain conditions. First of all, striving toward the normal ideal may lead to the value change called "containing disability effects," in which the effects of disability are seen as restricted rather than pervasive (see Chap. 5), by forcing the person to enter activities that he might otherwise avoid. In so doing, the person may become aware that these activities are really not precluded at all: "It was great . . . doing the things you thought you would never do again" (Ohnstad, *1942*:157). The person with a disability, particularly in the case of a recent injury, is subject to the same spread phenomenon as are the nondisabled majority (see pp. 118–119). He too will perceive his disability as extending far beyond the necessary limits, spreading into what could be unaffected physical and nonphysical areas. In the light of this, the push to act like anyone else serves the positive function of making certain activities accessible.

Secondly, it may be necessary to cling to the normal ideal before one can give it up, to try to be like everyone else before one can find the comfort and the reward in being oneself. This may be particularly true in a society that ill prepares its members for the eventuality of disability and, on the contrary, fosters the ideal of superman in many phases of its life, as in industry, sports, etc. We have not found any autobiographies in which the person was able to sidetrack this phase of the adjustment process. But it is equally important to note that we have not found in any autobiography that achieving the normal standards in activities impeded by disability was the primary basis for adjustment or acceptance of the disability.

Thirdly, to adhere to certain modes of behavior, though they might not be as natural where a particular disability is involved, may be recommended when (1) they involve little actual stress and (2) the natural alternative will be met with social disapproval. An enlightening case in point is teaching table manners to the blind child. This child should be cautioned against the tendency to put his nose close to the food or to use fingers or tongue in an attempt to find out what food is on his plate; it is easy enough to tell him what is being served. On the other hand, the blind child should not be discouraged from developing his own special and sometimes strange means of "space testing," because there is no adequate "normal" substitution for informing himself about his environment. "Blind children have been observed . . . clapping their hands, snapping their fingers, smacking their lips, and clicking or popping their tongues. All these slightly explosive sharp sounds produce high frequencies and help the child to know more about his environment, how big and spacious it is, how far away the walls are, whether it is empty or filled with objects, etc." (Lowenfeld, *1956:*60).[7]

Finally, adhering to the normal ideal may in some instances be worth the price of strain and pain, especially if the person does not feel that such achievement is all-important. To be able to do things in the manner of others or to look like others may smooth the way in social relations. A person may be justified in undergoing expensive and painful plastic surgery for purely cosmetic reasons just because certain aspects of his life will thereby be ameliorated.

The critical decisions concerning standards and goals must involve a careful weighing of the possible gains and possible losses. Because the issues are not clear-cut, because some of them pull in opposite directions, the matter is not a simple one for mechanical solution. It takes wisdom based upon accumulated scientific findings and upon the art of sifting the important from the superficially attractive. In the foregoing discussion, the dangers of uncritically maintaining normal standards have been stressed more than certain positive effects of these standards, primarily because in the total process of adjustment more weight must be given to the former. Furthermore, in the common sense of adjustment to disability, the need for reëvaluation of standards is generally neglected.

It is certain that, when the implications of maintaining the normal ideal as a standard are better understood, some of the procedures in current rehabilitation practice will be modified, for the implications are crucial to the central problem of what to work toward and how to get there. Cruickshank has made the point that education for the cerebral palsied "has permitted feelings of inadequacy as a result of overstress on normalcy" (*1955:*334). Meyerson has challenged on the same grounds the educational philosophy of teaching deaf children. His statement of some of the issues is so incisive that it bears verbatim recounting:

Everyone will agree that speech and lip-reading are useful tools for the deaf child. In their finest development they enlarge the life space of the child tremendously, permit increasingly finer differentiations or growth, and reduce

[7] From B. Lowenfeld, *Our Blind Children,* 1956. Courtesy of Charles C Thomas, Publisher, Springfield, Ill.

the communication barriers between the child, his family, and the world. For reasons that are presently unknown, however, not every deaf child learns to speak and lip-read. For reasons we can only conjecture, many who do learn, after 12 to 15 years of continuous drill, later do not use their hard-won skills. Perhaps they discover the deceit of the implicit promises held out to them that "if only you learn these skills and behave like other people, society will accept you." Perhaps many discover that their speech and lip-reading are good only in a limited circle of family and friends. Outside of it they may experience great difficulty in understanding or being understood. They may discover that others are amused or annoyed at their voices.

Is a child necessarily a less valuable child if he uses other modalities and communicates by finger-spelling or pad and pencil? Is nothing else so important as speech and lip-reading? It is true that in some schools there is a tendency to establish a status hierarchy of "good" oral pupils and "poorer" manual pupils, but there is no psychological justification for this. Perhaps parents should evaluate a school by determining whether its students have anything worthwhile to communicate beyond being able to say "a top, a ball, a fish." Perhaps they should ask if the children have learned to solve problems by themselves, whether they have learned to take turns and respect the rights of others, and whether they have "good" adult power figures with whom they can easily identify [Meyerson, 1955a:163–164].[8]

Lillian Smith (1954) has even insisted that sameness and normality (in the sense of typicality) have no place in human beings.

In certain quarters the philosophy of rehabilitation is absorbing the view that instead of normal behavior being the golden guide for "what to do and how to do it," the abilities and disabilities of the person himself far more wisely fulfill that function. The counsel given in a small illustrated booklet to the patients at the Institute for Physical Medicine and Rehabilitation on the question of standards of performance should be more generally applied:

There are hundreds of ways of doing all these things [that make us independent]. Maybe with your disability you won't be able to do them the same way you used to do, but that certainly doesn't mean you can't learn to do them some other way. And that's why our people are here—to teach you to do these things the best possible way with your disability [Rusk and Taylor, 1946:85].[9]

The account is told of Alice, severely crippled with polio, who learned to ascend stairs:

[8] Reprinted by permission from Lee Meyerson, "A Psychology of Impaired Hearing," in Psychology of Exceptional Children and Youth, to M. Cruickshank (ed.). Copyright, 1955, Prentice-Hall, Inc., Englewood Cliffs, N.J.

[9] H. A. Rusk and E. J. Taylor, New Hope for the Handicapped. Harper & Brothers, 1946. By permission.

. . . [Alice] learned to do at least one thing that seems practically impossible for a person with her limitations: Alice is able to walk upstairs on crutches without using a handrail. Her technique is to go up the steps backwards balancing herself on her two crutches as she pulls up her lifeless legs. She balances herself on her two crutches, pushes down on their handles, thus lifting the entire weight of her body. As her feet reach the step level, she swings them backward and catches her heels on the step [Rusk and Taylor, 1946:92].

Had the "normal" way of ascending stairs been Alice's model, her own techniques would probably never have been discovered.

The goals of rehabilitation and education need, therefore, to be evaluated and reëvaluated. We need to ask, Are the goals set reachable, and if so at what price?

Group Identification

As we have seen, "as if" behavior is in many instances a direct expression of the fervent wish to change one's group identification from the handicapped group to that of the favored majority. Paradoxically, the very attempt to hide the disability often prevents the person from feeling a part of the company of mankind in general. Concealing the disability does not eradicate it; it still remains in the eyes of the person as the barrier to his acceptance by the sought-for group. The stigma of disability that prompts his efforts to cover up at the same time negates his efforts. Not accepting the truth, he has to pay the consequence of being in the ambiguous position of the marginal man who belongs fully to no group (see p. 16). Like the man without a country, he will wander in his search for acceptance that cannot be his until he accepts himself.

A person threatened by identification with a particular group will also avoid contact with that group. Thus, the person who wants to forget his economically meager past will not wish to associate with people "on the other side of the tracks." Such contact reminds the person of his intolerable conflict resulting from deceit; it reminds him of his guilt and of his implicit "belongingness" to that group from which he has separated himself but whose hurt he well understands. Such contact may also threaten the person with discovery, for by the mere fact of contiguity he fears that likeness will be exposed; he may also sense that a person like himself will see through his mask. A similar psychological situation has been explored among the Jews (Lewin, 1948: Part III) and among the Nisei (Yatsushiro, 1953) for whom "the Americanization process was so thorough that in many cases there developed . . . a feeling of hostility toward 'things Japanese,' including frequently their unacculturated immigrant parents" (p. 205).

So it is with the person with a disability whose overpowering wish is to be considered nondisabled. Such a person will "look the other way" at a social gathering to avoid meeting the eyes of a person visibly disabled. He is likely to resist the employment of a person with a disability in his own place of work; he will tend to become hypersensitive to behavior and mannerisms that earmark a person with a handicap.

The *principle of vigilance* operates. This principle, formulated by Bruner and Postman (*1948*), refers to the tendency of the person to respond to threatening material with increased alertness in certain circumstances. It accounts for certain experimental findings on prejudice. Thus, Allport and Kramer (*1946*) whose work was verified by Lindzey and Rogolsky (*1950*) found that persons high in prejudice not only saw more faces as being Jewish than those low in prejudice but also were more accurate in their detection. Though these studies dealt with how majority-group members perceive minority groups, the explanation of the findings applies to a minority-group member who has reason to be alerted to identifying characteristics of his own group. "The question of racial [or in our context, disability] identity is of small importance to the person free from prejudice. Yet it is of considerable importance to the bigot [or to the person threatened by group identification], and for this reason the bigot apparently learns to observe and interpret both facial features and expressive behavior so that he can more swiftly spot his 'enemy' " (Allport and Kramer, *1946*:17).

By the same dynamics, a person who wishes to conceal his disability will notice disability-revealing mannerisms in another person. Moreover, he is likely to resent those mannerisms that advertise the fact of disability, for in wishing to conceal his own disability he wishes others to conceal theirs. Thus it is that the person who is hard of hearing and who strives to hide this fact will be annoyed at the old woman who cups her hand behind her ear. Flaunting the disability is a threat to him because it stirs up the guilt of having scorned his own group membership as well as the possibility of his own exposure. He may prefer surreptitiously to realize the other person's secret and to maintain a gentlemen's agreement that both should play their "as if" roles to having the other person challenge his pretense by confiding his own. He may even develop an active dislike for persons who have a disability and will resent being classed with those who are more severely disabled than himself. One reason why those hard of hearing were moved to establish separate organizations from the deaf was just this desire to avoid identification with a more stigmatized group (Barker *et al., 1953*:189).

Some of these reactions to group identification are seen in Frances Warfield's (*1948*) personal document. It will be recalled that Frances was terrified lest others should discover her imperfect hearing.

She feared exposure by members of her own group:

> . . . I was terribly afraid of deaf people—they didn't like me; I couldn't talk
> loud enough; I was too shy. Moreover, I thought they might be on to my
> secret. I thought that, being deaf themselves, *perhaps they could tell by looking
> at me I didn't always hear* [p. 9, italics added].

She felt uncomfortable in the presence of other deaf persons:

> Marge Martin gave me the willies. She was very pale, with blond hair and
> staring pale-blue eyes. She reminded me a little of Alice Hart, the girl who had
> been electrocuted years ago, back home. Marge talked in a flat voice that was
> sometimes so faint no one could hear it and sometimes so shrill that people
> turned to look at her. That was because she couldn't hear herself accurately,
> people said, and therefore couldn't regulate her voice. . . .
> Whenever I met . . . [her] on campus I smiled and sang out, "Hello, how
> are you?" heartily and hurried past. I didn't want to stop and talk to her if I
> could help it. *It was embarrassing.* You didn't know whether to shout or
> mouth words silently, and it gave you a funny feeling to have her watching
> your lips [p. 43, italics added].

She felt her secret would be revealed if she associated with other deaf
persons.

> Besides, I didn't want to associate even casually with Marge. *Somebody* . . .
> *might get the idea we were alike,* that our voices sounded alike, or something
> [p. 43, italics added].

She preferred mutual pretense on the part of others who were hard of
hearing.

> I went through a series of glubglub part-time maids before I found Poppy, a
> large, plush-upholstered Negro with a rich, plushy voice. Then I had to fire
> Poppy; I heard her telling the back elevator man he'd ought to speak up, her
> young lady didn't hear too good. Poppy was followed by a middle-aged Irish
> woman named Vera, and at last I was safe in my own home, thank goodness.
> Vera was hard of hearing herself. We played our game together. When Vera
> suggested peas for dinner and I ordered cheese instead, she never let on it
> wasn't cheese she'd wanted all along. When Ellen Pringle telephoned and
> Vera's note on the pad read "Miss Trinket called" I said Mrs. Pringle sounded
> exactly like Miss Trinket and, anyhow, people should learn to speak up in this
> world [p. 119].

Not only does a person who views his disability as a stigma tend to
feel uncomfortable in the presence of other persons with disabilities but

he may also resist association with persons who excel in precisely those characteristics wherein lie his lacks. For example, a man disturbed by his own shortness will furtively be interested in the height of a prospective associate, and should the latter be of notably tall stature, will silently mark this against him. The person wishing his deficiency to remain obscured does not welcome a contrast that accentuates it. Thus he is hounded on both sides; he resists the association of others like him and of others unlike him. The resistance is a demonstration of the point made by Horney (*1937*) that the person who does not believe himself lovable is unable to love others. Fromm (*1939*) and others have also asserted that we should love ourselves, for self-love and the love of others go hand in hand.

The discussion can be summarized in two propositions: (1) there is a positive relationship between self-acceptance and acceptance of others; (2) there is a positive relationship between self-acceptance and felt acceptance by others. Experimental support for the first proposition is found in the studies of Sheerer (*1949*), Berger (*1952*) and Fey (*1955*), the correlations between measures of self-acceptance and acceptance of others ranging from $r = .36$ to $r = .69$. Evidence for the second proposition is provided in the work of Fey (*1955*), who found that subjects with high self-acceptance tended also to feel accepted by others ($r = .71$). It is noteworthy that the degree of self-acceptance bore no relationship to the degree to which the subjects were actually accepted by the others as measured by a sociometric device ($r = .07$).

It is always significant in science to observe, because of lawful relations, the same psychological phenomena manifested in situations that appear very different. For this reason it is relevant to note the behavior of members of a government housing project who resented having to live with "low-class" people and who for various reasons could not move (Festinger, *1953*). It was observed that severe limitations were placed on the kinds of contacts they could have with the surrounding community because they imagined that outsiders would also look down on people from the project. Thus the project residents, because of their shame over having to live in the project, remained clearly in a state of relative social isolation both from members of the project (own group) and from people in the town (respected group).

We should now like to offer a clinical demonstration of the fact that acceptance of one's disability is a prerequisite not only for group identification with other persons who have disabilities but also with other persons who are not regarded as disabled. The following sequence captures some of the phases that Noreen passed through in her gradual acceptance of kinship toward other persons with disabilities (Linduska, *1947*). She had contracted polio at the age of 24.

At first, even though dangerously ill, she refused to consider the possibility of polio and insisted that her ailment was "just the flu" (p. 22). Later in the hospital Noreen vacillated between recognizing and denying her illness. On the one hand she inquired about the Sister Kenny treatment and combed all the newspapers for every account of polio that was printed. On the other hand she continued to attribute her paralysis to various other diagnoses, such as diphtheria, streptococcic sore throat, malnutrition, and even mental alienation.

Noreen's gradual willingness to recognize herself as a polio patient is seen when, many months later, as a convalescent who had learned to sit but not yet to walk, she began writing magazine articles about her experiences with polio. However, she still resisted her new group identification and avoided answering the letters from her readers who had a disability, rationalizing that people should not segregate themselves for the sake of sympathetic company (when actually desiring sympathetic company is a healthy and honorable motive and need not imply segregation). When she was asked to become a regular contributor to a monthly magazine for the disabled, she became troubled: "I then realized that I had slipped into a different group of society and I didn't like it" (p. 129).

The true beginning of a feeling of identification with persons who had a disability is seen when, during convalescence, Noreen attended a Sister Kenny rally and felt a sudden kinship with the crippled children on the platform:

I couldn't ascend the platform, so the nurse helped me to a chair in the front row. It wasn't bad. I munched the peanuts, and out of the corner of my eye, I watched the rest of the hall fill. Then the children who were to sit on the platform began to arrive, and a strange kindred feeling arose midway when our glances met. I saw a little boy with a chromium-plated brace on his back and his arm stuck out on a shelf extending perpendicularly from the body. They put him in the front row [p. 162].[10]

But this feeling of group belongingness was unstable and gave way to strong resistance against it when the unreality of her present situation loomed forward in the wake of her reaching out for her past, normal existence:

. . . Suddenly the peanuts stuck in my mouth, and my whole body surged with an emotion I could not identify. I began to breathe faster, and I simply could not decide whether to laugh or cry.

What kind of a crazy, upside-down cockeyed dream was this! CRIPPLED

[10] Noreen Linduska, *My Polio Past,* copyright 1947 by Noreen Linduska. Used by permission of the publishers, Farrar, Straus, and Cudahy, Inc.

CHILDREN! Remember Father's Elks' parties? Remember the Girl Scouts! Remember the Woman's Clubs! Hey! Just a moment! I don't belong with crippled children! I'm on the wrong side of this fence! [p. 162].

Soon after, in describing a splash party in the hospital swimming pool, Noreen was able to feel a real identification with polios:

In our own bathing suits, we polios were rolled off the hospital carts which conveyed us to the pool . . . [p. 167].

It is no accident that Noreen's glimmering feelings of kinship with the minority group were concurrent with her awareness that crippling was an adjustable state, one that still provided tremendous scope for meaningful activity. During the rally, Noreen was lost in thought:

Who said that cripples are unfortunate? Do they, or do you? . . . Polio is not sad—it is just darned inconvenient . . . [pp. 164–165].

The morning before the rally, Noreen had visited the children's polio ward and realized that the world had room for differences:

. . . Here I was in a roomful of the tiniest "victims" as the newspapers called them. . . .
In this room were the little shoes that would be lifted into the Orthopedic School Bus that used to pass our house every morning as I was running down the front stairs to catch the 7:45 "L." These little shoes wouldn't fit into roller skates or skis or be exchanged for soldiers' boots. These would know a different world than that of being center-fielder on the local dry goods baseball team. It wasn't sad—it was simply different, and I knew undramatically that there is a place all picked out in this world for every one of those baby faces [p. 157].

It is equally significant that as Noreen began to appreciate the adjustable side of crippling, there were major shifts within her system of values: moral imperfection became far more important and deplorable than physical disability:

Why and when had physical perfection become so important, when mental imperfection, more easily remedied, went along so unnoticed. Little crippled boys were given sympathy because they could not walk, but how about the little boys who had never been taught to read or write. How about the minds of the children who lived in the same room where the adults in the family slept. Would their minds be crippled? Would somebody pity them if they could run very fast but didn't believe in the future of honesty? Would they be pitied if they lacked whatever it takes to love the dark-skinned children whom they had gone on strike to ban from their high schools? Would they be pitied if they grew up to think that sex was the only thing in life worth working for, and that to be a pin-up girl in a movie studio was the greatest honor a woman could achieve? [pp. 158–159].

This is in sharp contrast to her prepolio outlook where physique and good health had been key criteria for status judgments:

. . . I had belonged to a generation of laughers. My "crowd" was gay and alert. We liked everything new, and if it wasn't new enough, we would invent something that was! I liked to move about all the time. I was thrilled with tennis and volley ball and swimming—and I adored dancing. I had made a hobby of the Russian Ballet ever since I had written an eighth grade term-paper about it. I had secretly been vain about my grace and I loved to remember the man who tried to persuade me to become a part of his adagio team. I had always wanted to be a dancer, but not that kind. The fact that my parents did not approve of dancing as a career did not keep it from being a secret ambition.

Good health was the most important thing in the world, and we even unconsciously scoffed at people with too-frequent sniffles [pp. 176–177].

Noreen was further along the path of adjustment than was Jay, a young man also convalescing from polio. He was greatly troubled by the anticipated pitying attitudes of people outside the hospital. Noreen was better able to take this prospect objectively and to concern herself with its coping aspects. Her adjustment was strengthened by a reëvaluation of the meaning of life involving a reconsideration of the relative importance of significant values.

Jay vividly described the deep struggle against being pushed into an alien group, that of the handicapped. His resistance against being dislocated from his former position was so great that he could not begin to see what his new circumstances had to offer. As long as he felt that he did not belong to the group with a disability, he would continue to feel that he did not belong to the "other half" either. The price for refusal to acknowledge membership in one's own group is great:

. . . When you are healthy all your life, and suddenly in the best years of it, you slip into the other kind—you are naturally unhappy. You are out of your element, a fish out of water. You find yourself where you do not belong. You remember how the other half lives, but you can't live with it. You won't concede your former position—you won't even turn your head to see how comfortable the new category might be. You liked the old places, and there you want to stay—there you don't belong any more, but there you want to stay—so you do—miserably! [p. 194].

Physique, which was a central value for Jay, provided the foundation for his powerful resistance against belonging to the disabled group. For

Noreen, physique was becoming a relatively superficial characteristic, other values being of far greater importance. Consequently, she was now able more comfortably to accept her disability with the result that she was also able more comfortably to feel a part of the nonhandicapped group as well. In answering Jay, she said:

. . . "When you once belong to a group, you always belong. You belong to it because of a lot of reasons you have nothing to do with—race, religion, position, education, inherited traits and talents. Those things are not physical, but they make you belong someplace. Sometimes these uncontrollable factors combine and people of unlike religions or talents make up a group—but somewhere there is a common, compatible factor. Just because you can't hop off a chair or go running down some stairs doesn't mean that you belong to a different group—the common factors are never that shallow" [p. 194].

To sum up, the preceding analysis revolved around the following points:

1. During the initial phase of her illness, Noreen refused with all the psychological maneuvers she could muster to accept the fact of her disability.
2. Her prepolio values provided a strong foundation for this resistance. Health had been all-important, with physical skills and grace in close second position.
3. But the facts of her illness were unrelenting.
4. And something was being done about her condition. She was massaged, hot-packed, etc.
5. Gradually she became less preoccupied with the threatening, succumbing aspects of disability and more involved with ideas of coping with it.
6. Concurrently, changes occurred within her value system. Moral and personality values became more important than physique, which was but a shallow characteristic.
7. These changes helped Noreen find her locus within the group with disabilities and consequently also within the ranks of the normal majority.

But the pendulum must not swing the other way. To accept one's disability and oneself as a person with a disability by no means implies an all-absorbing interest in disability-connected problems. Too much preoccupation may be as much a sign of maladjustment as ostensibly too little. Generalizing to all group memberships, Lewin correctly points out: "If an individual's membership in any one group, e.g., the Jews, is of dominant interest to those around him in all situations, or a dominant value for him in all situations then he is living in an unhealthy totalitarian social setting from the point of view of group dynamics, no matter whether this dominating membership is his family, his race, his religion, or his nation" [or, we add, his disability] (Lippitt, *1945*:26).

But accepting one's disability and oneself as a person with a disability does imply a certain feeling of kinship with others who have the disability, a feeling of knowing such a person a little even though he is a stranger, in the same way that meeting an American abroad makes for an immediate tie, albeit a temporary one. This hypothesis may be integrated within Heider's (*1958*) theory which relates sentiments to unit formation (see pp. 262–263). Accepting one's disability allows the factor of similarity to bring about unhampered the formation of a group, which in turn arouses a positive feeling toward the other person. This phenomenon is seen in the personal experience of Louise Baker (*1946*), an amputee:

> I have met a great many crippled people since then and some of them have developed into real friends. Even the most casual contacts, however, have been rewarding. One-leggedness is a common ground on which individuals of vast difference in background can meet and communicate. I have had fascinating conversations with handicapped persons whose lives were so divergent from my own that in the normal course of a two-legged life, I never even would have crossed their pathways.
>
> A jolly drunk who sold newspapers on a city corner and who happened to wear a peg leg, gave me a full, though perhaps slightly alcohol-flavored, account of himself one day while I waited for a bus. Similarly, I've learned all about the private lives of a taxi driver, an ex-policeman, a sculptor, a factory worker out on parole from a woman's reformatory, a little one-armed Negro orphan, a Japanese fruit peddler, an architect, etc., etc. We speak to each other. We flaunt our fraternity badges. Whatever our limping walks in life we are all people of parts—missing. We stand on common ground. We may remain transients; we usually do. We meet; we pass on; but we enrich each other in the passing [p. 156].[11]

Accepting one's disability and oneself as a person with a disability does mean that belonging only to the majority is not all-important, for in belonging to the minority as well one belongs to humanity, a group that knows no majority-minority boundaries.

The Eclipse of Behavior Possibilities

The insecurity of the person who tries to forget and conceal his disability is yet further increased because he does not allow himself to clarify what he can and cannot do. We have seen (pp. 21–24) how

---

[11] Reprinted by permission from *Out on a Limb* by Louise Baker, published by McGraw-Hill Book Company, Inc. Copyright 1946 by Louise Baker.

Frances bluffed her way through all kinds of social occasions, instead of asking for more light in order to lip-read, or for someone to speak louder or to repeat (Warfield, *1948*). Frances figured out elaborate techniques to cope with "dinner lulls," intermissions at concerts, football games, dances, and so on, in order to protect her secret. But they served only to make her more uncertain, and in turn more cautious, and in turn more uncertain. Thus, Frances had it down pat that at a dinner party she should (1) sit next to someone with a strong voice; (2) choke, cough, or get hiccups, if someone asked her a direct question; (3) take hold of the conversation herself, ask someone to tell a story she had already heard, ask questions the answers to which she already knew (Warfield, *1948*:36). But what if she were placed next to a mumbler? What if, after her coughing, the person persisted in asking questions? What if? The uncertainty and panic snowball. Behavior resulting from new and uncertain situations follows (see Chap. 4).

The person does not allow himself to clarify his behavior possibilities because, in order to do so, he must first be able to acknowledge, "this is my limitation. . . ." Only then will he realistically be able to study the requirements of different situations toward his more able functioning in them. Only then will demarcation between what he can and cannot do become more sharply defined. Only then will he realize that confidence in the self which is essential to the adequate meeting of new situations that inevitably present themselves.

Compensation as Indemnity

Overcoming of inferiority is also sought by way of compensation. Compensation has been defined as "the individual's attempt to make up for an undesirable trait and the consequent discomfort by emphasizing or exaggerating a desirable trait" (Maslow and Mittlemann, *1951*:575). In order to avoid semantic confusion, let it be noted that compensation is sometimes used in a fundamentally different meaning. Sommers (*1944*), for instance, applies the designation "compensatory reaction" to those individuals who recognize and accept the limitations of their disability and concentrate on what they can do. It is in the former sense that we shall use the term "compensation"—i.e., as an indemnity, a way to "make up for" a shortcoming in order to redeem oneself.

The concept of compensation was given a prominent place in adjustment theory at the instigation of Alfred Adler (*1917a, b*), who felt that organic or constitutional inferiority was basic to man's striving for adaptation to the world in which he lives. In compensating for his inferiority, the person may either be led to constructive achievement or to a neurotic power drive.

That compensation occurs cannot be denied, but to consider it the spring of all or even most motivation is questionable. Also questionable is the view that compensation, as a prodder of achievement, is a way toward mental health. These issues are especially germane to the psychology of disability because of the readiness with which all behavior is linked with the disability. Thus, accomplishment tends to be seen as compensatory, *particularly* when the achiever has an obvious disability.

Cutsforth (*1948*), a clinical psychologist who is blind, deplores the approval that educators and social agencies for the blind place upon compensation: "The attempt to compensate for the feelings of inadequacy drives the individual ofttimes to the achievement of successes, but never to personality adjustment" (p. 67). A person with a physical limitation has, in fact, nothing "to make up for"—that is, unless he feels inferior because of it. The following admonition captures the essential devaluating presupposition underlying the adjustment theory of compensation: In order not to be especially bad, the person with a disability (or any minority-group member) must be especially good. The theory of compensation that includes "making up for" as part of its dynamics is actually a theory of shame and guilt.

The fact that a disability imposes limitations in certain situations does not mean, perforce, that the person has to sing better, or write better, or do something else better. It means only that he, like everyone else, has to engage in and pursue those activities which he can do and finds rewarding. He will not join the track team, because there is no sport where there is no challenge. But he may become a radio ham, not because he must "make up for" his limp, but because mechanical and electrical matters interest him. Had he been sound of limb, it is possible that his mechanical interests might have directed him toward piloting an airplane. But this does not mean that being a radio ham is second choice to piloting—*not necessarily*. Now that he has explored radio, he may find it more challenging than piloting, even if the choice were his to make. Moreover, his initial move toward radio need not have been primed by compensatory forces. When a person is unsuitable for one undertaking, he may seek another and pursue it because the experience is satisfying rather than compensating. The person who cannot become a doctor because of limited financial means chooses instead to become a biologist, not necessarily because he is compensating, but because limited financial resources is but one among other important considerations. All major decisions take into account a vast array of factors in order to lead to the best choice. The final decision is not compensatory *just because* it has included considerations of limitations.

Actually, if the prime motivation to be a good radio ham continued to be compensatory, the person's full satisfaction of achievement would be spoiled by the interminable fermentation of inferiority feelings over the fact that he is a cripple. His achievements, no matter how great, would not alter the fact of his disability, and as long as he felt that this fact had to be compensated for, so long would he continue to suffer the apology for himself. Byron, the great British poet, Talleyrand, the great French states-man—each was born with a club foot. Byron evidently showed as much ambition to excel in violent exercises as the most robust youth of the school. Though both rose to the heights of world fame, it is reported that neither could ever forget for a moment that he was lame, and both suffered the ignominy of attempts at dissimulation and feigning (Hentig, *1948a*:75–76).

In only one sense would we propose that compensation as a principle of mental hygiene has anything to recommend it. The driving force that pushes a person to new pursuits may produce major alterations in the individual's system of values. The new areas may reveal satisfactions and values which become more important than the old ones that led the person to compensate. A person who paints *because* he limps may dis-cover that art is a significant value too, that a person's worth need not arbitrarily be connected with his physique.

EFFECTS ON PERSONALITY

Opinion and Research Findings

One might suppose that a stigmatizing, underprivileged social position would predispose the individual toward feeling inferior as a person. As a matter of fact, feelings of inferiority are mentioned with considerable frequency by experts and laymen alike as characterizing disabled groups.

A study of the expert opinion of professional workers with the handi-capped revealed that feelings of inferiority (with a frequency of about 25 percent) headed the list of behavior characteristics mentioned by 26 authors in general articles about the handicapped (Barker *et al.*, *1946*:71).

A study of the opinion of high school students revealed that when the stimulus subject was represented as crippled he was rated as feeling more inferior than when he was represented as able-bodied (Ray, *1946*). Specifi-cally, high school students were presented with six photographs of college boys to be placed in rank order according to a number of behavior and personality characteristics. One of the college boys was photographed sitting in a wheel chair and this picture was presented to half of the subjects; to the other half, the same picture was presented with the wheel chair blocked out. When depicted as crippled as compared to able-bodied, the stimulus was judged to be more conscientious, to feel more inferior, to be a better friend, to get better grades, to be more even-tempered, to be a better class president, to be more religious, to like parties less, and to be more unhappy.

However, when we turn to the research literature on the *actual* feelings of persons with disabilities, a far less clear-cut picture is found. In some studies, the disabled groups earned scores indicative of *greater* self-respect than their "normal" controls. For example, the postpoliomyelitis cases in Seidenfeld's (*1948a*) study showed a greater sense of personal worth on a personality test than the groups on which the test was standardized. And in Arluck's (*1941*) study, both the cardiac and the epileptic subjects more often *felt superior* to most children in respect to attitudes, feelings, and interests than did their normal controls, as measured by a self-rating scale.

In other studies no relationship was found between specific physical characteristics and inferiority feelings. Sommers' (*1944*) blind adolescents, for example, came out just as high on sense of personal worth as the norms for the standardization population. And negligible correlations were found between inferiority feelings and height or weight of men and women in another study (Faterson, as reported in Paterson, *1930*).

On the other hand, studies do exist that show a relationship, albeit a low one, between feelings of inferiority and physical defect. In Arluck's (*1941*) study, the epileptic subjects, but not the cardiac subjects, tended to feel that they were inferior in respect to their *behavior,* though not in respect to their *feelings,* more often than did the normal subjects. The hospitalized tuberculous but not the hospitalized amputees in a study by Shelsky (*1957*) tended to be more self-rejecting than the control subjects who were also hospitalized but for minor illnesses. The findings in this case were based on a self-rating scale utilizing an adjective check list. In still another study by Faterson (*1931*), the Minnesota Rating Scale for measuring inferiority attitudes was administered to a group of entering university students and the resulting scores were correlated with degree of physical defect as determined from each student's medical report. A physical-defect score was obtained by giving one point for each physical defect reported on the medical blank, such defects being included as fallen arches, menstrual disorders, heart murmurs, poor posture, nasal obstruction, orthopedic defects, diseased tonsils, insomnia, tiredness, etc. The correlations between inferiority feelings and physical defect for men and for women were low (under .25) but positive. (Note that the physical-defect score included deviations such as insomnia and tiredness which might easily have a large psychosomatic component.)

No matter how the studies are grouped, the data cannot be ordered so that scores of inferiority are in any systematic way related to disability or to such aspects of disability as type, duration, or degree.

Oversimplified Connection Between Disability and Inferiority Feelings

To attempt a clarification of the preceding problem, several considerations need to be taken into account. First of all, disability is not the only characteristic that places a person in an inferior status position. Underprivileged minority status touches those of particular races and religion, of low socioeconomic level, and of slower mental development. Even children are placed in the psychological position of inferior status, and women too in some respects. In short, all of us have within us the experience of being looked down upon as individuals or as part of a larger group.

But, the protest might be made, a person with a disability has the stigma of a disability superimposed on whatever other depreciating characteristic he might have; he has a greater load of inferior status to bear and a more persistent one. Ought not this fact lead to more pronounced feelings of inferiority? Evidently not. And the reason is an important one. *Psychological processes do not add up in a simple way.*

For clarification, let us consider the relationship between *degree* of disability and adjustment. One might assume that the greater a person's disability, the more difficult it is for him to accept it or to achieve good adjustment. But the facts provoke serious question of this. Though some studies (Brunschwig, *1936;* Kammerer, *1940;* Landis and Bolles, *1942*) have shown a relationship between degree of disability and poor adjustment, other studies (Springer, *1938;* Donofrio, *1948;* Tracht, *1946*) have shown no relationship, and still others (Macgregor *et al., 1953:*70; Miller, *1958*) have shown the reverse relationship.

To explain these inconsistencies, it may be postulated that a person with a mild disability may, because he is *almost* normal, have a greater push to hide and deny his disability, thereby thwarting his own adjustment, whereas a person whose disability is so severe as to be undeniable has little recourse but to grapple with the problem of accepting himself as a person with a disability. Support for this hypothesis may be drawn from the point made by Heider (*1958*) that a near approach to what we desire seems to make its attainment more possible, and from Dembo's (*1931*) observations in experiments on anger that the subjects were more disturbed when they *almost* succeeded in the task (throwing rings on a peg) than when the failure was more clear-cut. The observation has also been made that the child with cerebral palsy who has a mild handicap appears to have more severe adjustment problems arising from disturbed parent-child relationships than does the child with a severe cerebral palsy involvement (Miller, *1958*). On the other hand it may also be postulated that a mild disability, by imposing fewer frustrations owing to the barrier of physical limitations, makes adjustment easier. Doubtless there are other factors associated with degree of disability, some favoring and some hindering good adjustment, the resultant effect being quite removed from the objective fact of severity. Notice that we have moved from the *physical* fact of degree of disability to *psychological* concepts, such as need to hide the disability, perception of probability of goal attainment, and frustration, in order to account for the associated personality and psychological behavior. Such psychological concepts are known as *intervening variables* and are necessary for the understanding of somatopsychological problems (see pp. 377–380).

By like reasoning, we cannot say that frequency or intensity of social devaluation is related in a direct or one-to-one way to personal feelings of inferiority. With increase in social devaluation may come an increased need for a new look into one's values, which, as an important first step in the process of adjustment, may do much to counteract the destructive power of inferior social status.

Furthermore, inferior status is not the only psychological situation in which a person with a disability is placed. At times he may be looked up to and may even enjoy an exalted position (see Chap. 3). The majority group may sometimes bestow genuine commendation, as when the person is acknowledged who achieves in spite of his disability, and certainly respect, encouragement, and acceptance from family members and close friends are not infrequent. That salutary status and acceptance by others are not foreign to members of minority groups is undoubtedly an important prophylactic against the deluge of feelings of worthlessness.

In an important study by Langdon and Stout (*1951*) on well-adjusted children, it was discovered that despite tremendous differences in the background and physical characteristics of these children, many of which could be considered as social or physical handicaps, there was one outstanding similarity: the children were loved by their parents in an atmosphere of warm though not necessarily demonstrative acceptance. Of the 261 well-adjusted children, some wore glasses, one used a hearing aid, a few were described as overweight, some underweight, several were left-handed. One was said to have a spastic condition, another a heart lesion, another to be diabetic. The children were oldest, youngest, in the middle. Some were from poor homes and some from middle-class homes and higher. Several children came from one-parent families through divorce, separation, or death. There were children of mixed religious beliefs. There was such a diversity of discipline procedures as one can hardly imagine, ranging all the way from "They do what I say or else" to "We want them to want to do what is right." Yet all these children were well adjusted! And all the parents, without a single exception, expressed in some way the following thoughts as being most important of all: Loving them and letting them know it, thinking of them as people and treating them so, appreciating what they do and trusting them and telling them so, and above all letting them know they are wanted. This study is important in showing that conditions commonly accepted as being deleterious to personality development do not necessarily bend the twig into a deformed tree; the tree may flower and prosper because of deeper psychological soil made rich by growth-promoting interpersonal relationships.

The thesis presented here does differ from Alfred Adler's (*1917b*) theory, which holds that ". . . the possession of definitely inferior organs is reflected upon the psyche—and in such a way as to lower the self-esteem, to raise the child's psychological uncertainty. But it is just out of this lowered self-esteem that there arises the struggle for self-assertion . . . the predisposed child in his sense of inferiority selects out of his psychic resources expedients for the raising of his own value . . . among which may be noted as occupying the most prominent places those of a neurotic and psychotic character" (p. 3). The Adlerian doctrine would lead one to expect a high incidence of neurotic and psychotic tendencies in individuals with a physical disability and specifically of marked feelings of inferiority. The available objective evidence, however, supports none of these expectations and forces one to the conclusion that there has been a gross oversimplification of the connection between physical impairment and maladjustment.

Moreover, even should inferiority feelings in an individual case history be associated with defective physique, we must in order to understand and evaluate those feelings ". . . deal with the individual in relation to and as part of the family, and with the family in relation to and as part of the individual's cultural environment" (Sommers, *1944:*98). As Allen and Pearson (*1928*) have pointed out, "When the relationship between the child and its parents and its effect on the development of the former's personality is studied, it becomes evident that this feeling of inferiority has causes other than the physical defect, although these causes are associated with and conditioned by it" (p. 234). Sommers' (*1944*) intensive study of blind adolescents clearly reveals that the feelings of the individual with regard to his own inferiority, incompetence, uncertainty, and the manner in which he accepts his defect are conditioned principally by the attitudes of those around him, especially his parents.

Our position must be further clarified on one point. It does not assert that physical disability plays no role at all in the development of inferiority feelings or other problems. It does imply, however, that the objective fact of disability is an extraordinarily poor criterion for judging which individual is unduly beset by self-abnegation and which individual is not, and that the common association between inferiority feelings and atypical physique is a gross oversimplification unwarranted by the facts.

Indeed, physical disability, through social derogation, does produce psychological problems. Some of these have already been reviewed in this chapter. And the problems are not easy to solve, for they are weighted with frustration and hurt and sorrow and their inherent conflicts pull the person in different directions. But persons with disabilities do solve them, evidently about as well (or as poorly) as do the nondisabled who are also faced with the same psychological problems though their specific content may differ in some respects. Some factors important in the process of solving the difficulties stemming from a stigmatizing personal character-istic are discussed in Chap. 5.

Thus far we have been concerned with efforts to escape the stigmatizing effects of disability, efforts that are first attempts and often persistent but not soundly adjustive, for they function to sidetrack negative attitudes associated with disability rather than to overcome them. The discussion dealt with forgetting, concealing, idolizing normal standards, group identification, the eclipse of behavior possibilities, and compensation as indemnity. It was seen that these phenomena were prompted and guided by a basic rejection of the disability when it is seen as a devaluating characteristic which makes of one an inferior person. At the same time, the person has a need to accept his disability; in spite of all, he would like to feel comfortable with himself as a person with a disability, and to have others accept him as such. The undercurrents of these feelings, long repressed, may be stirred into consciousness by the gradual recognition that pretense produces nothing but repeated failure, shame, guilt, and estrangement from oneself and others. Pretense gradually becomes recog-nized for what it is, an insult added to an injury. It is then that efforts to accept the disability become more clearly the honorable and realistic method of choice.

The value changes implied in these efforts are discussed at length in Chap. 5. In the following chapter, attention will be given to the fact that, along with inferior status, disability may under certain conditions also bring with it a position of respect. It is well that we examine these condi-tions, for within them lie important clues for aiding adjustment to dis-ability.

Chapter 3

Salutary Status Position

FAVORABLE, PUBLICLY EXPRESSED ATTITUDES TOWARD PERSONS WITH atypical physiques are not infrequent. In one study (Mussen and Barker, *1944*), students were asked to rate cripples in general on 24 personality traits. The median ratings fell nearest the following descriptive phrases:

Conscientiousness: Tries harder than most
Self-reliance: Tendency to have more than average degree
Kindness: More than average
Emotional restraint: Tendency to be reserved; seldom lets the world know his feelings
Persistence: Quite persistent; gives up only after definite proof of impossibility
Mental alertness: Intelligent; more alert than average
Originality: Tendency to be more creative than average
Religiousness: Tendency to be more religious than most people
Impulsiveness: Inclined to ponder possible results of behavior
Unselfishness: Marked tendency to be unselfish; generous, altruistic
Friendliness: Average
Trustworthiness: Average
Disposition: Average; for the most part moderately cheerful
Tolerance: Average
Courage: Average
Self-pity: Average
Social poise and tact: Average ability and interest in getting along with others
Vitality: Average amount of vitality, energy, pep
Self-confidence: Average
Submissiveness: Average amount of ascendance and submission
Realism: Given to reverie occasionally
Aggressiveness: Tendency to be mild; gentle in approach to others
Social adaptability: Finds it somewhat difficult to adjust to new situations
Sensitiveness: More sensitive than average

Ray's (*1946*) data (detailed on p. 51) support the preceding study in showing that publicly expressed attitudes toward cripples are frequently favorable. Covert attitudes, of course, may in some if not many of these instances still remain negative.

When the subjects of Strong's (*1931*) study were asked whether they liked, disliked, or were indifferent to persons with a variety of physical characteristics, the most common response was "indifferent." Cripples and blind persons were more frequently checked as being liked than disliked, whereas the reverse was true for deaf-mutes. The following percentages represent the responses of 2340 professional men and businessmen between the ages of 20 and 60.

	Liking	Disliking	Indifferent
Sick people	22%	28%	50%
Very old people	45	11	44
Cripples	29	19	52
Side-show freaks	4	77	19
People with gold teeth	4	46	50
People with protruding jaws	6	42	52
People with hooked noses	4	38	58
Blind people	25	16	59
Deaf-mutes	16	25	59

These percentages may be compared with the following:

People who borrow things	3%	77%	20%
Negroes	13	32	55
Socialists	8	41	51
Athletic men	74	1	25
Conservatives	50	12	38

The evidence seems clear that publicly expressed attitudes toward persons with physical disabilities for the most part are not unfavorable, are frequently mildly positive, and may even indicate respect. Yet positive feelings toward persons with disabilities have been given little attention.

Positive attitudes in general are more apt to go unnoticed and unnamed because they do not disturb our sense of well-being, of what "ought" to be. So it is that the nomenclature of maladjustment is much richer and more differentiated than that concerning good adjustment. The list of pathology extends long and wide, whereas normal adjustment is modestly described under the relatively undifferentiated classification, normal adjustment. We shall find, however, that once we trouble ourselves about the untroubling positive status aspects of disability, their still waters run as deep as the turbulence of inferiority.

COPING VS. SUCCUMBING

A woman, in musing about injured war veterans, remarked, "When I thought of the courage it took to ignore those handicaps, I felt humble. I felt that anyone who overcomes a handicap like that wins an added amount of respect from everyone" (Dembo, Leviton, Wright, *1956*:24). In contrast, others in thinking of severe disabilities feel, "It wouldn't be worthwhile to live." "I'd go into hiding and not show my face for the rest of my life" (Dembo, Leviton, Wright, *1956*:24).

What are some of the immediately underlying differences between these two points of view? In the first instance, the person, although appreciating the seriousness of the disability, focused on the adjustable or coping aspects. She saw the difficulties associated with a disability as something that could be faced in some way or overcome. Those who voiced the second kind of comment saw the difficulties as a quagmire through which there was no path. Perhaps one doesn't even seek a path, for one is so consumed with the suffering of the disabled state that one is dragged down by despair. The difficulties are in command and one succumbs to them.

One's orientation toward coping with or succumbing to difficulties has contrasting effects on the evaluation of a person with a disability. When the person with a disability is coping with his problems and the black side of things is held in check, he is placed higher on the scale of adjustment than in the reverse situation. A person with a disability who is seen to make the most of what he has, to arrange his life in accordance with his abilities, is respected and even admired. Further positive attitudes may also be differentiated, such as feeling that the person has courage, or ambition, or stamina, etc. Even should the person die as the result of his injury, the fact that he "put up a good fight"—i.e., that he was occupied with coping with his problems—makes him a person of strength and dignity. In contrast, when preoccupation with the undermining or succumbing features of the situation is typical, the person tends to be devaluated. His situation may be looked upon with horror and even derision, and he may be pitied or even contemptuously disregarded.

Of course, concentrating on the coping possibilities does not imply glossing over the difficulties themselves. Disregarding difficulties could lead only to unrealistic behavior on the part of the person with the disability or, if others should ignore his difficulties, it would make him feel that they are taking his situation lightly. Actually, coping means coping with the difficulties rather than managing because of blissful ignorance or pretense. Indeed, the difficulties must be realistically appraised if continued failure and discouragement, the most effective impetus to succumbing forces, are to be avoided.

Coping, even when half-hearted, may provide the spark for the adjustive change designated as "enlarging the scope of values" in the case of what has been called all-inclusive suffering (see pp. 108–115). Coping may also provide the opportunity for "containing disability affects" (see pp. 118–128), for it leads to new learnings and solutions that overcome difficulties. The person who becomes blind, for example, must learn to go from his bedroom to the kitchen, and *in trying* discovers that visual cues are not the only stimuli the world has to offer. "Then you perceive suddenly that there is order and reason and communication within the vast darkness which had seemed only chaos" (Ohnstad, *1942*:42).[1] The way Karsten Ohnstad relearned to write soon after he became blind illustrates well how coping is the true mother of invention. He became impatient with having to depend on the nurses for doing his writing, and after trying unsuccessfully to produce a legible product on his own, he discovered that he needed something to hold his paper steady and to keep the lines straight across the page:

. . . I found a medical-chart holder—a flat piece of metal with rubber-tipped clamps at the top. The rubber clamps held the paper firmly in place. As a guide for making a straight line, I laid an envelope across the sheet and folded the left end under the chart, so that it could slide up and down along the edge without becoming crooked. A rubber band slipped around the entire chart held the envelope in place at whatever point I pushed it. It worked! When I made a *g* or an *f* or any letter that dropped below the line, I lifted the edge of the envelope until I had made the loop and then dropped it again. The lines were no longer run together. Completing a line at the right-hand side of the sheet, I pulled the envelope downward the approximate distance of the line, and there it remained, held fast by the rubber band. I handed the letter to a nurse and glowed with the pride of accomplishment as she read it word for word rapidly and without hesitation [Ohnstad, *1942*:48–49].

Psychologists increasingly are concerning themselves with the positive strivings in man, with the factors that lead him to face and cope constructively with his problems. Among the investigators who have recently given particular attention to this emphasis are L. Murphy (*1956*), in her research with children, and Maslow (*1954*) and Rogers (*1951*) in their work with adults. The emphasis was explicitly recorded in the proceedings of an Institute on Psychology and Rehabilitation (Wright, *1959*). Among the 12 principles and assumptions defining rehabilitation listed therein are included (1) the importance of stressing the "assets of the person," his stabilizing and maturity inducing characteristics, and (2) the necessity of

[1] Karsten Ohnstad, *The World at My Fingertips,* Indianapolis, The Bobbs-Merrill Company, 1942. By permission.

dealing with "reality factors," those difficulties within the actual social and physical environment with which the person with a disability has to cope.

In summary, coping serves the person in various ways. As a value in itself, it enhances his status. It also makes possible adjustive changes in the outlook of the person with respect to his disability.

Attractions and Aversions as Expressions of Coping-Succumbing

One type of affect aroused by the perception of coping or succumbing associations—namely, the aesthetic reaction to disability-connected symbols—can be taken as typical and discussed at length. Reaction to the sight of blood, an exposed stump, braces and crutches, etc., is sometimes matter-of-fact and even positive, sometimes strongly antipathetic. One might, for example, turn away from the sight of blood when it signifies a crushing accident, suffering, and pain but be quite calm about it when it connotes the life-saving material for the blood bank. One might be bothered by the sight of a stump and consider its exposure indecent, or see it as well healed and ready for a prosthesis.

The same holds true for aesthetic reactions to prosthetic devices. During Harold Russell's (*1949*) initial reaction to his handlessness, he thought of hooks in terms of their devastating implications—as "claws" and "flippers," "hollow in sound." An old-time amputee, on the other hand, thought of his hooks as loyal friends who had served him well; to him they were "nice shiny little hooks." Harold notes: ". . . The prospect of going through life with steel claws terrified me. That would mean I'd be openly advertising the fact that I was a cripple and a freak. Besides, they were gruesome and repulsive to look at" (*1949:*42).[2] He therefore looked toward the cosmetic artificial hand in the hope that it would cover up his handlessness. Desperately he asked an old-time hand amputee, "Were they [the cosmetics] any good? How well did they work? Did they really look like the genuine article?" (p. 43). The old-timer replied:

"Ah reckons they ain't so hot, son, else more folks'd be usin' 'em." He chuckled and clacked his hooks together like a seal clapping his flippers; they gave off a dismal, hollow sound. "No, suh! Gimme mah nice, shiny little hooks anytime! Yuh c'n do anythin' with 'em, positively anythin', suh!" [p. 43].

Harold continued to be filled with horror at the thought of going through life with hooks until he discovered for himself that the hooks worked, whereas the cosmetic hands did not. It is noteworthy that from

[2] Harold Russell with Victor Rosen, *Victory in My Hands,* copyright 1949. Used by permission of the publishers, Farrar, Straus, and Cudahy, Inc.

then on he thought of the hooks as hooks or artificial hands or working hands, and of the cosmetic prosthesis as "phony hands."

It didn't take me long to discover my mistake. The "cosmetics" looked all right, though the gray gloves gave me a clammy feeling and reminded me of pall-bearers hauling a coffin. What was more important, however, was that they didn't work. To begin with, only the thumb and index finger could be moved at all; the other three fingers were stationary. Then the normal position of the two functional ones were open. That meant that when I wanted to grasp something and hold onto it I had to exert constant pressure in order to keep the fingers closed. That was both tiring and disturbing. If I relaxed for just an instant, I'd drop whatever I was holding. I was under steady physical and mental strain everytime I picked up something.

The following morning I went back to the workshop. I traded the phony hands for a pair of hooks. Maybe they didn't look so good, but they worked. I found that out right away. I pulled out a cigaret and lit it. It took a little struggling, but I was able to do it, which was more than I could say for the hands. I left the shop feeling that maybe things weren't going to be so bad, after all [pp. 99–100].

Though at this point Harold still had a long way to go before he could approach full acceptance of his hooks, the groundwork was well laid. The hooks had become secured within the frame of coping rather than of succumbing.

By the same dynamics, Noreen Linduska (1947) was able to see her braces as aesthetically pleasing, whereas they were abhorrent to an outsider. When Noreen described them as beautifully chromium plated, a woman felt that she was being "gruesome" (p. 189).

Another incisive example is the reaction of Karen and her mother when they saw Karen's crutches for the first time. Karen, now 7, had never walked. For years she had been slowly conquering the limitations of cerebral palsy by diligent application toward self-help in feeding, washing, and dressing, and by development of sitting balance, active reciprocal motion, etc. After what seemed like interminable waiting, the crutches finally arrived. They were glorious, because they meant not incapacity but tools with which to walk:

. . . I [Karen's mother] threw the package on the couch and scampered off for a pair of scissors. It took a few minutes but finally I was down to the box. I took the box and placed it on the floor in front of Karen. Reverently I raised the lid. I looked at Karen. She was staring down, spellbound.

There in all their gleaming beauty were our crutches. "Isn't the wood beautiful," she said in a hushed voice.

Lifting her out of the bars, I sat her on the ottoman. My hands trembled as I lifted the crutches from their box. Wood or wings? [Killilea, *1952:*215].[3]

Of course, the perception of succumbing aspects and the resultant aversions may be invested with quite widely differing emotional contents. An example of deeply morbid preoccupation is the reaction of Miss M., observed in an experiment on the emotional reactions of nondisabled persons to a cosmetic hand (Cattell *et al.,* 1949). The subject was in a small group that included a young man wearing a cosmetic hand prosthesis. Unable to bear the sight of the hand, she left; when interviewed later, she spontaneously said:

"It nauseated me. That's why I ran out. The sandwich [which she had been eating] began to smell . . . I smelled it again. The look of the hand where it came to the ridge . . . discolored, yellow-greenish" (grimaces and shows disgust and shrinks from the discussion and has to be encouraged to go on) [p. 62].

After continued discussion Miss M. pointed out that "It looked like nothing. It looked like death" (p. 63).

What is important to realize is that Miss M.'s marked aversion to the yellow-greenish color is comprehensible when seen as linked to emotional contents that destroy the person, in this case the association of death. To be sure, negative reactions can be aroused by other than succumbing features; for example, the cosmetic hand may be rejected because it does not fit the build or personality of the wearer. But where there is aversion and not just disapproval or regret, the evaluator is overwhelmed by the perception of succumbing rather than coping aspects. What may be gruesome to one may be gratifying to another, for in the one case it signifies troubles and heartaches and in the second case solutions and adjustments.

Underlying Conditions

The pressing question, then, concerns the conditions that give focus to the coping rather than the succumbing possibilities in situations involving serious difficulties. One important condition concerns the *position* of the person with respect to the disability situation—i.e., whether he is an intimate part of it or an outsider looking in. In general, the *inside* position is characteristic of the person with the disability himself, persons close to him such as family and intimate friends, and those directly involved in

[3] Reprinted with permission of Prentice-Hall, Inc., from *Karen* by Marie Killilea. Copyright 1952 by Marie Lyons Killilea.

his welfare, such as rehabilitation workers and vocational counselors. Typical of the *outside* position is that of strangers or persons who feel little connection with the fate of the person with the disability.

In the former case, the person and those concerned about him not only wish for success but are actually faced with the necessity of coping with the difficulties; both wish and *necessity* persistently emphasize various coping possibilities.

In contrast, the need to cope with disability problems may not be felt by the stranger or the casual acquaintance. Such a person sees only the hardships imposed by the disability. Moreover, he may in many instances overestimate the extent of the limitations because he views them from his own vantage point rather than from that of a person with the disability. If he could assume the inside position, he would not, for example, be puzzled when a blind person attends the movies for, after all, he himself enjoys the radio without benefit of visual stimulation. Yet, because of his outside psychological position, many a sighted person remains incredulous. The emphasis on the succumbing as against the coping possibilities is one important factor, we believe, in the surprise, if not doubt, of many persons when informed that handicapped and nonhandicapped *groups* are for the most part indistinguishable with respect to health of personality.

There is yet another factor—namely, the *requirement of mourning* (see pp. 242–243)—that predisposes the outsider toward emphasizing the aspect of succumbing to difficulties. When the security of the outsider depends upon maintaining his high status with respect to physique, he will have a need to emphasize the negative aspects of disability and to expect and even demand that a person with a physical disability pity himself. Thus, the lack of a need to perceive coping possibilities and the existence of a need to perceive succumbing aspects may combine in the outsider with such uncontested force that he pitilessly "pities" a person with a disability. Other outsiders, although they may genuinely wish the person success, may not have the opportunity to become aware of coping possibilities.

Implications for Rehabilitation and Education

Originally, agencies on behalf of persons with disabilities were organized to give comfort to the afflicted, to make the lot of the handicapped somewhat easier. Increasingly, the efforts of organizations are being directed away from charity and toward constructive effort.[4] Fraternal and social

---

[4] Allan (*1958*) presents a comprehensive and enlightening review of current rehabilitation activities as shared by the many disciplines and the broader community.

organizations of all kinds are making tangible contributions toward rehabilitating persons with disabilities rather than merely solacing them. The focus on succumbing to disability leads to charity, the focus on coping to rehabilitation.

The best rehabilitation procedures contribute enormously toward bringing into focus the possibilities of coping with difficulties. For example, the emphasis on what Rusk and Taylor (*1953*) have called "activities of everyday living" directs the person to deal with the concrete here-and-now demands of getting along. When a paraplegic patient learns to move from the bed to the wheel chair, from the wheel chair to the floor, he is learning something more important than a new physical skill; he is learning that he can improve his situation and that in coping with the many "little things" he is coping with the biggest thing of all: gaining self-respect. It has been said that working with daily-activity skills is the basis for all subsequent rehabilitation processes. This is as true for the restoration of self-respect as it is for the restoration of physical independence. The emphasis on coping is caught in the following two rules stressed by the Institute of Physical Medicine and Rehabilitation at Bellevue Hospital, New York, namely: "You can't disable ambition" and "You still have a lot more ability than you have disability."

Success stories can also aid a person with a recent disability by highlighting the reality of coping successfully with the attendant difficulties. The story is told of a Marine flying officer whose left heel and entire right foot were amputated by the propeller of an enemy plane while he was parachuting from his own destroyed plane. Upon landing in the water, he inflated his life raft, applied a tourniquet, and waited to be picked up by a crash boat. When later he was asked what he thought of when he was administering first aid he answered, "I thought of an article I had read about Alexander de Seversky and how, although he lost a leg in the First World War, he was able to continue flying, and became one of the great men of the world in aviation. I thought, if he could do it, I could, too!" (Rusk and Taylor, *1946:*12).[5] What this Marine officer realized was that the world still could reserve a useful place for him, that all the important things of life were not lost with his foot.

Without a doubt, some success stories serve to augment the feeling of self-pity. Inspirational stories about a person with a handicap may exude self-aggrandizing feelings on the part of the writer that kindle the flames of devaluation in the reader. It is enlightening to read the following account with the eyes of an amputee, sensitizing oneself to the emotional undertones of the message rather than to the straightforward intellectual

---

[5] H. A. Rusk and E. J. Taylor, *New Hope for the Handicapped,* Harper & Brothers, 1946. By permission.

statement. It is a news story about Pete Gray, the baseball player, who lost his right arm when he fell from a truck at the age of six: "Gray is an inspiration to practically every wounded veteran. The mere fact that a one-armed ball player has crashed the big leagues opens up new and electrifying vistas for each of them. If he can overcome his handicap in such fashion, there is hope for them all" (Rusk and Taylor, *1946:*140). Particularly the last phrase, "there is hope for them all," carries the sting of "You poor fellow, don't worry, there is still hope for you."

In contrast, consider the following account of Bill Talbert, the United States Davis Tennis Cup star, who must daily remember the fact that he has diabetes. "In the fourteen years Talbert has played tournament tennis, he has competed in some five hundred events, has traveled more than three hundred thousand miles, and taken more than ten thousand insulin injections. Diabetes has not interfered with either Talbert's tennis playing or his personal life, for he has learned to live with his disability" (Rusk and Taylor, *1946:*131). There is no pity in this description. But there is an awareness that the disability plays a role in Talbert's life, a role defined by his efforts to cope with its impositions.

Even more than success stories, knowing or seeing how others with like problems manage successfully may provide the realization that it is possible to do so. Pearl Buck received such support as a parent of a retarded child when she needed it most:

> I learned at last, merely by watching faces and by listening to voices, to know when I had found someone who knew what it was to live with sorrow that could not be ended. It was surprising and sad to discover how many such persons there were and to find how often the quality I discerned came from just such a sorrow as my own. It did not comfort me, for I could not rejoice in the knowledge that others had the same burden that I had, but it made me realize that others had learned how to live with it, and so could I. I suppose that was the beginning of the turn. For the despair into which I had sunk when I realized that nothing could be done for the child and that she would live on and on had become a morass into which I could easily have sunk into uselessness [Buck, *1950:*31].[6]

The positive psychological effect of seeing others *like oneself* manage is an important reason for at least some of the rehabilitation workers to have disabilities similar to those of their patients. An occupational therapist with a hook prosthesis can teach arm amputees a good deal more than the mechanical use of prosthetic devices. He can teach them not only that it is possible to become physically independent but also pride in achievement that stems from acceptance of a disability:

[6] Reprinted by permission of Harold Ober Associates, Inc. Copyright, 1950, by Pearl S. Buck.

. . . Sure, it was easy for her [an able-bodied occupational therapist] to show me how to turn on a water faucet or drop a coin in a box. All you did was thus and so, and then they'd demonstrate for me. That didn't mean much to me. Of course they could do it themselves. They had hands. But if someone with hooks had demonstrated how to open a window or turn a faucet not with hands, but with hooks, he would have made a deep and lasting impression on me. Then I wouldn't have left Occupational Therapy every day saying to myself, That's all very fine and wonderful, *but*—[Russell, *1949:*104–5].

Parenthetically, an occupational therapist who himself has the particular disability is likely to have worked out tricks and short cuts that may not be a part of the nondisabled therapist's repertoire:

. . . they taught me in Occupational Therapy to pick up a cup of coffee by slipping my hook through the handle. That was all wrong. I had no control over it that way. The weight of the liquid would pull it down. To keep it from spilling I'd have to steady it with my other hook. After awhile I learned by myself that it was better to grip the handle between the prongs of one hook, thus leaving the other free [Russell, *1949:*103].

The difference between perceiving difficulties in terms of coping and of succumbing provides one important basis for evaluating educational projects, such as films and publications, which are intended to develop more favorable attitudes on the part of the public. If the project predominantly portrays suffering or succumbing, and minimizes the coping possibilities, the dominant emotions it arouses will be devaluating pity and/or fear. Unfortunately there are many instances where the emphasis is on the wrecked lives of paraplegics, on the horror of cancer, on the devastating effects of blindness, and so on. To be sure, many projects, primarily designed for fund-raising, have been based on the assumption that giving is most effectively stimulated by pity. This assumption is in itself questionable and should be subjected to experimental test. In any case, because emphasis on the catastrophic effects of disability ill prepares the public for the eventuality of coping with disability problems themselves or for satisfactory interpersonal relations with others who have disabilities, such propaganda is of questionable value.

Sometimes the educational effort is aimed at arousing the audience to follow certain health practices. For example, a cartoon selected for a Pulitzer award portrays a small boy on crutches watching from the sidelines other children vigorously playing football. It is captioned, "Wonder why my parents didn't give me Salk shots?" The psychological soundness of such propaganda is highly questionable. The cartoon arouses pity, yes, but does it accomplish the purpose of shaping helpful attitudes and prompting constructive action? As an alternative, it is proposed that the public can be educated toward the importance of safety and of medical care by information concerning precautionary measures and treatment procedures rather than the horrors of disease, disability, and neglect. In terms of our theoretical framework, it is the aspect of coping with the problem that should be pointed up rather than the possibility of succumbing to it.

There is some experimental evidence supporting this thesis in a study of the effectiveness of different kinds of information in producing attitudes and behavior in accord with a set of recommendations (Janis and Feshback, *1953*). Three types of information varying in the amount of fear-arousing material were presented in an illustrated lecture on dental hygiene: The Strong Fear presentation emphasized and graphically illustrated the threats of pain, disease, and bodily damage. For example, it was stated that "if you ever develop an infection of this kind from improper care of your teeth, it will be an extremely serious matter because these infections are really dangerous. They can spread to your eyes, or your heart, or your joints and cause secondary infections which may lead to diseases such as arthritic paralysis, kidney damage, or total blindness" (p. 79). The Moderate Fear presentation described the same dangers in a milder and more factual manner. The Minimal Fear variation rarely referred to the unpleasant consequences of improper dental hygiene. Instead, it substituted relatively neutral information dealing with the growth and functions of the teeth. Each of the three presentations included the same recommendations as to the proper toothbrush and toothbrushing practices, and the importance of dental consultations. Translating into our terminology, we can say that the Strong Fear presentation emphasized succumbing potentialities whereas this emphasis was almost absent in the Minimal Fear presentation.

The three types of lectures were heard by equivalent groups of high school students as part of the school hygiene program. In order to observe changes produced by the illustrated talks, questionnaires about dental hygiene beliefs and practices were administered to the subjects one week before the experiment, immediately after the experiment, and again one week later.

The results suggest that "under conditions where people will be exposed to competing communications dealing with the same issues, the use of a strong fear appeal will tend to be less effective than a minimal appeal in producing stable and persistent attitude changes . . ." (p. 86) and conformity to recommended protective actions. The specific results follow.

1. The fear appeals were successful in arousing affective reactions. Immediately after the communication, the group exposed to the Strong appeal reported feeling more worried about the condition of their teeth than did the

other groups. The Moderate appeal, in turn, evoked a higher incidence of "worry" reactions than did the Minimal appeal.

2. The Strong appeal evoked a more ambivalent attitude toward the talk than did the other two forms. Though the students exposed to the Strong appeal were more likely than the others to give favorable appraisals concerning the interest value and the quality of the presentation, they nevertheless showed the greatest amount of subjective dislike and made more complaints about the content.

3. The three forms of the illustrated talk were equally effective with respect to (*a*) teaching factual content, as assessed by an information test, and (*b*) modifying beliefs concerning the proper type of toothbrush.

4. In *practice* the greatest amount of conformity to the recommendations was produced by the Minimal appeal. The Strong appeal failed to produce any significant change in dental hygiene practices, whereas the Minimal appeal resulted in a reliable increase in conformity, as compared with a control group. Similarly, more of the students of the Minimal appeal group went to the dentist during the week following the experiment than of the Strong appeal group.

The investigators conclude that "when fear is strongly aroused but is not fully relieved by the reassurances contained in a mass communication, the audience will become motivated to ignore or to minimize the importance of the threat." (Janis and Feshbach, *1953*:92). Implications for propaganda and education concerning other threatening situations such as the atom bomb are also drawn in the study.

More research is needed utilizing different contents, subjects, and types of succumbing and coping materials. Nevertheless there seem to be sound theoretical support and some experimental evidence for centering on coping. Rusk and Taylor's *Living with a Disability* is an admirable example of depicting problems of disability as problems of coping and adjustment (*1953*). This is also true of such films as *A Place in the Sun,* which shows children with cerebral palsy learning activities of everyday living, such as eating, shoe-lacing, writing, sitting.

Films that picture the person with a disability managing the ordinary affairs of living also offer excellent training for the recently disabled. The psychological impact that such a film can carry is seen in Harold Russell's (*1949*) experience two months after he lost his hands:

. . . *Meet McGonegal* was the story of a man who had lost his hands in World War I. McGonegal . . . had been faced by the same problem I was up against and he had licked it. . . . There was no plot to the movie, at least not in the ordinary sense. But for me it had a tremendous impact. It told me that any handicapped person could get along fine and take a normal place in society if he really wanted to. The picture showed a typical day in Charley McGonegal's life: It showed him dressing himself, shaving, brushing his teeth, combing his hair, eating breakfast, smoking, drinking, reading, shooting a game of pool and writing a letter—with a fountain pen, like a grownup, instead of with a pencil, like a child.

It was the most exciting movie I had ever seen. When it was over and the lights went up again I said to myself, if he could do it, I can do it, too [pp. 105–106].

The difficulties and problems in these films are not minimized or sugar-coated, but they are understood in the light of the efforts of the individual to meet them rather than succumb to them.

Coping is not only desirable from the educational point of view but is also very much in accord with reality. Though such feelings as fear, help-lessness, and hopelessness may overwhelm the person in his initial adjust-ment to disability, his will for growth and personal integrity most often shifts the balance in favor of coping with his problems. He may not cope as successfully as we would like, but he does think and act in terms of managing the difficulties that beset him.

EXPECTATION DISCREPANCY

It is of far-reaching consequence that the expectations concerning the behavior and adjustment of persons with a disability are often discrepant with the apparent behavior and adjustment—that is, with what the subject observes. We shall call this the *expectation discrepancy*. The "subject" as used here will apply to the person whose expectations and other per-ceptions we are examining, be he the person with the disability or the person viewing him. The expectations can be worse than the apparent reality or better.

The subject who has these discrepant expectations will react with some feeling appropriate to the gap between the expected and apparent state of affairs and to the direction of that gap. Where the expectations are worse than what he observes, he may be:

Surprised—"Despite their severe disabilities, the mental health of the veteran paraplegics as a group is surprisingly good."

Incredulous—"It's unbelievable, but he can even shave with those hooks!"

Where the expectations are better than the presenting facts, the subject may be:

Anguished—"I felt sick. The last hope that I might again see perfectly was gone."

Disappointed—"I had hoped this final operation would be successful, but she still can't bend her knee."

Assuredly, there is a wide gamut of emotional reactions to expectation discrepancy. Such feelings as amazement, wonder, curiosity, dismay, horror, frustration, futility, etc., could be added, but there is little in the way of research to assist us in delimiting the possibilities. It seems reasonable that if the direction of the expectation discrepancy is in accord with the subject's wishes, a positive affect emerges, such as "pleasant surprise" or hopefulness. If, however, the expectation discrepancy runs counter to his wishes, a negative feeling is experienced, such as disappointment and frustration.

Though it might appear that a positive reaction would be typical in cases where the state of affairs turns out to be better than anticipated, we must not forget that the subject, under certain conditions, might wish a worsening or a maintaining of the unfortunate situation. In the case of the person with a disability, this occurs when he does not wish to get well, when secondary gains are contingent upon his remaining disabled. In the case of someone else, this occurs when the principle known as the "requirement of mourning" operates (see pp. 242–243). Then it is that the subject may actually feel dismayed should he perceive the person with the disability as "better off" than he expected and quite content to find the reverse.

In addition to the subject's immediate reaction to the discrepancy between his expectation and presenting fact, he has a need to explain it, to fill in the gap, so that there is a reconciliation between the two halves of the equation, i.e., expectations on the one hand and the apparent reality on the other. How this reconciliation takes place also has important consequences for the evaluation of a person with a disability, but first we need to inquire as to the conditions giving rise to expectation discrepancy.

Conditions Underlying Expectation Discrepancy

How does it happen that there is a discrepancy between what the subject expects of the behavior of a person with a disability and what at some later time he experiences of that behavior? Several conditions may be mentioned:

1. *Spread*—the subject perceives the person (or himself) as a "disabled person." That is, the person is seen as disabled not only with respect to physique but with respect to other characteristics as well—e.g., personality and adjustment (see pp. 118–119). This spread appears to be particularly fluid when the subject is in a comparative frame of mind—that is, when he is evaluating the person with respect to some preconceived standard

(see pp. 128–133). Because of "spread," the subject *expects* the lot of the person with a disability to be *worse* than the apparent reality. Such spread, then, often accompanied by devaluation, becomes paradoxically a condition for the subsequent wonder and admiration at the proved accomplishments of the person with a disability.

2. *Position of the subject*—when the subject is in the position of an outsider—that is, when he is actually little concerned with the fate of the person with a disability—he will view the problems attendant upon the disability from his own perspective. This means that he will see the problems of the situation in terms of his own "equipment" as a person with the usual physical advantages and be unable to discover new ways of meeting these problems (see pp. 63–64). In their insolubility the problems loom large indeed, and hence the expectations may be worse than the actuality. Were the subject closely aligned with the disability situation, either as the person with the disability himself or one close to him, then the necessity of meeting the problems of living would reveal to him the pertinent truth, "there is more than one way to skin a cat." When coping is enhanced, negative expectations are reduced and sometimes may even be underestimated.

3. *Requirement of mourning*—when the security of the subject depends upon physique as a high status value, he will tend to insist that the lot of a person with a disability is an unfortunate one (see pp. 242–243). Exaggerated negative expectations are part and parcel of this need and point to an important source of expectation discrepancy.

4. *Wish for improvement*—Sometimes the wish that all will be well is so strong as to lead to unrealistic expectations of marked improvement or eventual recovery. Even though current difficulties may be played down because of this same wish, the fact that the hopeful expectations cannot materialize means a discrepancy with reality that is at best disappointing and at worst heartbreaking. We should also expect that a person with such a strong wish would show other differentiating emotions; for example, he is less likely to be amazed or surprised at the positive adjustment and accomplishments of a person with a disability and more likely to be pleased than would the outsider who does not actively entertain the wish for improvement.

5. *Blurring of perception owing to anxiety*—Both the expectations and the apparent reality may remain obscure because of the tide of anxiety that keeps the subject, as it were, in a daze. Then it is that such emotions as worry, depression, antipathy take hold, and emotions arising from expectation discrepancy, such as anticipation, surprise, disappointment, etc., cannot appear until there is a clarification and differentiation of one's expectations and the apparent reality.

Reconciling the Expectation Discrepancy

It is part of the nature of man to search for explanations and connections so that his experiences in the world about him become comprehensible. So it is in the case of expectation discrepancy. It is disturbing to the subject when his expectations do not match the presenting facts, and he feels a need to reconcile the two. This may be accomplished by such cognitive changes as *expectation revision, altering the apparent reality*, and *anormalizing the person*. These means will be illustrated by several different cases of expectation discrepancy.

Let us consider the frequently occurring expectation discrepancy where the performance of the person outstrips the expectations of the subject. Assume that the subject in question is in the position of an outsider who, faced with the discrepancy, attempts to explain it. Because of this, he may cease ruminating about succumbing to the difficulties, i.e., emphasis on all the things the disability denies, and instead become concerned with the coping aspects, i.e., the ways in which the person has managed. In so doing, the subject begins to recognize the adjustment possibilities of a paraplegic, a blind girl, or an amputee, and is then able to agree with Miers (*1953*), for example, that ". . . my athetosis . . . is not half the nuisance you think. Straws for drinking, a typewriter for putting my thoughts on paper, an electric razor, in the main cut down this disability to life size" (p. 7). Not only will the coping aspect of difficulties have become dominant, but the subject will have also shifted his position to that of the insider.

These two shifts give a new direction to the original amazement over the adjustment of the person with a disability. The *expectations* of the subject have been *revised* upward so that he is no longer incredulous. This does not mean that he is left with a simple nonchalance of fulfilled expectations. He may now, for example, feel respect for the persistence shown by the person with the disability in meeting his difficulties, or he may feel that it took courage or ambition or earthy common sense regarding the realities of life to do so. These positive feelings emerge when coping with as against succumbing to the difficulties is in the field of concern.

Although this perceptual change for resolving the discrepancy is to be desired, the social-psychological position of the subject is not always conducive to such a shift in emphasis. For example, there may be little opportunity for the subject to learn just how the person with a disability does manage. This is particularly true if the subject is an outsider, for not only does he lack ready opportunity for coping discoveries but he has little need, other than that produced by the gap, to create such opportunities. Instead, the subject may seek other means at reconciliation.

He may, for example, *alter the apparent reality* by doubting the evidence concerning the adequate adjustment of the person with a disability. Thus, he may feel that the person is shamming, simply acting *as though* he were managing, when actually he is not. He may suppress evidence regarding the coping aspect of difficulties and high-light evidence bearing upon the succumbing aspects: for example, he may not "see" how well the child with braces gets around but may notice primarily that the child walks with a halting gait. He may tend to attribute all the discomforting aspects of the person's life to the disability, though they may have little actual connection and, in spite of all indications that the person has arranged his life in accord with his abilities and is living satisfactorily, he may insist that the person's lot is lamentable. Chevigny (*1946*), as a blind adult, sometimes could not help feeling that the world "doesn't want to be convinced that I am not altogether helpless, despite the plain evidence to the contrary" (p. 76). Unfortunately, this means of fitting together the expected state of affairs with the apparent state is probably not infrequent. Where the "requirement of mourning" (see pp. 242–243) is felt to insure the security of the subject, this method becomes a cunning maneuver. Altering the apparent reality requires some fluidity in the perception of the reality, i.e., what is perceived cannot be bound too tightly to the objective reality but must be responsive to the manipulations of the wishes and beliefs of the subject.

Finally, the discrepancy may be reconciled when the subject *"anormalizes"* the person, i.e., attributes to him certain unusual characteristics, even supernatural ones, so that the ordinary expectations do not apply. It is very much like the kind of anormalization one might experience in the event of winning the sweepstakes; the incredibility soon becomes cloaked with a strange feeling that one has been blessed or fated to win in the face of overwhelming odds. Similarly, when the subject expects the blind man to fumble and stumble and instead finds him well oriented, it is easy for him to chalk off this discrepancy by appraising the blind man's sensory apparatus as literally "out of this world."

Anormalization of persons who are deaf also occurs, as will be seen in the following fictionalized events:

In Gian-Carlo Menotti's contemporary opera, *The Medium,* the title character and fraud, Madame Flora, intones about the deaf-mute boy she has taken into her home: "Just because he cannot speak we take him for a halfwit, but he knows a great deal. He knows more than we think. There is something uncanny about him. He sees things we don't see." Her vague apprehensions are ambiguously justified in the course of the opera. Assuming that the deaf-mute is the real medium for inexplicable phenomena, she is frightened into killing him, and thus brings about her own downfall.

Madame Flora's recitative is taken up in full chorus by a whole group of inhabitants of a small town in Georgia, in Carson McCullers' novel, *The Heart*

Is a Lonely Hunter. The spiritually desperate characters come to regard Mr. Singer, a deaf-mute who lives in their community, as a kind of God substitute, and attribute to him many of the characteristics traditionally ascribed to deity. The author simultaneously points up the irony of the equally anguished concerns of Mr. Singer's own life, so remote from the supernatural vision of him conjured up by the needs of the other townspeople that his eventual suicide becomes a poignant mystery and defeat to them.

The same idea again finds expression in a popular movie, *Flesh and Fury,* where the boxing skill of a champion prize fighter seems mysteriously to hinge upon his status as a deaf-mute. When his hearing is restored, and he has learned to articulate, he finds himself at a total loss in a championship match, as inept in the face of his opponent as the shorn Samson before the Philistines. Fortunately, a blow in the course of the fight deprives the hero of his hearing long enough for him to win the bout [Maisel, *1953*:216–217].[7]

The person with a disability himself may feel a kind of supernatural intervention when he is carried through what appeared to be insuperable difficulties. Karsten Ohnstad (*1942*) describes the problem that confronted him when, in crossing a busy thoroughfare, his usual sound cues were disrupted by wind and the rumbling noises of trucks. Upon arriving safely at the curb, he felt that in some way he had been magically protected (p. 68).

When Karsten gained thorough *control* over traffic hazards by using a white cane, the anormalization became even more a part of his very person:

. . . The cane was a nuisance, clattering against everything and catching in my trouser cuffs as I twirled it idly about like a baton; but at street corners it proved its worth. Car drivers saw it and stopped. I held it out before me and walked across the pavement with an assurance that I had never felt before. I was a worker of miracles. I was the Moses of the metropolis. I held out my staff over that roaring, honking sea, and lo! the traffic parted, and I stepped up on the opposite curb sound as a dollar [Ohnstad, *1942*:69].

The factor of personal control is probably conducive to the feeling of deification in contrast to the kind of anormalization in which the person is felt to be a pawn of fate or subject to control by other supernatural events. Such personal deification was experienced by Raymond Goldman (*1947*) when, unable to walk because of polio, he mastered the "unattainable" through the strength of his own will:

. . . Other children learn naturally and without conscious effort to move about and crawl and stand up. Not I. I had to achieve those things so deliber-

---

[7] Edward Maisel, *Meet A Body,* by permission of the Institute for the Crippled and Disabled.

ately, at the cost of so much pain and sweat and tears, that the attainment of each was a separate triumph. I stood almost in awe of my own power to accomplish. I was like a god [p. 38].[8]

Anormalizing the person with a disability means that he transcends the laws of ordinary mortals so that expectations relevant to normal persons do not apply. There is one important difference between the quality of deified eminence and that of the esteem generated when, through concern over coping with difficulties, expectation revision takes place in which higher though entirely normal expectations are maintained. In the former case, the person with a disability is viewed as a different kind of person; he is set apart from normal persons and his accomplishments are seen as resulting from some kind of mystical intervention. In the latter case, the person with a disability is very much a part of the group of normal human beings, and his accomplishments are "understood" in terms of natural behavior.

Conditions for anormalizing the person appear to be favorable when the perceptions of the two sides of the equation are difficult to change. Again let us turn to blindness as an illustration: (1) When a sighted person has the position of an outsider with respect to blindness, he expects that the locomotion difficulties attendant upon blindness are insuperable. Moreover, this perception is difficult to change. (2) When such a subject sees a blind person unperturbably getting about there is a discrepancy with what he expected. Moreover, this perception is also difficult to change. Seeing is believing, and he cannot deny that the blind person has safely crossed the street, mounted the stairs, and located his books.

In these circumstances, it is perhaps comprehensible why the person who is blind should be looked upon with reverence and felt to be equipped with unusual powers. In fiction, the most frequent stereotype of the blind is that of the idealized and abnormally good person (Barker *et al.,* *1953*:274). In religious practices, the blind have been accorded privileged positions (Barker *et al., 1953*:273). Modern Turkey regards the sightless as indispensable assets to religious ceremonies and funerals (Maisel, *1953*:23). In Greek legend many clairvoyants are blind (Hentig, *1948b:* 23). Among the Koreans it is believed that the blind have acquired an inner vision and they are therefore held in high esteem (Maisel, *1953*).

For a review of the factors important in resolving expectation discrepancy, the case of deafness serves well. Commonly, with respect to a person who is deaf, the subject holds higher expectations than are borne out by what ensues because the deaf person, looking just like anyone else,

---

[8] The selection from Raymond Goldman, *Even the Night,* copyright 1947, The Macmillan Company, is used with the permission of the publishers.

is expected to act like anyone else. The subject expects the person who is deaf, for example, to be able to communicate with him but discovers that he cannot.

Reconciliation of this expectation discrepancy is then initiated. Depending upon his social-psychological position with respect to the disability situation, the subject may revise his expectations downward. This is easier to do when the subject has an objective rather than a more personal, wishful interest in the welfare of the person. In such circumstances, the subject seeks honest understanding of "what is wrong" and may discover that his expectations were unrealistic in the light of the newly uncovered facts. If in the process of expectation revision the difficulties of deafness are seen in the light of coping rather than succumbing, positive evaluation of the person will occur.

However, there will undoubtedly be strong resistance against lowering the expectation level where there is an overpowering wish for the person to hear better, this not infrequently characterizing the subject who is in the position of an insider. In this case, the subject may alter the apparent reality. He may regard the discrepancy as a temporary one that will be erased through the efforts of continued cures; the apparent reality is looked upon as eventually rising upward to close the gap. In the meantime, insofar as the gap still gapes, the apparent reality will be perceived as progressively better. Thus the person with a hearing impairment and those close to him will after surgery tend to feel, as long as the apparent reality is sufficiently fluid, that there is an improvement, though this may not at all reflect the true state of affairs. Eventually, it is possible for the forces of objective reality to become so great as to make such mobility of the apparent reality difficult and the subject may then turn to a reëvaluation of the expectation level.

There are instances of expectation discrepancy in which both the expectations and the apparent reality resist change. This is true of some outsider subjects, where neither need nor opportunity exists for the comprehension of the difficulties incumbent upon deafness or for upward shift in the apparent reality. The discrepancy is resolved by anormalizing the person, and he is dubbed queer or strange or even bewitched. Anormalization that reconciles a discrepancy in which the expectations are lower than the apparent reality leads to sanctification, but where the expectations surpass the apparent reality anormalization leads to vilification.

This discussion has permitted, perhaps, some glimpse into the significance of expectation discrepancy for the social evaluation of persons with disabilities. Clearly, further investigation of the conditions underlying expectation discrepancy and its reconciliation is indicated. We have pointed out the probable significance of such factors as the position of the subject, his wishes, opportunity for reëvaluation, fluidity of apparent reality, direction of the gap, etc. Of course, the concepts have application to nondisability situations as well, just as do the concepts of marginal position, new situations, value systems, etc., discussed elsewhere in this volume. The attitudes and behavior of adults toward children, for example, frequently can be understood in terms of expectation discrepancy. Recollection of such an incident with an analysis of possible conditions contributing to the expectation discrepancy and of the means taken toward its reconciliation is a worth-while exercise. One must ponder apt illustrations from nondisability situations before one can realize with the conviction of fact rather than supposition that the social psychology of disability is truly a *general* social psychology, the laws of which have bearing upon diverse fields not restricted to problems of disablement.

In addition to the coping-succumbing dimension and expectation discrepancy as factors in the high regard of the person with a disability, there are two others that should be explicated, namely, the significance of suffering and outstanding success.

SUFFERING AND UNDERSTANDING

Regardless of the various viewpoints expressed by the psychiatrists and psychologists, those who have worked closely with the physically disabled know that having once made the emotional adjustment to their disabilities, they possess a depth of understanding, patience, and tolerance which is rarely found among those who have not endured some soul-torturing experience. They have been forced to discard the superficial and to find the fundamentals. They have discovered what Robert Burton wrote over three hundred years ago: "Deformities and imperfections of our bodies, as lameness, crookedness, deafness, blindness, be they innate or accidental, torture many men; yet this may comfort them, that those imperfections of the body do not a whit blemish the soul, or hinder the operations of it, but rather help and much increase it!" [Rusk and Taylor, *1946:*224].

The point of view that deep understanding emerges from suffering has more or less vigorously been advanced through the ages by philosophers, poets, writers, and scientists. It is one of the important factors that evokes respectful regard for persons disabled in some way. In its more general application it is represented by the belief that life should not be made too easy for children in school and society, because only through frustration and tribulation can the fullness of creativity and wisdom be realized.

Not only professional personnel, but many laymen and persons with disabilities themselves connect suffering and even great misfortune with fundamental improvement in the person. In one study on values, for example, the subjects were asked whether they would wish tragedy for their child (Dembo, *1953a*). About half the subjects answered affirmatively on the ground that in this way depth of understanding is reached. In another study, virtually none of the subjects (40 men in the professions) expressed disagreement with the statement: "I believe we are made better by the trials and hardships of life." Even when other subjects (an experimental group of 50) were confronted with a presumed group consensus toward disagreement, only one third went along, whereas two thirds took a position supporting the statement (Crutchfield, *1955*).

Persons with disabilities have, in looking over their lives, also expressed the feeling that, through the manifold experiences of living with a disability, they have gained a profound awareness of truly human values. Harold Russell (*1949*), who lost his hands as an adult, puts it this way: ". . . this seeming disaster has brought me a priceless wealth of the spirit that I am sure I could never have possessed otherwise. I have enjoyed a life that has been full and rich and rewarding, a life that has had a meaning and depth it never had before" (Russell, *1949*:278). Raymond Goldman (*1947*), who faced infantile paralysis as a child, deafness as an adolescent, diabetes as an adult, puts it this way: "Now, I thought, I could understand the true meaning of life, could see a *reason* for the physical and mental anguish I had had to endure, could see the *reward* for the struggle I had made. How else could one gain victory except through defeat? . . . How else could one know happiness except through suffering and despair?" (p. 159).

In the following account we are brought into a life experience that arose because of a disability. It took place within three years of a man's blindness and because it did so very much to challenge his understandings and shape new ones that carried him far in his own adjustment, it is reproduced here at some length. The world could well learn the lessons of that one incident and the revaluation of fundamentals that followed in its wake. It is told by Chevigny (*1946*), who became blind at the age of 40:

. . . one noon I was walking up 53d street on my way to the restaurant I usually frequent for lunch. I heard a genial hail; it turned out to be someone I knew only as Billy, the office boy at a publishing house where I am acquainted. I said hello in return, we fell into step—he was going to lunch too —and I suggested he join me. Billy hesitated, then asked, "Are you sure they'll serve me?" "Of course," I answered, "why shouldn't they?" The next few minutes were among the most profoundly embarrassing I ever passed. Billy had to tell me a fact about himself of which I was completely unaware; he is a Negro.

My embarrassment arose in my instant realization of the predicament in which I had placed him. . . . Then what seemed a brilliant solution occurred to me. I said, "You were on your way to lunch—why don't you take me to the place where you're going?"

"That's a thought," Billy said, and we changed the direction of our walk. Then I remembered my own problem. Would Bill's restaurant admit Wiz [the Seeing Eye dog]? I put the question up to him and it was his turn to be embarrassed—for me. He didn't know about the policy of his restaurant regarding dogs. He was shocked at the thought that any restaurant would exclude a man with a Seeing Eye dog. I had my hand on his arm as we walked and I felt his muscle stiffen as he said, "They'd better let you in. If they don't, they'll have a little trouble putting the roof back on when I get through raising it." It was a remark that filled me with profound shame. I hadn't offered to raise any roofs for him. Yet the reasons for his exclusions from restaurants had infinitely less justification than the reasons for mine.

This story might seem more dramatic had we had the argument we expected on reaching the restaurant, but we didn't. We were courteously shown to a table, I put Wiz under it, and we ordered lunch. But it was eaten in silence, both of us being much too preoccupied with the consideration of the separate accidents of fate that made our relations with the world difficult.

Walking back to my office, alone with Wiz, my mind was busy with the implications of this scene. There was the thought of Billy's kindness; it was no different from that given me by any other man. And had I not been told, in so many words, that he was a man marked out from the majority I would have attached no undue importance to it, I would not even have sought to detect any difference in him. But there was another thought, one almost terrible in its significance.

Were the whole world blind, there would be no race prejudice. There couldn't be. The only sense which could have told me that Billy is what is called a Negro was my sight. No other sense detected any difference. I had nothing but Billy's own word for it. It was a concept shaking to the intellect. The whole structure of the majority-minority relationship was perceived in a clear light; its foundation is that which can be seen, and nothing else. The color of hair, the shade of skin, the shape of nose—what can perceive them but the eye? It takes hearing to perceive what is in the heart and mind, and civilized man is too busy using his eye to listen [pp. 254–256].

My inmost dislike has always been for seeming different from the rest of my fellow men. Every act of my life has been in the direction of making myself as close to the norm as possible. I therefore could not now accept the notion that I had suddenly [when blindness occurred] become inherently peculiar, and that is the feeling which drove me forward to reattaining as much of my old position as I could.

It was a nice comfortable position, my old one, very normal and ordinary. The tabulated card that represents me in the files of the Census Bureau has always, in passing through the electric tabulating machines, dropped into the pockets containing the biggest and fattest bunches of cards. My height and weight were average, I belonged to the white race, there was nothing exotic or unusual about the church I attended, my politics were ordinary enough, and

I was neither rich nor poor. The only time my card ever fell in with the smaller package of cards was in tabulating professions; but even as a writer I was distinguished by being neither very good nor very bad. I was safe in the bosom of the majority. . . .

Now suddenly an important difference had developed between the majority and me. . . .

That I resented it shows that my thinking was of the very stuff of which intolerance is made. I was of the majority and I thought like it. That means I was conscious of such things as differences between people and classes and groups.

It took a long time, and not until after the meeting with Billy did I fully realize that I was carrying with me the very body of fixed notions against which my resentment was now directed. Those fixed notions were based on sight, that sight I no longer had; . . . Now, if I wanted to do it, I could get to the heart and the mind of a man right away without first reading into him a whole set of attributes because I could see the color of his skin or the shape of his nose.

I think a good deal of the inward part of my adjustment formed about that time. . . . What happened was that there didn't seem any longer to be too much need to belong to the majority, to be a regular. The important body to which to belong was mankind itself, every member of which laughs when tickled and bleeds when pricked. That there is such a body—well, that too I had merely been told; now I could know it emotionally.

The rich experiences with friendships of the past previous months fell into place with these new concepts. The friends who so magnificently came to my assistance were Christians, Jews, and men of no faith at all. Their political beliefs were as varied. Yet when they came to my bedside as I lay in the hospital and offered the means to erase worry from my mind about both the present and the future, their thought was only that I was a fellow man who needed help. They defended me from the tragedy of my position; I can do no less, when the need arises, than to defend them from the tragedy of theirs.

These are among the understandings of living I have gained under blindness. As a writer they are of great importance to me and have added much to my desire to express what I know and feel. They are of even greater importance to me as a human being; I still can hate, but only ideas—not people [pp. 258–261].[9]

A hundred new thoughts occurred to Chevigny that day. And in the end not only did he attain higher social values but he also made possible an inward adjustment that was fundamental and satisfying. He realized in the depths of his emotional core that one does not have to belong to the majority group in order to be as worthy as any man. He realized that sight, the queen of the senses, may also become the servant of malice that

[9] H. Chevigny, *My Eyes Have a Cold Nose,* Yale University Press, 1946. By permission.

divides man against man on the basis of the most superficial criteria. And in so realizing, he and others through him gained that which is priceless.

Chevigny is a man of high intellect. Could the ordinary person with a disability reach such fundamental understandings? Harold Russell (*1949*), on the basis of wide observation, thinks so. He is convinced, for example, that racial intolerance wanes in the sick and disabled in general:

> During my tour . . . I visited dozens of Army and veterans' hospitals. I talked, not only with hundreds of amputees like myself, but with paraplegics, spastics, and the badly mutilated. I also visited several Canadian Army hospitals. I carried away one more conclusion from these hospitals: Neither differences of nationality, race, nor religion counted for much among the sick or disabled. All were united by the common bond of illness and suffering. It was only among the so-called healthy that I found the seeds of disunion and hatred [p. 237].

As far as we know, there are no objective studies on this point. Clearly, much is needed in the way of research that will sharpen our understanding of the connection between certain kinds of life experiences and the attainment of deep understanding of what really matters. We would support the hypothesis that "soul-*searching*" experiences are essential for the attainment of depth of understanding of the truly important, but we at least question the role of "soul-*torturing*" experiences. Although there is good evidence that one *may* rise to great heights of emotional understanding from the depths of despair, this may not prove to be the course par excellence. The course may be too thorny, too tortuous, so that the soul-torturing of too few will find the light through the darkness. Soul-searching experiences need not be predicated upon soul-torturing experiences, but what they do require needs further theory and test. It is the *process* of adjusting to the suffering (see Chap. 5) that leads to sifting out the trivial from the important and in this way to deeper understanding of the basic underpinnings of human values.

OUTSTANDING SUCCESS

Just as an inferior position with respect to a single characteristic may lead to devaluation of the total person (see pp. 131–132), so outstanding success in a particular area may spread so that the person in general is looked up to. Henry Viscardi (*1952*), dwarfed by misshapen legs, remembers how much becoming an expert marbles player did for his standing in the gang:

> In the years that followed, under the tutelage of Marble Bags I gradually became the immies champ of our block, and my self-esteem grew along with

my big bag of marbles. In later years I was often to think with pride of that little achievement, as I watched amputees and paraplegics regain a feeling of personal dignity through mastering the art of doing something well with their hands [pp. 27–28].[10]

When special achievement becomes sufficiently prominent, it may serve the person well by becoming the organizing characteristic for status evaluation around which other characteristics of the person will be seen.

Since a physical disability has in our culture a high potency, however, any special achievement has a very deft competitor in becoming a *stable* organizing characteristic for status evaluation. Franklin Roosevelt may be admired by countless persons—but one must note that being President of the United States is sufficiently distinctive to make insignificant the fact of disability. Henry Viscardi was a champion marbles player among his friends, but an "ape man" to many of those who did not know him as a person. One usually cannot wear one's laurels for all to see, not even in the manner of a titular appurtenance such as M.D. or Ph.D.

Of course, apart from its social reward, high competence of any kind is potentially a strong asset in personal adjustment. "Any measures designed to encourage the development of some areas of excellence will help to reduce if not prevent an inferiority complex" (White, *1948:*156). Needless to say, the potentialities of the individual must always be the guiding factor, for pressures to achieve where the "stuff" is lacking are likely to weigh down the person yet further with inferiority feelings.

As was mentioned earlier (pp. 65–66), success stories may be helpful in counteracting devaluation of the person by emphasizing the possibilities in his situation for coping and by leading to the realization that the individual is not a disabled person but a person with a disability. Physique becomes subordinated to other characteristics that have given status to the person. Persons with loss of limbs who have made outstanding contributions in diverse fields are: Bill Stern the sports broadcaster; Alexander de Seversky, the aircraft designer; Al Capp, the cartoonist; Herbert Marshall, the actor; and Jimmy Savo, the comedian. All these persons lead normal, busy, profitable, and interesting lives and are known first as respected individuals so that the disability is put in its place when it is disclosed. If among persons who rose to fame one were to point out those who have lost limbs, are blind, deaf, paralyzed, etc., the list would become long indeed. Such a list taken from an earlier German compilation has been reproduced in Boorstein (*1935:*106–110). It includes the names, and in some cases short biographies, of almost 500 cripples.

---

[10] Henry Viscardi, Jr., *A Man's Stature.* Copyright, 1952, by Henry Viscardi, Jr. Used with permission of the John Day Company.

The contribution of outstanding success to the development of healthful attitudes toward disability may be seen as being mediated by the following: (1) it highlights coping possibilities, (2) it subordinates physique as an organizing characteristic for status evaluation. At the same time, as we have previously stressed (pp. 65–66), the uncritical use of success stories may carry its own defeat by actually connoting devaluation of persons with a disability.

DILEMMA OF CONTRADICTION IN STATUS

Finally, it should be mentioned that perceptions and beliefs that bring about inferior status exist side by side with those that bring about salutary status. This juxtaposition may lead to a complex admixture of devaluating pity and respect in the same social relationship, as exemplified in an incident recalled by Karsten Ohnstad (*1942*) while he was a pupil at the school for the blind:

> The woodworking room was one of the favorite stops of visitors to the school. They swelled our heads with admiration for our work, then deflated us with pity. One of them looked sadly at my basswood box.
> "Is he blind?" she asked the instructor.
> "Yes," said the instructor, as sadly as she. "He's blind."
> I could feel the woman looking at me incredulously. There was a long pause.
> "And he has such fair skin," she mourned, finally [p. 129].

In important relationships such as marriage, contradiction in the status of the person with a disability may lead to disturbing conflicts. A person who is deaf, for example, may be held in great esteem because of his accomplishments as a writer but may be regarded by some as unsuitable as a marriage partner. A similar dilemma with respect to other minority groups has been described by Hughes (*1945*). The point has been made that being a Negro "tends to overpower, in most crucial situations, any other characteristic which might run counter to it. But professional standing is also a powerful characteristic. . . . In the person of the professionally qualified Negro these two powerful characteristics clash. The dilemma for those who meet such a person is that of having to choose whether to treat him as a Negro or as a member of his profession" (p. 357). Such dilemmas bring out clearly that status is not an abstract quality attributed to a person; it always has to do with social standing within prescribed roles.

Not only does the dilemma challenge the nondisabled person. Inconsistency of social attitudes also brings about situations of psychological uncertainty for the person with a disability in which he is unsure as to how he will be received and what is expected of him (see pp. 99–105).

The conditions under which a person with a disability may be respected and admired have been reviewed. Recognizing the coping endeavors of the person is one of these. Expectation surpassed in reality is another. The belief that suffering leads to deeper understanding is a third. Success so outstanding that it becomes the distinctive characteristic of the person is a fourth. That salutary status is part of the social climate confronting the person with a disability may well contribute to the significant fact that feelings of inferiority are not generally more characteristic of the "disabled" as a group than of the nondisabled (see p. 52). Yet feelings of self-depreciation do exist and must become a relatively unimportant feature in the healthy personality. Before embarking upon an analysis of the changes conducive to self-acceptance, we should like to examine two psychological problems important in understanding adjustment to disability—namely, frustration and uncertainty.

Chapter 4

Frustration and Uncertainty

PSYCHOLOGICAL ANALYSIS CAN FOCUS EITHER ON FACTORS OUTSIDE THE person or on those within the person. The question of social status, for example, was viewed on the one hand in terms of the attitudes of others toward disability and the restrictions and facilitations imposed by society and on the other hand in terms of the person's feelings about himself. To take another example, behavior stemming from overlapping situations was seen in terms of an external set of circumstances as well as its origins within the person.

This variable emphasis can be understood in terms of what Heider (*1958*) refers to as the problem of attribution. He points out, for instance, that when more or less everyone reacts to a situation in the same way, the source of the behavior—its underlying conditions—is usually placed in the environment. Thus, if a problem is difficult for all people of a particular age, the problem is appraised as difficult, not the person as stupid. Conversely, where there is personal variability, the attribution of the behavior is to the person. If in this case most persons could solve the problem, the troubles of a particular person with it would be attributed to his deficiencies rather than to the nature of the problem. With a full psychological analysis, however, the nature of the problem and the psychological processes in the person must both be examined. Actually, this is just another way of expressing the commonly accepted dictum that behavior is a function of both the person and the environment. Thus the conclusion follows that any behavior under consideration can be partialed between these two arenas. The double-barreled approach of person and environment will also be taken in the following discussion.

FRUSTRATION

"By a frustrating situation is meant any situation in which an obstacle —physical, social, or conceptual, personal or environmental—prevents the satisfaction of a desire. . . . It includes only those situations where the subject himself accepts the obstacle as impassable, the solution as impossible" (Barker, *1938*:146). This psychological definition is more or less the one connoted in common usage.

It is commonly and perhaps naturally assumed that a physical disability augments frustration. Thus, few persons would see anything contestable about such statements as: "The handicap of seriously defective vision or no vision is so obviously shackling, so frustrating, so dispossessing, that when borne by a child small wonder those who love him feel he is intolerably afflicted" (Stern and Castendyck, *1950*:73). With greater frustration, it is also assumed that one should find more frustrated persons among those with physical disabilities, more who show irritability, regression, restlessness, and other negative effects. Yet somehow none of these intuitive connections is borne out by experimental test or systematic observation. The word "systematic" should be emphasized, for certainly the casual and haphazard glance at everyday experience seems to verify these a priori connections. Let us first look at research using persons with disabilities as subjects, and then attempt to integrate the findings into a clearer understanding of the meaning and management of frustration as applied to problems of disability.

Two Studies

Kahn's (*1951*) study is important because it exercised a degree of scientific care in investigating the problem of the effect of disability on behavior in frustrating situations all too rarely found in disability research. Kahn used three groups, each of 15 children between the ages of 9 and 11: a group with normal hearing, a moderately hard-of-hearing group with loss of 15 to 35 decibels, and a severely hard-of-hearing group with still greater losses. The first two groups attended public schools; the severely hard-of-hearing children attended a special day school. The subjects were equated on age, sex, school grade, socioeconomic status, and intelligence level.

The children participated in two tests of frustration. One, known as "The Children's Form of the Rosenzweig Picture Frustration Study," is a projective test consisting of 24 pictures (Rosenzweig *et al.,* *1948*). The children were directed to write down what they thought the child in each picture would answer to the person talking to him. The second was a realistic test of reaction to frustration. The children were directed to arrange 16 blocks according to a specific pattern before them. The test was discontinued when the child had been thwarted by ten of the designs.

The reactions of the children in the two situations were rated on a dozen categories: Behavior was rated as extrapunitive when aggression was directed toward the external world, as intrapunitive when aggression was directed against the self, and as impunitive when the child tried to avoid blame and aggression entirely by passing over the frustrating situations lightly. In addition, the behavior was rated according to the degree to which it showed "obstacle-dominance" (concentration on the barrier itself), "ego-defense" (defense of the self) and "need-persistence" (emphasis on solution). Finally the behavior was evaluated in terms of six variants of ego-defensive scores.

The main overall findings may be summarized as follows: ". . . few differences exist between the groups in terms of response to frustration. What differences do appear . . . seem to indicate a consistent tendency [though slight] for the hard-of-hearing children to meet frustration more constructively than the non-handicapped children" (p. 58). Specific results are:

1. There is a negative correlation between hearing loss and ego-defensive responses (r = −.34), as well as between hearing loss and obstacle-dominant responses (r = −.24), but the correlation between need-persistive responses and hearing loss is positive and significantly high (r = .37).

2. As for the direction of blame, externally aggressive responses are positively related to hearing loss, while internally aggressive and impunitive responses bear a negative relation to hearing loss. The most severely handicapped children tend toward greater use of extrapunitive responses. When confronted by the "realistic" frustration situation, the hard-of-hearing children are likely to abandon extrapunitive responses in favor of responses which indicate that they accept responsibility for failure. Such response tendencies seem to indicate that the hard-of-hearing children meet frustration with a realistic acceptance of the extent of their responsibilities.

3. The evidence strongly suggests that unwarranted suspiciousness (as manifested in undue emphasis on extrapunitive responses) is not an invariable feature of the hard-of-hearing child's personality.

4. Hard-of-hearing children do not have lower thresholds for frustration. The findings taken in toto may reasonably be accepted as an indication of at least average emotional maturity of these children so that as a group they can be expected to have "sufficient emotional reserve to withstand and overcome the adversities of the deprivations inherent in their handicaps" (p. 64).

A second study dealing with the management of frustration as related to disability was carried out by Fitzgerald (1950). Initially, the line of reasoning that guided the research was: (1) limitation of normal mobility and activity implies the presence of a frustrating situation; (2) increased frustration, according to the frustration-aggression hypothesis, results in an increased tension state (see Dollard, et al., 1939); (3) therefore, the reactions of the crippled might be expected to deviate from normal because of increased tension. Thirty adolescents with moderate to severe crippling conditions and a comparable group of nondisabled young people served as subjects.

Contrary to expectations, reaction to frustration, as established by behavior with difficult form boards, was not differentiable on grounds of physical status. Instead, the investigator concluded on the basis of interviews with the subjects that the ability to perform a task under stress is more closely related to personal feelings and attitudes about home than to status as a physically handicapped or physically normal adolescent. Thus, subjects who felt dissatisfied with their home life did more poorly than those reporting fewer deviant home conditions. The experimenter, however, retained the frustration-aggression hypothesis as applied to disability by his interpretation of the following findings: the male but not the female subjects with crippling conditions tended to reveal lower aggressive urges and sadder feeling tones in stories (elicited by use of the Thematic Apperception Test) than did their nondisabled counterparts. He hypothesized that the male adolescent who has a disability is frustrated in his ability to carry on the usual masculine role and consequently inhibits the feeling of aggression, expressing it instead as states of unhappiness. This same resultant would not hold true for females, since a physically dependent status does not conflict as markedly with the feminine role.

The fact that these two well-executed studies did not show subjects with disabilities either to have lower frustration thresholds or to react less adequately to frustrating situations than their nondisabled counterparts forces one to reëxamine the common-sense connections between disability and frustration.

Evaluating the First Common-Sense Notion

The first assumption that must be considered is that persons with disabilities are more frequently frustrated than the nondisabled. The few available studies, however, actually belie the *generality* of this assumption.

Shere (*1954*) studied the parent-child relationships of 30 pairs of twins, one of whom in each pair was a cerebral-palsied child. The pairs included 10 pairs of identical twins, 9 pairs of like-sex fraternal twins, and 11 pairs of boy-girl twins, ranging in age from 1½ to 16 years. The disability of 12 of the cerebral-palsied twins was judged to be mild to moderate, nine considerable, and nine extreme. This study is one of the few systematic twin studies found in disability research.

The following findings, based on several rating procedures, are relevant to the present discussion. They are statistically reliable at the 5 percent level of confidence, which means that in only five cases out of 100 would they be expected to result from chance.

The behavior of the parents toward the twins differed only in certain areas.

They tended to be more understanding of the potentialities of the cerebral palsied twins and to get along with them with less friction.

They tended to expect the twin not cerebral palsied to assume more responsibilities and to act in a more mature manner than their age or capabilities would warrant.

Moreover, the parents appeared to be aware of the problems of the cerebral palsied child but to be oblivious to those of his twin.

It is believed that the lack of conformity exhibited by the twin not cerebral palsied and the consequent disciplinary friction with the parents was part of the behavior pattern of the rejected child.

In other areas the behavior of the parents was actually more desirable toward the child not cerebral palsied than it was toward his twin.

The child not cerebral palsied was accepted in an objective matter-of-fact way, accorded a place in all family activities, given help when necessary, protected from real dangers, encouraged to participate in new activities, and allowed to govern his own activities as much as possible.

On the other hand, the parents tended to overprotect the cerebral palsied twin; to prevent, consciously or unconsciously, his growing up; to give him little or no active part in forming family policies; to direct his activities in a loving but usually arbitrary manner.

The behavior of the twins differed. The child not cerebral palsied was more curious, more ready to explore than was his cerebral palsied twin.

However, the latter was more cheerful and less stubborn and resistant to authority.

He was less easily excited and less prone to violent emotional outbursts.

He was more willing to wait his turn without becoming impatient.

He was not as sensitive to either flattery or disparagement as his twin and was not unduly jealous.

This list leads to the important conclusion that, among these children, those with cerebral palsy experienced fewer frustrations in their relationships with their parents than did their nondisabled twin. We must remember, of course, that the subjects were still children, and whether the benign environment will persist in adulthood is uncertain. Also, how the children fared outside the home was not investigated in this study.

The ecological study by Barker and H. Wright (1955) is even more startling in its findings, for it covers naturally occurring situations both inside and outside the home. The three findings most pertinent to the topic of frustration are based on behavioral observations throughout a day in the lives of 12 nondisabled children and 4 children with appreciable disabilities. The children were between 2 and 11 years of age. The number of children is small, but the consistency of the findings and their theoretical implications give them an importance of the first order.

1. For each of the children, there was a relatively low frequency of episodes ending in success, frustration, and failure. Summing the percentages for these

three experiences yields a median of 2 percent for the group. Thus, "life for these children appears to have been less a matter of high ups and low downs than one might be led to expect from the amount of attention often given to these outcomes of action in research and writings on children's behavior" (p. 298). (The rating "success" was reserved for episodes in which there was clear evidence of pride in having accomplished something difficult. Satisfaction in goal accomplishment without especially crediting the self was rated as "attainment," or as "gratification" where credit was bestowed upon another.)

2. For every child the percentage of good endings (attainment, gratification, and success) is higher than the percentage of bad endings (nonattainment, frustration, failure).

3. There is no suggestion of difference between the nondisabled children and the children with disabilities; a contention that motor disability necessarily implies more frequent occurrence of bad episode endings is simply not supported.

The far-reaching implications of these findings and of some complementary ones are conveyed in the following major conclusion: "The outcome of behavior episodes in so far as it is related to release of tension, success, failure, frustration, etc., is in children virtually unrelated to motor and intellectual abilities. The fact that the 2-year-olds and the 10-year-olds, the physically disabled and the normal children were perceived to experience the same episode outcomes would seem to indicate that some governing apparatus is functioning to protect the weak and disabled from too great [negative] psychological consequences of their limitations" (p. 465).

The protective governing apparatus may be placed within two foci—namely, environmental accommodations on the one hand and adjustive changes within the person on the other. Examples of the former are: considerations in the home that take into account the special needs of each person, school curricula geared to individual and group differences, architecture that accommodates the varying physical attributes of people, legislation on behalf of persons with disabilities. These are frustration-reducing accommodations. Of course, the social environment, through mistaken notions or even through "malice aforethought," can make life for persons with disabilities unnecessarily frustrating. How the positive and negative environmental factors balance out can be expected to vary to some extent with times and places. Nevertheless, it seems certain that the environment is benign more often than our fears would allow, though to be sure it is also more deleterious in many instances.

In addition to environmental accommodations are the adjustive changes within the person. The person does not simply remain in a frustrating situation "taking it on the chin." Varying reactions to frustration have been discussed elsewhere (Rosenzweig, *1938*), but here we can note that considerable learning often takes place in coping with frustration. The person learns about the sources of the frustration, what he can and cannot do, the nature of the physical environment and its human inhabitants, all of which are important differentiations of his reality.

One of the general consequences of such learning is that he adjusts his goals (usually referred to in this context as the level of aspiration) to his experience of success and failure. With success, his aspirations usually rise; with failure they decline. To be sure, this balancing mechanism of the level of aspiration may be counteracted by other factors (see p. 337 and Barker and Wright, *1952*), but it is certainly not typical for a person to continue to concentrate on unattainable goals.

Besides lowering one's goals in accord with one's abilities, the person may meet frustration by substituting a goal that is attainable and that in effect brings about the same satisfactions. This implies that essentially the same need may be satisfied by means or subgoals of entirely different character. For example, when the person is unable to participate successfully in sports, he may substitute goal activities that do not require physical agility and still enjoy the satisfaction of such broader needs as that of group belongingness or achievement.

Still another constructive reaction to frustration, similar to the former in some respects, is to find a way to circumvent the difficulty, to discover new ways to accomplish the task at hand. This restructuring of paths to goals is seen in process when Wally, unable to push his wagon straight up the incline, turns it at an angle and with the help of other adaptive maneuvers, achieves his goal. For a recording of this incident see pp. 5–6.

The pendulum must not, of course, swing from the position where disability is equated with frustration to the opposite, where frustration is never seen to stem from disability. The following incident, one of many that could have been selected, shows that (1) the person is unable to reach his goal because of limitations imposed by his disability and (2) the totality of circumstances makes it difficult to alleviate the frustration by a shift in goals or in means. It is the same 4-year-old Wally whom we met trying to push his wagon up the bank. He is unable to walk because of a polio attack a few years before. The scene is a backyard shed where he and his cousins, Ben and Jim, ages 6 and 8 respectively, are playing:

Both Jim and Ben were on an old auto seat in the southwest corner of the shed. Between that and the doorway where Wally was, lay quite a bit of debris, including some heavy electric wire.

Ben said invitingly and commandingly, "Come and get on this, Wally," meaning on the auto seat. Wally paid no attention to them but crawled away toward the door from the shed into the Wolfson's garage.

Ben came to Wally and said shortly, "I'll carry you." He picked Wally up under the arms and proceeded to drag him across the debris and wire to the auto seat.

As he squirmed, Wally protested loudly, "I don't want over there." Wally's reluctance seemed just to make Ben more insistent. He dragged him over and dumped him on the end of the auto seats.

Wally, with impotent anger, said, crying as he said it, "Take me back, I don't want over here. Take me back."

Jim said in a lofty and quite nasty way, "You can take yourself over. You can take your *own* self over."

This enraged Wally. He shouted, "You big shit-ass, you. Goddamn it, you take me over."

Ben and Jim joined forces and taunted, "Take yourself over."

Wally, whipped into a frenzy, yelled, "Goddamn it," again. "You *will* take me over."

The two boys together teased, "No. Take yourself over."

Wally slipped off the end of the auto seat. Crying and shouting, he tried to make his way back to the shed door, crawling over the debris. He got entangled in the heavy electric wire that was in the way.

Jim and Ben took hold of the wire and pulled on it to pull him back. One of them said playfully, "We've got a big fish on this wire."

Wally took hold of the wire but his strength was not sufficient to counterbalance that of the other two boys. He was in a frenzy. "Goddamn you," he yelled, angry and crying.

He fumbled around, evidently for something to throw at the boys. Wally picked up a corn cob and threw it at them as hard as he could. One of them immediately threw it back at Wally. Wally threw another corn cob. They threw one back at him. Jim and Ben were teasing Wally; they were not angry.

Wally was really angry and obviously wanted to throw something at them to hurt them. He got hold of the handle of the big ax. He said fiercely, "I'll throw *this* at you," as he tried to lift it. It was too heavy for him to really lift adequately.

Ben immediately, recognizing Wally's real anger, came and took hold of the ax and pulled it away from him.

Wally picked up a piece of a bushel basket that was broken and threw that at the boys but didn't hit them. Then he found a short heavy board and pulled it up and started to throw it at them.

Ben came and easily took that away from him.

Wally pulled himself loose from the wire. He crawled over to the doorway and got out of the door, crying and whimpering as he crawled toward the kitchen door.

His mother appeared at the kitchen door. I [observer] heard him call to his mother from the ground, "They've been teasing me," complaining bitterly [Barker and H. Wright, *1948–1951*].[1]

---

[1] One of a series of records.

That Wally was frustrated to the point of tears and that he could do little about it is clear. It is also clear that if he were sound of limb he could have run away and have avoided much of the unbearable frustration that ensued.

In analyzing this incident more specifically, the problem of attribution clearly arises. To be sure, Wally's limitations prevented his escaping the ordeal, but there was no doubt in his mind that the behavior of Ben and Jim was *the source* of his misery. That is to say, though the disability was one of the factors that made the situation a frustrating one, it was not viewed as *the causal* condition. The importance of source or causal attribution to the meaning of an experience of frustration has been stressed by Heider (*1944*). He points out that "usually frustration leads to aggression only (and not always even then) when the origin of the frustration is attributed not to one's own person, or to impersonal causes, but to another person" (p. 367).

For the sake of completing the picture, however, it is necessary to add that there are many times when a disability may be held *responsible* for one's failures. Sometimes this belief may actually be the case and sometimes it serves as a convenient rationalization. In any event, ascribing failure to the disability may act as an excellent protection against the greater personal indictment that the failure and frustration were the resultants of inadequacies of the ego, such as motivation and character, for which the person is more deeply responsible (see Heider, *1958:*112).

The main theme of our discussion is that though a disability may act as a barrier to the achievement of certain goals, the person in adjusting to this reality tends to alter his aspirations and way of life in such a way that oppressively frustrating situations are avoided. Add to this the many environmental accommodations that take special needs into account and we can no longer be surprised to find no more frustration in life histories among persons with a disability than among the nondisabled.

This is not to say, of course, that there are not many persons with disabilities who are frustrated. Unfortunately, the person-environment-governing apparatus is not foolproof, either for persons with physical limitations or for those without. The world has all too many persons who are excessively frustrated, distraught, bothered, unfulfilled. The therapeutic focus must then be placed on personality and/or environmental factors that require change in order to facilitate adjustment.

Why does the common-sense notion that sees in disability frustration heaped upon frustration persist with such tenacity? The reasons are varied, but fundamental is man's proclivity to view the situation of another from his own perspective. Especially when he has no need to do so, it is difficult for him to see with another person's eyes. In empathy we often react the way we think we would feel in such a situation without realizing that adjustive forces within our own psychic economy would so alter the meaning of the situation that the emotional reaction would be correspondingly different.

Thus, in the following scene, as Lila is viewed laboriously building a tower, probably most persons would feel an "anticipatory" frustration that in fact was not there at all. Lila is 8½. Cerebral palsy has affected her hand and arm movements so that only with a great deal of patience and persistence does she manage to accomplish tasks requiring fine movements. It took Lila more than two minutes to place the six blocks one upon the other, a task that could ordinarily be completed by a child her age in a fraction of the time:

Lila picked up the red block carefully and set it down directly in front of her.
Then she slowly picked up the orange block. She laboriously placed it on top of the red one.
Lila carefully picked up the yellow block. As she picked it up, it fell out of her hand. She picked it up again. The yellow block was carefully put on top of the orange one.
Then she picked up the green block. It took her almost twice as long to put the green block on top of the yellow one. Finally she got the green one fitted on top of the yellow one.
She picked up the blue block. She laboriously tried to put the blue one on top of the green one but the tongue and groove didn't match. She looked at it for a moment.
Then she slowly took the blue one off. She put it down on the desk. She turned it around in her hand. Then again she carefully tried to put it back up. This time she put it on so that it fit securely in place.
She took the smallest block, the purple one, and carefully put it on top. After a few moments she got it in place.
As soon as she got the block in place, she banged her hand and squealed in delight [Barker and H. Wright, *1948–1951*].[2]

Lila would have been frustrated only if her goal had been to complete her task in short order, for then she would have been blocked by her physical limitations. Instead, the goal itself was molded in terms of the reality of her situation.

A second reason for the association of disability with frustration has to do with the fact that the nondisabled person, being uninitiated into the specific ways of circumventing limitations, tends to perceive the disability as an insurmountable barrier to the achievement of many goals. For example, many persons would be certain that the following activities are closed to those who are blind: playing ball, mowing the lawn, traveling, roller skating, and so on, until the list becomes frighteningly long. It is

[2] One of a series of records.

with surprise and admiration that many learn that none of these activities is denied, because the manner of carrying them out can be appropriately modified.

Also, physique as prime mover (see pp. 124–128), the phenomenon that gives to disability such a central position that it is held accountable for unrelated events in the life of the person, plays its role in reducing frustration to the fact of disability. Accordingly, whatever failures and frustrations the person with a disability may experience tend to be seen as disability-connected.

Finally, the presumption that disability brings about frustration leads the observer to expect frustration, an expectation that conditions him to highlight evidence supporting the expectation and to suppress or distort facts that conflict with it. This is a case of "selecting the facts that fit and fitting the facts that do not." We shall meet it again in a discussion of expectations and the interpretation of social relations (Chap. 7). Through this selective phenomenon, perception becomes pressed into the service of one's biases and expectations. Recognizing this danger, Kahn (*1951*), in his experiment on frustration in normal hearing and impaired hearing children, took precautions against it. By deleting the identification of the subject from the record of behavior in the frustrating situation, the research workers could rate the behavioral accounts according to frustration indexes without the biasing influence of their expectations.

The oversimplified linkage between disability and frustration would not be so disturbing to the person who has a disability were it not for the fact that often an attitude of devaluating pity accompanies it. Because this linkage is supported by the common sense of perception and cognition, it is necessary to bring about understanding through reappreciation of the basic truth, ignored perhaps because it is so familiar, that life is a process of adjustment, of mutual accommodations between the person and his environment.

Evaluating the Second Common-Sense Notion

The generality with which "frustration" is judged to be a negative experience makes one realize how natural this evaluation is. Mowrer (*1938*) points out that frustration is also a negative term to the clinician who sees in the life histories of delinquent, criminal, and disturbed persons relatively severe and persistent frustration as an unvarying antecedent. Nevertheless, a second look reveals that frustration is an inevitable part of life and a third look leads to the conclusion that it is capable of leading to highly desirable as well as to undesirable results.

To begin with, it appears obvious to many psychologists and educators that learning cannot be achieved without some frustration. If gratification were contemporaneous with the arousal of desire, the ultimate in frustration-free situations, the self could hardly be differentiated from the surrounding environment. It is in the solving of problems, not in the ready acquisition of goals, that insights are attained.

Besides, blocking certain activities releases energy for other purposes. This is one of the bases for advocating sublimation as a psychological mechanism important in adjusting to the restrictions of the social and physical environment. Thus some psychologists, notably psychoanalysts, hold that sublimating sexual impulses renders the psychic energies serviceable to other endeavors, such as art, science, and creative enterprise in general, the main problem being to channel the available energy to constructive rather than to asocial uses. Undoubtedly there are more or less permanent renunciations demanded of all members of a group as the price they must pay for the gains of social living, but these "cultural privations" may be turned to constructive outlets.

Furthermore, the fact that catastrophe and other unplanned, trying events do inevitably occur requires that the individual develop a tolerance for frustration if he is to remain undefeated by them. This tolerance doubtless cannot arise in the absence of prior experience with frustration. Rosenzweig believes that frustration tolerance can be fostered by allowing the child to experience small amounts of frustration—amounts that he can negotiate without reacting inadequately. Extreme deviations from this optimal dose will produce difficulty. If the child is overindulged, he will develop insufficient frustration tolerance. If, on the other hand, he is frustrated beyond his ability to handle it, areas of low frustration tolerance or complexes may be created and the ground prepared for behavior disorders (Rosenzweig, *1938:*153).

In a significant study on improving children's reactions to failure (Keister, *1937*), the training program was designed to introduce the children to progressively more and more difficult tasks, thus enabling them to build up mature and desirable responses to later situations difficult for them. During the training, the child was encouraged to persist longer in the face of tasks that were difficult for him, to depend less on an adult for help, to offer fewer rationalizations in the face of failure, and to attack a problem with a certain amount of composure. The children who experienced the training showed marked gains, whereas a comparable group of untrained children showed little change in their habitual response to frustrating situations.

Analyzing the effects of frustration from another point of view, Barker (*1938*) considered two different kinds of problem: (1) the effect of frustration upon ability to overcome the difficulty from which the frustration arises; and (2) the effect of frustration upon ability when an individual gives up and turns to other activities: in other words, what is the effect of a frustrated need upon the intellectual level of behavior not directly related to the satisfaction of that need? In both cases, as Barker points out, the reaction may reflect either a lowering of intellectual (cognitive) functioning, as when regression occurs, or it may reflect creative behavior of a high order.

In the following experiment (Barker, Dembo, Lewin, *1941*), for example, though the typical reaction was one of regression and primitivization, some of the children showed an increase in their level of constructiveness. Thirty nursery school children were observed individually on two occasions: first, in a standardized playroom, where the child's play was rated by observers on a constructiveness scale; secondly, when the room had been enlarged and the old toys incorporated into play materials greatly surpassing them in attractiveness. After the child became thoroughly interested in the new toys, the situation was changed to a frustrating one by making them unobtainable by placing a barrier of wire netting in front of them so that they could still be seen but not played with. The old toys were available, and play with them was compared with the previous play in the standard situation on a constructiveness level.

Barker (*1938*) makes clear that the constructive level of behavior is depressed when the person is torn between preoccupation with the goal he is frustrated in reaching and the goals in which he is currently involved. Conscious awareness of this double concern is not a prerequisite, for, though there may be repression of one, conflict still persists.

On the other hand, constructiveness may be enhanced when the stepped-up tension stemming from frustration is deflected toward other goals that are able to satisfy the same needs (substitution; in the case of repressed needs, sublimation), and when it raises the energy level of a person otherwise only lethargically interested in an available activity (p. 149). In addition, frustration may stimulate the person to new solutions of his current difficulty. His efforts, however, cannot be so intensely concentrated on the goal or its barrier that he becomes shortsighted for lack of adequate perspective. Rather, along with his persistence, he must achieve the flexibility that comes with a sufficient degree of relaxation to enable him to survey alternatives and not be bound to a limited number of them. Krech and Crutchfield (*1948*) present a succinct yet comprehensive analysis of the sources and consequences of frustration under the proposition that "the frustration of goal achievement and the failure of tension reduction may lead to a variety of adaptive or maladaptive behaviors" (pp. 50–62).

With respect to the problem of adjusting to disability, it seems to us that one of the most common and powerful factors militating against the constructive substitution of means and goals in coping with frustration is what has been referred to as "idolizing normal standards" (see pp. 24–40). If the person feels that he is valued according to the degree to which his goals and behavior are the same as they would have been without his disability, then, depending on the limitations imposed by the reality of his disability, he is a ready candidate for overwhelming frustration. The following protocol of a counseling session with a 16-year-old boy suffering from a quadriplegic cerebral palsy shows the depths of despair that can result from frustration stemming from rigid adherence to the standards of the nondisabled state:

SUBJECT: "I just don't know why the doctors let me live when I was born. I'm no use to anyone the way I am."
COUNSELOR: "You feel that you are of no value to society and that discourages you."
SUBJECT: "Yes, I know what I want to do and I can talk O.K., but every time I try to do anything I'm stymied. I can't walk or even eat without some help."
COUNSELOR: "You feel, because of your physical condition, that you can't do many of the things you want to do and you feel frustrated when this happens."
SUBJECT: "It's worse than that. When I can't succeed in something and when I know I could succeed if I weren't a C.P. (cerebral palsy), I get more than discouraged because I'm so helpless. You're stuck and you hate yourself for being stuck" [Cruickshank, *1948*:81–82].

Some will hold that in such an extreme case of helplessness overwhelming frustration is inevitable, and yet we must remind ourselves that it was this boy's vision of his accomplishments unfettered by his disability ("I know I could succeed if I weren't a C.P.") that was crucial in making rigid his aspirations so that appropriate modifications could not bring satisfaction.

Disturbance may be created not only in frustrating situations, where the goals and the way to reach them may be clear but blocked, but also in what have been described as new psychological situations. This problem will be examined before we proceed to a discussion of adjustive changes within the person which, in enabling the person to live more comfortably with himself, also bear upon frustration and uncertainty.

UNCERTAINTY ARISING FROM NEW PSYCHOLOGICAL SITUATIONS

Puzzling over a problem, being on thin ice, applying for a job, being in an unfamiliar town, entering a social situation well under way, all have in common the fact that in certain respects the situation psychologically is a new one. This means that the directions toward a desired goal are unknown and that the behavior one embarks upon is simultaneously positive and negative, i.e., each act may place one closer to the goal (positive) or move one further from it (negative). Such a situation provokes cautious behavior and, to the extent that the situation is a dangerous or crucial one, anxiety and insecurity as well.[3]

Situations that are psychologically new in the sense that they are perceptually unclear, unstructured, or ambiguous arise in regard to a person's disability when: (1) the person is unsure as to whether he will be able to manage physically. (For example, he may not know whether the building has steps that he must negotiate but that he may be unable to manage.) (2) the person is unsure of his reception by others. (For example, he may not know whether he will be accepted or rejected, shown sympathy or devaluating pity, reacted to with fear or trust, helped or ignored, etc. See Chap. 9 for many illustrations of this.) (3) the person is unsure of what kind of person he himself is. (For example, he may have difficulty in reconciling his physically imperfect body with personality characteristics that are acceptable and even complimentary. See p. 157 for the anguish and the conflict suffered by a young woman every time her mirror image shattered her self-illusions.)

Whether or not a physical disability in general tends to increase the frequency with which new psychological situations are encountered requires ecological investigation. Some psychologists have taken a firm position that it does (see Meyerson, *1955b:*48). But relative frequency is always difficult to establish and depends on many inconstant conditions. If one argues, for example, that the able-bodied person is not troubled by unknown architectural features (as whether a building has steps or an elevator), one can counter that the able-bodied person might more frequently engage in activities that would involve other kinds of uncertain physical-geographic situations. Whether in greater or lesser degree, nonetheless, the problem of uncertainty resulting from new psychological situations seems especially prominent in the case of particular physical disabilities: for example, deafness, blindness, and epilepsy.

The following account shows the extreme consequences of uncertainty created by seizures that overtake the person without warning:

---

[3] For a more detailed and systematic account of the properties of new psychological situations, see Barker *et al.* (*1953:*30–37), the thinking therein stemming from the work of Lewin (*1936, 1938*). The concept of new psychological situations and their derived behavior, namely, behavior characterized by conflict, emotionality, alertness, and instability, has been applied to a variety of cases such as adolescents (Lewin, *1939;* Barker *et al.,* 1953), autocratic groups (Lippitt, *1940*), and persons with disabilities (Barker *et al., 1953;* Meyerson, *1955b*).

When I have an attack, I sort of go into my shell. I stay at home, am absent from school and just sit around thinking. I am afraid that I might get another attack any minute. When a few days have passed since my attack, I may go out of the house, perhaps for a walk. But I am still very anxious about my physical condition and make sure that I get home quickly. It takes about a week before I feel like returning to school and seeing outside people. Even when I'm back at school I can't help thinking about getting an attack there, or in the street or in the subway. It seems as if I'm always ready to jump within my shell, as I like to put it, at the slightest disturbance [Arluck, 1941:64–65].

In this case, the persistently "new" psychological character of the person's surroundings was not due to his never having experienced them but to his inability to structure his situation in a stable way because at any moment events could shift dangerously beyond his control. The tension, caution, conflict, frustration, alertness to every cue—behaviors derivable from the forces characterizing new psychological situations— are apparent. Whenever a situation occurs in which the consequences of behavior are seemingly unpredictable or uncontrollable, and in which benefits and harms occur in an apparently inconsistent, fortuitous, or arbitrary manner, insecurity of the deepest sort may be expected. The fact that most persons with epilepsy, however, are able to control seizures with proper medication means that they need not be beset by insecurity stemming from unexpected physical attack. Nonetheless, uncertainties of social reception as well as ambiguities resulting from an unstable self-image (for example, one that vacillates between identification with the healthy and with the sick) may give to the life space the character of frequently occurring new psychological situations (Lewin, G., 1957).

It is most important to distinguish between unknown situations that are difficult to avoid, as in the case of uncontrollable seizures, and those that arise because the person himself has not accepted his disability. Much uncertainty and tension stem from the fact that, in hiding his disability, the person at the same time prevents clarification of his behavior possibilities (see pp. 48–49). The overwhelming anxiety that can be self-imposed in this way is seen in the account by Raymond Goldman, who, hard of hearing, could not tell when the teacher would call upon him or what point in the text the recitation had reached (see pp. 31–32 for incident). If only Raymond had allowed himself to inform the teacher of his hearing difficulties so that appropriate steps to meet them could have been taken, he would have been spared much of the uncertainty of a perceptually confused situation. For example, he could have been placed in a strategic position to speech-read more adequately; someone could have followed along in the text with him, and so on.

That the uncertainty of new psychological situations faced by a person with a disability is frequently independent of the fact of his disability also must be recognized. Because the following incident clearly illustrates this and because it also demonstrates a type of behavior commonly occurring in new psychological situations, it is recounted in full. Karsten tells about the time he and a girl, both blind high school students, were out together for the first time. Especially prominent is cautious, exploratory, trial-and-error behavior. Underlying tension and resulting frustration may be presumed.

. . . I found a small brick alcove jutting out from the wall with a high concrete step at its base. I brushed the snow from a small area, and we sat down on either side of it about three feet apart. The girl was a bit timid, I thought. For a long time we sat in silence. Snow settled on my hat. The cold air pried into my overcoat and through my shirt. I rummaged about in my brain trying to find something to talk about.

"It's kind of cold out tonight," I said finally.

The girl drew her coat more closely about her.

"Yes," she said, her head still turned straight ahead.

I shivered. I turned up my collar and wished that I had put on my winter underwear.

"I think it will be warmer tomorrow though, if it doesn't turn colder," I went on. Words came out of me like a dull razor sawing through dry whiskers. The girl took a handkerchief from her purse and blew her nose cautiously.

"Yes," she said.

I had a vague feeling that things were not progressing. I put my hands in my pockets and curled my toes, trying to find a warm spot by the heel. There must be other interesting subjects that we could talk about!

"You live quite far from here, don't you?" I asked.

She deliberated.

"Yes," she said.

I was uncomfortable. I managed to keep some warmth in my hands and feet, but the concrete I was sitting on did not seem to warm up at all. We sat staring into the snow. The girl moved uneasily, but I said nothing. It was her turn to ask questions. I did not want to hog all the conversation. Snowflakes clattered loudly on the crown of my hat. I wondered what Ben and his girl were talking about on the other side of the building. My companion blew her nose again and turned slightly.

"Do you like that new song we are learning in chorus?" she asked.

I fumbled about for a brilliant answer. Our conversational infant needed a verbal whack that would put life into him.

"Yes," I replied.

She deliberated again.

"I think the sopranos sing a little flat, don't you?"

"Yes," I said.

We lapsed into another long and profound silence. My thoughts moved sluggishly, like broken ice on a prairie river. It was getting late. In a short time the girls would have to leave. Impulsively I put my hand on the concrete behind her back and leaned forward.

"My lips are kind of puckery tonight," I said nonchalantly.

"Are they?" she brightened. Her voice was like chocolate and raspberry jam. She leaned toward me. Her face was not over two feet away. "What do you suppose makes it?" she asked.

I took my hand from behind her back and turned the other way again.

"I don't know," I said, rubbing my lips reflectively. "Been practicing too much on my cornet, I guess. . . ."

We were half buried in snow when Ben and his girl came around the corner again. When the girls were two blocks or more away, Ben and I started trudging slowly along. Ben was silent. I wondered what he was thinking of—most likely of all the things he and his friend had talked about.

"What sort of a girl was she, Ben?" I asked.

Ben plodded along.

"Yes," he said hollowly.

I waited. He seemed unaware of my presence.

"I said: 'What sort of girl was she?' "

"Yes," Ben repeated mechanically.

I shook my head sadly and blew a cloud of steam inside my collar to thaw my cheeks. Together we trudged along over the drifts toward home [Ohnstad, *1942*:146–148].[4]

Situations that are psychologically new differ from one another in an important respect: some are crucial and even dangerous to the person and some are not. Being on thin ice, either literally or figuratively, is an example of a new and dangerous psychological situation. Working through a problem in automobile mechanics or in room decorating is an example of a new but relatively safe psychological situation. It is safe even though the directions to the goal are unknown and even though one is bound to make false steps in spite of caution. The safety accrues either from the fact that the inevitable false steps are reversible or because the worst eventuality, failure, is not crucial to the security of the person. As applied to disability, this means that a psychologically new situation may, with adjustment, shift from one that spells danger to one that is far more innocuous.

First, as to the matter of reversibility. The person can develop facility in structuring otherwise unknown situations. If he has a hearing impairment, for example, he can ask people to face him, to speak louder, to repeat. If he is blind, he can begin to use a white cane or ask someone to accompany him when he goes to town the first time. Obviously, these facilities are not independent of the person's acceptance of his disability, which, as we shall see in the following chapter, is contingent upon important changes within the value system of the person.

As for the matter of how crucial the situation is, this too, in many instances, is subject to reëvaluation. For example, if the person's self-esteem hinges on whether he can converse like any normally hearing person, on whether he can find his way around town unaided, on whether he can walk as far as the next man, then these situations are crucial and any perceptual unclarity will give rise not only to cautious behavior but to anxious behavior as well. But if, as a result of adjustive changes, he is able to accept his limitations, then failing to keep up with the others is simply not decisive to his ego. He may remain alert as to how he can best manage, but the emotionality of conflict and frustration need not be prominent accompaniments.

It is not so much the situation that is psychologically new as such that one wants to avoid (though to be sure a superabundance of such situations with the problem solving required in them may become burdensome). If all situations were well structured—that is, if the directions to goals were always known—man would neither be alerted nor challenged to make new discoveries. Probably the notion of optimum balance between the known and unknown is applicable here. But it is true that the psychologically new situation that is also a major threat to the person ought either to be avoided or altered where possible unless some purpose is served by entering it.

In this chapter, frustration and uncertainty as problems commonly associated with disability were briefly examined in terms of their sources, certain positive and negative aspects of their consequences, and the conditions that mitigate their deleterious effects. The common-sense notion that oppressive frustration is a probable if not inevitable accompaniment of disability has been challenged by a review of pertinent research findings and theoretical considerations. Environmental accommodations and changes within the person must become the two foci in understanding how frustration as a problem-solving situation is often met satisfactorily. One of the main impediments to the adequate solution of frustration-producing situations as far as disability is concerned is the high value placed on "normal" standards of behavior. Likewise, diminishing or even eliminating the danger in many new psychological situations is at least to some extent within the power of the person himself on the one hand and of the group on the other.

The main attitude or value changes that have positive adjustive effects are discussed in the following chapter. These apply not only to the person with a disability, though the focus of the discussion has been placed there, but to the nondisabled person as well. Specific suggestions as to how the "other person" may avoid difficulties in ordinary relations with a person handicapped in some way are presented in Chapter 9.

Chapter 5

Value Changes in Acceptance
of Disability

WE HAVE SEEN HOW A PERSON WHO FEELS ASHAMED AND INFERIOR BE-
cause of his disability avoids identification as a person with a disability.
By keeping his disability to himself, he tries to prevent it from becoming
a social fact, hoping that thus he will not suffer rebuff from others and
society. In one sense he is correct in his basis for this course of action for,
having a disability, he will be ill received by some persons and meet
discrimination in some situations of possible importance to him, as, for
example, in employment. By hiding his disability, then, it seems possible
to avoid these negative experiences. If it is not possible actually to conceal
the disability, then the person, as long as he himself feels inferior because
of it, tries to act as though the deviation makes no difference, tries to
outdo himself in maintaining normal standards, and in general tries to
appear as much like a nonhandicapped person as possible. But, even
should he be able to conceal his disability, he cannot in his own eyes feel
the security of being a complete, worthy individual, for admission that a
difference exists is a prerequisite to the further step of accepting the difference as nondevaluating.

If, as was already shown, the cultural attitudes toward atypical physique
are conflicting, viewing it on the one hand as a sign of inferiority, and on
the other hand as neutral or even as an indication of virtue and goodness
meriting special reverence, why is it that the person with a disability
focuses on the personally more devastating side of the conflict? It is just
because the first view is such a threatening one that it demands a hearing.
And when in this hearing the individual in some way associates disability
with punishment or idolizes the normal ideal, he receives confirmation of
his dreaded feelings that disability is and ought to be a sign of inferiority.
Moreover, as we shall soon see, under certain conditions an inferior
position on one characteristic tends to spread to other characteristics and
to the total person. These and other factors taken up in Chapter 10 contribute to the upper hand that disability-as-personal-inferiority assumes

at first and that determines the more primitive efforts of escaping the intolerable rejection of the self.

The maladjustive reactions to disability, however, are important first efforts in the process of accepting one's disability and oneself. Gradually and intermittently, the individual may become aware of the strain that nonacceptance of his disability imposes, and of how, in spite of all his efforts to the contrary, his deviation is real and has personal and social effects. Frances Warfield (*1948*), who admitted her hearing loss only to her medical and quack therapists, who devised elaborate schemes to hide her impairment, at the same time perceived well the foolishness of such acting *when the actors were other people*. She spoke of them as "silly ostriches . . . who didn't fool anybody but themselves" (p. 26). It may take a longer time and a deeper personal upheaval to admit the foolishness in oneself, for the admission carries the obligation of altering one's behavior, of giving up the methods one wants desperately to succeed, of examining anew the values one holds dear and by which one lives. This chapter will deal with the kinds of value change that appear significant in the process of accepting one's disability and oneself.

WHAT KIND OF ACCEPTANCE?

The importance of accepting oneself has become a cardinal principle among psychotherapists ever since the far-reaching role of such psychological processes as repression and guilt have become more clearly understood. Unfortunately, the concept of acceptance has also become a ready-made cliché purporting to guarantee adjustment, though if one becomes serious about the connection in the particular context, one often wonders what kind of acceptance and what kind of adjustment are meant. When a patient in psychotherapy becomes aware of his hostile feelings and defiantly begins to insult his associates and cater almost exclusively to his own needs, is that accepting himself? At the moment he may be accepting his hostile feelings, but he is also accepting the premise that they need no controls and that "he is as he is and is fine." Does acceptance require that the *status quo* be supreme and sublime, that changes in and about oneself are unnecessary? We think not.

When a person accepts his state, it does, however, sometimes mean that he prefers it, that if it were his to choose, he would select it over other alternatives. There certainly are persons among underprivileged racial and religious minority groups who are glad that they are Jews or Negroes or Indians, for example, who wish their children to continue to be, who accept their group membership in this sense. The book *It's Good to Be Black* culminates in the young Negro girl's conviction that she could be proud that she was black (Goodwin, *1953*). Moreover, she felt "genuinely sorry for everybody in the world lighter than the brown pair of . . . shoes laced on my dancing feet" (p. 256). Perhaps the opinion that a person with a disability may be glad about his condition will be viewed more dubiously. But even this can be the case, and before we rest comfortably with the diagnosis, "Aha, secondary gain, rationalization" we must again remind ourselves of the blinding force with which our own values prescribe our evaluations.

In any case, the problem of acceptance as dealt with here is not concerned with the conditions that will bring about preference of one's own state over others. Nor does it deal with the other end of the scale, that of acceptance in the sense of resigning oneself to the inevitable. Resignation connotes a bowing to misfortune, patiently uncomplaining, rather than feeling all right about it. We are more concerned with the conditions facilitating acceptance of one's disability as nondevaluating. The disability may still be seen as inconveniencing and limiting. The person may still strive to "improve the improvable" where improvement will facilitate certain aspects of his life. He may exercise daily to graduate from crutch-walking to cane-walking, but he will not abandon his crutches prematurely in order to be as much like a normal person as possible. He will not feel debased as a person and suffer the strain and shame of hiding and pretense.

Dembo and co-workers (*1956*) have made a careful beginning in tracing the process of what they have called "acceptance of loss." By loss is meant the absence of something valuable, felt as a personal misfortune. The following discussion is a development of their analysis of the changes within the value system of the person that are instrumental in overcoming the feeling of shame and inferiority resulting from disability as a value loss. These changes may be designated as: (1) enlarging the scope of values, (2) containing disability effects, (3) subordinating physique, and (4) transforming comparative values into asset values. These value changes are interdependent in the sense that affecting one will affect another, but for clarity they will be considered separately.

ENLARGING THE SCOPE OF VALUES

Enlarging the scope of values means the emotional realization of the existence of other values. This is of especial importance during the period of mourning following the loss of something cherished, whether the loss be physical normality, a loved one, or something else.

Conditions Underlying Mourning

The psychological shock reaction to physical impairment has been described as a period of mourning comparable to that of bereavement (Dembo *et al., 1956;* Cholden, *1954;* Blank, *1957*). The aptness of this designation becomes apparent when one realizes that the conditions underlying mourning are similar in both instances. It has also been observed that the blind sometimes refer to their "dead eyes" and the deaf to their "dead ears" (Blank, *1957:*12).

One of the most pervasive conditions producing mourning is the inability or unwillingness of the person to sever ties with the endeared state that was. By mourning his loss, he brings the past into the present and in this way does not give up the past.

The person also needs time to begin to absorb the new changes about himself into his self-concept. As Blank has pointed out, the shock reaction to loss ". . . seems to be an emergency defense against the threat of dissolution of the ego by eruption of overwhelmingly painful affects. The affects are thereafter allowed to emerge bit by bit so that they can be handled by the ego piecemeal . . ." (p. 11).

In addition, a perceptual factor contributes to the persistence as well as existence of mourning. In the sheer act of comparing the present with the past, one is prone to attend to the changes and to ignore the common denominators. Perceptually, the things that are different stand out and the remainder, in its sameness, becomes obliterated. In the case of disability, the difference is the *disability* and thus the loss is seen as the main feature of the new state.

A person with a disability feels his loss in terms of personal and social satisfactions now denied him (Dembo *et al., 1956*). Mourning for personal loss is expressed in the following ruminations as Harold Russell (*1949*) realizes for the first time that he has no hands:

I looked up and saw my arms. For the first time. Their ends were wrapped in bandages. They were pulled up over my head and fastened to a wooden frame above the bed. I couldn't move them. I could hardly move my body at all. It made me think of the days before I went to the Army, when I worked in the market. My arms reminded me of two sides of beef hanging on hooks. . . .

Then it hit me.

It was my *hands* that were gone. Those things at the end of my arms. Those things with five fingers on them. They hadn't been much to look at. Quite ugly, in fact, and dirty most of the time.

Suddenly I knew how useful those hands had been to me. I had always taken them for granted. Like my eyes, legs, ears, tongue. They had always been there when I needed them, ready to work. If I wanted to cut and weigh a piece of meat, if I wanted to drive a golf ball, if I wanted to write a letter to Rita or pull the ripcord of a parachute, they were always there to serve me. I never had to ask, Will you do this for me? They were always there, by my side, prepared, willing, unhesitating, obedient, loyal. A pair of stout, strong friends, not beautiful, but dependable. . . .

I tried not to think about them. . . .

But I kept coming back to my hands. I couldn't get them out of my mind. What wonderful, efficient machines they were. Hands. So simple. Just some bones, muscles, nerves, blood vessels and skin. Nothing to them, really. And yet, how valuable, how perfect, how cunningly contrived to do so many marvelous things. Like pitching a ball or painting a picture or caressing someone you loved [pp. 4–5].[1]

The social loss content of mourning may be conveyed in the following: "People might stand my presence but not accept me as they used to." "I never had to depend on others. Now I will be a burden." "People will pity me." "Others will go ahead while I will be left behind."

In mourning, the loss aspects dominate the emotional stage. In extreme bereavement, "the loss seems to pervade all areas of the person's life. Whatever he thinks about, whatever he does, he is troubled, pained, and distressed. There is no differentiation between areas of the person which are and are not injury-connected. All that matters are the values affected by the injury and they are lost. No other values in life are important or even existent" (Dembo *et al., 1956:*36). In the grip of such an emotional onslaught, the person may become apathetic, numb to all conscious feeling. Goldman (*1947*) captures the essence of this state in his recollection of the period following the death of his wife:

. . . I tried not to look back; I couldn't look forward, for ahead was a wall of blankness. It is difficult to put into this chronicle the record of my emotions. I seemed to have none; I was empty as a wormed shell. I no longer felt even the twisting pain of grief. . . .

. . . I wanted to die . . . to be rid of the galling burden of futile struggle. The thought of taking my own life never once entered my mind. . . . Just passively I wanted to die [p. 168].[2]

Pearl Buck (*1950*), upon learning that her retarded child could never be normal, was overcome with a despair so profound that it threatened to destroy her thought and feeling:

[1] Harold Russell with Victor Rosen, *Victory in My Hands,* copyright 1949. Used by permission of the publishers, Farrar, Straus, and Cudahy, Inc.

[2] The selection from R. L. Goldman, *Even the Night,* copyright 1947, The Macmillan Company, is used with the permission of the publisher.

. . . there was no more joy left in anything. All human relationships became meaningless. Everything became meaningless. I took no more pleasures in the things I had enjoyed before; landscapes, flowers, music were empty. Indeed, I could not bear to hear music at all. It was years before I could listen to music. Even after the learning process had gone very far, and my spirit had become nearly reconciled through understanding, I could not hear music. I did my work during this time: I saw that my house was neat and clean, I cut flowers for the vases, I planned the gardens and tended my roses, and arranged for meals to be properly served. We had guests and I did my duty in the community. But none of it meant anything. My hands performed their routine. The hours when I really lived were when I was alone with my child. When I was safely alone I could let sorrow have its way, and in utter rebellion against fate my spirit spent its energy [pp. 29–30].[3]

Black despair may also occur in the recently injured person when the experience of loss and change from one's former state is so overpowering that the suffering seems boundless, not only in extent but also in time. Then the idea of suicide may present itself or, more moderately, the gnawing feeling that one's present state is worthless. This period in the case of blindness has been described as follows:

The shock [of sudden blindness] consists of depersonalization followed by depression. The depersonalization usually lasts two to seven days. The patient is immobile, or almost so, facial expression is blank, there is a generalized hypoesthesia or anesthesia, and mutism [,] or speech is meager, slow, muted. Superficially, the condition may resemble catatonia. But the patient does not utter the delusional or dissociated remarks of a schizophrenic; rather, he is likely during the acute stage, or more often later, to say that he has no feeling or that he feels as if he were unreal or the world were unreal. . . . the depression which follows may be an acute reactive depression or an agitated depression . . . and it is a state of mourning for the loss of the eyes [Blank, *1957*:11–12].

Mourning may also express the need to make a public pageant of grief. This may be associated with a bid for sympathy, indulging in self-pity, or fulfilling the formal requirements of propriety.

That the mourning reaction to loss, though common, is not the only reaction is seen in a study of World War II amputees (Randall, Ewalt, and Blair, *1945*). It was found that severe depression (mourning) was the preponderant reaction immediately following the injury in the case of noncombat casualties, but in the case of battle casualties the modal reaction was the feeling of being lucky, with depression, though common,

[3] Reprinted by permission of Harold Ober Associates. Copyright, 1950, by Pearl S. Buck.

taking second place. These results can be accounted for by the likelihood that the battle casualties felt that they easily could have been worse off; instead of comparing their present injured state with their previous able-bodied state, the comparison was with their anticipated annihilation. The difference that stands out in these circumstances is not the loss aspect of the new state but rather its gain. The percentage of cases (76 battle injuries, 24 noncombat injuries) reacting variously to injury as determined by social histories from Red Cross files, Rorschach "blind" analysis, and psychiatric examinations follows:

	Immediately Following Injury		In Base Hospital	
	Battle	Noncombat	Battle	Noncombat
Shame	0	0	11	33
Self-pity	1	0	9	0
Lucky	42	0	7	0
Worry about family	16	13	0	0
Depression	30	61	13	21
Psychiatric	4	13	3	8
No emotional response	7	13	57	38

The reaction of the battle cases is more favorable in both phases. In the second phase the feeling of both "lucky" and depression decreases, and the feeling of shame and self-pity increases. Finally, it is apparent that depression was not the only prominent reaction. How many of the "no emotional response" reactions can be considered symptomatic of what we have called mourning is not known. An important study of the conditions underlying various psychological reactions to the stress of surgery (other than amputation, e.g., appendectomy, colostomy, etc.) has been reported by Janis (1958).

During mourning there is a combination of factors in which the need for the lost values, the perception of difference with the compared state, and even the propriety of mourning concentrate the energies of the person on the *loss aspects*. It now becomes clear why the first step in the adjustment process or in overcoming mourning entails enlarging the scope of the values to encompass those that are still available to the person. Only then can the person look to the satisfactions existing in the present and begin to see that he and his life have something to offer.

Overcoming Mourning

How the scope of values is enlarged is of fundamental importance. We do know that the values presumed lost may be perceived in a new way, in which their essential aspects are retained and not in fact denied. For example, the person may come to realize that though he can no longer run and skip, he can now carry on the essential value of locomotion by means of his prosthesis, the crutches, or the wheel chair. We also know that values heretofore undiscovered may become meaningful as the person struggles with his suffering and reacts to his own feelings and to the behavior of others. "Faith," for example, may begin to make sense to the person; or he may begin to appreciate the value of brotherhood and service to others; or in case of asocial perceptions, he may begin to feel the value of selfishness, revenge, power. In any case, his horizon becomes structured with things that matter in one way or another. Although the lost values may still be important, a necessary condition toward overcoming devaluation has been realized.

But what causes such reëvaluation? At first the person is submerged in a surrounding gloom and then he begins to see that there is meaning to life, that worthwhile experiences still await him. What produced this shift? Several processes appear significant.

Dembo and her co-workers (1956) suggest that the essential value, *life*, may be regained at the moment the person decides to give it up. Here we again have the important role played by the perception of what constitutes change or the difference between two states. In a contemplation of suicide, the characteristic that differentiates the two states, before and after, is *life*. Life, for the moment at least, may then occupy the person's energies instead of the pervasive suffering. This may provide the first hold, the feeling of strength and hope called the "stamina experience" and lead to new awareness of the positive in life.

The factor of perceptual difference with a compared state is also in evidence when a person, in seeing others who are worse off, first realizes his assets. G. Barr, himself an amputee and the head of a pharmaceutical goods company many of whose employees have handicaps, has observed: "It is valuable psychologically to have different types of disabled workers together in the same company. . . . The blind man considers himself much better off than his deaf-mute co-worker. The deaf-mute would not trade places with the infantile paralysis victim who cannot walk. The infantile paralysis victim feels sorry for the one-armed person. Each one, when he sees someone else and realizes the limitations forced upon the other fellow by handicaps he himself does not have, feels he is not so badly off" (Rusk and Taylor, 1946:188).[4] This contrast phenomenon is of therapeutic value when, through it, the person becomes aware of his own assets or abilities, and particularly that these enable him to partici-

[4] H. A. Rusk and E. J. Taylor, *New Hope for the Handicapped.* Harper & Brothers, 1946. By permission.

pate in his own way, as others can in their own way, in the multivaried world.

Even when the person may believe that nothing matters now, many values remain at the unconscious level and may be aroused. Dembo *et al.* (*1956*) give an example in which the depression of an amputee was eased when a close friend ridiculed and scolded his self-pity. This resulted in awakened pride as a remaining value.

In less depressed states, the sheer necessities of living may contribute to the turning away from the past and dealing with the here and now. The paraplegic, for example, has to attend to bodily needs. His needs prod him to try to move, to turn over, to sit up; and in coping with these problems he may find a challenge that assuages his rued loss and leads him to devote his attention to the problems at hand. We can see, now, the important place, in the process of enlarging the scope of values, of mastering "activities of daily living" that modern rehabilitation introduces early to the patient. The problem still remains, however, of how soon and how much of the patient's physical and psychic energies should be deflected to problems of the external world.

It is also likely that a satiation factor enters, helping the person to overcome his absorption with his loss. One can maintain an emotional state only so long. One can, for example, be ecstatically happy, but the peak wanes with time even when the circumstances remain the same. Similarly, a person may be deeply depressed over a loss, but in time there is an ebbing of depression. Sometimes, as was previously noted, this is accompanied by a numbness. The person feels wrung dry and feels no more. It is as though he were satiated with emotion and even satiated with preoccupation with the loss. One has mourned and mourned and mourned. One becomes tired of mourning. Suddenly the person is ready for something new, something different. The dominance of loss now is abated and, in his search for diversion, he rediscovers the wider reality. Satiation may be one important factor permitting a person "to snap out" of a feeling of hopelessness and grief by himself.

Though it is necessary to leave the state of mourning behind as one adjusts to the facts of disability, it would be a mistake to conclude that this should be done with dispatch. There is good reason to believe that the period of mourning can be a healing period during which the wound is first anesthetized and then gradually closed, leaving the least scarring. Lack of recognition of the psychological value of mourning is the basis for an indictment against one of the military rehabilitation centers for the blind where, "because of an enthusiastic and efficient attempt . . . made there to help the blinded soldier master problems of external reality," it was believed that the inner work of mourning could not be accomplished (Blank, *1957:*12). This, then, is an issue clearly affecting the nature of rehabilitation in centers treating the newly injured.

The issue is by no means closed, for there hardly is enough study to permit conclusive statements. The views presented are rather of the order of hypotheses requiring continued research for their clarification.

It is significant that certain societies seem better able to prepare their members for bereavement (Volkart and Michael, *1957*). One example of variable cultural mores affecting the psychic ease of meeting bereavement is the matter of "replacing" the one lost. Some societies have instituted obligatory remarriage or adoption, this serving to reëstablish the role vacated by death. Our society, on the other hand, tends to emphasize the loss aspects of dealth. One even should not speak ill of the dead. However, the period of mourning during which homage is paid to the dead and healing takes place is halted at a year, a formality that encourages the person to resume fully the affairs of the living. Whether "the year" is generally and optimally satisfactory and whether it has equal relevance with respect to mourning a physical loss touches upon important social-psychological issues. Surely this is an area in which research is needed.

Mourning, clearly, is not a state through which one passes and then leaves behind. It is experienced intermittently after the deepest pangs are mitigated. Moreover, "one should not draw any strong inference about psychiatric diagnosis and ego strength from the severity of the symptoms in the shock stage" (Blank, *1957:*12). As the outlook of the person is further altered by the value changes to be discussed in the following pages, mourning becomes less persistent until finally the person is able to look upon his loss with unconcern or a feeling of tenderness rather than hurt, "with that tenderness which old people not infrequently feel toward the reminiscences of their youth," now gone, but still a part of them (Dembo, Leviton, Wright, *1956:*39). During the later phases of adjustment to disability, after the person has found a first hold and can carry on in meaningful activity, further enlargement of the scope of values is necessary before he can reach what may be called self-fulfillment.

The following dynamic processes important in overcoming mourning have been considered: comparison of one's state with other worse states, arousal of dormant values, satiation, involvement in necessities of living. There are others, but these are sufficient perhaps to demonstrate the important practical and theoretical problems involved in overcoming mourning.

SUBORDINATING PHYSIQUE

Even when the person does not doubt that life is worth-while he may be unduly troubled because of the supreme value that he places on physical competence or normality. He may, for example, recognize that life means comfort, friendship, work, and so on but still feel degraded because he falls below the standards of physical normality. The person, then, is less troubled when physique becomes a relatively minor value.

Dembo *et al.* (*1956*) describe two examples of value change in which physique becomes less important. In the first of these, physical appearance matters less and in the second, physical ability matters less. In both instances, other values matter more and become the important determinants in the evaluation of the person:

1. *The problem of appearance.* It is proposed that devaluation resulting from damaged appearance will be diminished to the extent that surface appearance is felt to be less important for the evaluation of the person than personality. This shift is facilitated when the person is convinced of the fundamental importance of nonphysique values, such as kindness, wisdom, effort, coöperativeness. Earl Schenck Miers (*1949*), a man with cerebral palsy, has expressed this relative subordination of physique values to personality or character values: "The intolerance of ignorance, the ruthlessness of avarice, the insanities of lust for power and domination, the unfeeling heart that must nurture the shameless, all-consuming pride —such handicaps as these are most to be regretted and most to be avoided, for from them come much of the world's eternal suffering."

Actually, the perception of the physical appearance may itself change when it is seen in the light of such personality variables. Thus, whatever the objective conditions of the surface appearance may be, when one reacts positively to the person, the appearance may be felt to be attractive, and vice versa.

In certain circumstances, as among strangers, the influence of personality recedes to the background and that of surface appearance becomes a focus of attention. On the other hand, many people naturally judge a person's attractiveness in terms of personality. This is especially true among persons in close relationships, where the personality of the other is felt. It is also true that some people show little concern with physical appearance because other aspects of life, being much more highly valued, command a good deal more of the available time and energy. We are not advocating, of course, neglect of personal grooming, but we are asserting that placing personality above physical appearance will reduce devaluation of persons with visible disabilities.

2. *The problem of ability and achievement.* Dembo *et al.* introduce the problem as follows:

To call someone disabled implies that performance determines the evaluation of the person. In our society, people are frequently compared with each other on the basis of their achievements. Schools, for example, are predominantly influenced by the achievement or product ideology. High grades are not given to the one who worked hardest but to the one who performed best. Under certain circumstances, of two persons who reached the same performance level, the one who did so with greater ease is considered the better. He is seen as potentially a better producer than the one who had to work harder. Thus, effort is not only considered a positive value, but paradoxically, sometimes as a liability.

If one would follow the maxim which also exists in our society to the effect that, "All that is expected of you is that you do your best," it would mean that the person would not be compared with others in regard to ability; it would mean that only his own state matters and thus that it does not matter whether he lost or lacks ability. Actually, one wishes to say, a person does not lack ability; he can only *have* it. In everyday life we do evaluate as equally good citizens those who pay taxes according to their financial state. The injured who applies himself with effort contributes the most that he can as a *person*. Though the unsatisfactory physical tools of his body may have limited his production [along specific lines] his personal contributions are at the maximum. As a *person* he is not different from the noninjured [Dembo, Leviton, Wright, *1956:*40].

In the preceding discussion physical appearance and ability were both subordinated to personality factors within the person over which he has more control. One may wonder what happens to the person who cannot claim merit via effort, moral fortitude, or other personality traits. That he still remains a devalued person is clear, for comparison with a standard still exists, albeit the standard now pertains to character and personality. If instead of physical shortcomings we had been discussing acceptance by a person of his personality shortcomings, such as indolence or selfishness, we might first raise the moral question of whether one should strive to accept these attributes; if affirmative conclusions were drawn, subordinating these traits as values would be indicated. In considering physical disability, however, devaluation of the person will be diminished insofar as physical achievement and physical appearance become unimportant as compared to effort and other personality traits. In the words of Shakespeare:

> In nature there's no blemish but the mind;
> None can be called deformed but the unkind:
> Virtue is beauty, but the beauteous evil
> Are empty trunks, o'erflourished by the devil.
> (*Twelfth Night,* Act III, Scene 4)

CONTAINING DISABILITY EFFECTS

Spread

If a person who was below standard in one characteristic felt inferior *only* in that regard and not in general, his feelings of inadequacy would not be destructive of the personality. They may, in fact, be salutary, for recognizing one's real limitations is an admirable prophylactic against futile effort, costly of time and morale.

Unfortunately, so sane an appraisal of personal liabilities is not the rule. Physique (as well as certain other personal characteristics) has an enormous power to evoke a wide variety of impressions and feelings about the person. In fact, physical deviation is frequently seen as *the* central key to a person's behavior and personality and largely responsible for the important ramifications in the person's life. This spread holds for both the person with the disability himself and those evaluating him.

To begin with, the physical disability is perceived as spreading to other physical aspects of the person. Thus, because a blind person cannot see, it is sometimes taken for granted that he cannot hear, though of course there is no necessary connection. A mother of a deaf child stated that she would rather have her child deaf than blind, because "a blind child has blindness to face as well as deafness."

Overprotection on the part of those close to the person with a physical limitation may in some measure be a consequence of spread. The parent of a blind child may keep him confined to crib or carriage because she feels that without sight the environment is a source of endless danger. Because the child cannot see, *ipso facto* he cannot get around at all.

The spread not only affects additional physical areas but also involves social abilities and events as well. We have seen how Frances regarded perfect hearing as the open sesame to all the worth-while things in life, from marriage to career, and impaired hearing as the impenetrable barrier (see pp. 21–24). Others may look upon the person as less worthy, less acceptable, and the person himself may concur. Thus, physique affects the perception not only of abilities but also of acceptabilities.

So it is that the evaluation of the total person is affected by a single characteristic. Physique has unusual potency in this regard, partly because it is so intimately connected with the identity of persons, the "self" (see Chap. 6). In the development of the self-concept, one's physical attributes become intricately a part of the "I," the "me." However, the fact must not be overlooked that even what may objectively be entirely independent of the person may also become connected with the person in such a way as to affect evaluation of him. A case in point is such a situational factor as unemployment, often seen as due to personal qualities (Ichheiser, *1949*).

Disability effects are not always easy to contain. It is not simply a matter of learning that the person is actually restricted only in this way and that. How often do mothers talk in front of their children about matters not for their ears, though the mothers know better! Because the child is small, unlearned, and unaccomplished, the mother acts as though he does not understand. Even if the mother should be cautioned about this, she easily slips into the old pattern. The following is an example of the persistence of spread in the face of ongoing objective evidence that the person is not restricted in the assumed ways. Karsten Ohnstad, a blind man, is in the library with a companion. One librarian always talked to the companion as if Karsten weren't there at all! Karsten recounts:

"What book does he want?" she would ask, looking straight at Oscar who was standing beside me.
Oscar would turn to me. "What book did you say you wanted?"
"Les Miserables by Hugo."
Oscar would turn back to the librarian. "He wants *Les Miserables* by Hugo."
The librarian got the book. "Does he want to take it with him?"
"Do you want to take it with you?"
"Yes, I want to take it with me."
Oscar would turn wearily back to the librarian. "Yes, he wants to take it with him."
The librarian put the book on the table. "Does he want it signed in his own name?"
"Do you want it signed in your name?" Patient Oscar.
"Does he . . ." began the librarian.
"No, he doesn't," I said. "He's changed his mind. He doesn't want a book." I hurried out of the building.
"Now whatever do you suppose got into him?" I heard the librarian asking Oscar [Ohnstad, *1942*:62–63].[5]

Pertinent Research Findings

In one experiment, mentioned earlier in another connection (p. 57), (Mussen and Barker, *1944*), college students were asked to rate cripples in general on 24 character and personality traits, such as conscientiousness, self-confidence, etc. The task was seen as a sensible one by the subjects, and this reaction alone has important implications. If one pauses to consider that nothing more was said about the group to be rated than that they were cripples, it is amazing that the task could be executed at

---

[5] Karsten Ohnstad, *The World at My Fingertips,* Indianapolis, The Bobbs-Merrill Company, 1942. By permission.

all. Yet it was possible for these subjects to make judgments about a wide range of personality traits, simply knowing one characteristic about the group, and a physical rather than a personality characteristic at that.

In a second experiment, also referred to previously (p. 51), half of a group of high school subjects were shown a photograph of a college boy sitting in a wheel chair, and the other half were shown the same picture with the wheel chair blocked out (Ray, *1946*). The college boy in the wheel chair was judged to be more conscientious, to feel more inferior, to get better grades, to be more unhappy, than when depicted as non-crippled. Again the single fact of physical deviation was able to affect the perception of the kind of person being judged.

A similar phenomenon occurs in regard to other characteristics of groups—nationality, for example. Katz and Braly (*1933*) studied the racial stereotypes of college students by having subjects select from a list of traits those most typical of ten ethnic groups. One of the important findings that has not been stressed because it is so easily taken for granted is that the subjects felt able to rate groups with which they had had no contact (for example, Turks).

The interesting question is, How can subjects generalize from a single characteristic, such as crippling, so that a vast array of expectations as to personality and behavior are evoked? Fruitful empirical data on this question could be obtained directly by asking the subjects themselves to elaborate and explain their judgments. What, for example, would a particular subject say who rated cripples as having a marked tendency to be unselfish? One subject might say, "They have suffered so much that they have become more sensitive to people's wants." Another might say, "This is one way they try to be accepted by others."

Such responses suggest that the subject's impressions need not necessarily be arbitrary ones but may have their origins in the way he views disability. He is able to generalize from the physical characteristic because this represents for him a crucial deviation that affects a person in ways he presumes to understand. That is to say, the subject's judgments are partly based on hypotheses as to crippling as a value loss. He sees, for example, that crippling leads to suffering, which is a necessary prerequisite for sensitivity to others' needs. If he regards crippling as a state to which one can adjust, his judgments could be expected to differ markedly from the case where he regards crippling as an overwhelming calamity.

Even subjects who rate cripples sometimes favorably and sometimes unfavorably are likely to hold not arbitrary and discrete impressions of cripples but impressions that are coherent in terms of underlying attitudes toward crippling. One can see that if a person describes those with orthopedic handicaps as trying harder than most and also as being more sensitive than the average, he is not necessarily being inconsistent. Many of our impressions of one another or of groups have a meaningful character (Asch, *1952*). To explore by further questioning, the attitudes of subjects who have atypical physiques and those who do not is a promising procedure for arriving at some of the rational roots sustaining attitudes.

At the same time, we do not wish to deny the existence of what may be called rather arbitrary impressions of a person. There is reason to believe that a type of spread occurs from one characteristic of a person to others with little in common other than the fact that they are also positive or also negative. Such spread properly belongs with the phenomenon known as the "halo effect," a term introduced by Thorndike (*1920*), and is related to Heider's (*1958*) unit-forming factors (see p. 262), as well as to Dembo's (*1953b*) "comparative values" (see p. 128). In this instance, the hypotheses of the evaluator probably are afterthoughts, the evaluations being formed independently of them.

In his series of well-known experiments, Asch (*1946*) has contributed considerable understanding to the problem of how we form impressions of personality. He distinguishes between qualities that furnish the key to a person and those that are subsidiary—i.e., between central and peripheral characteristics. In one experiment, two groups of subjects were read a list of personality traits, identical with the exception that one group heard the person described as "warm" and the other group as "cold," thus:

1. Intelligent — skillful — industrious — *warm* — determined — practical — cautious
2. Intelligent — skillful — industrious — *cold* — determined — practical — cautious

If the character traits "warm" and "cold" are central aspects of a person, they should affect the total impression of personality. That this is the case is shown in the accompanying tabulation, which reports the results obtained when the subjects were asked to select from a check list of pairs of traits, mostly opposites, the quality that best fitted the impression they had already formed. The positive terms of each pair appear in the tabulation.

	Warm N = 90	Cold N = 76
Generous	91	8
Wise	65	25
Happy	90	34
Good-natured	94	17
Humorous	77	13
Sociable	91	38

	Warm N = 90	Cold N = 76
Popular	84	28
Reliable	94	99
Important	88	99
Humane	86	31
Good-looking	77	69
Persistent	100	97
Serious	100	99
Restrained	77	89
Altruistic	69	18
Imaginative	51	19
Strong	98	95
Honest	98	94

The "warm" person was described as being generous, wise, happy, good-natured, humorous, sociable, popular, humane, altruistic, and imaginative much more frequently than the "cold" person. There was also a set of qualities that was not affected by the warm-cold variable, e.g., physical attractiveness, reliability, strength, seriousness, etc. Thus, though the central characteristic affects the impression of the total personality, it does not function as an undiscriminating "halo effect." Duplicating this experiment utilizing "crippled–physically normal" as the variable would demonstrate that physique is a central characteristic of a person that gives rise to notions as to the kind of person he is through the subjects' hypotheses concerning the social-psychological significance of physique.

In a second experiment Asch (*1952*) showed that the order in which the characteristics of another are experienced may make a real difference in how he is viewed (p. 211). Two series of identical personality traits differing only in their order of presentation were read to separate groups:

Series *A*: Intelligent — industrious — impulsive — critical — stubborn — envious

Series *B*: Envious — stubborn — critical — impulsive — industrious — intelligent

The order of traits is merely reversed, Series *A* opening with positive qualities, Series *B* with questionable qualities. In general the subjects' impression of *A* is that of an "able person who possesses certain shortcomings, which are not serious enough to overshadow his merits" whereas *B* impresses the majority as "a 'problem' whose abilities are hampered by his serious difficulties." Apparently, first impressions of a person are especially potent in that they set up a *direction* that exerts a continuous effect on later impressions of that person. "The view formed quickly acquires a certain stability; later characteristics are fitted to the prevailing direction when the conditions permit" (Asch, *1952*:212–213).

Determining the precise conditions that give to physical characteristics their central organizing position requires continued research. On the basis of the evidence above, it might be postulated that visible handicaps are especially potent insofar as they present the person to others *first* in terms of his physique and thereby condition subsequent impressions.

Ichheiser (*1949*), in a penetrating consideration of the image of the other man, stresses visibility as a main determinant of social reality. He points out that coercion is more objectionable when it is evident in outright violence than when it is invisible. Likewise, bodily appearance assumes a major role because the *visible* appearance of an individual, and not his invisible personality, constitutes the main basis of identification. Ichheiser offers the following dramatic sketch as an example.

Suppose Jane Doe would change all her inner personality characteristics, such as her attitudes, opinions, tendencies, character, temperament, and whatever else. At the same time, suppose she would retain unchanged her bodily appearance. Then, obviously, she would continue to be considered and identified as "the same person." Other people would probably say that Jane Doe has radically changed, but it would be still Jane who has changed. If, on the other hand, Jane would maintain all her inner personality characteristics but would by some miracle altogether change her bodily appearance so that she would look like Susan Smith, then she would cease, in terms of social reality, to be "the same person." People would then, obviously, consider and identify Jane as being Susan, and they would probably wonder why Susan talks and behaves like Jane [*1949*:17].

In a study of the social usefulness of the cosmetic glove for arm amputees, Cattell, Dembo, *et al.* (*1949*) have contributed valuable material on some of the conditions determining centrality of physique. The conclusions are based on data derived from several lifelike experimental settings. In one setting the experimenter, an observer who took notes, and an amputee with a cosmetic hand prosthesis went to a store as ordinary customers. The salesman did not know that he was the subject of a psychological experiment. The amputee engaged the salesman in conversation and tried to draw his attention to the cosmetic hand by putting it on the counter, by gesturing, scratching his face, smoking, etc. The contact lasted between 5 and 20 minutes, after which the amputee left, and the experimenter and observer approached the salesman for an interview designed to elicit his reactions to the cosmetic hand.

The cosmetic glove is designed to approximate as closely as possible the appearance of the natural hand. Though on closer inspection the cosmetic hand is noticeably different from the natural hand, in casual contacts 80 percent of the subjects, not recognizing the cosmetic hand as such, were completely unaware of any difference. The investigators account for this by distinguishing between the *region of visual presence* and the *region of visual concern*. The region of presence encompasses those objects that are perceived but not inspected, the region of concern those which command the focus of attention. The cosmetic hand, when in the region of presence, matches the normal hand sufficiently not to be noticeable, whereas when it becomes a part of the region of concern, obvious differences emerge. In casual contacts we do not usually concern ourselves with the hands of the other person. Thus, "during a first meeting with someone, which may be the initial stage of a lasting relationship, the cosmetic hand is seen as useful, because it allows the non-wearer to get to know the wearer as a person before the fact of a prosthesis and feelings about the injury and amputation come into play" (Cattell *et al., 1949:*28).

Undoubtedly, too, variables within the beholder will influence the prominence of physical characteristics in another. The principle of vigilance (see pp. 41–42) is relevant. If the person is anxious about health and physique, or if he is alerted to bodily facts for other reasons, such features will become outstanding qualities.

Apparently, the observer need not be aware of the physical characteristics of another for them to influence his impressions. Winkler (*1931*) presented action pictures of healthy and crippled children to 200 physically normal subjects who were to judge them according to personality traits. Some of the crippled children were not consciously recognized by the subjects as being crippled. Unfavorable judgments regarding the non-disabled children constituted 46 percent of all judgments about them, whereas of the judgments made about the children *who were not recognized as crippled* 60 percent were unfavorable. Possibly the postures of crippled children, although not sufficiently peculiar to be consciously recognized as crippled, served as a stimulus for an unconscious negative reaction. Other evidence supports the validity of these findings (Barker *et al., 1953:*77).

The next chapter discusses two other psychological factors, "the self-connection gradient" and the "status-value gradient," which are believed to be significant determiners of spread from a single attribute to the total person.

Theoretical and Social Missteps

That the effects of physical disability are seen as spreading beyond the narrower physical confines into diverse areas of the person's life is well established. Actually, the unconditional central role of physique has led to one-sided theories about adjustment to handicap and has created difficulties in interpersonal relations involving persons with disabilities.

Let us consider the marked inclination to "understand" a person's accomplishments solely in terms of his disability. We have called the rationale for this the theory of *compensation as indemnity* (see pp. 49–51). Because it is felt that a person attempts to make up for an undesirable trait by emphasizing a desirable trait, *all* his efforts are seen as devoted to that end. The following is representative of this kind of thinking: "A well-known psychologist brought together some very interesting and enlightening factual information concerning some famous personalities who achieved greatness and distinction through relentless effort to compensate for organic inferiority and physical limitation" (Wilson, *1950:* 192). The author then goes on to mention several accomplished sportsmen who achieved, it is supposed, *because of* their physical deficiencies—e.g., Annette Kellerman, who "compensated for her frail body by rigorous swimming and became one of the great women swimmers of all time" (p. 192). To us, it is still a moot question whether Annette Kellerman's performance should be seen primarily as compensatory, but the issue is even more clearly drawn in the following remarks, made specifically to illustrate the principle of compensation:

> The record in the field of intellectual accomplishment is even more amazing. Robert Louis Stevenson was racked with tuberculosis and kept moving from one health resort to another. Charles Darwin was so sickly that he was limited in his work to only a few hours each day. Lord Byron's whole life was altered by his club foot. Edgar Allan Poe was the victim of a lung condition. The philosopher Kant carried on his writings in a state of continual pain caused by gout and his sunken chest. The philosopher Nietzsche, conscious of his frail body, conceived a philosophy of the superman. Aristotle and Demosthenes were physical defectives. The poet Goethe always complained that his life was all pain and burden, and once stated that in his whole life of seventy-five years he had not even four weeks of general well-being. Beethoven was pockmarked and snubnosed. He was continually harassed by asthma and digestive disorders, and at the age of twenty-eight, became deaf . . . [Wilson, *1950:*193].

This passage clearly exemplifies how the undisciplined spread of the effects of disability can distort the meaning of crucial aspects of a person's life. The disability is seen not only as entering everywhere but as being the critical element in the events of life. Surely, the fact that "Charles Darwin was so sickly that he was limited in his work to only a few hours each day" is not sufficient to account for his absorbing interest in evolutionary processes. A review of his intellectual and emotional life most certainly would reveal that physique played a role, but as certainly not *the* role, not the one factor primarily responsible for the directions assumed by his life.

When it is assumed that disability effects spread in unbridled fashion, it is hardly conceivable that a person might pursue an area of work simply because he finds it satisfying. Every effort, every interest is presumed to be a compensation for the person's physical deficiency. The theory of compensation as indemnity gives to physique a central organizing role to which life motivations are dynamically linked. The view emphasizing containment of disability, on the other hand, includes physique as but one among an array of factors that determine the direction and intensity of the person's efforts.

The intrusive power of atypical physique to dominate our perception of the person can also be seen in the unbalanced emotional evaluation of the state of disability. When disability is seen to dominate the entire life, it is interpreted as a tragedy from which there is no respite. Thus it is that a person may feel, "I would rather be dead than stone deaf or blind or . . ." On the other hand, the recognition that deafness or blindness permits a life of competence and enjoyment requires putting the physical characteristics into a subordinate place of sharing with other factors, consequences, and effects.

The unrestrained spread of physique is again seen in the attitude that persons who have a disability stand apart from, rather than are a part of, the community of others. It is said, for example, that "a handicapped child can never have the satisfaction of being just like other children." Does this mean that his physical difference is always so central that it looms as the major feature of every situation? Clearly not. A more accurate statement of group identification might read: "A handicapped child can feel just like other children, even though at times he may feel different in certain particulars. This is true of all children." To see a handicapped child first and foremost as a child and only secondarily as a handicapped one is a significant adjustive sign in a parent. Too often the child's difficulty is attributed to his handicap rather than to the preëminent circumstance of his relative immaturity or some other pertinent condition.

Such titles of books and pamphlets as *Understanding the Disabled* help to foster the invidious tendency to perceive disability as creating psychologically different kinds of people. All too readily is it assumed that persons with disabilities take a great deal of knowing before they can be understood or accepted on the usual level.

The role of atypical physique as prime mover also leads to difficulties in interpersonal relations. Sources of tension that arise in social contact must be adequately evaluated in order that one's efforts be focused correctly in alleviating them. Yet when a person who is physically deviant is involved, the source of difficulty is often laid to the disability, even though other events and personality characteristics may be more immediately responsible.

Misperception of this sort occurs both in the person himself and in the nonhandicapped. The person may attribute to his crippling the fact that he is not invited to someone's house, when actually the host may not enjoy him as a person irrespective of his physique, or may wish to invite him on a more suitable occasion. This feeling of being reacted to as a stereotyped version of a deaf person or a crippled person is one important factor in the belief of some persons that they can never be understood by the nondisabled, that forever a chasm exists between them.

The following incident took place when Henry Viscardi, dwarfed through congenital malformation of the legs, was 7 years old. By this time he had had several harsh experiences which taught him that except for those who knew him he was an object of pity, to be ostracized and ridiculed. He jumped to the conclusion that he could not enter the church because he was crippled—and it was a wrong conclusion:

But as we stopped by the holy-water font a man at the church door looked at me sharply and whispered something to papa. The other people stared at us too.

What is wrong? I wondered. *Do you suppose crippled children* are not allowed to come to church any more? [Italics ours.]

Papa took my hand and led me outside. "Let us go for a walk in the park," he said, smiling brightly.

My eyes were smarting. "What's the matter, papa?" I finally said. "Why didn't we stay for Mass? Is it because I'm crippled?" I could hardly get the words out.

Then Papa threw back his head and laughed. And he laughed again.

"Oh, this is very funny," he said.

I did not think it was funny, and I wished I had never come to church with him. I had a salty taste in my mouth.

Then he put both his hands on my shoulders and looked right into my eyes. "Oh, this is very funny—no children allowed at eleven o'clock Mass. What a way to run a church!" I laughed too, just to be polite [Viscardi, *1952*:24–25].[6]

From the point of view of social reality, the person is sometimes reacted to in terms of physique alone. There also are times, however, when he is reacted to primarily in terms of personality characteristics. And sometimes impersonal circumstances are the main determining factors. But the basis is often ambiguous, and the emotional nature of attitudes about physique interferes with clarification. In the following example, Karsten Ohnstad

[6] Henry Viscardi, Jr., *A Man's Stature*. Copyright, 1952, by Henry Viscardi, Jr. Used by permission of The John Day Company.

was very sure that the girl stopped writing to him because he was blind. Was he right?

A letter arrived from an unexpected source—from the pretty blonde girl back home. I listened with a glow of pleasure and embarrassment as I sat on my bed while my favorite nurse read the letter aloud. I had not expected to hear from the girl. . . . A nurse wrote the reply I dictated. The blonde girl had said in her letter that she would write again. I waited—one week, a month. I made a decision. She had written purely out of sympathy. I took her letter and tore it to bits. This, I decided, was part of my new education [Ohnstad, 1942:29–30].

There simply is not enough evidence for a reliable verdict as to the circumstances surrounding the girl's silence, and such ambiguity repeats itself in the life of every person with a disability.

Ambiguity of social position is, of course, true of all minority groups. The Jew or Negro, for example, has to pit the possible circumstantial or personality reasons for his lack of acceptance in a particular situation against what may be equally possible prejudicial reasons. And such ambiguity is well known to everyone, even to those among the favored majority. Everyone has occasion sometimes to wonder whether *he* was rejected or whether the discomfiting incident was the product of non-personal factors. And many times the person does not pause to wonder but simply takes it for granted that the explanatory key turns upon his disability, his race, his poor manners, or whatever else is an emotional touchstone. Sometimes he may be right. Not infrequently he is wrong.

All persons, those with a disability and those without, must be educated to the more cautious yet more veracious understanding that, though a physical disability is a physical fact whose psychological effects radiate to other areas of the person's life, the effects can be contained more precisely within those areas that are dynamically linked or "caused by" disability factors. Not all of life is influenced, let alone determined, by disability. The person with a disability must be encouraged to pinpoint the values now lost to him so that they become but dots in the large map of the world, in which vast areas remain relatively intact and accessible. He will then realize that he is not a disabled person but a person with a disability, that life has a multitude of meanings, opportunities, and frustrations, only some of which are disability-connected.

COMPARATIVE VALUES AND ASSET VALUES

The reaction to something, be it a person, thing, event, or performance, may be favorable, unfavorable, or neutral. But such judgments may be brought about through at least two distinct psychological processes, involving what Dembo has called *comparative values* and *asset values* (Dembo, Leviton, Wright, *1956*).

If the evaluation is based on comparison with a standard, the person is said to be invoking comparative values. The standard may represent the presumed average, as when a person is judged to be bright or stupid; it may represent certain "ought" characteristics, as when a person is judged to be a good father or a poor father; it may represent certain formal requirements, as when a person is evaluated for membership in a social club.

On the other hand, if the evaluation arises from the qualities inherent in the object of judgment itself, the person is said to be invoking asset values. What matters is the object of judgment in a setting that has its own intrinsic purposes and demands. The person's reaction is then based upon how appropriately the situational demands are fulfilled rather than on comparison with a predetermined standard. Consider the following illustrations: A person may enjoy the musical performance of his acquaintance without comparing it with the performance of anyone else. He sees the situation as one in which the performer is playing for pleasure and the listener is to listen for pleasure. In these circumstances he is able to enjoy the assets of the performance itself. A second listener, evaluating on the basis of comparative values, does not enjoy the musical performance because he constantly compares it with the playing of a great virtuoso. He cannot appreciate what this musician has to offer, because the music is felt not to be up to a certain standard. Other terms that may clarify the conception of asset values are "intrinsic values" and "substantive values."

Some persons appear to be very comparison-minded, always sizing up others in comparison with themselves, for example, or with some symbol of status such as wealth or education. It is not by accident that these persons are called status-minded, for evaluations of status and prestige require the standards of comparative values. There are other persons who hold predominantly asset values and employ comparative values only in special circumstances. When, for example, such a person is called upon to hire a new member to his staff, he will offer the job to the better of two candidates according to predetermined standards. In this case, the nature of the situation demands comparative evaluation. When, however, the asset-minded person is not subject to a comparative frame of reference, he may well be satisfied with the rejected applicant. He now is no longer comparing the person against a standard; he is simply appreciating his qualities for their own worth, much as he can enjoy a summer day without comparing it with other days. To be sure, the evaluation of the summer day will be affected by one's experience with other panoramas. If one has been having consistently beautiful sunsets, one may be rather blasé toward the same beauty the following evening, instead of being uplifted as one had been on the first occurrence. But the evaluation itself at the time of evaluation is not a comparative one, and the thing is enjoyed or disliked because of its inherent qualities in a situational context.

The person with a disability has much to gain psychologically if he can look upon physique in terms of its inherent or essential characteristics—that is, what it permits him to do and what it restricts him in doing—without basing his evaluation on comparison with other individuals or with his previous nondisabled state. The perception of what physique permits and restricts depends, of course, upon knowledge of what other persons can do. A person would not think of his hearing impairment as a restriction if everyone else were similarly affected, just as we do not mind not being able to hear high frequencies. Nevertheless, when physique has the function of an asset value, the person is able to appreciate those inherent satisfactions that are but disappointments the moment physique is taken as a comparative value.

This analysis may arouse skepticism. But incredulity shades into understanding when one considers that walking in itself is always a remarkable achievement. Aren't we pleasingly amazed when the toddler takes his first faltering steps? Why? Surely, if we consider that almost all babies in their second year of life embark upon such an expedition it is not remarkable at all. Such emotional nonchalance, however, is forced upon us only when comparative values form the basis of our evaluation of baby behavior, but when "norms" of whatever kind are not a part of the picture, we can thrill at the first tooth, the babbling, the uncertain steps.

Parent-educators, particularly since the 1930's, have been strongly urging parents to enjoy their children, to accept them as they are without attempting to mold them into an ill-fitting pattern of the boy or girl they would like. This principle, translated into value terms, states: Regard the characteristics or attributes of your children as asset values. Then you will be able to enjoy your children for themselves rather than for their relative position in the group or on some other predetermined standard of behavior.

Let us look in on 5-year-old Raymond crawling for the first time since polio struck him almost a year and a half earlier. He is sitting on the floor with his toys surrounding him:

On one momentous occasion I gave the engine a great shove, failed to hold on to it, and it rolled away beyond my reach. I hesitated to call Celia [the nurse], for she fussed, but I wanted my engine, and I decided to try to go after it myself. I placed my hands, palms down, on the floor in front of me. I moved my legs from the hips, moved them more than I had ever moved them before, until they were behind me and under me and I was on my knees. I put my right hand forward and pulled my right leg forward. I put my left hand forward and pulled my left leg forward. I repeated the actions and soon I was across the room where my fire engine waited for me.

. . . I remembered the act and the emotion, the ineffable joy that flooded me, the sense of power, of achievement, of a miracle wrought. . . . Later I was to feel the crushing weight of shame, but the memory of what happened to me that day helped me to bear up and struggle on. I crawled six feet across the carpeted floor and the course of my life was charted.

When I reached my fire engine, the enormity of what I had achieved flashed upon me. I twisted my body around and sat down. My eyes filled with tears of happiness. I had been over there and now I was over here, and I had done it all myself! (Goldman, *1947*:10–11).

Raymond was exalted by the wonder of his accomplishment because at that moment his evaluation of himself and his behavior was asset-determined. He was not comparing his achievement with a norm, a standard of behavior. He was just savoring it for what it was—a sense of power. "I had been over there and now I was over here, and I had done it all myself!"

Physique as an asset value provides a sound basis for the commonly heard dictum, "It is not what you have lost, but what you have left that counts." It is significant that when Harold Russell, who lost both hands in World War II, first began to realize the truth of this dictum he also began to take himself in hand with these admonitions: "I would have to stop regarding myself as a freak. I would have to stop sneaking into dark corners and hiding my hooks. . . . I would have to realize that I had nothing to be ashamed of" (*1949*:142). It is significant because these admonitions express the dim recognition that physique can become an asset value, a view that would free him of shame and inferiority. Gradually shamming and shaming no longer pursued him and he was able to share with McGonegal, the man who lost his hands in World War I and whom he grew to admire, the insight that "self-respect and real pride are better fed by achievement than by concealment" (p. 108).

Dembo (*1953b*) has developed further the theory of comparative values by showing that not only is the evaluation of the disability by the holder of comparative values different from that of the holder of asset values but that *other* characteristics of the person, and even the total person, are also evaluated differently. She points out that when we compare an object with a standard, we are interested in only certain characteristics of the object (e.g., physique). Because these characteristics are within our field of concern, they become potent and have the power to impose their properties upon our perception and evaluation of other characteristics not being compared at the moment and which, therefore, are vague and unstructured. If physical normalcy is taken as a standard and a disability is viewed as far below standard, other vague characteristics and the person himself are regarded as below standard. In a diffuse sort of way the person comes to be regarded as an inferior being.

For a perceptive view of such devaluative spread, let us again consider some of the recollections of Harold Russell (*1949*). His first reaction upon awakening in the hospital was one of aversion (see p. 61). During that first week he shuddered with horror at the thought of "hooks" for hands. He was revolted by a civilian visitor without hands: "He was fat and chubby and he kept scratching his bald dome with the claws. It gave me the creeps" (p. 41). The prospect of going through life with "steel claws" terrified him, for it would mean that he would be openly advertising the fact that he was a cripple and a freak. During this early struggle, Russell felt so totally worthless that he vowed he would not marry his girl, because "How could I let her throw herself away on me, a helpless cripple?" (p. 44). He longed to be wrong in his picture of himself and instead to believe that he was a man in spite of all that. In his fantasy he sought proof of real love from his girl:

> My reason told me I should and must give her up, but all my instincts told me I should cling to her, that she could be my ultimate salvation. If only I could be sure she loved me—*really* loved me—not out of pity, not out of loyalty, not out of a sense of duty! To know that I was still desired, to know that a woman could still love me as a man, that was the all-important thing. That knowledge, I felt, could lift me over the highest hurdles. It could give me new hope and courage. It could make me into a human being again, instead of a helpless freak.
>
> But I knew that could never be. I knew that no matter what she said—no matter how fervently she proclaimed her love—no matter how many times she told me she still wanted to marry me—I knew that I would have to give her up. There was no other way [Russell, *1949*:45].

What has happened here? Because Russell felt so abnormal with respect to a major physical characteristic, because at this time his disability was *the* thing of importance, occupying his entire thinking, the horror and aversion spread to himself as a total person, and he became a useless freak, a travesty on the human being he had been.

The following reminiscence of Noreen about her prepolio days helps to enlighten the phenomenon of comparative values and diffuse spread:

> . . . I am simply inconsolable at horse-races or relays of any kind, for worrying about the unhappiness of the contestant who comes in last. At gala night-club scenes in the movies, I always search out the background for extras

who sit at the gay tables with unconscious envy painted on their pretty faces as they watch the star perform. At weddings I watch the least of the bridesmaids, and at graduation exercises, the little girl whose dress has the widest hand-made hem [Linduska, *1947*:15].[7]

Why does Noreen's heart go out to the person who is last, an extra, a lesser bridesmaid, or a girl with the widest handmade hem? These may be facts, but they have no necessary connection with being unfortunate. The wide hem may belong to the girl who is brimming over with the anticipation of marrying her beloved after graduation. The contestant who comes in last may be pleased to have been part of the race at all. Not everything that can be rank-ordered involves a contest. But for Noreen, relative position on this characteristic or that meant so much that it spread to the evaluation of the total person. Being below par on one characteristic spelled being the underdog.

It has been noted that "even social workers accustomed to dealing with all types often find it difficult to think of a normal, pretty girl as being guilty of a crime. Most people, for some inexplicable reason, think of crime in terms of abnormality in appearance, and I must say that beautiful women are not often convicted" (Monahan, *1941*:103). At this time we are able to suggest two hypotheses for this "inexplicable reason." In Chapter 10 the question of "requiredness" in attitudes toward disability is discussed. There it is pointed out that one a priori connection relates disability to wrongdoing, both being negative in character (see p. 258). A second explanation, drawing upon the properties of comparative and asset values, argues that the social worker finds difficulty in thinking of a pretty girl as guilty of a crime when he holds beauty as a comparative value. Then, when the girl's beauty is in the field of concern, its property of being above standard spreads to other characteristics of the person so that the social worker would also see a moral girl. The spread effects are incompatible with a below-standard characteristic such as criminality.

It is certainly possible that both factors, that of a priori requiredness and that of diffuse spread, play a role. Yet it is possible to disentangle them if one would select an "asset-minded" rather than a "comparison-minded" social worker and discover if the difficulty described above existed to the same degree. If it did not, it would be legitimate to give considerable weight in the phenomenon to the asset-comparison nature of values, whereas if it did, a priori requiredness would be the telling condition.

[7] Noreen Linduska, *My Polio Past*, copyright 1947 by Noreen Linduska. Used by permission of the publishers, Farrar, Straus and Cudahy, Inc.

ACCEPTANCE AND ADJUSTMENT

The preceding sections have outlined the kinds of change within the person's value system that are significant in his acceptance of a disability. The resulting acceptance frees the person of devaluation because of a disability and also frees him to seek satisfactions in activities that befit his own characteristics as a person rather than those of an idolized normal standard. The assumptions made and the consequences presumed lead us to expect that a person who *in these terms* accepts his handicap would be well on his way toward becoming well adjusted. The final verdict, however, must await scientific exploration.

To begin with, it must be borne in mind that there is quite a jump between accepting one's disability in particular and accepting oneself in general. The self-accepting person has been defined (Berger, E., *1952*, as modified from Sheerer, *1949*) as one who:

1. Relies primarily upon internalized values and standards rather than on external pressure as a guide for his behavior.
2. Has faith in his capacity to cope with life.
3. Assumes responsibility for and accepts the consequences of his own behavior.
4. Accepts praise or criticism from others objectively.
5. Does not attempt to deny or distort any feelings, motives, limitations, abilities, or favorable qualities which he sees in himself, but rather accepts all without self-condemnation.
6. Considers himself a person of worth on an equal plane with other persons.
7. Does not expect others to reject him. . . .
8. Does not regard himself as totally different from others, "queer," or generally abnormal in his reactions.
9. Is not shy or self-conscious.

It is not difficult to reason that a person who enlarges his scope of values, confines disability effects, subordinates physique as a value and, particularly, regards physique as an asset value also will show beneficial effects with respect to most if not all of the nine self-accepting criteria. Value changes do not occur in isolation. A major change in outlook with respect to part of the self reflects or affects the self-concept in general (see Chap. 6). Yet, experiment and systematic observation must remain as the supreme court, where fact may be sifted from fancy.

Likewise, it must be borne in mind that there is also a jump between accepting oneself and being a mentally healthy person. The emotionally mature person has been characterized as follows (Saul, *1947:* Chap. I):

1. He is independent and responsible.
2. He has little need to regress.
3. He is giving and productive, although still able to receive normally.
4. He is cooperative rather than egotistical and competitive.
5. He is in relative harmony with his conscience.
6. He is reasonably free of inferiority feelings and his anxiety is at a minimum.
7. His attitudes toward sexuality show a balance between freedom and responsibility.
8. His hostility toward others and toward himself is minimal but is freely available for defense and constructive use.
9. His grasp of reality is clear and unimpaired by the emotional astigmatisms of childhood.
10. He is discriminating and highly adaptable.
11. He not only has the *capacity* for such attitudes and functioning but also the ability to *enjoy* them fully.

Again, it is not difficult to reason that there is a necessary connection between these characteristics and self-acceptance. Although adjustment involves a broader spectrum of characteristics than self-acceptance, they appear on conceptual grounds to be mutually consistent. But, again, actual data must be the prime witness.

Unfortunately, what appears to be the most relevant study lacks adequate data for final evaluation of the issue of acceptance and adjustment. Landis and Bolles (*1942*) interviewed 100 handicapped women 17 to 30 years of age. On the basis of the interview data, the subjects were rated on General Adjustment, Adequacy of Adjustment to Handicap, and Method of Adjustment to Handicap. With respect to the latter, four styles of reaction were distinguished: withdrawal, substitution, obliteration, compensation.

Of these four, obliteration comes closest to what we have described in Chapter 2 as denying and concealing, but none of them applies to the kind of basic value changes we have included in our conception of acceptance. Substitution might, but there are no indications that the substitutions were brought about by containing disability effects or subordinating physique as a value or changing physique to an asset value. As a matter of fact, about half the subjects who used this method reported that the substituted activities were merely unsatisfactory escapes or "time killers."

The authors evaluate these four types of adjustment with respect to both personal satisfaction and social acceptability. On both counts, obliteration is placed first, substitution second, with the remaining two lagging behind. Unfortunately, aside from general statements relating method of adjustment to general adjustment, very little is given in the way of actual data. All we know is that of the 17 subjects whose method of adjustment to the handicap was rated as withdrawal, only 5 were rated as showing adequate general adjustment, whereas of the 16 subjects given the obliteration rating, 15 rated as showing an adequate adjustment. Comparable figures on the other methods of adjustment are not given, nor are data relating method of adjustment to adequacy of adjustment to handicap.

Seemingly the relatively high rating of the obliterative style of reaction runs counter to the argument presented in Chapter 2, which undertakes to show the futility of "as if" behavior. However, there are difficulties in interpreting the high rating in the light of the following facts: (1) The Rorschach records of the ten subjects who were rated as most maladjusted showed no significant difference in the number of neurotic signs as compared with the Rorschach records of the ten subjects who were rated highest in adjustment. (2) Except for the withdrawal type, the Rorschach test gave no evidence of consistent tendencies in the personality make-up related to any of the other three types of adjustment to handicap. Add to this the possibility if not probability that the girls who denied any limitations whatever would also tend in an interview to deny any troubles whatever, thus accounting for the spuriously high adjustment ratings, and we have reasonable grounds for feeling that the present evidence is inadequate and future research on this issue is imperative.

Acceptance of a disability has been discussed in terms of four kinds of change within the value system of the person. Clearly there may be others, and certainly these are interrelated. Thus, enlarging the scope of values appears to be favorable to subordinating physique, for in the perspective of other values physique may become one of lesser rank. Subordinating physique is also apt to lead to some containment of disability effects; for if physique becomes less significant, its effects become less involved. The converse is also true: containing physique at the same time tends to deflate it. The inauguration of these three value changes facilitates the ultimate transformation of physique from a comparative to an asset value. In turn, the emerging asset character of physique hastens the process of subordinating and containing for, stripped of comparative standards, the importance of physique is diminished, and spread is impeded.

Not all these value changes are to be recommended in all circumstances. In regard to physique, we sometimes urge the reverse of "subordinating," as when we educate our children to appreciate the importance of good health rather than to neglect it as inconsequential. On the other hand, there are strong indications that we overvalue certain physical attributes. Physical fitness is a case in point. It has been noted that there is "no real evidence in humans that unusual physical fitness imparts immunity or resistance to disease" (Rusk and Taylor, *1946*:199). Moreover, though it is commonly acknowledged that there is a relationship between physical fitness and ability to work, we know that motivation and training may be far more important in a particular situation. Similarly, with respect to containment, the test of reality is always in order. If a person continues to attempt the impossible through ignorance of the actual limitations imposed by his disability, overcontainment has occurred. A more realistic widening of the effects of disability may well be indicated.

The various value changes may be recommended in the following circumstances:

1. Enlargement of the scope of values is indicated in the case of all-inclusive suffering where the problem is to see as valuable those aspects of life not closed to the person.
2. Subordination of values is indicated where the importance of the value has been overrated.
3. Containment of the effects of disability is indicated where diffuse spread has occurred and where, on the basis of available fact, the disability need not have disabling effects.
4. When a value retains substantial importance, as in the case of physique, what is required for full acceptance is transformation from a comparative to an asset value in situations that do not require a comparison frame of reference.

It is our judgment that the asset value change is the one *par excellence* that will bring about the full and lasting feeling of the dignity of the individual.

The kernel of feeling epitomizing the state of comparative values on the one hand and of asset values on the other can be described as, first, "I am nothing but an incomplete, injured person who has always to mourn his loss," and in the second case, "I am as I am, and though I don't have all the possible assets which can be *imagined,* my life is full" (Dembo, Leviton, Wright, *1956:*39–40).

Chapter 6

Development of the Self-Concept

THE KIND OF PERSON YOU THINK YOR ARE BECOMES ENDOWED WITH RE-
markable powers. It influences, and often decisively, the way one
perceives the intentions of others (see Chap. 7), the choice of associates
(see pp. 40–43), the goals set for oneself (see pp. 24–40), and much
more. The self-concept, then, is an important part of one's world or life
space and has been so recognized by our eminent psychological fore-
fathers who have given serious attention to its development.[1] Contemporary thinkers are continuing the investigation of this important area.[2]
In broad outline, we shall attempt here to describe how the concept of
the self is formed and the forces that direct its fate, with particular
reference to problems of disability. That aspect of the self-concept which
pertains to attitudes and experiences involving the body is referred to as
the "body-image."[3]

The composition of the self-picture is an intricate one, for it is made up
of the variety of personal characteristics that define for the person his
psychological *identity:* the person develops a notion about his own body,
what satisfactions it gives him and denies him; he discovers that he has
certain interests and abilities, likes and dislikes; he begins to think of himself as shy or outgoing or in-between, as irritable, or calm, or anxious; he
learns something of the way in which he affects others, that he is likable
or resented, for example. All these perceptions and evaluations make up
that separate entity in the individual's world variously designated as the
"I," the "me," the "self," and the "ego." For our purposes, no distinctions
between these terms will be made, though some psychologists have made
them. Freud (*1933*), for example, distinguishes the superego or "con-

---

[1] The interested reader is referred to Adler (*1924*), Freud (*1933*), Lewin
(*1935, 1936*), McDougall (*1918*), and Sullivan (*1953*).

[2] Allport (*1943*), Ausubel (*1952*), Bronfenbrenner (*1951*), Lecky (*1945*),
Murphy (*1947*), Sherif and Cantril (*1947*) offer critical or integrated accounts
of the development of the self-concept.

[3] A broad survey of thought and research concerning body-image phenomena
may be found in Fisher and Cleveland (*1958:* chap. 1). The authors also
formulate a theory of the "body-image boundary dimension" and describe a
series of research studies, including some dealing with physical disability, which
stemmed from it.

science" of the person from the ego, whereas Sherif and Cantril (*1947*) see no need for this separation. Ausubel (*1952*) makes a distinction between the body, the self, the ego, and the personality.

It is well to keep in mind that the boundary between what is the self and what is not a part of the self, even in the mature person, is not as sharp as it might seem. One's children, for example, are felt to be a part of oneself, though at the same time there is recognition of their independence. Even an object may become so intimately bound up with the emotions of a person that, should it become necessary for the two to become disjoined, as when the person moves from the house in which he has lived for many years, the person feels that he is leaving behind a part of himself.

DIFFERENTIATING THE WORLD AND INTEGRATING THE SELF

Journal accounts of the behavior, vocalizations, and verbalizations of infants and young children have provided some of the earliest source material for studying how notions about the self are formed. A concise and well-illustrated review of such accounts has been written by Sherif and Cantril (*1947*). Later investigators, notably Piaget (*1926, 1932*), and Gesell and Ilg (*1943*), collected their observations under more controlled conditions and ordered them systematically.

Psychologists generally agree that the young infant does not make any distinction between what is himself and what is not. If he should happen to pull his hair or scratch at his face, he will cry out, but he does not realize that *he* is pulling *his* hair or scratching *his* face. With the maturation of his nervous system and increased commerce with his environment, however, *differentiation* takes place in which there gradually emerges a very special part of the universe which is felt as the self or "I." For example, the baby's interest in his hands initially appears to be no different from his interest in other objects, such as a rattle or crib post. Soon, however, new experiences emerge. Not only can he control the wiggle in the fingers but, more than that, he feels the wiggle in a way different from the wiggle of the rattle. In time he will realize that the hand is a part of himself whereas the rattle is not. Psychoanalytic theory places special importance on the physical self both in the differentiation of the person from other realities and in the continuing development of the ego. Fenichel (*1945*), an exponent of the Freudian viewpoint, presents this emphasis in these words:

In the development of reality the conception of one's own body plays a very special role. At first there is only the perception of tension, that is, of an "inside something." Later, with the awareness that an object exists to quiet this tension, we have an "outside something." One's own body is both at the same time. Due to the simultaneous occurrence of both outer tactile and inner sensory data, one's own body becomes something apart from the rest of the world and thus the discerning of self from nonself is made possible. The sum of the mental representations of the body and its organs, the so-called body image, constitutes the idea of I and is of basic importance for the further formation of the ego [Fenichel, *1945*:35–36].[4]

This process of self-identification is hastened by the fact that the baby meets resistance in the external world. His needs are not and cannot be satisfied the moment they arise: it takes time for the bottle to be warmed and gastrointestinal tensions to subside. The unsatisfied needs not only sharpen self-awareness but prompt the baby to search for ways to gratify his needs and, as a consequence, the baby's world becomes yet further differentiated. It may very well be, as some have asserted, that frustration is a necessary experience in personality development, for if all needs could receive immediate gratification, there would be no differentiation between the self and external reality.

Learning about the self occurs through various modalities. There is, first of all, the direct sensory experiences of the baby, as when he discovers the different relations to himself of the hand in contrast to the rattle. Since vision is presumed to serve more efficiently than the other senses for the differentiation of external objects from one another, as well as of the self from other objects, it has been hypothesized that among the congenitally blind there should be some delay (but not necessarily a permanent defect) in the development of ego functions (Blank, *1957*:7).

Secondly, the child learns about himself through the leads given him by others. He learns that he is a boy and has a certain name and is an American, for example. He also develops certain attitudes about these facts, and therefore about himself, through contact with the viewpoints of his associates. That the self-concept is a social looking glass expresses the belief of most psychologists that ideas and feelings about the self emerge largely as a result of interaction with others.

Not always is the self-knowledge gained directly through the senses consistent with that socially induced. According to Rogers, when the person denies the former in favor of the latter, the conditions become favorable for neurotic ego development (Rogers, *1951:* Chap. 11). Part of the therapeutic process then becomes one of attribution, i.e., notions about the self must become more correctly ascribed to evidence directly

[4] By permission from Otto Fenichel, *The Psychoanalytic Theory of Neurosis,* New York, W. W. Norton & Company, 1945.

experienced on the one hand and to evidence socially mediated on the other.

The fact that knowledge about the self is built up through sensory experience and through the viewpoints of others, as well as through inferences based on these sources, makes it possible for the body to become invested with significance beyond its concretely apprised functions. Body parts begin to assume such connotations as good and bad, clean and unclean, adequate and inadequate. The hands, for example, may not only be regarded as tools for grasping and manipulating but also contaminated by shame and evil should the child have been traumatized when caught masturbating or in fecal play.

Psychoanalytic theory gives especial prominence to the symbolic meaning of body parts and considers these meanings to be crucial in adjustment to disability. The problem of adjusting to amputations, for example, is felt to be largely a problem of dealing with castration anxiety. (See pp. 271–272 for a more detailed discussion of this.) Such was the interpretation given to the following remark of a patient: "Even though the eye is useless and I will look better with a glass eye I don't want any part of me cut out" (Blank, *1957*:17). When the patient was analyzed within this theoretical framework it was reported that she mastered the problems of surgery and the use of the prosthetic eye. Representative of psychoanalytic theorizing is Blank's analysis of the significance of blindness: "The factors of particular interest underlying the maladaptations and personality disturbances of the visually handicapped are: (1) The unconscious significance of the eye as a sexual organ, including the equation of eye with mouth and with genital. (2) The unconscious significance of the eye as a hostile, destructive organ, including the equation of eye with piercing phallus and with devouring mouth. (3) The unconscious significance of blindness as castration, a punishment for sin" (Blank, *1957*:1). Without debating the specific symbolic associations attributed to the eyes in this statement, it is undoubtedly true that the meaning of the body and its parts has significance that extends far beyond the concrete apprehension of function and appearance.

The ever-enlarging array of facts and attitudes about the self, whether or not their symbolism ranges far afield, is not built into the self-picture in a haphazard way. There is good reason to believe that at least in many if not all instances, new self-attributes are *integrated* within old ones either by modifying the meaning of the former or the latter or both.[5] This

---

[5] Ausubel (*1952*) apparently would disagree with the generality of this statement as applied to what he calls "satellization" or the period of dependent identification of the child with his parents. This "attitude of subservience is an extremely potent force in value assimilation. It makes possible unquestioning and unconditional acceptance before any criterion of reasonableness need be

holds true for attributes pertaining to the body as well as those pertaining to other aspects of the self. In this way a certain stability and consistency of the self-picture is achieved. This notion is central to such "organismic" theorists as Goldstein (*1939*) and Lecky (*1945*).

The principle of integration through modification of the old and the new applies, as psychology has clearly established, not only to the self-concept but to all sorts of perceptions, beliefs, and even behavior. A clear demonstration of the principle appears in a study in which college subjects were asked to form an impression of a factory worker on the basis of a list of traits presented to them (Haire and Grunes, *1950*). The inclusion of "intelligent" as an attribute was disturbing to these subjects, who, having had a well-organized picture of a working man that was generally somewhat patronizing and snobbish, found that an intellectual trait did not easily fit in with their existing system of beliefs and values. They either had to ignore this trait, tamper with its meaning, or revamp their total concept of a factory worker. There are many other studies directly dealing with perceptual and cognitive phenomena that show the interacting process between part and whole in the service of integration.

Returning to the self, we get a glimpse of the process of differentiation and integration with specific reference to body image in the following account. Billy was born without arms. Attached to his right shoulder was a small part of a palm and three tiny fingers, and to his left shoulder were two webbed appendages. When Billy was about two years old, he was led to believe, through discussion he had heard from time to time about his body as well as information gained through his own senses, that his right hand, with which he could feed himself and hold things, was his good hand, whereas his left hand, which was practically useless, was his broken hand. The development of this perception is seen in the following incident told by his mother:

. . . in the playground, one of the children noticed Billy's lack of arms for the first time and kept asking over and over if his arm had broken off. He was too little to understand a real explanation so I finally said, yes, it had broken off, and walked away. I thought no more about it, because similar incidents had happened so often, until that night when I was giving Billy his bath. He felt his little two fingers that protrude from his left shoulder anxiously, as if to reassure himself that he, too, has something there. Then he held up his right arm and said, "This good hand, other broken hand" [Bruckner, *1954:*140].[6]

---

satisfied" (p. 137). In our judgment, integration need not require a reasonableness that adheres to adult logic, but is rather a "fitting-in process" in which new facts or attitudes or values are assimilated by being attached to existing beliefs so that the old and the new cohere as a Gestalt.

[6] Leona S. Bruckner, *Triumph of Love*. New York, Simon and Schuster, Inc., 1954. By permission.

Sometime later Billy denied not having an elbow because (and we interpret) this fact was simply inconsistent with his existing belief that his right hand was his good hand:

One day as she [Karen, Billy's sister] was doing something, and Billy was trying to copy her, she noticed that he could not do it. She looked truly surprised as she said, "Mother, I just noticed that Billy doesn't have an elbow and he can't lift his hand up high like I can."
I hadn't thought that Billy had heard her because he was so absorbed in what he was trying to do. But he immediately answered her.
"I do so have an elbow and look at me lift my hand up high. See, Karen" [Bruckner, *1954:*146–147].

It is certain that once Billy learns more precisely what an elbow is, he will recognize its absence in his own anatomy, but once having perceived this, other changes in his self-picture will take place in order to effect the necessary integration. He may realize, for example, that his right hand is not, in fact, a "good hand"; though it is better than his left, it still has major shortcomings. How this will affect other attributes of his self-concept, his self-esteem in particular, will depend upon the further direction the integrating forces take. We shall have more to say about this shortly.

At this point it is important to note that the principle of integration need not imply a self-picture that is integrated in all its aspects. The findings of one study, for example, suggest that the ideal self is a complex rather than a unitary entity, making it possible for inconsistencies to persist without tension (McKenna, Hofstaetter, and O'Connor, *1956*). It is more than likely that not only the ideal self but also the self in its existing structure consists of subparts, each of which may be fairly well integrated but not necessarily related to every other part in an integrated way. For example, Mr. A. may consider himself a handsome man but a scoundrel: his appearance self and moral-behavior self are relatively independent, by which we mean that a change in either of these subparts of the self has little effect on the other. Subparts, however, may show a high degree of interdependence and therefore integration, as when a person feels himself a scoundrel *because* he is repulsed by his appearance. We believe that personality descriptions in terms of the relatedness of subparts of the self would provide pertinent data about the individual.

Schilder (*1953*) asserts "that single sensations [about the body] do not stand helter-skelter side by side in memory, but are ordered into a total image of the body—or, to use Head's expression, into a schema. Every new stimulus is met by previously fixed structures, by a body-image . . ." (p. 93). Our only difference with this point of view is to take the more moderate position that integration of a new stimulus or sensation need not require ordering into a total image of the body, but rather a subpart may be sufficient.

INTEGRATION AND SELF-EVALUATION

A Two-Way Process

One of the most interesting and direful facts about the integrating process is that frequently congruency is established between what we might call a single attribute of the self on the one hand and self-esteem on the other. This fact has been encountered earlier in the discussion of the phenomenon of spread (see pp. 118–119). Self-esteem refers to the more or less general evaluation by an individual of himself as a worthy or unworthy *person*. The perception of a single attribute may be molded by self-evaluation, or the evaluation of the self may be affected by a single attribute in such a way as to bring about the necessary integration.

Both processes may occur, and both are seen very clearly in Raymond Goldman's (*1947*) life history. It may be recalled that Raymond was the boy whose legs became disabled from infantile paralysis at the age of 4, and who in his teen years struggled against increasing deafness. The first example shows that even what objectively may be a startlingly clear and unambiguous fact concerning the self, namely the gross condition of one's legs, may be distorted by the power of the general evaluation of the self. The scene is the doctor's office where 8-year-old Raymond is waiting to have long leg braces fitted. His self-esteem at this time glistened with the high and mighty omnipotence of a childish ego. All along he had been king-pin in a world in which he had been loved and lauded and protected:

> Most of the seats were occupied by waiting patients and their mothers. It was the first time I had ever been close to a large group of children—there were about ten or twelve in the room—and I regarded them with curiosity. They were all crippled and deformed, and I saw what braces were like. There were different kinds. The little girl who sat across from me wore one on her head. It protruded from the neck of her dress in the back and ended in padded circular fingers that gripped either side of her head just above the ears. When she wanted to look to one side or the other she had to turn her whole body from the waist. The boy who sat beside her wore braces on his legs as did nearly all the children. But each brace differed from the others and I wondered what my braces would be. Did they hurt? I wanted to ask the boy who sat next to me, but so deep a hush lay over the room that I did not dare. . . .
>
> I preferred looking at the folding doors to looking at the children. I couldn't bear the sight of them; they were ugly and sickening. I almost hated them. Their legs were thin and misshappen. Their faces, somehow, were too old and

wise. I felt that way, *not realizing that I was there as one of them.* [Italics added.] If someone had reminded me that *my* legs were thin and deformed, dangling there helplessly from the edge of the chair, and that *my* face, perhaps, revealed a kind of wisdom that only long, deep suffering can impart, I would have been shocked [Goldman, *1947*:24].[7]

Even though Raymond could not walk and pain was still a frequent intruder, even though he had watched other children run and play, a deformed body image was simply out of keeping with his self-evaluation as a lovable and powerful person. Integration between these two attributes of the self was achieved by not recognizing on the conscious level that his body was deformed! There is some evidence, however, that subconsciously Raymond was aware of his own deformity, and in fact hated it. For example, the deep aversion he felt toward the other crippled children in the doctor's office seems explicable on the basis of such awareness.

The next example shows both how a single attribute is molded by self-evaluation and, conversely, how the perceived attribute, through its evaluatory connotations, largely determines the person's self-esteem. The following incident took place a short time after Raymond's visit to the doctor (previous incident). It is Raymond's first day at school:

I finished my lunch and dropped the remains into the can that I was able to reach. Other boys came to drop their refuse in the can. One of them stopped to look me over.

"What's the matter with you?" he asked me.

"Nothing," I said.

"Can't you walk?"

"I can walk a little," I said. "I can crawl real fast, though."

"Jiminy Christmas!" he exclaimed.

I took this to be an expression of admiration. I looked up into his face, eager to be friendly. No one else had spoken to me, though many had looked at me intently, and I was grateful for this attention.

We attracted the attention of other boys and soon a crowd was gathered in a semicircle around us.

"Lemme see, will you?"

"Quit shoving or I'll—"

"This kid can't walk. He says he can crawl real fast though."

I was pleased and honored. It was like one of my dreams.

"I can even crawl up and down steps," I told them. "They won't let me crawl here because I'd get dirty."

The boys began to laugh. I wondered what was funny about that statement. Through my mind flashed the weeks and weeks of efforts before that feat had

[7] Selection from Raymond Goldman, *Even the Night,* copyright 1947, The Macmillan Company, is used with the permission of the publisher.

been accomplished. Now my boast—and I had really said it boastingly—was greeted with laughter.

"That's pretty good, fellas! He can crawl up and down steps!"

I felt easier when I heard that. So they did think it was pretty good! Their laughter, then, had been prompted by admiration.

One of the boys leaned down and touched my leg. He circled it with thumb and forefinger.

"Look how skinny!" he shouted triumphantly. "I can wrap it with two fingers!"

"Let's see!"

"Sure 'nough!"

"Gee, what skinny old legs!"

A feeling of inferiority began to batter against the bulwark of my illusions. I sensed the ridicule before I comprehended it. I had never been fully conscious of the fact that my legs were emaciated. Now I looked down at them and then at the legs of the other boys. The damnable hammer of comparison beat the truth into my consciousness.

"Let go my leg!" I said, letting anger rise to cover rising horror.

"Why? Does it hurt?"

"No. But let it go."

"Who says so?" the boy demanded, but he released my leg and stood up. "Let's see you crawl."

"No."

"Jiminy!" he said. "Those ain't legs. You got broomsticks!"

That prompted another sally of laughter. The room echoed a jeering repetition of "Broomsticks!" I looked at my tormentors with burning eyes. I saw them through a film of tears. I wanted to kill every one of them, to hit them and claw them and bite them. In my hand was an imaginary dagger, sharp and glistening. I saw myself leaping from the bench and slashing right and left with the murderous blade. My victims screamed and fell, bleeding, dead at my feet.

The boy—perhaps it was the same one—reached down and grasped my leg again. I flung myself forward off the bench, grabbing him as I fell. The boy went over backward and we went down with me on top. I heard his head hit the concrete and I was glad. I sat astride him, pounding my fists into his face, screaming with tears streaming down my face.

Then I felt myself being lifted up while my fists were still flailing.

"Stop it! Stop it! Behave yourself, Raymond!"

I suddenly realized that it was Mr. Stevens' [the principal's] voice and that I was on his arm. I buried my face in his shoulder and sobbed [Goldman, *1947*:35–37].

Following this incident Raymond Goldman was a changed person. "A few ill-mannered boys had implanted in me the seed of shame from which I was to conceive a monster" (p. 38). Thereafter, until more maturing forces took hold, Raymond suffered the hurt and shame of inferiority. The perception of a single attribute, that his legs were deformed, had the power to annihilate fairly thoroughly the general esteem he had heretofore felt.

If we examine the foregoing incident in order to reveal more explicitly what was happening in the process of alignment between attribute and self-evaluation, three phases may conveniently be distinguished:

1. Self-evaluation dominates perception. When Raymond went into the lunchroom, he felt proud of himself and his accomplishments. Ambiguous social events were integrated within this scheme and interpreted accordingly. Thus, when Raymond became the center of attention through staring and queries, he basked in illusory glory, for was not all this admiration over the wonder that he was?

2. There is temporary incongruence between self-evaluation and outside events. Then the boys began to laugh. To Raymond the laughter was puzzling, for it seemed inappropriate for a hero who, by dint of *sheer perseverance,* had accomplished so great a feat as crawling. But his self-esteem remained unshaken and his uneasiness allayed when that segment of the comments made by the boys that could be seen as consistent with his high self-regard was partialed out; he latched onto the statement, "That's pretty good, fellas! He can crawl up and down steps!" Raymond was then again able to interpret the laughter as being prompted by admiration, the laughter being sufficiently ambiguous to be fitted into the pattern of his highly valued self.

3. Single attribute dominates self-evaluation. Then came the turning point when the events outside Raymond's skin were not so malleable. The children pointed out how skinny his legs were, that two fingers could wrap around them, and that they were broomsticks. What is more, they were unrelenting in their jeers until Raymond was all but bludgeoned into perceiving the stigmatizing aspects of his physique. We would like to speculate as to what might have gone on in Raymond's mind as these invectives were being hurled at him:

They call my legs skinny, and broomsticks. They are not skinny! I can prove that they are as stout and shapely as anybody's. See—look at mine and look at yours. Oh no! They are skinny! They are broomsticks! I have broomsticks for legs. You shouldn't have broomsticks for legs. They asked me if I can walk. I can't walk but I can crawl. That's just as good as walking. No it isn't. I *should* be able to walk. I'm ashamed. It's awful. It's horrible!

Notice that, before Raymond's new perception of his legs could affect his self-esteem, the perception had to take on an evaluative quality of good and bad, what should be and what should not be. Although Raymond sensed the ridicule before he could comprehend it, the ridicule had the power to bewilder *but not to shame* until the ridicule became *attached to* his own perceptions of what should be and what should not be.

Integration then took place along many paths: fact with fact—Raymond perceived his legs as broomsticks. Fact with value—he perceived that his legs should be stout and shapely and not like broomsticks. Evaluated fact with self-esteem—he perceived his self as inferior in keeping with an inadequate physique.

The integrative process is one reason why the self-concept is difficult to change. The very thing that is to be changed has considerable power in molding the experiences impinging on the person to fit its own image so that they are interpreted as not conflicting with that self-concept. It takes a lot of convincing before a drastic remodeling of the self-concept can take place in either a negative or positive direction (Rogers, *1951*). Just as Raymond had to be "bludgeoned" into perceiving the abnormalities of his physique, so it took years of internal struggle before he became convinced that he was still a man for all that.

The resistance against positive change in the self-concept is especially interesting since it runs counter to what would seem to be the wishes of the person. Would not everyone rather feel better about himself? The resistance, however, is simply one of the consequences of the integrating process. Once self-abnegation involving the total person has taken place, then the old and new events tend to be interpreted in harmony with a negative self-concept. Raymond, for example, could no longer really think of his performance as accomplishments because such an evaluation, which previously had fitted in well with his high self-regard, now had nothing to which it could be anchored. In the same way a foreigner who feels ashamed because of his place of birth sees primarly what to him are the devaluating features of his extraction such as poverty or poor education, to the exclusion of possibly worthy aspects, such as good culture and diligence. The therapeutic problem involves identifying the worthy aspects of the upsetting characteristic in question, of giving them sufficient weight to effect a change in self-concept, and of reintegrating the negative features accordingly. This process may be designated as the *principle of positive identification*. Concretely, in the case of disability, it means highlighting and identifying with the coping aspects of the disability (see Chap. 3).

Two Gradients in the Spread from Single Attribute to Self-Evaluation

Once again we encounter the phenomenon of spread, and once again we raise the question of how a single fact about a person can become so potent as to print its negative (or positive) stamp on the person as a whole. Previously, this phenomenon was related to the "halo effect" (see

p. 121) and to "comparative values" (see pp. 131–132). Here we should like to approach the problem from the point of view of the structure of the self-concept by isolating two general factors—namely, the "self-connection gradient" and the "status-value" gradient.

SELF-CONNECTION GRADIENT.   It is known that attributes of the self differ with respect to how central they are to what may be called the "essence of the self" or the "essential me." One's blood type, for example, typically is quite alien to this central core, whereas one's ability and appearance are typically very close. A close connection between the attribute in question and the self-core is often expressed by the verb "to be," as in the following: I *am* smart; you *are* good-looking; he *is* dishonest. A weaker connection is often expressed by the verb "to have," as in the following: I *have* false teeth; you *have* a clear complexion; he *has* fine motor coördination.

What makes for closer or weaker connections with the self-core is a challenging problem requiring further investigation. A few leads are, however, immediately apparent, several of them directly related to what has been called ego-involvement. From the perceptual point of view, it appears that events involving the face and torso are more closely connected with self-essence than events connected with the appendages. Thus it is to be expected that adjustment to a facial disfigurement would in general involve a greater problem from the point of view of the self-connection gradient than adjustment to a leg disfigurement, for example. This is also at least one reason why we speak of a girl as being pretty if her face is pretty but not generally if her hands are pretty. The face seems to be a more intimate part of the person than the hands or legs. How close the identification between face and self can be is seen in the case of a little boy who feared that if he wore glasses nobody would know him.

Evidently, too, there is less connection with the self-core when a body attribute may be looked upon as a tool than when it is looked upon as a personal characteristic (Dembo, Leviton, Wright, *1956*:22). For example, false teeth may be thought of as a tool for eating, albeit inferior to the original equipment, or they may be thought of as bespeaking one's decline—i.e., as a personal characteristic.

Also, certain personal characteristics about the self appear to be more crucial to one's identification than others. People identify themselves as men or women, for example, and not as broad-headed or long-headed. Since sex identification is often a central personal characteristic that serves to define the person to himself and others, it can be expected that any circumstance that alters or endangers this identification will have marked effects on the self-concept. The same little boy who faced the prospect of wearing glasses expressed the fear that he could not be a rough-and-tumble boy any more, an a priori connection which, threatening the child's sex identification, made him envision himself as a strangely different person.

To take another example, leg amputation is sometimes viewed as a symbol of castration. Feeling "half a man" points to one of the main areas of adjustment, an area that often has wider implications for personal well-being than the sheer ability to get around. In one intensive study on the role of sexual impotence in the concept of self in male paraplegics, it was pointed out that, compared to nonimpotent male paraplegics, the impotent group appeared less adjusted to their disability and more upset in almost all other areas of their personality (Berger, 1951). Parenthetically, we should like to say that this study deals almost solely with succumbing aspects of paraplegia, carefully detailing the personal and interpersonal disturbances effected by the physical trauma, as if the concept of self does not have anything to do with the strivings of the person, with his efforts to meet the impact of his disability. In the personality sketches drawn for the 30 subjects there is no mention of any constructive forces, of the resources within the patient that will enable him to cope adequately, of what the patient is "becoming," to use the expression of Gordon Allport.

Another personal characteristic high on the self-connection gradient is often symbolized by the kind of work one does. One's very essence may be felt to be that of a scholar, a miner, or a musician. The self-concept, then, might be expected to suffer stress when circumstances—retirement or injury, for example—force one to give up the work. Preparing for retirement in advance means reshaping the self-concept to fit a new role. If adjustment is to take place, other personal, positive attributes must assume a high position on the self-connection gradient. Unfortunately, the science and practice of mental health have not as yet seen the equal necessity of preparing for disablement.

Personal characteristics, of course, carry with them status implications. But independent of the status value of a personal characteristic, there is variation as to its connection with the self-core. This point is clarified in the following section, which deals with the status-value gradient.

An examination of cases in which the body becomes so detached from the self that it is looked upon or felt to be an object is revealing. For instance, Bettelheim (1943:431) reports that as a Nazi prisoner he was able to endure the torture and indignities inflicted upon him because right from the beginning he became convinced that these horrible and degrading experiences somehow did not happen to him as a subject, but only to him as an object. There is also a psychotic separation between the body and the self in which the person *disowns* the body as not being his or as belonging to another person. A more familiar example of body-person separation is the physician who, examining a patient, maneuvers him and treats him as he would any other object coming under serious scrutiny. For him, physique has been removed from any connection with feelings, attitudes, or essence of the other person's self.

In this last example, the separation is effected in a second individual, the physician, rather than in the person himself. Undoubtedly, body-self separation occurs less readily in the person himself than in the second person who, intentionally or not, more easily remains cut off from the personal qualities of the former. Thus it is that without qualms a stranger can stare at a person with a disability just because this person is, for him, an *object* of his attention. Should their eyes meet, the body-person separation is destroyed, for "eyes are the mirror of the soul," and the stranger looks away.

It is also noteworthy that the person himself resists such separation all the more when it denotes a loss of integrity of the "essential self." He resents being stared at *when* he feels "like a monkey in a zoo." On the other hand, in the case of the prisoner, he could maintain integrity only by dissociating his body from his self-core.

In terms of adjustment to disability, clinical records indicate that disowning the defective part is deleterious to the goals of rehabilitation. The person who feels psychologically that the withered limb is not a part of himself will not be able to make most effective use of it. In this connection, a study of patients with facial disfigurements (Macgregor, *et al., 1953*) indicated that persons reared not to mention and to otherwise hide their deformity never integrated it well into the body image, whereas those who were reared to regard the deformity realistically were able to give a fairly accurate description of themselves. Moreover "a poorly integrated deformity seemed to favor dissatisfaction with the operative result, whereas a clear concept of the body image seemed rather to predispose to postoperative satisfaction" (p. 199). Similarly, a study of amputees has shown that an individual's adjustment to a prosthesis is dependent to a considerable degree upon his self-concept (Fishman, *1949*).

The disability must become an integrated part of the self, not severed from it, though research will have to show whether its optimum position on the self-connection gradient is at a distance from or closer to the self-core. Clearly, the development of theory and research is also needed to identify further the conditions determining position on this gradient.

STATUS-VALUE GRADIENT.   Attributes also vary with respect to their relevance for the evaluation of personal worth or self-esteem. In the American culture, for example, success and achievement commonly have a higher loading of status value than diligence or coöperation. One of the determiners of status value may very well turn out to be the degree of connection with the self-core (as well as vice versa), but undoubtedly there are other determiners as well, for the relative status value of two attributes may sometimes be the reverse of their position on the self-connection gradient. Thus, a man may enjoy high status because of his political influence rather than ostracism because of his reprehensible character, even though this second attribute may be more tied in with the core of the self than the first.

In the preceding chapter, several value changes were discussed that have the potentiality of reducing the status value of physique: enlarging the scope of values, containing disability effects, subordinating physique, considering physique as an asset value. Also, perceiving the coping aspects of a disability in contrast to its succumbing aspects has significantly different effects on its status value (Chap. 3, p. 59).

When the effects of disability are felt to be widespread, it would seem that the disability has greater possibilities of assuming a high position on both gradients. At the same time one has to be most cautious in concluding that a severe disability will automatically have a more drastic consequence on the perception of self than a mild one. An excellent example of more than a minor disability having a relatively insignificant effect on the perception of the person (though it deals with interpersonal perception rather than self-perception) occurred when a father, confronted with the news that his son lost a leg, rebutted:

"Lost a leg, has he? What's so bad about that? Rest of him's in good shape, hain't it?" [Viscardi, *1952:*143].[8]

And as we have seen in the example of eyeglasses presented in the preceding section, even a mild disability may affect areas in the person's life that are closely tied to his self-core and important to his status.

In answer to the original question concerning how an evaluation of a single attribute becomes imposed on the evaluation of the total person, we may now stipulate two functions. The power of a single attribute to influence self-esteem will be greater (1) the closer the connection between it and the self-core, and (2) the higher the status value it possesses.

Two conclusions follow. First, since a disability is a negatively evaluated condition, and since physique almost always has some connection with the self-core (though in specific cases its position on the self-connection gradient may be low) and since physique in most cases has some status-value relevancy (though in some cases a low value) for most people self-esteem will be threatened by disability. Because of the danger of false generalizations, we must note that this conclusion does *not* state that

[8] Henry Viscardi, Jr., *A Man's Stature.* Copyright, 1952, by Henry Viscardi, Jr. Used with permission of The John Day Company.

persons with disabilities tend to feel more inferior than the able-bodied, for, of course the able-bodied may also feel inferior about particular attributes (see pp. 52–56).

Secondly, though shame stemming from the negatively evaluated aspects of disability ordinarily must be experienced, such shame can be but a tiny voice in a chorus whose main themes speak of the coping aspects of the situation. When the coping aspects are attended to, new *positively evaluated attributes* will appear which, through the principle of positive identification, establish high positions on the self-connection and status-value gradients, thereby building up self-esteem. For example, the person may feel proud because he has managed to earn a living in spite of severe handicaps. Such personal attributes as perseverance, independence, intelligence, moral stamina, etc., may give genuine support to an ego that may be undermined by the negatively evaluated attributes of the disability itself.

AGE OF OCCURRENCE OF DISABILITY

During the life of an individual, the body, of course, undergoes change. It grows, matures, and ages. The change may occur gradually, as during childhood and adulthood, or more suddenly, as during adolescence or as a result of disability.

Before raising the question of what happens to the self-concept when there is a sudden change in physique, it should be realized that typically even a gradual change is first consciously recognized not gradually but all at once as a sudden and startling fact. This occurs when the meaning of the changing physical trait is of such a nature as to effect major modifications in the self-concept. Thus the wrinkles and the greying hair that had been accumulating over a period of time may not even be perceived until the person suddenly realizes, "I am getting middle-aged!" To take another example, many an adult remains happily unaware of what to others is an unmistakable increase in weight, interpreting their blunt remarks as inconsequential and meaningless jests, until he is shocked into the realization, "I *am* fat. Is that I? I once was so slender and youthful. It couldn't be."

Often, however, what are looked upon as major changes or "turning points" in a lifetime are brought about by special events that significantly alter the self-concept. Marriage, parenthood, graduation, victory or defeat in important areas, commonly represent such events. Raymond Goldman's first day at school was a turning point for the same reason (see pp. 145-147). Subjectively, the person may feel a strangeness about himself, a kind of unfamiliarity, and more extremely he may feel like a different person. Ordinarily, however, he still recognizes himself as the same person in spite of remarkable changes. The property of integration, which requires that the new feelings and notions about the self be absorbed within the old ones (see pp. 139–148), makes possible the feeling of continuity between the past and the present in a life history. It is this property which cautions us against the generalization that a physical trauma, even a major one, must create a violent upheaval in the self-concept.

Because of man's tremendous need to simplify so that he can understand, generalizations continue to be made to the effect that it is easier to adjust to a disability when one is "born that way," or when it is acquired in childhood, or in adulthood. There are several good arguments for each of these alternatives. In the case of congenital disability, one does not have to cope with alteration in the self-concept and therefore on this score adjustment is facilitated. On the other hand, in the case of adventitious disability one is not faced with the possible stigma of hereditary defect. Also, one could argue that the adult is better able to adjust to a disability because of his greater maturity, in contrast to the child, who is more vulnerable; or the reverse could be stated—namely, that the child, being more plastic than the adult, can more easily accommodate changes in his self-perception. One could add that the child is not burdened with earning a living and with the heavy demands for independence that confront the adult. Also, one could point out special psychological stages in the life cycle that affect adjustment to disability incurred at that time. Thus, on the basis of certain phases of psychosexual development, the conclusion has been stated that "all other factors being equal, we expect blindness occurring at age nine or ten to be less traumatic to the ego than at age five or age thirteen" (Blank, *1957*:17).

Probably all the aforementioned factors, as well as others, bear upon adjustment to disability. But evidently their weighting or correlation with age varies with the groups studied, for research has simply not shown with any consistency that adjustment to disability is easier or more difficult at certain ages of incurrence than at others. The overall status of the findings in regard to deafness may be taken as representative of research with other disabilities. Barker *et al.* (*1953*) summarize 13 studies analyzing adjustment in terms of age at loss of hearing with the statement that the findings of these studies are inconsistent. "A few tend to show greater problems of adjustment when loss of hearing occurs at young ages; others tend to show the reverse. Most of the relationships are statistically unreliable" (p. 233). Even though, in the case of hearing, loss at an early age carries with it the special and difficult problem of learning language, nonetheless age of onset as such does not appear to be a crucial factor governing the psychological outcome of the adjustment process.

The fact remains, however, that a disability incurred after the self-concept has already achieved some structure requires that the new state be integrated within the old notions about the self. In a study dealing explicitly with the effect of disability on the self-concept, Shelsky (*1957*) asked his subjects to describe themselves as they were before the disability and as at the time of the survey. The particular disabilities involved were tuberculosis and amputation. All the subjects were adults, still hospitalized, and were examined at least two months posttrauma, the average length of time since determination of the disability being about six months. He found that both groups of patients did recognize some difference between their present and past selves but far less than one might have expected. The amputees described themselves as having been more active, adventurous, and energetic, and less awkward than they were at present, these being realistic perceptions of the effects of loss of a limb. This realism is also seen in the perceptions of the tuberculous patients as having previously been more healthy and active. They also saw themselves as having been more foolish, impulsive, and hurried than at present.

It seems that these subjects did not, at least on the conscious level, experience any violent upheaval of the way they perceived themselves as persons. Of 300 possible traits, including such commonly assumed disability-related characteristics as *anxious, complaining, confused, dissatisfied, high-strung, irritable, moody, nervous*—or, to take a sample of positive attributes, *adaptable, contented, courageous, enterprising,* and *inventive*—the subjects evidently felt that only a very few differentiated their former from their present selves. For the most part, the acknowledged changes related to realistic and very clearly disability-linked attributes. Moreover, the results did not show these changes to have major consequences for traits not directly related to the disability or for one's general self-evaluation as expressed by such feelings as contented, capable, self-confident, etc.—at least not on the conscious level.

One could reasonably argue that effects on the personality as a whole and on the less obviously involved personality areas were repressed or that such effects require more time to become apparent than these recently involved patients had. Also, one could question the advisability of considering a group of persons who have a disability in common as psychologically homogeneous, since real consequences for the self-concept may be obliterated by the intragroup variability. As a matter of fact, the process of integration makes certain that there will be a significant relation between emotional reactions to disability and the premorbid personality with corresponding differential effects on the self-concept which, if added together, may well cancel each other out. In a study of tuberculous patients, for instance, Wittkower (*1949*) points out that for *conscientious* individuals to be ill, unfit, and dependent tends to be incompatible with high and rigid self-imposed standards of fitness and social responsibility. *Dependent* persons, on the other hand, seem to feel no urgency to get better. As for *rebellious* individuals, their resentment at fate and confinement may more or less obliterate immediate concern about the illness. If the diverse personalities were treated as a single group, one could see how these differential reactions could become buried in the statistical treatment.

In support of the principle that age as such is a poor psychological index of the effects of physical trauma on the self-concept and that personality factors already formed are the important variables, Bard (*1952*), referring to emotional reactions in radical mastectomy patients, concludes:

It is true that the loss of a breast constitutes a blow to femininity, but femininity has a different meaning to each woman. To the patient who is extra-maritally promiscuous, femininity means something quite different than it does to the woman who is as yet chaste and unmarried at a relatively late age. The statement that postclimacteric women will have a more emotionally tranquil course than will younger women who have not fulfilled their goals of marriage and motherhood is an equally meaningless generality since the breast acquires individual meaning to each woman based on her resolution of fears pertaining to the achievement of heterosexuality and motherhood. Some women integrate the breast into a framework of self-esteem in feminine function. Others, on the other hand, integrate the breast as a defense against a feeling of worthlessness as women. These resolutions and defenses are active throughout the life of the woman and do not mysteriously disappear with menopause. The impact of breast amputation upon a woman, therefore, will depend less on her age than upon the character defenses which it disrupts [p. 1147].

Just how traumatic to different kinds of personalities is the advent of a major disability we do not know. In a study of facial deformities, Macgregor *et al.* (*1953*) mention that "disfigurement which occurred during adulthood always seemed to have a disorganizing effect on the integration of the person" (p. 195). But to what extent for different personalities is an important psychological question.

It may be that more often than even wishful thinking would allow man absorbs the fact of a disability in such a way as to keep the major outlines of himself as a person intact. There is good reason to believe that the kind of person one is as differentiated in the self-concept has a stability that resists a general overhaul (see p. 148). Because new experiences are partly and sometimes largely interpreted in terms of the existing self-concept, it is not surprising that damage to the body can also be accommodated within this framework.

Yet where the essential "I" is inextricably associated with the intact body and where the status value of body-whole, body-well, and body-beautiful is high, traumatic consequences for the self-concept appear inevitable. In fact, the consequences may be so traumatic that the person may be unable to integrate his new physique into the self-concept at all. This anguished difficulty is effectively described by Katherine Butler Hathaway (*1943*), who suffered from a tubercular infection of the spine and was bedridden throughout her middle childhood:

> When I got up at last . . . and had learned to walk again, one day I took a hand glass and went to a long mirror to look at myself, and I went alone. I didn't want anyone . . . to know how I felt when I saw myself for the first time. But there was no noise, no outcry; I didn't scream with rage when I saw myself. I just felt numb. That person in the mirror *couldn't* be me. I felt inside like a healthy, ordinary, lucky person—oh, not like the one in the mirror! Yet when I turned my face to the mirror there were my own eyes looking back, hot with shame . . . when I did not cry or make any sound, it became impossible that I should speak of it to anyone, and the confusion and the panic of my discovery were locked inside me then and there, to be faced alone, for a very long time to come (p. 41).
>
> Over and over I forgot what I had seen in the mirror. It could not penetrate into the interior of my mind and become an integral part of me. I felt as if it had nothing to do with me; it was only a disguise. But it was not the kind of disguise which is put on voluntarily by the person who wears it, and which is intended to confuse other people as to one's identity. My disguise had been put on me without my consent or knowledge like the ones in fairy tales, and it was I myself who was confused by it, as to my own identity. I looked in the mirror, and was horror-struck because I did not recognize myself. In the place where I was standing, with that persistent romantic elation in me, as if I were a favored fortunate person to whom everything was possible, I saw a stranger, a little, pitiable, hideous figure, and a face that became, as I stared at it, painful and blushing with shame. It was only a disguise, but it was on me, for life. It was there, it was there, it was real. Every one of those encounters was like a blow on the head. They left me dazed and dumb and senseless every time, until slowly and stubbornly my robust persistent illusion of well-being and of personal beauty spread all through me again, and I forgot the irrelevant reality and was all unprepared and vulnerable again [pp. 46–47].[9]

And yet the person cannot comfortably remain one kind of person when "looking in the mirror" and another kind of person when he is able to suppress the disturbing facts of his physical self. The integration that will allow the person to continue to think well of himself, however, requires important reëvaluation of physique as a value (Chap. 5) with concomitant changes on the two gradients described in the present chapter.

[9] K. B. Hathaway, *The Little Locksmith,* copyright 1943, Coward-McCann, Inc. By permission.

CONCLUSIONS FOR CHILD-REARING PRACTICES

We have attempted to give some indication of the processes of differentiation and integration in the development of the self-concept and how self-evaluation and the evaluation of a single attribute become reconciled. Now we shall consider the problem of self-evaluation and integration from the point of view of the prevention of psychological trauma:

Using Raymond Goldman's (1947) childhood as an example, we might agree that the following were undesirable:

1. Raymond's denial of his own deformities during the period in which he regarded himself as a paragon.
2. Raymond's denial of his own worth at the time when he was forced to recognize the disabling and pitiful aspects of his disability.

Each of these defied the evidence of reality. That the first occurred was a good guarantee that the second would occur also, because it indicated that the disability as a *negatively evaluated fact* could not be assimilated into the self-concept without threatening it. To avoid this, gross distortion became necessary. The inevitable occurred, however, when Raymond's schoolmates denied him the bliss of his pretense and insisted that he acknowledge the inferiority of his legs. What had heretofore been a stable and high self-esteem gave way to an even more undeniable reality; his self-esteem plummeted and shattered to the depths of despair and shame. Raymond's "wakening to shame and the consciousness of reality was inevitable. If it had not happened that day under those circumstances, then it would have happened another day under other circumstances" (p. 38).

We should like to ask in what circumstances would Raymond have been better prepared to face his deviations without having had to pay the price of his sense of personal worth. The main principle offered is that negative or devaluating aspects of disability must be brought to the young person's awareness, along with the coping aspects, by those who know and love him. This principle may be referred to as *realization amid interpersonal acceptance*. Accordingly, it was important for Raymond to have talked and thought about the fact that his legs were in fact emaciated and inferior to those of most children in order that he could have relegated these devaluating aspects to a position of relative impotence by feeling and understanding that he was loved and accepted *in spite* of his crippling. In terms of the previously described self-connection gradient, this would mean that the devaluating aspects of physique became further removed from the self-core: "I and my crippling are not the same because I am loved though my legs leave something to be desired." A comparable shift on the status-value gradient, especially if accompanied by the value changes described in the preceding chapter, permits a healthful integration of the disability into the self-concept.

The principle of realization amid interpersonal acceptance is best effected when the person close to the child discusses disability-connected matters in the framework of their coping aspects and in situations where this topic comes up naturally. Lowenfeld (*1956*) advises parents of blind children as follows:

. . . When he [your child] has recognized that he cannot see, he may ask you why this is so. If you tell him that he is blind because his eyes do not work, but that he has his hands with which he can feel, his ears with which he can hear, his nose with which he can smell, and his tongue with which he can taste, his attention will be focused on what he can do rather than on what he cannot do. Telling him alone would of course not be enough, but by the time he asks this question, he should have experienced so many things with his senses that your reply will be accepted by him as satisfactory [Lowenfeld, *1956*:88–89].[10]

The following is a concrete account of how one mother made a start on bringing her son to the realization that he was blind. Davey, now 4, had been blind since birth:

We came out of the house, and spring was in the air. Things smelled sweet and new, and the sky was bright with stars.

"Smell, Davey," Al [his father] said, drawing his breath in deep. "Doesn't it smell sweet?"

"Um," said Davey, inhaling with gusto.

"Um," Mary Sue [sister] echoed, sniffling up her small nose with short brief sniffs.

I hugged her against me, and then I glanced up at the sky.

"Look, honey," I said. "Look, Mary Sue, up at the sky. See the stars."

Davey put up his hand. "I want to see the stars, too," he said.

I looked over at Al, and his face was blurred in the dark or maybe it was my sudden tears that made it seem blurred. For a minute, my throat closed over, and I knew a pain so sharp I thought I could not bear it. But then I knew that this was my opportunity, the time I had been seeking for. So I put Mary Sue in Al's arms, and I sat down on the steps beside Davey.

"Listen, honey," I said, and I turned his face toward me. Then I stopped, and for a second, there were no words to say. But then the words came, and I said them. "Davey, some people in this world can't see things with their eyes. Those people are called blind people. They have to look at things with their fingers, the way you do. Annabel [a blind social worker whom Davey knew and loved] is like that, and you are, too."

"But couldn't I touch the stars?" said Davey, and there was, of course, no

[10] From B. Lowenfeld, *Our Blind Children,* 1956. Courtesy of Charles C. Thomas, Publisher, Springfield, Ill.

loss or sorrow in his voice. He had found that very beautiful things could be seen with his fingers. He was only four years old, and so he did not miss color or light when he had shape and substance.

"No, honey," I said, and I did not want to cry, not any more. "No, some things in this world are too far away to touch, ever, and the stars are like that. Those things you'll have to learn about by hearing of them. Understand?"

He nodded his head against my shoulder.

"Sure," he said. But, of course, he didn't. He probably never would, not completely. But I had told him [Henderson, *1954*:112–113].[11]

In this brief scene, several important ideas were introduced: the meaning of blindness, Davey is blind, other people are blind too, blindness entails certain restrictions (disabling aspects) and thus certain aspects of life must be met in a different way (coping aspects). But these marks of difference from others were brought out with a deep but simple feeling of love and acceptance. One such scene may not be enough, for ideas sometimes "sink in" slowly and may require repeated exposures for the self-picture to be positively imprinted with full values that are able to withstand assault.

In Raymond's case, however, a comparable scene apparently never took place (Goldman, *1947*). That he was different in some ways from other children and would continue to be different was never mentioned. He was praised for coöperating with the exercises and striving to crawl, etc., but no special reference evidently was made to the shortcomings of his legs. "They [his parents] entered into a fine conspiracy of cheerfulness, hope, and courage, and throughout my childhood I was treated the same as my brother and sisters" (p. 6). Raymond came to identify being loved with being perfect as epitomized in the frequent scenes in which his parents, nurse, and older sister "kissed me [being loved] and said lovely things about me [being perfect] to each other while I listened from my seat in childhood's heaven" (p. 11). Whatever subconscious awareness he had of his own physical inadequacies was counterbalanced by an active fantasy life in which he envisioned "a personal vigor and physical strength that were Gargantuan. I dashed about the city streets, uprooting tall trees with my bare hands. Or, more constructively, I ran like the wind on my own fleet legs to spread the alarm of fire to every inhabitant" (p. 3).

Through the techniques described in Chapter 11 Raymond could also have been prepared for the prejudices he would inevitably experience. Storytelling, role playing, and discussion would have all been in order. Not only would these have equipped him with certain social skills but, in exposing him to the negative aspects of his disability, the necessary

---

[11] Lois T. Henderson, *The Opening Doors*. New York, The John Day Company, 1954. By permission.

reorganization of the self-concept would have been taking place in a protective atmosphere. The companionship of other children with disabilities in an accepting atmosphere of the home or nursery school would have provided the opportunity for "the mental and emotional experience of recognizing another human being as possessing simultaneously a recognizable disability and a lovable self" (Garrett, *1955:*447). This, as in group counseling, favors the assimilation of the negative aspects of disability within a self-concept that could remain positive.

Being brought face to face *for the first time* with one's shortcomings in a hostile and rejecting environment can be such a devastating experience that precautions must be taken to avoid this, particularly in childhood. It makes all the difference in the world if painful facts about the self are first realized in a friendly and accepting atmosphere. In the former case there is a cementing between the self-core and the negative fact, whereas in the latter case there is a separation. (A particularly favorable relationship for the accomplishment of this separation exists in therapy, where the patient is unconditionally accepted.) Therefore, if by the age of 8 Raymond already had come to some grips with some of the displeasing aspects of his physique in his own home where he was loved and accepted, his self-concept would have had a far greater inner strength to stand up against the barbs being thrust at him by the boys who were so unfriendly on that first day at school. He still would have fought and cried, but the strong core of his self-esteem would not have been shattered.

Chapter 7

Self-Concept and the Perception of Interpersonal Relations

"BELIEVING IS SEEING"—ILLUSTRATED

HAROLD RUSSELL (1949), THE SOLDIER WHO LOST HIS HANDS, REACTED differently in the following two situations involving discussion of his injury:

SCENE I. *In a bar during Russell's first pass to town from the hospital.*

We had just ordered our first round when I noticed someone at the bar staring right at me. I tried to ignore him, but he wouldn't stay ignored. I could feel him watching me. Presently he came over. He was a blubbery hunk of fat and had three or four chins dripping down his vest. He pulled up a chair and made himself at home. Apparently he believed that everyone loves a fat man. He ordered a round of drinks for all hands.

"Thanks, mister," I said, "I still got one."

"So you'll have another! On me, Joe! Always good to have reserves on hand. That's how we win battles." He winked and looked around us, trying to milk a laugh. None of us made a sound. He squirmed momentarily, then shifted to the subject that he was really interested in. "Tell me, sergeant, how did—"

"—you lose your hands?" One of my buddies finished the question for him.

SCENE II. *Sometime later in a restaurant shortly before Russell was ready for discharge from the hospital.*

The night we were at Ruby Foo's [restaurant] I was wielding my chopsticks at a great rate—I'd learned how in Boston's Chinatown—when a man came over from another table.

"I was noticing," he said, "how well you managed those things."

"These?" I held up the chopsticks.

"No—I—er—mean those—" He swallowed hard and nodded at the hooks. "Well—*those*—"

"Oh! You mean, my hooks?"

He sighed with relief. It was obvious he had been embarrassed to call them by their right name.

"I couldn't help noticing how skilful you are with them," he said. "You can just about do everything with them, can't you, sergeant?"

"Everything," I said, grinning, "except pick up a dinner check."

That drew a laugh. I could see the man relax at once. That made me relax, too [p. 151].[1]

"Why, how did you know what I was gonna ask?"

"Maybe you'd like to tell me how you lost your teeth?" I said.

"Just tryin' to be sociable—" he said, backing away nervously, beads of sweat glistening all over his fat face, his tiny opossum's eyes darting from one to another. "No offense in-in-intended—I—I—I'm sure—no offense—"

"Scram!"

"Before I give you these!" I added, shaking my hooks at him [pp. 122–123].

What was the difference that made a difference to Russell, so that in the first incident he felt he had been insulted, whereas in the second he actually had enjoyed the situation? Was the difference in the *other* person, in the one case blustering and pitying, and in the second more reserved and respectful? Perhaps to some extent, but there is evidence that in the interim between the two scenes Russell *himself* had undergone change, a change that drastically affected his perception of the intentions of others. Russell, after many experiences in which he felt self-conscious and like a freak on exhibition, in which he froze up in regard to discussion of his hooks, began to arrive at important new understandings. He notes:

. . . Gradually, it began to seep through my skull that folks were not just being morbid and inquisitive, but that they were genuinely interested in me. When a stranger offered to buy me a drink it wasn't cheap charity, but a kind of acknowledgment of a debt he felt he owed to all who had served. I began to notice, too, that I wasn't the only GI who was being offered free drinks. Almost every man in uniform, whether disabled or not, was getting his share of them [p. 150].

Moreover, this changed perception paralleled significant transformations within Russell's system of values, heralding progressive acceptance of his disability. The following introspections point to the kinds of reëvaluations occurring in his outlook on life:

Containing disability effects (see pp. 118–128):

Sooner or later, I had to face the problem of how I was going to earn a living. After giving it a great deal of thought, I discovered a startling fact: my

---

[1] Harold Russell with Victor Rosen, *Victory in My Hands,* copyright 1949. Used by permission of the publishers, Farrar, Straus and Cudahy, Inc.

hands had not been as important as I thought. *There were lots of occupations where I wouldn't be too seriously handicapped* [Italics ours] [p. 147].

Subordinating physique (see pp. 115–117):

. . . That was the great lesson of his [Franklin D. Roosevelt's] magnificent fight. That was the innermost secret of his triumph. He had overcome not only his physical handicap but his spiritual one, as well. He had accepted his disability. For what he had missed he had gained something immeasurably more valuable. He was the master of himself and his destiny [p. 142].

Transformation to asset value (see pp. 118–133):

. . . I would have to realize that I had nothing to be ashamed of. . . . I began to see that it's not what you've lost that counts, but what you have left [pp. 142–143].

As long as Russell damned his disability with the epithets degrading, devastating, and disgusting—any social interaction, real or imagined, which so much as touched upon his disability would signal personal threat. At the time of the first scene, this was Russell's phase in the process of accepting his disability. When, however, the meaning of his disability began to change, as indicated by the value transformations indicated above, social interactions correspondingly appeared different to him.

That social perception is a function, among other things, of self-perception is strikingly shown in Goldman's reminiscences in which the *same* situation was first interpreted in one way and then antithetically, *only* because his self-concept had undergone fundamental change. In the first example, Raymond Goldman (*1947*), crippled from polio and now 8 years old, is meditating about the feelings of other persons toward him. Until recently, he had known little of shame. His family had been loving, and his efforts to do things had been greeted by praise and encouragement. But now he had become fully aware of the fact that he was not like other children. During his first day at school he had been taunted and ridiculed (see pp. 145–146 for incident): he "learned" that he was "a pariah among the strong and straight." What had before seemed like kindness and admiration was now defiled by pity and scorn:

. . . I knew now why strange women on the street smiled at me when Christina [his sister] wheeled me along in my gocart, sometimes stopping to chuck me under the chin or pat my head. It was because they pitied me, not because they admired me. I knew now why children along the way stopped their play and stared at me. It was not because they liked me and wished they could play with me, but because they were disgusted by the sight of a boy my age riding in a gocart [p. 39].[2]

The second example, ten years later, reveals the reverse direction in which a previously negatively interpreted relationship now is viewed positively. This change, as in the case of Harold Russell, reflected basic adjustive value transformations during Goldman's struggle with acceptance of disability (see pp. 27–35 for an analysis of this struggle):

. . . When I had played ball with the boys, wearing heavy braces, passers-by had often stopped to watch me. I had thought they were pitying me and I had hated them for it. Now I knew that I should have been grateful to them for that meed of recognition of my striving [p. 94].

The problem of self-concept and the perception of interpersonal relations is not, of course, limited to the way in which a person views his disability. It has the widest application. For example, Maslow (*1939*), in his studies of personality and social behavior, has reported that women low in dominance "can not 'take' compliments in spite of . . . their need and hunger for them. This is because they are apt at once to discount the compliment as untrue and seek suspiciously for other motives. Often, for example, they may think the compliment is making fun of them, holding them up to ridicule, or else trying to get something out of them" (p. 21).

As Santayana is reported to have said, "The empiricist . . . thinks he believes only what he sees, but he is much better at believing than at seeing" (Korzybski, *1951*:176).

INTERPRETATION OF SOCIAL RELATIONSHIPS IN THE FRAMEWORK OF PERCEPTION

The problem concerning the relationship between feelings about the self and the interpretation of the behavior of other people toward oneself is part of the larger problem of variables within and without the person that influence perception (Witkin *et al.*, *1954;* Blake and Ramsey, *1951;* Symposium, *1949*). Experiments on the role of expectations or mental set help to clarify the problem.

In Kelley's (*1950*) experiment, subjects were asked to rate an unknown instructor, after he had led the class in a 20-minute discussion, on such traits as conscientiousness, popularity, intelligence, humor, etc. Some of the students had been informed that the instructor was reputed to be

---

[2] Selection from Raymond Goldman, *Even the Night,* copyright 1947, The Macmillan Company, is used with the permission of the publisher.

"rather cold" and the other students that he was "very warm." One of the main results was that the warm-cold variable produced large differences in the evaluation of the behavior of the instructor. Students given the "warm" prior information consistently rated the stimulus person more favorably than did those given the "cold" prior information. Thus, the information as to whether the instructor was a warm or cold person geared the subject to select and highlight those aspects of his behavior that were in harmony with that concept.

Of course, the conditions within the person do not always primarily determine the interpretation of another's behavior to the exclusion of objective events. Clearly, the conditions "out there" affect one's perceptions. Kelley's experiment, in addition to demonstrating the potency of expectations for evaluations, also demonstrated the influence of the instructor's behavior itself. It happened that two instructors who were very different in personality and behavior served as the stimulus person in the several groups of subjects used. There were marked differences in the *degree* to which the warm-cold variable was able to produce differences for the two instructors. For example, even though the "warm" observers rated instructor *B* more favorably on the popularity and humor scales than did the "cold" observers, he was still rated as "unpopular" and "humorless," which evaluations agreed with his typical classroom behavior.

There is further experimental evidence to indicate, however, that what may objectively be determined as solid and irrefutable evidence may still be denied or distorted when the subject has a strong expectancy of contrary fact. An experiment by Bruner and Postman (*1949*) is particularly relevant. Subjects were presented with playing cards, some of which had suit and color reversed (e.g., black hearts and red spades), for brief exposure periods. Initially, almost all the subjects saw nothing unusual about the trick cards. Congruence between color and suit was effected by misperceiving either the suit or the color at exposure levels well above the threshold for such recognition. Thus, a red six of spades was reported with considerable assurance as being either the red six of hearts or the black six of spades. An equally significant fact, however, is that with increase of exposure time the percentage of correct recognition of the bizarre cards progressively increased. That is, expectations held greatest sway under conditions of ambiguous stimulus information and became less influential as the stimulus input became more reliable. The complexity of the interdependence between stimulus and person variables for perception is seen in the following hypothesis offered by Krech and Crutchfield (*1948*:95–98): If the stimulus differs but slightly from the expectation, the perception will tend to be assimilated to the expectations; however, if the difference between the stimulus and expectation is too great, the perception will occur by contrast to the expectation and will be distorted in the opposite direction.

It is to be noted that on the environmental side the degree of ambiguity or unreliability of the stimulus information can vary: the more clear-cut and reliable the input information, the more effective it will be in structuring the percept. The degree of ambiguity has been controlled in the laboratory by the use of such experimental techniques as dimly illuminated pictures or words, tachistoscopic (briefly exposed) materials, ambiguous drawings, etc. As for the person, the strength of expectations can vary: the stronger the expectation for certain events, the greater its potency in structuring the percept. Expectancy strength has been controlled in the laboratory by information, past experience, and other kinds of set.

In summary, it can be stated that as the features of the environmental stimuli become more ambiguous, the subject's perceptions increasingly adhere to his own expectations. The expectations become an organizing principle according to which facts are made to fit. It is especially important to understand the factors that influence expectations concerning the behavior of others toward oneself since such behavior is often perceived according to one's expectations.

THE ROLE OF SELF-CONCEPT IN EXPECTATIONS

The opening section of this chapter illustrated the significance of self-perception for social perception. The expectations of Russell and Goldman in the situations where the behavior of others was positively evaluated clearly differed from those in the situations evoking negative evaluation. In turn *these expectations depended upon how they felt about themselves, their self-concept.* When they viewed their disability with shame and derision, they could expect only that others felt likewise; this is what they saw in the questioning, the staring, the help of others. When they were able to accept their disability more fully, it became sensible that others could view them as self-respecting, worth-while, and even admirable. Instead of ignoring this expectation as a possibility, they could then entertain it, and once entertaining it, they could see the corresponding positive attitudes in the behavior of others.

There are several reasons why the self-concept plays a role, often decisively, in the interpretation of social relationships. An important one is that it is a necessary (though not sufficient) part of the total situation. The subject sees that the other person is reacting to him and therefore he must take himself into account as an object of stimulation. The kind of "account" he takes of himself is usually drawn from his self-concept, for in most social situations there are few other clues as potent in defining the kind of person one is. He has a full and deep experience of himself and sees himself in a more or less incisive way, even though upon further introspection he may well become ambivalent and confused. In a particular situation he feels that he is right or wrong or at least in between, that he is competent or not or at least in between, that he is handsome or not or at least in between. He does not have as direct access to the other person's regard of him.

It might seem that all that is necessary when one is interested in the behavior and intentions of another person is to attend to his *actual* behavior, inasmuch as that is the direct expression of what he is feeling. That this is not always the case is indicated by sound research. The well-known problem and experiments on the interpretation of human emotions from photographs are particularly relevant (Woodworth and Marquis, *1947*:354–360). Though the findings indicate that the emotion portrayed is not often mistaken for its opposite, they also show that a knowledge of circumstances leading up to the emotion may be an important condition of emotional recognition. To take Asch's example: "The sight of the relaxed face of a man who is watering his garden has one physiognomic quality; the same expression has a wholly different value if the man has just committed a murder" (*1952*:194). In the case of an emotion directed toward me, *my* characteristics as an "object" of stimulation to the other person, and usually available to me via the self-concept, are a highly relevant part of the surrounding conditions.

A second set of factors leading to the preëminent position of the self-image in the interpretation of social interactions is that the clues reflecting the attitudes of the other person are often ambiguous and difficult to pin down. There are several reasons for this. First, such attitudes as respect, warmth, annoyance, disapproval, which the subject senses or tries to sense because of their vital personal relevance, are expressed in multifarious ways. The affection of one person may spill over effusively, whereas in another it may receive satisfying expression in comparatively restrained ways. In addition, the same overt behavior may reveal different underlying emotions, particularly when the behavior in question is a relatively small unit so that further elaboration in terms of causes, consequences, and implications are cut off from view. For example, the same obstreperous behavior of a child may be judged to be an expression of fatigue, stubbornness, anger, or the struggle for independence. Furthermore, attitudes toward another are complex and often conflicting. It is possible for a mother, for example, to become irritated with the demanding behavior of her child but at the same time to love and to cherish him. Similarly, the attitudes toward a person with a disability not infrequently reflect both positive and negative feelings, either simultaneously or at least in rapid succession. For example, the person with a disability may be admired for his success at meeting his situation and pitied because he is still a cripple. Psychoanalytic theory and clinical experience leave no doubt that ambivalence toward others occurs frequently, perhaps even typically, and is a consequence of the multifaceted aspects of our relationships to other persons.

Sometimes, however, a person may have independent information as to how another person feels about him. The information may be hearsay; it may be based on repeated and unequivocal past experience with the other person. In certain circumstances he may wish and be able to set aside his own self-image and substitute the picture of himself as drawn from the perspective of the other person.

Nonetheless, because of the particular relevancy of the self-concept in social interactions and of the ambiguity of the environmental stimuli (i.e., the behavior of the other person), the self-concept acquires an importance that surpasses its actual effectiveness in gauging correctly the attitudes of others. The person comes to expect certain attitudes and feelings toward himself, expectations rooted in his self-concept.

EXPECTANCY STRENGTH

The *strength* of expectations largely determines the degree to which they affect perception. This holds true for expectations in general, whatever their source, and not only those arising primarily from the self-image. Because of our special concern with problems of acceptance of disability and because of the special role of the self-concept in social expectations, we shall largely restrict our examples to expectations anchored to the self-concept.

The work of Bruner (*1951*) provides a soundly considered and well-integrated conception of some of the important determinants of the strength of an expectation. His work forms the basis of our application to disability-connected problems.

Bruner's fundamental proposition is that perceiving begins in an organism tuned to select certain features of his environment by an expectancy or hypothesis or set. These several terms are used to give the flavor of the highly generalized state of readiness to perceive in a given way. The assumption is that "we are always to some extent *prepared* for seeing, hearing, smelling, tasting some particular thing or class of things" (p. 124). Whether any organism is ever completely "untuned" need not concern us here. Our concern is more with those conditions that affect the power of the "tuning" to channel perception into meaning and evaluation, for in the process of acceptance of a disability it is the tuning that largely determines the key to understanding.

Bruner offers three propositions concerning the concept of expectancy strength: The stronger an expectation, (1) The greater its likelihood of arousal in a given situation; (2) The less the amount of appropriate information necessary to confirm it, and (3) The more the amount of inappropriate or contradictory information necessary to refute it.

The expectations with which a person enters a situation, therefore, not only put the spotlight on what he will see but also, as a function of their strength, delimit the degree of incompatibility with objective fact that can be tolerated. Thus, when a person has a strong feeling of shame and inferiority, the more often will his experiences tend to bear out his expectations that he is indeed to be pitied and cast aside. He will see confirmation in even the most modest evidence, and disruption of the expectation would require considerable proof to the contrary. Expectancy strength can now be seen as of central importance in determining whether acceptance of a disability will proceed as a matter of course or whether it will meet difficulties along the way as the struggle is tested in life's experiences.

What, then, are some of the conditions that strengthen or weaken an expectation? Bruner (1951) proposes five such determinants. In his exposition he has carefully attempted to tie them to experimental findings.

1. *Frequency of past confirmation.* The more frequently an expectation has been confirmed in the past, the greater will be its strength: It will be more readily arousable, require less environmental information to confirm it, and will, conversely, require more contradictory evidence to negate it than would be required for a less frequently confirmed expectation.

The significance of past confirmation for expectancy strength has been demonstrated in a variety of experiments. For example, in the playing-card experiment described above, the fact that it took a far longer exposure time to recognize the cards that had suit and color reversed than those that did not is explained by a strong expectation for normal suit and color combinations built up through many past confirmations (Bruner and Postman, 1949).

Laboratory experiments have also shown, however, that frequency of confirmation does not operate in a simple way to increase strength by uniform increments. Sometimes a single contrary experience can markedly weaken or even wipe out an expectation that previously had many confirmations. Again we draw upon the playing-card experiment. Once the subject "caught on" that suit and color might be reversed, an expectation for incongruous as well as normal cards was established that served to weaken measurably the initial sole expectation. For a clinical example, the life history of Raymond Goldman (1947) may be recalled. During the first four years of his disability, he had many, many experiences in which he was respected, lauded, encouraged, and loved. His expectation that others felt positively toward him was hardly if at all contaminated by doubt until his first day at school, when in one "fell swoop" the violence done to his self-concept correspondingly affected his expectation (see pp. 145–146 for incident).

The conclusion is warranted that expectancy strength is a function of frequency of past confirmation in which the confirming or infirming power of a single experience varies enormously, depending upon what it does to the cognitive outlook of the person. This does not contradict the common-sense feeling that frequent exposure to devaluating experiences in the important areas of life, such as home, school, and job, provides fuel for the smoldering conviction that one is an object of pity. It simply forces recognition of a second common-sense feeling—namely, that frequency as such is not everything and that one experience can be more effective or destructive than another. It would be unfortunate if frequency alone mattered, for then therapy would have the impossible task of altering the attitudes and percepts of an individual that had been built up over a life-time of experience.

2. *Monopoly.* The smaller the number of alternative expectations held by the person concerning his environment, the greater their strength will be.

Bruner (*1951*) describes the relevant experimental evidence and points out that though it is rather scanty, it is unambiguous (p. 129). He mentions the study in which less exposure was required for the recognition of words having to do with food when the subjects were given the instruction to find such words than when they were told to find food words *or* color words (Postman and Bruner, *1949*).

Applying this determinant of expectancy strength to disability problems, we may compare the person whose expectation that others will look down upon him has full reign with the person in whom this expectation is shared with such others as "My disability may not matter to them"; "they may not even notice me"; "they may admire my accomplishments." In the former case, the expectation of devaluation will be confirmed by less evidence than in the second case, and also it will be more tenaciously retained in the face of contradictory information. This suggests that exposing the person to alternative and more positive attitudes toward disability facilitates psychological rehabilitation.

3. *Supporting context.*[3] A particular expectation is embedded in a larger system of supporting hypotheses and beliefs. The larger or more integrated the number of supporting hypotheses, the stronger will be the expectation. Bruner cites one experiment in support of this—namely,

[3] Bruner's term for this is "cognitive consequences."

that a reversed letter is less easily detected when it is embedded in a meaningful word than in a nonsense word. In the former case, the supporting context of a meaningful word strengthens the incorrect expectation that all letters are facing correctly (p. 129).

This determinant points up a crucial step in adjustment to disability—namely, that the overcoming of shame and inferiority may be facilitated when supporting hypotheses are eliminated. Examples of hypotheses supporting disability as a sign of personal inferiority are:

1. My disability is a punishment.
2. It is important to conform, not to be different.
3. Most people are physically normal.
4. Normal physique is one of the most important values.
5. Physique is important for personal evaluation.
6. A deformed body leads to a deformed mind.
7. No one will marry me.
8. I will be a burden on my family.
9. My deformity is revolting.
10. I am less valuable because I can't get around (or see, or hear) as others can.

Which of these supporting beliefs can be eliminated is a challenging issue to consider. Some of them may be discarded or at least weakened through factual and scientific knowledge: e.g., "most people are physically normal"; "a deformed body leads to a deformed mind." Others require basic changes in one's value system or outlook on life: e.g., "normal physique is one of the most important values"; "it is important to conform, not to be different." Even the last hypothesis, that because of a disability one is less valuable than others or than one "would have been," a hypothesis regarded as almost axiomatic by many, is challengeable. Pearl Buck (*1950*) learned this through suffering for her helpless, retarded child, and meeting that suffering:

So by this most sorrowful way I was compelled to tread, I learned respect and reverence for every human mind. It was my child who taught me to understand so clearly that all people are equal in their humanity and that all have the same human rights. None is to be considered less, as a human being, than any other, and each must be given his place and his safety in the world [pp. 51–52].[4]

Parents may find comfort, I say, in knowing that their [retarded] children are not useless, but that their lives, limited as they are, are of great potential

---

[4] Reprinted by permission of Harold Ober Associates, Inc. Copyright, 1950, by Pearl S. Buck.

value to the human race. We learn as much from sorrow as from joy, as much from illness as from health, from handicap as from advantage—and indeed perhaps more [p. 57].

And because Pearl Buck challenged hypothesis 10 and others, she was able to say to all parents of atypical children and to mean what she said:

Be proud of your child, accept him as he is and do not heed the words and stares of those who know no better. This child has a meaning for you and for all children. You will find a joy you cannot now suspect in fulfilling his life for and with him. Lift up your head and go your appointed way [p. 59].

4. *Motivational consequences*. Expectations satisfy the needs of a person in varying degrees. The more relevant the confirmation of an expectation may be to the satisfaction of needs, the stronger the expectation will be: it will be more readily aroused, more easily confirmed, less readily repudiated.

Bruner (*1951*) cites various lines of evidence substantiating the role of motivational support in strengthening expectations and also calls attention to the complexities involved (p. 130).

With regard to disability problems, this proposition gives to what has been called "secondary gains of disability" a theoretical position of significance. A disability may serve many purposes. The person may wish to insure continuing financial compensation that his disability provides; he may welcome the dependency facilitated by his disability; his disability may satisfy a masochistic need for punishment; it may afford him social sanction for avoiding competitive striving, which he fears. All these are motivational supports that will lead a person to cling to expectations confirming the *disabling* aspects of his disability. He will also resist such value changes as containing disability effects and subordinating physique, for example, for these bring out the abilities and positive strivings of the person instead of the disabling aspects.

By the same analysis, the counterparts of these motivational supports should strengthen those expectations in which the disability is minimized. The man who has a strong need for independence, for example, will on this account expect fewer limitations from his disability. He will also require less convincing evidence that disability effects can be drastically contained. The point is a simple one. When a disability is satisfying for one reason or another, it becomes magnified through beliefs and expectations. When a disability runs counter to the important needs of the person, its disabling aspects are correspondingly diminished through beliefs and expectations.

5. *Shared Verification*.[5] An expectation may be strengthened by virtue of its agreement with the expectations of other observers to whom the perceiver may turn.

A pertinent experiment in support of this is that of Asch (*1952:* Chap. 16) on the modification of judgments by groups. Subjects were asked to report verbally in small groups the relative lengths of lines that perceptually were clear-cut and stable. In the main experiment, all the subjects but one had been instructed unanimously to oppose the critical subject by reporting incorrect judgments at certain points, leaving the critical subject a minority of one. In these circumstances, though the input information was clear-cut, the critical subject of each group became generally insecure and yielded to the incorrect majority in one third of his responses. When, however, a partner was introduced who was to support the critical subject by consistently giving the obviously correct responses, the majority effect was markedly weakened. In only one eighth of their responses did the critical subjects yield. The presence of a single confirming voice served to strengthen the subject's conviction and enabled him to follow more consistently and independently his own sensory information. Festinger (*1954*) has developed a theory of social comparison processes based on hypotheses that stress the importance of shared verification in supporting one's judgments. One of the corollaries, for example, states that in the absence of both a physical and social comparison, subjective evaluations of opinions and abilities are unstable.

Applying the factor of shared verification to disability problems, we may conclude that if a person is surrounded by the judgment that a disability is a horrible calamity which denies all the important satisfactions in life, then it will be more difficult to change this expectation in the person himself than if his social verifiers supported a more moderate view.

Having examined the self-concept and expectations as influencing the perception of social relations, we may wonder how one ever manages to be on the right track, to perceive the intentions of others correctly, to have harmony in social relations. Ichheiser (*1949*) has written a perceptive analysis of sources of misunderstandings in human relations with emphasis on cognitive factors. We wish now to discuss how understandings can and do take place even though in many social situations we see things in some measure as *we* are rather than purely as *they* are.

EXPECTATIONS AND SOCIAL UNDERSTANDING

There are several factors that lead the person, *p*, and the other person, *o*, to see things sufficiently alike to allow for mutual understanding. First,

---

[5] Bruner's term for this is "social consequences."

as we have noted previously, there is the role played by reality itself. Under clear-cut environmental conditions, expectations play a less dominant role. In some social situations the behavior of another has such a firm and indisputable structure of its own that it forces its own meaning on the interaction in spite of the fact that the self-concept and consequent expectations may be at variance with it. This may be more apt to occur after several exposures to the other's behavior just because expectations do play a directive role. The following example is illustrative:

Mary, a young woman who required bed rest for several days during an illness, rejected the genuine attempts of her friends to help, as in meal preparation, caring for the children, providing transportation to the doctor. Each offer was resisted until finally Mary said, "Everyone's been so nice to me. It makes me feel that they like me." Mary, who for a long while had regarded herself as unworthy, at first could only interpret the help as mere formality. It was only when the offers were made repeatedly and effected over her protestations that she could accept the help for what it was, an expression of real friendship. The property of the behavior of those close to her finally impressed its own character on her perception.

There is another factor, also mentioned earlier, that enables people to understand each other. There are times when the person structures himself as an object of stimulation to others not in terms of his self-concept but on the basis of independent clues, such as information. Thus, when a thief is sure that his friend knows nothing of his irregularities, he may take not his self-image but the honest version of himself as the basis for interpreting the social interaction. Likewise, when a person with a disability knows that the employer has an exaggerated notion of his limitations, he may interpret his lack of promotion accordingly rather than in terms of any aspects of his own self-concept.

Moreover, satisfactory interpersonal relationships need not require identity of perception between the person himself, p, and the other person o. In many situations, p's picture of himself as an object of stimulation may sufficiently match o's picture of p to permit harmonious interpretations. For example, o may agree to some extent with p's notions as to p's capability. It is also possible for p up to a certain point to misinterpret o and still manage well together. Suppose p senses an annoyance in o that he mistakenly attributes to fatigue. Although o may truly be annoyed, the source of the annoyance may be entirely different—displeasure with the task at hand, for example. Yet both may be able to accept the undercover friction without delving further.

Finally, a social interaction is a process that unfolds in the give and take between the participating members. This means that the reality—i.e., what actually occurs—is not charted independently of the person's wishes, fears, and expectations but to some extent is actually shaped by them. In this way not only the reality as perceived but the reality as is may be made to fit the person's expectations and self-concept. When Goldman (*1947*) became aware of this he became overwhelmed with the implications:

> I've discovered something else: the gym teacher was embarrassed when he began to talk to me today. It was almost as if he felt the shame that he expected me to feel. But when he saw that I was not ashamed, his embarrassment disappeared. Is that a manifestation of a kind of power that human beings hold over each other? His attitude was in *my* control, it was *I*, not *he*, who determined what that attitude toward me should be. What kind of power is that? How far can one use it? What is its source? [pp. 94–95].

Russell (*1949*) also began to realize that "the only way I could expect to feel at ease with them [people] was if they felt at ease with me, and the only way for them to feel that way was for me to be at ease with myself" (p. 150). And once feeling at ease, he was able to establish social techniques that put others at ease. Let us compare the following two situations involving his hooks, the first when he was beset with embarrassment and shame, the second when he felt comfortable about his hooks and thought of them as "working hands."

The scene is Russell's first homecoming since his injury. He has just deplaned:

> When I finally got off I carried my bag in one hook and hid the other in my pocket. I hoped they [those meeting him] wouldn't notice the one with the bag right away. I tried to keep it out of sight, but the bag kept bumping against my legs.
>
> Rita [his sweetheart] spotted me first. She shouted and waved at me. Then mother and Fred [a sailor friend] began doing the same. My first impulse was to wave back at them. Then I realized how grotesque that would be. I kept the hook in my pocket. It was only a hundred yards to where they were standing, but it seemed like I was on one of those twenty-five-mile marches. And with every step I became more uncertain, more jittery, more scared. I wanted to go straight back to the hospital.
>
> Mother was the first to reach me. She folded me in her arms. "Darling! It's wonderful to have you back!"
>
> I kissed her. I started to put my arms around her. I caught myself just in time.
>
> She pushed me away from her and looked me over. "My, but you look fine!" she said. I noticed she was careful to avoid where my hands had been.
>
> Now Rita snuggled up to me. She gave me a long, tender kiss. I had a hard job not taking her in my arms. I didn't dare. It might ruin everything. Imagine having those hard, cold claws biting into your back! I could feel a shiver run through her body as she pressed against me. I knew that as soon as she was alone she'd let herself go. . . .

All during the ride to Cambridge I could sense Rita and mother stealing glances at the hooks. I felt like shaking them in their faces and shouting, "Here! Take a good look at them! Fascinating, aren't they?"

I was sitting next to Fred. He was driving. All the time he kept looking down at his hands guiltily as though he'd stolen something. That made me freeze up even more. I couldn't keep my eyes off the wheel and he kept taking one hand off it and sticking it in his pocket as if to hide it [pp. 129–131].

The second scene is after Russell had been discharged from the hospital. He is thinking about different ways to put people at ease when they meet him and his hooks for the first time:

First of all, I found it was extremely important to shove my hook out at a person when I met him, just as if I were shaking hands with him. That had the psychological effect of telling him I wasn't worrying about my hooks, so why should he? Or course, I knew that most people dreaded gripping that cold hunk of steel the first time and I could hardly blame them, so I was always careful to make that first handshake as casual, informal and friendly as possible.

Then there was the cigaret gag. That was invariably good for a laugh. Whenever I'd walk into a restaurant, bar, or party I'd whip out a pack of butts, open it ostentatiously, take one, light it and sit back puffing on it contentedly. That almost always attracted attention. People would stare and I could almost hear them saying, My! Isn't it wonderful what he can do with a pair of hooks? Whenever anyone commented on this accomplishment I'd smile and say, "There's one thing I never have to worry about. That's burning my fingers." Corny, I know, but a sure icebreaker. . . .

It wasn't long before my plan paid off. I soon found people were taking me and my hooks for granted. There would be that first shocked moment of confusion and bewilderment. Then I'd throw my hook out, we'd shake, I'd pull one of my gags and everybody would laugh. From then on everything would go smoothly [pp. 166–167].

The difference between these two episodes has snowballing effects. In the first, Russell felt ashamed and expected others to be revolted and to pity. He behaved accordingly, guiltily hiding his hooks, etc. And the events that followed bore out his expectations. Others did feel embarrassed; others did shy away from his hooks. In the second, Russell had made important headway in accepting his disability. He had already found out that he could talk and think about his handicap without feeling self-conscious or ashamed. Believing this, he could expect others to begin to accept his hooks; it thus made sense for him to try to put others at ease. And again the events that followed bore out his expectations. People began to take his hooks for granted. In both episodes, the social reality fulfilled Russell's expectations *as much because Russell's behavior helped form that reality as because he was set to interpret the behavior of others in certain ways.*

We should note once again that though expectations and self-regard have such a directive role, they do not control all social reality. Russell, no matter how good he felt about himself, perceived "that first shocked moment of confusion and bewilderment," for example.

This discussion of expectations and social reality brings us to several comments regarding adjustive relationships between a person with a disability and those around him. If, as there is a good reason to believe, the so-called nondisabled hold both positive and negative attitudes toward persons with disability, the positive attitudes will more readily be aroused when the person has accepted his disability and believes that others can accept it too.

It may happen that a well-adjusted person, in not looking for rejections, may not see the rejection that actually exists. But this unawareness need not be unfortunate. As Ichheiser (*1949*) has put it, it is highly probable that certain illusions possess a positive function and value. It remains a question whether all human relations would always operate more smoothly or with greater satisfaction if they were altogether free of illusions. In not seeing the rejection, the person may behave in ways more attuned to the positive chord in another and thus fan the "pilot light of the flame of love." Should the rejection be so strong as eventually to come through, the person's hurt would have a different quality from that which is heaped upon self-rejection. It might be a hurt of sorrow that others are unjust or do not understand him, or that certain activities and relationships are denied him, but it would not be a hurt that, indeed, he himself is to be rejected. At the end of his life story Russell (*1949*) states:

> People like to feel sorry for me. I suppose that's only natural, too. Once it used to bother me but it doesn't any more. It isn't important now what or how anyone feels about my being without hands. The only thing that matters is that I've learned to live without them and that I have mastered my handicap, instead of letting it master me [pp. 278–279].

Expectations concerning the attitudes of others toward oneself are crucial in the perception of those attitudes. To go one step further, the self-concept is crucial in determining those expectations. The self-concept is psychologically of such great importance that it can hardly be over-stressed, though to be sure other factors, such as environmental conditions and the actual attitudes of others, must not be understressed.

In the following chapter, the significance of the self-concept during the adolescent period is discussed, especially as it relates to physique and disability.

Chapter 8

The Adolescent with a Physical Disability

THERE ARE SEVERAL REASONS WHY THE PERIOD OF ADOLESCENCE DE-serves special consideration. First, it is a period during which the self-concept undergoes important changes. Secondly, physique plays an especially prominent part in this new look at the self; it assumes a high position on the status value gradient and a close connection with the self (see pp. 148–153). Thirdly, the psychological situation of the adolescent can be dynamically represented as overlapping both childhood and adult-hood, an overlap similar to that involving minority groups (p. 16).

HEIGHTENED IMPORTANCE OF PHYSIQUE DURING ADOLESCENCE

There are many reasons why physique is intimately bound up with re-formation of the self-concept during adolescence.

1. The striking physical changes of adolescence bring about a change in what others permit and expect of the young person. This may be illustrated by the expectations of parents and teachers for two pairs of girls, each pair consisting of girls who differ greatly in physical maturity (Barker, *et al., 1953*:30–33). Though of the same chronological age (13–14 years), one girl of each pair appeared to be a fully developed teenager, dressing accordingly, whereas the other looked like a child of 10 or so. The parents and teachers of each girl were asked to judge which of a list of activities (e.g., buy dress by self) they considered proper for the girl. The physically more mature girl of each pair was judged to be mature enough for adultlike activities more frequently than the physically less mature girl even though each pair of girls was in the same grade, of the same mental age, and came from the same socioeconomic background.

2. The young person looks at his physique in the new light of sex appropriateness. Not only do the more purely biological urges contribute to this awareness, but the values of society also bring tremendous pressure on the young person to examine himself in terms of the criteria of his sex role. Particularly during adolescence, these criteria follow rigid standards

as to what the feminine and masculine model should be. Marriage and children are deeply ingrained values of society and, in fact, are often necessary passports to full adult status. Small wonder, then, that the adolescent as he grows into adulthood keeps testing himself as to whether he can make the grade. His final score requires not one look at the self but many, as each experience with members of the opposite sex is assessed. The status value of physique assumes tremendous potency because of its identification with rigid and idealized notions of what is admissible to each sex. In one study, two thirds of the adolescent boys who were dissatisfied with their physiques were troubled with aspects that the authors describe as "sexually inappropriate," e.g., development around the nipple area, size of genitals, scanty pubic hair, fat hips, and facial blemishes (Stolz and Stolz, *1944*).

In the following personal account, the impact of sex appropriateness on the adolescent's evaluation of a physical trait and of himself as a person is dramatically clear. What had been a disturbing fact became a source of pride at the very moment that its significance changed from sexually inappropriate to ideally befitting the sex-role aspirations of the subject:

All through my grade school years, I was the tallest in the class, and, as a matter of fact, was rather proud of it. However, the summer before I entered Junior High School at the age of thirteen, I grew to just an inch below my present five-feet-eight. I towered above every girl and boy in our class; and it seemed to me that I was the tallest girl in the world. *None of my family's comforting words made it easier for me to walk across the room at school.* In high school, two girls taller than I entered the class. *But they weren't in our crowd,* so I continued to feel like a giraffe when I went out with the girls. I suppose the fact that several of the boys grew to six-footers helped dispel that shrinking feeling. But the crowning touch came in the spring of my junior year. The school paper published a list of characteristics of a composite "Ideal Girl." Lo and behold, my name was listed after "Ideal Height." I haven't felt too tall since [Sherif and Cantril, *1947*:228].[1]

It has been concluded that once the boy feels accepted as a man and the girl as a woman, they "become more stable and predictable. Teachers and parents say they have 'settled down'" (Sherif and Cantril, *1947*:237). Such acceptance is often not the smooth consequence of natural development we would like it to be. Doubts in the area of sexual adequacy are kept actively astir by the rigid standards of what constitutes appropriate physique, by the preconceived notions as to what the sexual relationship ought to be, by the necessity for postponing marriage long after sexual

---

[1] Reprinted with permission from M. Sherif and H. Cantril, *The Psychology of Ego Involvements,* copyright 1947, John Wiley & Sons, Inc.

maturity, and by the fact that *any* real or imagined physical deviation readily becomes the scapegoat for all personal difficulties.

3. Physique affects the new self-look during adolescence in yet another way. Unlike the younger child, the adolescent tends to regard his physique as the final edition of himself. He certainly is aware of physical decline with age, but that indefinite future is unrelated to his present state. He now is grown up, in the prime of life, and his physical equipment is the best that he can hope for. On the other hand, the child, realizing that he is growing and therefore changing, can more readily discount an unpleasant body image as a temporary imposition and look toward a more suitable physique that the benevolent future will bestow. The child's perceptions are, in fact, more amenable to the influence of wishes on the "level of irreality" than are the adult's (Lewin, *1936:*204). Carlson (*1941*), who was born with severe spasticity, recalls that as a child "I formed a passionate faith that a . . . miracle would be achieved when I grew up: that halting feet, shaking head, writhing arms and legs, and troubled speech would all be healed" (p. 19). But as an adolescent ". . . I became so self-conscious about my handicaps. . . . For the first time the realization that I was different from other people sank home" (p. 22).[2] The immutability of physique has the important effect of placing physique close to the self on the self-connection gradient, thereby giving to it a commanding role in the process of reëvaluation of the self during adolescence.

It has been pointed out that, through the convenient mechanism of displacement, somatic defects can be made the scapegoat of all adjustive difficulties and the causes of all anxiety feelings regardless of their original source. Because physique becomes a prominent and important characteristic during adolescence, it may very well fulfill this scapegoat function with surprising uniformity.

Although physique carries a particularly heavy emotional loading during adolescence, it is not correct to conclude that any single physical deviation will invariably *or even probably* produce distress. "The psychological consequences of deviation will depend on 'social and individual attitudes toward non-conformity,' the strength of intrinsic attitudes of self-acceptance and the possession of compensatory assets" (Ausubel, *1952:*102),[3] as well as the meaning of that particular deviation for the individual. To give a concrete example of the individuality of reaction to deviation, we again refer to the study of adolescents by Stolz and Stolz. Of the seven boys who were concerned about their shortness, four were

[2] By permission from E. R. Carlson, *Born That Way*, copyright 1941, The John Day Company, publisher.

[3] D. P. Ausubel, *Ego Development and the Personality Disorders*, 1952. By permission of Grune and Stratton, publishers.

actually among the shortest 15 percent of the 92 boys all through the adolescent period. But there were five other boys in the same short group who gave no evidence of being disturbed about it. And two of the seven were as tall as 20 percent of the total group (Stolz and Stolz, *1944:*87). This is one important reason why studies that correlate variations in physique such as size, strength, and attractiveness with adjustment measures almost invariably yield but slight, if any, relationship (Barker *et al., 1953:* Chap II). ". . . the reader should remember that just what the meaning of variation in somatic conditions will be to any boy or any girl can only be determined by a study of the individual" (Stolz and Stolz, *1944:*80).

OVERLAPPING SITUATIONS IN ADOLESCENCE

"In American society there is a child culture and an adult culture. There are ways and goals of behaving that are accepted as appropriate for children, and quite different ways and goals of behaving that are considered appropriate for adults. Correct ways for children to eat, sleep, dress, talk, and work, for example, differ in many respects from the ways that are correct for adults" (Barker *et al., 1953:*28). During the transitional period of adolescence the individual may be described as being in an overlapping situation, being a child on the one hand and an adult on the other.[4]

Uneven physical maturity, conflict between giving up the comforts of dependency and attaining adult status with its widening horizons, plus ambivalent adult attitudes toward the child's ambiguous status—these factors and others contribute to the stress of the overlapping situations in which the young person finds himself. Inconsistency in adolescent behavior not infrequently occurs because sometimes the determinants of adult behavior and sometimes the determinants of childish behavior win out. When the person cannot satisfy both his childish and more mature intentions at the same time, there is the likelihood that anxiety, frustration, and heightened emotionality will ensue. Also, the uncertainty of the adolescent's role may lead to exaggeration either of adult behavior or of the childish component, whichever is deemed the most valuable at the particular time. Not all overlapping situations lead to disruptive behavior, however, since it is possible for behavior appropriate to each to be compatible. This is seen, for example, in the adolescent who plays childish games (child situation) with the small boy left in his charge (adult situation).

---

[4] For a systematic account of the properties of overlapping situations and the consequent behavior in adolescence see Barker *et al.* (*1953:*37–45).

The concept of the overlapping situation has been found useful to describe not only the psychological world of the adolescent but also, as we have seen, that of the person with a disability who is exposed to the pressures of what may be called the "disabled determiners" of behavior and "normal determiners" of behavior (see p. 16). Where these determiners are incompatible, then inconsistent, emotional, and exaggerated behavior can be expected to result, depending on the particular constellation of forces. For example, a person with impaired hearing may show inconsistencies in his use of a hearing aid when he wants on the one hand to act as though he were nondisabled (normal determiners) and yet also to wear his prosthesis in order to participate in conversation (disabled determiners). Emotion may be expressed in the aversion a person feels toward his braces. And exaggerated behavior may be evidenced when a person with a wooden leg refuses help in situations of ordinary courtesy. We have used the verb "may" here because the same overt behavior may be due to divergent factors. Thus, help may be refused in situations of ordinary courtesy, not necessarily because of the operation of conflicting overlapping situations but because the person may want to take every opportunity to learn on his own.

For an adolescent with a disability, two of the more lasting and problematic kinds of overlapping situations will be those due (1) to the operation of "child" and "adult" determiners of behavior and (2) to the operation of "normal" and "disabled" determiners. The following two incidents are taken from the autobiography of Frances Warfield (*1948*), who, it may be recalled, struggled against a progressive hearing loss throughout her adolescence. The first is an example of overlapping situations in which child and adult determiners of behavior operate at the same time; the "adult" situation representing freedom and independence is clearly positive, the "child" situation clearly negative. The resulting behavior is an exaggeration of behavior symbolic of adulthood. The incident took place when Frances was visiting England upon graduation from college:

I began going alone around London, poised and journalistic, I and my one-dollar Certificate of Newspaper Credentials. Anna Mary [a college-mate] was jealous. If only she had a job ahead, she grumbled. If only she could be free and independent, as I was, to go around having adventures.

I loitered at No. 10 Downing Street, and was rewarded by a glimpse of the Prime Minister. Paying tribute to the Peter Pan statue in Kensington Gardens, I saw a man who might well have been Sir James M. Barrie. I walked up to the bar in a pub in Hammersmith and ordered Guinness because I'd read it was the ruin and solace of London charwomen. *It was dark, sickish stuff, but I forced it down, feeling every inch a roving journalist, smoking a Gold Flake cigarette.* That was the first time in my life I ever smoked a cigarette in public, though, like all my friends, I had been smoking surreptitiously for several years. Just imagine Aunt May's and Aunt Harriet's faces if they could have seen me standing in a London pub drinking Guinness and smoking a cigarette! Judas Priest. I was so tickled that on the way home I stopped in a swank shop in Bond Street and bought myself a small pipe [pp. 72–73, italics added).[5]

In the next example, the overlapping situations are directly related to Frances' disability. It is during adolescence that the conflict between the "normal-disability" determiners of behavior often becomes acute, for it is during this period that physique tends not only to assume a heightened importance but also to become rigidly standardized as to what constitutes appropriateness. As a person in the "disabled" situation, Frances should say, "What? Speak a little louder, please." As a person in the "normal" situation, she should carry on a smooth conversation. But Frances at this time in her life was both kinds of people. Though the former was negative and the latter positive, Frances' physical status did not permit her to act in accord with the normal determiners of behavior to the exclusion of the disabled determiners. Instead, the behavior required by each of the situations was modified by the other, resulting in such "solutions" as dominating the conversation and double-talk. Notice, too, the manifestations of emotionality resulting from the conflicting situations. Frances is now 14:

I had learned by experience to do all the talking when I walked along the street with a boy. Indoors I could keep voices raised by playing the victrola; outdoors I was in danger of missing what was said. I always walked fast, rattling on at random, trusting to luck that when a boy wanted to ask me to a dance he'd call me on the telephone.

But this time my tongue was tied—transfixed between fear that Roger was going to ask me to the dance (he'd be sure to mumble) and fear that he had already asked Pamela.

He said, "Hello." We scuffed along in silence. My heart jolted against my red sweater and my ears set up such a roaring that I couldn't have heard a fire alarm at ten paces. When we reached my gate, Roger asked me a question. It might have been about algebra. It might have been about football, fudge, or fiddlesticks. It might have been about going to the dance.

I opened my mouth but nothing came of it. What could I say? I certainly wasn't going to say "What?" Well, hardly. And risk the Seven Deadly Words? Risk having a boy—and Roger Evans of all boys—jeer, "What's the matter— cotton in your ears?"

Mentally I ran through my standard dodges—feeling faint, being absent-minded, and so on. They wouldn't do. A big dance was at stake. And I couldn't just stand there.

[5] F. Warfield, *Cotton in My Ears*, New York, Viking Press, Inc. Copyright 1948 by Frances Warfield. Used with permission of Viking Press, Inc.

I swung the gate back and forth. Suddenly I exclaimed, "Wrinkelohwrinkelletdownyourhair!" [Wrinkel was an imaginary childhood companion that always came to Frances' aid.]

"Say, what kind of lingo's that?" Roger demanded.

"Wrinkelingo."

"What's wrinkelingo?"

"Wrinkeli wrinkelthink wrinkelyou wrinkelare wrinkela wrinkelprune," I improvised glibly.

"Come again?"

I repeated it, swinging the gate confidently.

"Wrinkelprune yourself, smarty," he said.

"Yah, wrinkelsap." I swung the gate to and started up the walk.

Roger telephoned that evening and wrinkelasked me to the wrinkeldance [pp. 24–25].

The adolescent with a disability, then, has to cope with two kinds of persisting overlapping situations, that owing to his disability and that owing to his transitional status as a child-adult. The conflicting nature of the former will be reduced in frequency and intensity to the extent that the person has stripped his disability of shame and inferiority. It may then exist as being imposed from the outside, in which case the rebellion is against those forces instead of against the self.

The overlapping situation of childhood and adulthood may persist beyond the usual span of years, and in fact may recur as more than one episode in the lifetime of an individual. Whenever the individual is pulled, in crucial situations that are more than fleeting phases, by both the emotional patterns of childhood and those of mature adult self-responsibility, he is caught up by the need for reëvaluation of the self typical of the adolescent.

Moreover, whenever the "rites" of adulthood are denied or postponed (as may occur where a disability exists), the adolescent marginal position tends to persist. In very simple societies children have completed their acceptance of themselves and their roles in life by the time they are 6 or 7 and then must simply wait for physical maturity to assume a complete role (Mead, *1949:*361). In our society, the status of full adulthood is generally withheld until the advent of two outstanding circumstances: economic independence and marriage. For some individuals, additional accomplishments are necessary before they and others accept their claim to full adult status: parenthood, being a property owner, admission to a fraternal order, and other symbolic attainments fall in this class. For others, no matter how many symbolic prerequisites are attained, the dependency relationship between parent and child is never outgrown and consequently they do not *feel* adult. The establishment of a separate household, so much the American ideal, is the outward sign that the person has assumed the responsibilities of marriage, has become economically self-sufficient, and has become emotionally independent of parental authority.

Where circumstances prolong the period of economic dependence, postpone marriage, or disallow sufficient emotional separation from the parent, then the position of the individual as an adult, no matter what his age, is apt to be tenuous and, like that of the adolescent, marginal between adulthood and childhood. He may well continue to experience conflicts with parental authority resulting from such marginality, to feel devaluated as an incomplete adult, and to show inconsistent, exaggerated, and emotional behavior typical of conflicting overlapping situations. It may very well be that the fact of disability in many cases tends to prolong the adolescent period.

THE ADOLESCENT PEER GROUP

The discrepancy in the perception of adults and adolescents concerning the appropriateness of adult and child determiners of behavior in different situations is one of the keys to the understanding of the tremendous importance that the peer culture assumes during adolescence. The adolescent often regards the adult as being the barrier to his attaining the status of full adulthood. Until recently, in the adult-dominated world of school and home, he may have enjoyed the privileges of being an older and more responsible *child,* whereas now his self-esteem may be shaken by those same adults with whom he has no standing as an adult.

The simplest type of negative response to the perceived agents of frustration is direct aggression. "Hence arise hostile and defiant attitudes towards adults and adult authority, contempt for adult goals and values, and cynical philosophies of life" (Ausubel, *1952:*93). But the adolescent does not generally have the inner fortitude to carry on the attack by himself. Moreover, his deflated ego as a marginal adult needs propping up. The necessary support is found in the adolescent peer culture. "Through the force of numbers, precedent and organized resistance, it is able to protect the individual adolescent from excessive encroachments of adult authority" (Ausubel, *1952:*94). And "through its power to confer recognition and prestige, it provides a rich compensatory source of status which is partially capable of restoring damaged ego adequacy" (Ausubel, *1952:*93).

The demands for conformity of dress, behavior, and speech by adolescents have been commented upon by many authorities. These demands serve to delineate the group from both adults and children and to produce a group solidarity that may be helpful in the search for self-assertion and independence. The adolescent peer culture can provide strength and comfort to the adolescent who is a part of it. It also is a source of distress for the individual who strives to join but cannot either because he is rejected by the "gang" or because of inhibitions within himself. We do not know how many adolescents are outcasts, but probably many if not most adolescents for shorter or longer periods of time during these maturing years experience the loneliness of not fitting anywhere. If rather strict conformity to the adolescent fashions is a necessity, it is not difficult for *any* adolescent to notice some way in which he deviates. It might also seem, therefore, that the young person with an obvious disability is at a disadvantage in becoming part of a peer group. Unfortunately there are as far as we know no systematic data concerning membership in peer groups, either for adolescents with disabilities or for those without.

There is one experiment on deviation and rejection that is pertinent though it does not deal with *physical* deviation (Schachter, *1951*). The problem concerned the reaction of a group to the deviation of a member from the group norms, the deviation being in one case relevant to the group's purposes and in the second case irrelevant. Cohesiveness of the group also was varied. The experimental design itself is a good example of controlled research that at the same time is suggestive for experimental application to problems involving physical disability and will therefore be reported in detail here:

The experiment was conducted as the first meeting of a club. Four types of clubs were set up, each representing a different degree and combination of cohesiveness and relevance. In each club, paid participants deviated from or conformed to an experimentally created group standard. Discussion in each club was systematically observed. At the end of each meeting members were nominated for committees, and sociometric rankings of persons whom the subject would like to have remain in the club were filled out. These served as measures of rejection.

The four types of clubs set up were case-study, movie, editorial, and radio clubs. The first two were highly cohesive groups, being made up of students who were interested in them; whereas the latter two were low-cohesion groups, comprising students who showed little or no interest in joining them. There was a total of 32 clubs, eight of each type. Each club had from five to seven members and three paid participants who were perceived as fellow club members. All the subjects in the clubs were male college students.

In a typical meeting, each club member read a short version of the life history of a juvenile delinquent that ended as he was awaiting sentence for a minor crime. The leader of the club, in all instances the experimenter, asked the members to discuss and decide the question, "What should be done with this kid?" This question was relevant to the announced functions of the case-study and editorial clubs, but irrelevant to the movie and radio clubs.

The discussion was guided by a 7-point scale ordered along a love-punishment dimension that was made up of alternative suggestions as to ways of handling the delinquent. It was introduced to the club members as a convenient device for learning everyone's position and for channelizing discussion.

The case was written sympathetically to ensure that there would be a deviate position. In all clubs almost all members chose positions on the scale emphasizing love and kindness (positions 2–4), and the deviate chose the position of extreme discipline (position 7). After reading the case, each club member announced the position on the scale that he had chosen. Then came the three paid participants. The "deviate" chose a position of extreme deviation and maintained it throughout the discussion; the second, the "mode," chose and maintained the modal position of group opinion; and the third, the "slider," chose the position of extreme deviation but allowed himself gradually to be influenced, so that at the end of the discussion he was at the modal position.

The discussion, limited to 45 minutes, was largely a matter of thrashing out differences of opinion among club members. After 20 minutes, the leader took a census to ensure that everyone was fully aware of everyone else's position, and did so again at the end of the discussion. Then the leader turned the discussion to the future of the club. At this time the committee nomination blanks and sociometric questionnaires were filled out.

The finding most pertinent in our context is that the deviate—namely, the person who took an opposing position and maintained it in the face of increased efforts on the part of the group to change his position—was rejected in all experimental conditions. The rejection was less in the groups in which the task was irrelevant and the group cohesiveness was low. The deviate was rejected more strongly than the "mode" (the person who took the typical position of the group) and more strongly than the "slider," the person who started with a deviate position and shifted under persuasion to the modal position. The sociometric data revealed that the deviate was nominated for undesirable committee jobs rather than for desirable committee jobs. This could mean that the deviate is seen as less desirable as a group member and less competent as an officer than either the "mode" or the "slider."

This type of experiment should be carried out with physical disability as the deviation, since it is not possible to equate a physical deviation that is by nature unchangeable with an attitude deviation perceived as being capable of change by persuasion or other means. In such an experiment, the variable, relevancy, could be manipulated by the type of club used. A sports or social club of adolescents in the relevant case and an editorial club in the irrelevant case would permit the physical factor to be used as an independent variable. One could postulate that the results would show that, as in Schachter's experiments, rejection by the group of a person with a physical deviation is not all-pervasive and indiscriminate but is experienced most strongly in that group in which ideal physique is most relevant. Such a finding would support the personal experiences recounted by adolescents with disabilities who bring out that they suffer rejection most keenly in matters of courtship and marriage—i.e., the interpersonal relationship *par excellence* where conformity to standards is felt to be essential.

A careful analysis of several autobiographies of persons with disabilities (Baker, *1946;* Brown, *1955;* Carlson, *1941;* Criddle, *1953;* Goldman, *1947;* Ohnstad, *1942;* Viscardi, *1952*) strongly suggests that the conforming demands of the adolescent can make allowances for physical deviations in many kinds of group situations. In only one of the seven accounts did the adolescent lack group companionship, and that was the case of Christy Brown (*1955*) who was profoundly incapacitated physically because of cerebral palsy. Each of the other personal documents reports a good deal of activity at work and at play with other young people.

Yet these accounts also reveal a deep and sometimes overwhelming loneliness. Each of the adolescents had to face and in some way to cope with the rigid conformity demanded in the vital area of sex appropriateness. These young people were lonely not because of the lack of friends, but because they could not share in the attachments of boy-girl relationships. The conviction that they could never enter the adult estate of courtship and marriage dawned at adolescence and did not disappear until the horizons widened to include other values besides physical conformity as criteria for sex appropriateness.

The pattern of adequate companionship along with frustrating boy-girl relationships repeats itself in these personal documents. Carlson (*1941*), a severe spastic, had three faithful friends with whom he played and studied. He did not lack companionship, but he did miss social life and the feeling of manliness thereby denied him. It was not until his middle twenties that he enjoyed "a great increased sense of personal worth, thanks to having won the affection of a girl for the first time in my life" (p. 71).[6] And the feeling of being part of the community of men was his also for the first time: "He who has thought of himself as being cut off from the rest of mankind by his handicap suddenly discovers that the barrier has vanished, and he idealizes the girl who has released him from isolation" (p. 71). Even young Louise Baker (*1946*), a vivacious and popular girl with one leg, who was president of one group or another twelve times before she was graduated from high school, suffered the frustration of believing herself "all wrong" and unwanted because she

[6] Quotations from Earl R. Carlson, *Born That Way,* 1941, by permission of The John Day Company, publishers.

"knew" that she could never get a husband (though subsequently she did, and more than once).

There is, however, no systematic evidence to indicate that young persons with disabilities have more troubles in heterosexual adjustments than other young people. Landis and Bolles' study (*1942*), discussed earlier in a different connection, is the most systematic in this area. It investigated specifically the psychosexual development of women with physical handicaps as compared with physically normal women. The subjects were 17 to 30 years of age. Ratings were made on the basis of controlled interviews. On the characteristics listed below, the group with handicaps differed from the normal groups:

	Handicapped	Percentage of Physically Normal
First knowledge of sex differences before age 6	11	33
Complete sex information before age 15	11	26
Little or no preparation for menstruation	78	55
No history of masturbation	74	50
Extremely close to family	23	3
No evidence of homoerotic behavior	23	8
Never been in love	30	3
Never had dates with boys	28	1
First date before age 16	18	52
No evidence of masculine protest	43	26
Recalled a desire to be a boy in childhood	43	69
Attitude of disgust toward sex	7	21

Source: Adapted and abridged from Landis and Bolles (*1942*), p. 154.

From these and related data the authors conclude that, in comparison with physically normal women, those with physical handicaps are less autoerotic, are emotionally more dependent on their families, are less homoerotic, have fewer heterosexual contacts, give less evidence of masculine protest, have equal narcissism, and are less emotional about sex in general. These findings may shed some light on the fact that the blind adolescents in Sommers' study (*1944*) were no more concerned about finding a boy or girl friend than were the seeing controls. Even though the Landis and Bolles women with physical handicaps were slower in dating and falling in love than were their normal controls, they also were less emotional about sex in general and in some ways had fewer knots to untie, such as autoeroticism, homoeroticism, and masculine protest.

In sum, autobiographical accounts indicate that, during adolescence, persons with disabilities experience trying times in heterosexual adjustments but evidently this is equally true of adolescents in general. We are forced to conclude that there are many, many factors that enter into the creation and resolution of problems; that though physical deviation may not be the least of these factors, neither is it the greatest; and that some factors may balance out others in the resultant effect on heterosexual adjustments. The adolescent with a disability who is convinced that his difficulties in forming boy-girl attachments would be obliterated were it not for his disability would do well to realize that many if not all adolescents have problems in this area which may be no lighter than his own.

The knowledge that "someday you will meet the person meant for you," as Russell Criddle's (1953) mother often repeated, may be of small comfort to the adolescent who needs reassurance now, whose personal experiences spell a different conclusion, and for whom rigid standards of sex appropriateness are part of his own values. Yet, even though knowledge may offer little conscious support, it may become part of a subconscious sustaining repertoire, drawn and leaned upon as needed, and therefore ought to be made available to the young person. He should know that physical conformity will not always remain so important a criterion for sex appropriateness. He should know that, for most persons with physical disabilities, courtship and marriage are not forever closed, though they may have to be delayed.

Such data as the following may speak louder than words: In one study of almost 2000 employees with various disabilities, the marital status was reported as follows (Brighouse, 1946):

Type of Handicap	Percentage Married	
	Males	Females
Auditory	69	51
Cardiac	62	60
Hernias	78	
Orthopedic	52	52
Respiratory	53	57
Visual	64	54
Multiple	68	52
All physically handicapped	61	55
Physically normal control group	71	49

In another study on the personal and social adjustment of more than 400 former poliomyelitis patients whose present ages were 16 to 42 years, about 28 percent of the men and 41 percent of the women were either married or actively contemplating marriage (Lowman, C. L., as reported in Barker *et al., 1953:*130–131). The percentage of persons with varying degrees of disability among those married and among those unmarried was:

	Married	Unmarried
Very apparent	34	55
Moderately or slightly apparent	34	40
Not apparent or no deformity	32	6

Both sets of data show that heterosexual adjustment is within the realistic outlook for persons who have a disability. Although there is some relation between severity or apparency of disability and marriage, the relationship is not strong.

Where the nature of the disability, however, is of such proportions that the probability of marriage is very remote, the person himself has time to absorb this realization, and to go on from there. Christy Brown (*1955*), for example, the boy severely affected with cerebral palsy, recalls his adolescence as mostly being a series of frustrations. He was terribly lonely, and his life seemed without purpose or worth. He loved a girl and then another, but of this he could only dream and never really partake. These experiences, however, were not pervasive. Other experiences enabled him to scale the high walls that were still around him and, as he achieved some degree of physical independence, encouragement to write, and understanding from those who listened to him and respected him as a person, his old bitterness changed to an acceptance. In his account, published when he was 22 years of age, Christy Brown notes:

. . . I wanted so desperately to love and be loved, but—it was a bitter realization, but a true one, a necessary one. What good would it do me if I were to shut my eyes and turn my back on every unpleasant fact about myself? I was tempted to do that many times, but I was only putting off the final ordeal a little longer; it had to come sometime. It came: it made me sad, bitter for a time, but in the end it also made me stronger within myself. If I could never really be like other people, then at least I would be like myself and make the best of it [p. 128].[7]

At the time of the writing, Christy Brown had not achieved the adult

[7] Christy Brown, *My Left Foot.* Simon and Schuster, Inc., 1955. By permission.

prerequisites of economic independence and marriage. That this will protract the adolescent situation of being neither a child nor an adult is quite certain. That this will maintain his present conviction that he will "never be a normal individual leading a normal life" (p. 128) may very well be. And yet, it is also certain that Christy, as he continues to integrate his experiences within reëvaluations of the importance of things and the values in life, will continue to realize that "it was this very affliction, which I regarded in my worst moment as a curse from God, that was to bring a strange beauty into my life" (p. 124).

The adolescent who does not have age-mate companionship, whether he has a handicap or not, needs help in providing opportunity for such relationships. The crucial questions must uncover reasons for the isolation. Sometimes the basic causes may be removed from any physical disability itself, as when the individual withdraws within himself and does not welcome other children, or when geographic distance acts as a barrier to ready companionship. Sometimes the effects of a disability may directly act as a deterrent, as in the case of severe physical dependence, where the child is for the most part homebound, or in the case of a young person who avoids social relationships because of deep shame over his disability. The steps taken to ameliorate the situation in each of these instances will obviously be different.

Undoubtedly, data will eventually show large variations in adolescent peer life among the group with disabilities as well as among the group without. Probably most adolescents, for one reason or another and for briefer or longer duration, experience the gnawing feelings of loneliness. Assuredly, not all persons need to feel part of a sizable group to satisfy the need for support and companionship. One friend may be sufficient. Finally, it is likely that the adolescent with a disability is able to find age-mate companionship more easily than to establish his status as a man or woman. Evidently, a physical deviation need not threaten the peer group in its supportive and status-giving functions, even though it may threaten role suitability for marriage.

THE CASE OF RUSSELL CRIDDLE:
AN ADOLESCENT WITH A DISABILITY

Let us examine in some detail the adolescence of Russell Criddle (1953), who traces with utmost sincerity the course his disability took in the adolescent search for self-respect and independence against opposing forces. The vision of this boy, you may recall, became so seriously impaired at the age of 12 that he could not see to count his fingers at more than 2 feet in a good light, and in order to read ordinary print had to bring the book to within 2 inches of his eyes. Legally he was declared blind. During the next 17 years, when his vision was temporarily restored by a corneal graft, he fought a constant battle against being what people thought a blind person should be—namely, thoroughly incapacitated, overprotected, and ineligible as a marriage partner.

In the narration, the following significant points are detectable: (1) As Criddle's physique took on new meanings in adolescence, his self-concept became altered too. The processes of differentiation and integration are seen throughout these reëvaluating years. (2) Criddle was by no means an isolate. He had friends to play with and to study with. (3) Yet he often knew a deep loneliness. In his preadolescence, this was felt when his disability kept him from participating in group activities. During his adolescent years, the loneliness became more firmly welded into the conviction that he could not secure the affection of a girl. (4) He had contact with girls, but except for short-lived and tenuous emotional ties, the relationships were (until his middle twenties) strictly "at a distance." (5) Like other adolescents, he rebelled against adult—particularly parental—authority, and had his teen-age gang with whom to rebel. (6) But in his struggle to meet the conflicting demands of the "normal" and "disabled" overlapping situations he was on his own for the most part. His mother was a source of comfort, but "solutions" evolved directly from his own experiences. (7) Two main factors combined to protract Russell Criddle's position as an adolescent. The first of these was the girl problem, which denied him the status of a suitor and eventual husband. The second was his extended economic dependence on his family, brought about by the depression years and exacerbated by his disability.

The following account is divided into age groupings that span significant changes in Criddle's life.

Age 12–13. This was the period of Criddle's initial adjustment to his disability and reinstatement, to some extent, with his gang. He did not think of himself as tragic, for he had his mother's assurance, supported by childhood's belief in the future, that his eyes would get better. But the months following his accident had been lonely months. The fellows had come around often at first, but after a while their visits dwindled until the older boys seldom came at all.

Soon he came face to face with the awful social consequences of blindness when he was openly rejected by his gang. From then on he denied that he was blind, though he was willing to admit that his eyes were bad, for blindness meant to him exclusion, dependency, and inferiority.

Criddle was correct in believing that the overlapping situations of normality and disability were not as incompatible as the stereotype of blindness would make them. But he was not correct in believing that in the long run the incompatibility would be obliterated by attempts to conceal and even deny the latter and "acting as if" he were fully a part of the former. This solution, "acting as if," begun early in his career as a person with a disability, persisted for almost a decade until the wisdom of experience thrust upon him the folly of his pretense.

Criddle did become reinstated with the gang as a result of his own perseverance and the support of the gang leader, who ruled, "As long as you got guts you're still a member, even if you are blind" (p. 21).

The initial, almost complete isolation gave way to a fair amount of group participation:

> . . . I can remember sliding down a steep clay bank that provided a ten-foot chute into the river [with the other fellows]. . . .
> I was the bat boy at ball games, though we only had one bat. I can remember hanging by my heels from the high strut of a billboard, in a game of follow-the-leader. I was the only one in the gang who could hang by his heels.
> We played hide-and-seek. I could hide but I couldn't seek, so I gave the last one caught before me the privilege and pleasure of giving me ten punches in the arm, in exchange for his taking "it" for me [p. 31].[8]

There were other occasions, and frequent ones, however, when Criddle felt alone and out of things:

> . . . there were the long, lonely hours, too, while the gang was playing some game I could not join in. I never resented their playing in the woods, or going fishing, or doing any of the hundreds of things I could not do without spoiling their play. I learned to be realistic and to play by myself while I waited out the hours and days between games I could take part in [pp. 31–32].

With respect to his family, Criddle sensed the sympathy and understanding of his mother and in turn loved her deeply. Throughout this period and those to follow, she helped him extend his space of free movement in spite of pressures from the community to overprotect and inhibit him. Other forces worked at sharpening the incompatibility between the overlapping situations of normality and disability. His mother worked toward destroying the incompatibility:

> Mother knew what I sensed. That the difference between not being able to see and not being blind was in not being what people thought a blind person should be. She had a problem, too, in not being what mothers of blind children should be. The neighborhood felt that she was being criminally negligent

---

[8] Reprinted from *Love Is Not Blind* by Russell Criddle. By permission of W. W. Norton & Company, Inc. Copyright 1953 by Russell Criddle.

in the way she allowed me to go about, playing, swimming, crossing streets, and all, and they were not reluctant to tell her so. "If that boy gets killed," I heard one irate neighbor say, "his death will be on your hands."

"I know," Mother answered quietly, "and if he doesn't, his life will be on my hands. I must let him live, don't you understand? Bad eyes don't make a boy into an old man" [p. 36].

Criddle's father provided for the family, but otherwise during this early period entered little into his son's life. The two brothers were enough younger to have their own gangs and Criddle did not often join them.

Age 13–14. As a whole, this was a lonely year for Criddle. The other boys were at school, but no sight-saving classes were available and Criddle found "life in the world of adults unbearably lonely" (p. 46). Occasionally he still boxed, skated, and went swimming with the gang. Through his mother's efforts, he was able to get a newspaper route. Criddle recalls the affectionate relationships among the family members, and makes repeated reference in this and later years to his mother's wisdom in rearing a handicapped child.

Age 14–15. During this year Criddle became increasingly aware of girls as a special object of interest but had not yet fully realized the barrier character of his disability in this regard. This was his first year at a sight-saving school in a nearby community, which he attended until the age of 16. Evidently his days were well filled with the activities at school, but he refers very little to his peer life there. He did have his first "love affair" at this school with a girl two years his junior. When she confessed her love for another boy, Criddle did suffer intensely. But, because he still held the childish belief, inspired in part by his mother, that eventually he would be able to see as well as ever, he was able to assuage his ego by blaming his handicap. Moreover, during this early part of his adolescence, Red, a good friend and a physically unimpaired member of the gang, was no great shakes as a Don Juan either, and at social affairs outside of school "Red and I were quite satisfied both with the cool kisses that we got from the girls whenever one of them accidentally called our numbers [at kissing games], and with the necessity of going stag" (p. 52). Criddle also could chalk off his apparent lack of sex appeal to his relative youth.

Age 15–16. It was this year that brought about some of the most drastic changes in Criddle's concept of himself as an adolescent. His accustomed role as a child to be protected by his parents was jolted and the fear that he could never be loved by a girl descended upon him.

The rude awakening of a changed role between himself and his parents occurred when Criddle engaged in a boxing match with his father. This started as playful sparring and ended up as a serious battle for superiority, Criddle becoming the victor. With this incident the potency of his adult position greatly increased, and that of his child position weakened. The conflict over giving up personal security as the price of independence is clear:

> Bruised and horribly fatigued, I made my way to the old camp site. . . . The camp was gone, its ruins having been salvaged by another generation or another camp. It seemed to signify my lost childhood. I didn't want to have licked my father. I didn't want to lose the protection his superior strength had given me. I didn't want to grow up. I didn't want to know that now I no longer need obey him for fear of punishment. I didn't want to lose the protection of his authority over me. Now I was a man, but I no longer had him to go to, and I felt ashamed of the tears that burned on my battered face.
>
> I wanted to go to Mother, to have her nurse me as she always had, but when the fight was over she had run out of the front door from where she had been watching and had gone directly to Dad. She had disregarded me entirely, and I had to accept the fact that her first concern was for him rather than for me [pp. 60–61].

With the gradual estrangement between himself and his parents that grew in the succeeding years, Criddle increasingly needed affectional ties with a girl to fill the void. But the problem of girls, with which he had been so happily unconcerned, developed during this period into the anguished conviction that the love of a girl could never be for him. His earlier rationalizations no longer worked. The adolescent's regard of his physique as being the culmination of a series of changes prevented his seeking consolation in the hope of major improvement with his eyes. Repeated experiences of a subtle advance and a subtle rejection convinced him that he was an unwanted person in boy-girl relationships. Not so subtle rejections and the incident recorded earlier (see p. 4) made his conviction indelible, though his hope kept alive the remote possibility that he was wrong.

In coping with this conviction, Criddle began to reason that one need not have children and a wife to be happy, that in fact one could enjoy more of the "finer things of life" without the restrictions of a family. But again the rationalization proved but a shallow covering for the relentless yearnings underneath. The fact that he could not get a dance date still foretold a life of loneliness for which he saw no alternative. The close of this period sees the cementing of the irreversible connection between loneliness and celibacy. He could not peer into the future of more than ten years thence when physique would cease to be the all-important criterion of sex appropriateness, when he would have matured a little and girls would have matured a little, to make possible the fulfillment of his mother's repeated reassurances that someday he would meet the girl meant for him.

Yet, during this resigned 'oneliness, Criddle had friends. "Anywhere from six to ten boys used to gather in either Red's cellar or my sitting room, and spend an evening in good fellowship and sparring" (p. 58). As an antidote for his loneliness his father tried to help him ". . . by making me a man among his adult friends. He took me fishing a few times that summer and though I tried to pretend to like it, he knew that I was bored. He started playing checkers with me during the evenings that he was not working, and we would have a stein of beer with the game" (p. 57). His father's efforts offered little comfort, however, for besides being a poor substitute for the real thing, Criddle felt that his father resented him because of his handicap (as well as loved him in spite of it).

The ambiguous and shifting light in which the parent of an adolescent regards his son is seen when Criddle's father on the one hand extended the symbols of manhood to him in offering the beer, and on the other hand withdrew them in demanding a curfew. His adolescent conflict with his father grew with the belief that his father required exaggerated virtue from him because of his handicap. His mother, as seen by Criddle, ordered him little and understood him always.

Age 16–18. Criddle's adolescent turbulence continued unchecked. He started regular high school but, being two years older than his classmates, he had little to do with them outside school hours. At best they left him alone; at worst they rejected and ridiculed him (see pp. 245–246 for one of the more trying incidents). He bent every effort to hide his disability in order to be like anyone else, but only years later did he learn that such play carried no trumps. His gang life continued with an occasional evening of boxing and pinochle. He even made new friends and with the gang made a stab at such concrete admissions of adulthood as gambling and drinking which could, at the same time, represent frontal attacks against authority. "Occasionally we would all chip in for a gallon of wine or a bottle of cheap whiskey. We seldom had enough money to do much damage" (pp. 65–66).

Criddle also saw in his escapades a bitter reaction against the loneliness of not having a girl. With indignation he challenged his mother, "So I was playing a little penny ante. What's wrong with that? The other fellows have dates all the time. What am I supposed to do, stay home and listen to the radio seven nights a week?" (p. 67). Criddle's parents continued to worry about him and keep tab on him. Once when he had been gambling, for example, his father went to the others involved and raised a row. He told them that if it would happen again he would call the police. Criddle resented the childish position this implied even though he agreed with his parents that he was more than ordinarily derelict.

But the times that Criddle spent with his parents were also good. This point is important: though parents and adolescents may often quarrel, there are times, not necessarily infrequent ones, when the bond of kinship is strengthened by friendship. Criddle's father confided in him his own youthful derelictions, taught him how to play the bugle, and continued to play checkers and drink beer with him of an evening. All of this gave Criddle the feeling that, in spite of his father's resentments, he was his favorite son.

When Criddle joined the bugle corps with two of his cronies, his spare time was well occupied with practice and performance. He was even assured of the company of girls at the dance after the celebrations. But as emancipation from the family increased with these new exploits, Criddle's need for attachments with a girl could not remain dormant. He began to reason that if he could conceal his handicap until after the girl had learned to like him—then surely she could continue to like him!

This was a rather ambitious plan. That I could keep a girl from knowing about my eyes through the intimacies of courtship, even a rapid one, seems improbable. That I did seems a little fantastic even to me, now that I realize how little I could see at that time.

This concealment became habitual. I would refrain from exposing my eye condition as unconsciously as I would refrain from touching a fire; for it was just as painful. People would notice something odd about me, but it was often a long time before they realized what it was [p. 76].

Little did Criddle know that the adolescent, for whom physical conformity is the essence of sex appropriateness, could not see him as a person aside from his disability. He had to be hurt and hurt hard before his one hope in concealment, and with it his hope for happiness, was shattered:

I remember Mary. I just happened to be standing on the corner of Fourth and West Main when Mary passed on her way to school. The day before, I had found her in music class—a new face, a new voice, a new hope, naturally to be investigated. Bud told me that she lived just around the block from my house, that she was a good-looker, and that she carried a heavy typewriter to and from school each day.

And so, as I said, I just happened to be standing there when she passed. I had been happening to be standing there some twenty minutes.

I pretended to be tying my shoe. Then I fell in behind her. I followed her almost to Condon's store before I mustered enough courage to advance.

"May I carry your case?"

"Thank you," she said with genuine gratitude. "It is heavy."

She handed me the typewriter, and tossed her head to send long black curls tumbling over her shoulder. She smiled. I watched her out of the corner of my eye as we walked on. I could see a pert little nose, and she walked with a lilt, a sort of dance, but not ungraceful. Her whole personality seemed musical. I would probably have walked the rest of the way to school in silence if she hadn't spoken first.

"I know you. I saw you in music class yesterday. Your name's Russell."

"How do you know?"

"One of the girls told me."

I wondered if one of the girls had told her about my eyes.

"Did she tell you anything else?"

"She said you were a sophomore. I'm only a freshman. I take music with the sophomores, though."

"I know," I said, "and your name's Mary."

She tossed her head again, and laughed, and I fell in love.

"Have you got a steady?" she asked after two more blocks of silence.

"No, I just broke up. Have you?"

"Sure. He's the hired man next to my daddy's farm. That is, he used to be. My daddy doesn't have a farm any more. I was getting tired of him anyway."

"You're pretty," I said, trying to steady my voice.

She smiled her appreciation of my compliment, and said, "You're strong."

"Aw, this ain't heavy."

I held the typewriter at arm's length, to show her how modest I was.

We stopped at the Sugar Bowl that night. Mary had a soda (15¢), so I had a dish of ice cream (10¢). I only had a quarter.

Mary sipped her soda and looked at me for a moment, then, without warning, "You're nice."

I told her I was going to be a newspaper reporter some day.

"I think newspaper reporters are romantic."

We went to the movies on Sunday night, and had a soda afterward. We walked home holding hands.

She liked horses. "My daddy had the best team of anybody," she boasted.

I laughed.

She turned abruptly and faced me. "Well, he did. My daddy said so."

"I believe you," I said.

We walked on, swinging our hands in time with her lilting steps. Then, "What are you laughing at?"

"I don't know. You, I guess."

"You're an odd person," she said pleasantly, as we reached her front porch.

"What do you mean?"

"I don't know. Sometimes I look at you and you don't seem to see me."

"Let's just say I'm deep," I said, and we laughed.

"I think you're awfully nice," she said.

I wanted to kiss her, she stood so close. But I felt guilty, it wasn't right, not telling her about my eyes.

I managed to keep Mary from knowing my eyes were bad through two dozen sodas and three movies. I used every trick I had ever learned. I paid special attention to the color of her dress each morning, and then I would keep my eyes and ears and my sixth sense alert for anyone that might be Mary. I didn't take any chances. If I wasn't sure, I would greet whoever it was with familiarity. They probably thought I was nuts, but I didn't care. I always held her hand on the way to and from the movies at night, and she led me, without knowing it, so I didn't have to feel for curbs and steps.

She said she had seen me in the library one day and that I had fallen asleep. I knew I had been studying, but I didn't tell her that.

"Why didn't you wake me up? Prof caught me."

She laughed and tossed her head, and the black curls tumbled about, and I sighed with relief and ecstasy.

"Will you go to the firemen's ball with me?"

"Sure. I was afraid you didn't go to dances," she said.

I'll never forget that date. I thought I would have to sell my bike to get funds, but Dad came through with the most beautiful five-dollar bill I have ever seen. I took a bath every night for a week. I brushed my teeth until they bled. My hair was plastered down with vaseline in the hope that it would subdue the stubborn cowlick. Mother bought me a new pair of white flannels and had my coat cleaned and pressed. I used up almost a whole box of shoe polish on my best shoes. I wore Dad's brand-new hat, and his best necktie. I was the essence of perfection as I straightened my tie and knocked at Mary's front door.

Mary's mother answered. "Come in, Russell, Mary isn't quite ready."

I almost lost faith in the worth of living as I sat in the parlor with Mary's mother, waiting for her beautiful daughter, for it started to rain. The awful stuff hit the windows like hailstones. Mary's mother probably saw my anguish, for she said:

"I think it will stop. They are big drops."

She was right. The rain had stopped when Mary came into the room. So did time. She was wearing a pink dress, all stiff and crinkled, that flared out below her slim waist and almost touched the floor. Enough perfume floated in with her to glamorize a dozen girls.

I rose and helped Mary on with her coat. She had a pink ribbon in her soft hair. Her eyes were almost black. I had thought they were.

"Come right home after the dance, and have a good time, children."

"Yes, Mother. Good night."

The rain had left the air clean and sweet, and Mary's perfume, thinned by a soft breeze, wrought havoc with my co-ordination. The shower had washed some of the greasy smoke from the town and part of it was left suspended in puddles at our feet.

With my head in the clouds, I placed my number nine shoe directly into an especially large one, splashing Mary's beautiful dress with the filthy water. Mary uttered a little scream of anguish, and the laughter left her voice as she moaned a futile, "Oh dear!" I snatched my handkerchief from where I had folded it so carefully, and dabbed at the wilting organdie, smearing it around all the worse.

Mary groaned and pulled away. "Don't. Just let it dry."

We went on toward the hall. I kept apologizing, and she kept saying it was nothing. I felt miserable as I "led" her, just a thought ahead of me, so that I wouldn't have to feel for the steps up to the dance hall.

The gaiety of the ball soon dispelled the gloom. Nobody said anything about her dress, so I guessed that it didn't look too bad. Mary danced close, and it was evident to all that she was my girl. It was pure happiness for me. I felt that Mary must somehow know about my eyes, the way she had acted about the puddle, and besides, someone must have told her by this time.

We went to the Sugar Bowl during the intermission, and we each had two sodas and a little piece of cake. After the dance, we went to the restaurant for hot roast beef sandwiches and coffee. I was happy, indeed I was. Mary didn't pity me. No one would pity me any more. I had a girl, a beautiful girl that even Bud would have liked to have, if his steady didn't already have him roped and tied. I had solved all my problems. People would no longer pity me, and even if they did, what did I care.

Mary met me the next morning with a simple "hello" that told that I was her beau. I didn't feel breathless any more; I felt contented, and happy. I looked at her and thought how wonderful she was to be able to go with a guy that nobody else would go with. It seemed to me there was no need to tell her about my eyes, that she had probably known all the time. I felt differently now. I didn't care whether anybody felt sorry for me or not. I didn't care whether they thought I was stupid or not. I had a girl.

I met Mary after school with the same inexpressible feeling of intimacy with which I had met her that morning:

"Hello. Where's your typewriter?"

"I left it in school."

We walked quietly to Main Street. Mary acted angry. She had never been that way before.

"What's the matter?"

"Nothing."

But there was, I could tell. Her manner was chilly; the music was gone from her bearing, the lilt from her step; and she was quiet. She had never been like that before.

"If I did something, I'm sorry," I said.

"It's nothing."

We walked on, almost to Condon's store.

"I wish you would tell me."

She just said, "It's nothing," but she seemed to be melting a little. It wasn't in anything she said, but her walk was a little less stilted.

Neither of us spoke again until we reached her house, and she would have left me without even saying, "I'll be seeing you." I caught her hand.

"You've got to tell me. Something is wrong."

If I could have seen her eyes, I know I would have noticed that they were shiny with tears. There was so much compassion in her voice when she finally answered that I felt sorry for her.

"I'm sorry, Russ, honest I am. I knew you were kind of odd, but I didn't know you couldn't see."

She pulled her hand from mine, and with a sob, ran into the shadow of her front porch and I heard the door close behind her [pp. 76–83].

Criddle's misery was complete. He was now reconvinced, and this time without a shadow of a doubt, that no girl could ever love him. But more than that, he felt he was only part of a man. It was as simple as this:

It takes six sides to make a hexagon, and a hexagon can hardly be expected to fall in love with a triangle.

I'm a man in every respect but one, therefore I fall short of being a man by definition. I can't expect to be desired as a man. But I have the desires of a whole man. It's just nature [p. 113].

Fortunately, after two years in high school, Criddle began to find a place for himself at school, and this served as a substitute to some degree for his deepest pain at not being able to find a sweetheart.

Age 18–20. These two years were Criddle's first of relative peace since the age of 14. He still missed the love of a girl sorely, but his gradual acceptance by his classmates and his life on his father's farm to some extent took its place. As a senior he was elected, by popular vote of the student body, to become editor-in-chief of his high school paper. Of one boy he says, "His acceptance of me had made my adjustment in school easier. We were close friends, and an intimate understanding existed between us" (p. 111). Nor did Criddle lack the companionship of girls:

But though I was without a sweetheart I was not without female companionship. Girls seemed to respect and admire me. They liked me, as they told me all too often, but not in that way. They wanted me for sort of a big brother. They confided in me their conquests, their desires, and even their sins [p. 115].

Aside from his improved social relations at school, his father's farm, acquired during Criddle's sophomore year, kept time from hanging heavy on his hands. Moreover, he gained the respect of the farmers and participated in the square dancing and movies of the rural community:

My hands blistered and toughened, and I grew hard until I could spend a full day in the field and still have enough energy left for a square dance or a movie. I gained their [the farmers'] respect as a good worker, which is the ultimate as regards social status among farmers. I was respected. I was liked, too, I think, and I liked them [p. 125].

Criddle was busy. During this period he reports no adolescent "flings" or major eruptions with his father. But though his life was far from empty, though he was productive and acclaimed, there remained an incompleteness that kept begging for closure—his wish for a sweetheart was intense. Criddle believed that he would not feel passion toward a sweetheart; that he would not desire anything from her other than companionship, understanding and affection. He recognized that this was "a search

for someone upon whom to transfer the great love I had for my mother"
(p. 114). Though this incompleteness caused him great distress, it was
mild compared to the compounded sufferings he had to endure following
his graduation from high school.

Age 20–22. Upon graduation from high school, Criddle looked forward
to achieving economic independence and with it the dignity that was his
right. He achieved neither. The year was 1936, and times were hard.
After battling for employment, he did manage to hold two jobs briefly
but returned home sick and with the growing realization that his greatest
battle would be against society's proscription that as a blind man he must
live a life of asylum.

Emancipation from his family came slowly, and the inevitable parent-
child conflicts piled up. Just a short while before, Criddle had enjoyed a
fair amount of status as a promising reporter at high school and as a good
hand on the farm. Now he had no status at all, for since he was dependent
on his father, his father expected him to assume once again the subservient position of a child. He argued, in effect, "See, without my help
you suffer. I will help you if you will do as I say." He beat Criddle
violently whenever he stayed out after one o'clock at night or committed
some comparable misdemeanor. And Criddle's reaction was to earn his
board on the farm as his father directed but otherwise ". . . Dad's decree
that I should do this or that was all the incentive I needed to disobey"
(p. 152). And like the adolescent who sees the parent as the main source
of his frustrations, Criddle recalls "I suppose I was normal enough to
blame all my troubles upon my father" (p. 152). Also like the adolescent
who needs some source of support for his rebellion and deflated ego,
Criddle sought out companionship wherever he could find it, whether in a
saloon or a pool hall, whether in a card game or at a dance. In short,
Criddle, who at the age of 18 was ready to abandon the adolescent
patterns of behavior for a more mature way of life, now in his twenties
was plummeted back to the typical psychological situation of an adolescent with a consequent resurgence of adolescent behavior.

We tend to think of the adolescent as the one who strives for family
emancipation, and yet it is the parents, too, who work toward that end
in a way as uneven and ambivalent as the adolescent's striving for freedom. When, years before, his mother went to his father's assistance after
the fateful battle and left Criddle without comfort, she gave him a shove
toward independence. Now, when their relationships continued to go from
bad to worse, it was the father who ordered Criddle from the house.

The endless trail of job hunting began again. He did secure a few jobs,
but as soon as his supervisors discovered the condition of his eyes, he was
fired in spite of the fact, according to Criddle, that he could do a more
than adequate job. Society had the fixed notion that blindness so incapaci-

tated a man that the only possibility of functioning at all lay in the sheltered workshop. Criddle was revolted by what to him was a last resort, for it meant giving up, a helplessness and dependency that he despised. Instead he suffered cold and hunger and utter exhaustion; in humiliation he returned after three months to his father's farm rather than agree with society's verdict.

Age 22 to Maturity. By this time both Criddle and his father had changed in ways that made living together less strained. His father had learned, through the unsparing teaching of worry and remorse, that he could not impose his will on his son. Criddle had learned that he could achieve a greater freedom by admitting his handicap: "I know now that the longer I kept people from knowing about my eyes, the greater became the shock when they found out" (p. 159). And having been buffeted around on the outside, he also could appreciate the relief he found in farm life, where he was not repeatedly subjected to social prejudice. Both parents welcomed him back and asked him to stay a while.

Criddle stayed. He worked on the farm during the harvesting season and filled in during slack periods with selling radios and cutting mine lagging. He had found some semblance of peace of mind. "That half of the emotional barrier which had been within me was gone; I no longer pitied myself" (p. 196). And then Criddle fell in love, in spite of having resisted such an attachment for fear of being hurt again.

What drew these two people together? Winona was fat and Criddle nearly blind. And each was ashamed of the other! In humiliation they went out together because that was better than sitting home alone. Their loneliness brought them together, and values deeper than physique drew them together. They found they had good times together. They developed a deep respect for each other, and mutual understanding flowered. They overcame the adolescent hump that defined sex appropriateness in terms of rigid standards of physical conformity. At last Criddle looked forward to marriage and it was this that made him savor the sweet nectar of full adulthood. In spite of having become a resigned bachelor, he had felt that every self-respecting farmer *should* be married. His vision of complete status embodied the following:

My heifers. My cows. Rather I should say our cows. That is one thing about farming, I thought: it makes a real partnership of marriage. Men have survived all sorts of handicaps on farms, except that of being without a wife.

The horses stopped for a rest and I looked toward the house and smiled. The next time I broke sod on this meadow, Winona would be there, in the house, doing whatever was to be done, perhaps cooking dinner. And when I grew thirsty she would seem to know it, and come out with a bottle of cool water, and maybe a piece of bread and jam. She would stay for a moment, admiring my work, and I would feel proud. She would probably bring some sugar for the horses, and caution me not to work them too hard. Then she would start back to the house, and I would call her back and kiss her.

I sighed at my dreams and started the team again. They would stand all day, if I let them. Winona would be a wonderful wife. I smiled again as a car went up the road. Today was Thursday and Mrs. Bryant was going to Ladies' Aid. Winona would probably belong to the Ladies' Aid too. That meant that every other Thursday I would have to get my own dinner, or eat something she would leave covered on the table for me. I guessed that would be one of the things I would have to tolerate. But the meetings always ended about four in the afternoon, and she would be home in plenty of time to get a good hot supper [pp. 207–208].

The picture painted a blissful marriage in a setting of economic independence. Criddle's love for Winona provided all the motivation he needed to prove that he could support a family by establishing and operating a dairy farm. With the help of his father he built a stable, a barn, and a milk house. His emotional independence from his father leaped forward: "Arguments with Dad didn't seem so important any more. I could always cajole him, knowing that sometime he would go back to town and I would be boss and could run things the way I wanted" (p. 208). An interim of deep unhappiness and loneliness still lay in store for him, but the maturity he gained in this period of approaching adult status helped him to withstand the onslaught of status loss he was to suffer.

When intervening pressures led Winona to reject his love several months later, full adult status was again denied Criddle, but now, because he had achieved the important prerequisite of economic independence, he was less vulnerable to the conflicting pressures of a marginal person. Against his father's wishes and assuming full responsibility, he bought an adjoining farm that had a large farmhouse on it, for in the big house he saw a chance to have a home of his own. As a substitute for what he wanted most, he could at least "hire some widow, with a child or two, to keep house" for him (p. 220). Occasionally he went out on a binge and often drifted in search of a good time, for his need to establish himself as a man and an adult remained unfulfilled. It was when circumstances brought Winona to him again, when this time his romance ended in marriage, that he found a contentment "which could not be marred by pain, or fatigue or bitterness or any other thing" (p. 226). Economic independence, marriage, a home of his own—Criddle finally came of age.

This discussion of some of the problems and solutions that the adolescent may experience as his self-concept begins to incorporate the role of adult, provides a background for understanding some of the special problems that an adolescent with a disability may face. He, too, undergoes a change of self-concept in which adult determiners of behavior as well as childish determiners demand a hearing. He, too, will conflict with his parents as these determiners vary in potency. And he will need the support of a peer group against the adults who are felt to thwart him. For him, too, physique becomes evaluated in terms of rigid standards of sex appropriateness and, like other adolescents, he has an intense interest in all matters that have to do with the establishment of his status as a man or woman. As in the case of other young people, the period of adolescence may be prolonged by protracted economic dependence and celibacy. In addition, the adolescent with a disability has to cope with the conflicts engendered by the overlapping situation of "normal" and "disabled" behavior determiners.

Chapter 9

Grievances and Gratifications in
Everyday Relationships

PEOPLE LIVE WITH PEOPLE. THEY INTERACT WITH ONE ANOTHER IN THE give-and-take of daily living. The interactions may leave them annoyed or content, inspired or distraught, even though on more objective examination they may seem just small, routine affairs. But it is these small events of everyday living, with their frictions and uplifts, that somehow season the mood and condition the morale. They are important to the person himself and to his relationships with others.

Persons with disabilities frequently refer to ordinary incidents that arise with the nondisabled. They describe situations involving curiosity, staring, help, sympathy, devaluating pity, being treated differently, social participation, and being taunted. There is hardly an autobiography that does not bring up several of these incidents, sometimes as positive and sometimes as negative experiences. It is important to uncover psychological conditions that determine the acceptance or rejection of such relationships, for it is an impossible task to provide recommendations for each and every concrete social act that may arise.

The discussion will draw heavily upon the research of Dembo and her associates. The findings of this study appear in several papers (Dembo, Leviton, Wright, *1956;* Ladieu, Hanfmann, Dembo, *1947;* White, Wright, Dembo, *1948;* Ladieu, Adler, Dembo, *1948*), but for ease of reference, the research will here be referred to as the Dembo study. The basic method of this study was an interview, usually lasting about an hour and a half, aimed at uncovering the kinds of difficulties existing in the relationships between persons with and without disabilities. The subjects were 177 adults with visible disabilities and 65 nondisabled. Of those with disabilities, 100 were arm or leg amputees, 40 were cases of facial disfigurement, and the remainder were distributed among such orthopedic disabilities as poliomyelitis, transverse myelitis, osteomyelitis, and congenital deformities.

THE PROBLEM OF CURIOSITY AND
DISCUSSION OF THE DISABILITY

The investigators of the problem of curiosity regarding a disability point out that a disability as a characteristic and inseparable part of the body may be felt by the person with the disability to be a matter that he would like to keep private (White, Wright, Dembo, 1948). Yet its visibility makes it known to anyone whom the person meets. A visible disability differs from many other personal matters in that anyone can deal with it regardless of the wish of the person; anyone can stare at the disability or ask questions about it and in this way communicate his feelings about the disability to the person. It is its visibility that makes easy an intrusion into privacy, an intrustion that the person may feel powerless to control or at best able to control only by how he reacts or handles the situation.

The subjects of the Dembo study rejected curiosity about their disability for several reasons. For example, they spoke of wanting to keep their disability private, of the unpleasantness of being reminded of painful disability-connected memories, of the fear of being considered different, of outright resentment at morbid curiosity. At the same time, it became clear that the evaluation of communication about the disability depended upon the circumstances in which it took place. Eighty-four percent of the subjects neither fully accepted nor fully rejected questioning and talking about the disability with nondisabled persons. Even staring, though generally rejected, was still considered all right in certain circumstances by one third of the subjects—for example, when it did not persist.

Conditions Underlying Evaluation

Several important factors emerged as contributing to the reaction of the person with a disability to staring, to questioning of others about his disability, and to their talking about it.

Self-regard was discussed at length in connection with the interpretation of the behavior of another toward the self (Chap. 7). There it is pointed out that, when the person has a well-balanced, accepting attitude toward his disability, he is more likely to feel that others question him and stare at him because they simply wonder about him—how he gets along, or how his prosthesis works—than when he himself is ashamed of his disability. If, however, the person basically rejects his disability and himself, he will tend strongly to resist the curiosity of others, feeling that he is being regarded negatively, with aversion and pity. His self-concept defines for him the kind of person he is as an "object" of stimulation to others. He may also actively resist speaking of his disability because he views it as something to be ashamed of, a mark of inferiority, a skeleton to be kept hidden.

There is also the factor of *situational context* that contributes to the person's reaction. The subjects sometimes urged that others should not talk about the disability unless it comes up naturally, meaning that reference to the disability should be part of a broader conversation or should arise out of the demands of the situation. Such references are less likely to be felt as an intrusion into privacy. They are also less likely to be felt as emphasizing the disability as such, but rather may be seen as secondary to the purpose of the broader context. The peculiarly distasteful experience of being stared at can be partially attributed to the fact that it is not seen as emerging from a situational context; instead it is an expression purely of the needs of the onlooker. Staring often goes on in an extremely unstructured situation, so unstructured that it lacks a situational context. Under such ambiguous conditions the worst anxieties of the person may come to the surface and determine the nature of his perception. Should "extended looking" be required by the situation, as when a doctor examines a wound, the activity is no longer thought of as staring.

Besides the situational context, there is also a *personal context*, representing the more lasting relationships between two persons. This accounts for the marked tendency on the part of persons with disabilities to make a distinction in favor of talking about the disability with friends or family members rather than with strangers. The person with a disability recognizes that his friends see him more frequently as a person whose personal qualities are more important than his bodily appearance. He has less fear that "it is not I but my disability" that is uppermost in the other person's mind. Staring on the part of strangers represents in the extreme an impersonal context. The very act of talking is to some degree symbolic of a human relationship, but staring is a thing one does not ordinarily do to another person. One does not talk to a monkey in a zoo or to a freak in a sideshow—one only stares. As a result the relationship is easily perceived as one of a person (the nondisabled) to an object—a curiosity.

The wish to be and to appear to be well adjusted, which may lead to strong resistance against talking about the disability, sometimes may act to diminish that resistance. The subjects often brought out their wish to be considered "normal" and especially the wish to prove that they were not defeated by their disability. Trying not to mind the curiosity of others is a way for the person to prove that he is not sensitive, that he is not ashamed, that the disability did not make him maladjusted. Thus, along with the feeling of being hurt that questioning and staring may produce, there is a struggle against this feeling. He will, however, restrict the discussion to a superficial level of factual information and to casual feelings. If the conversation is carried on with an understanding person, the experience, especially in its cumulative effects through repeated occurrences, may make it possible for the person to discover that talking about his disability was not nearly as difficult as he had thought. In this way, even a superficial level of discussion may provide an opening wedge for change in the meaning of disability.

There are indications that the person *has a desire to be understood,* that he needs and wants to talk about his disability with persons with whom he feels secure and in situations that enhance his security. He wants to talk because basically he wants to be accepted as he really is, with his actual needs and feelings, and not as he appears to be on the surface. He may also feel a need for reassurance that he is worthy as a person or that his attitudes and behavior toward others are justified. He may feel a need to recognize more clearly how the disability has affected his life and how he can manage more satisfactorily. However, it may be extremely difficult for him to give expression to this need, for at the same time he may be weighed down by the overpowering wish to be nondisabled and to be treated as such. Moreover, those around him may also feel uncomfortable and embarrassed in regard to the disability. There is thus a pretense on both sides; both try to act as though the disability did not exist.

This pretense causes an emotional strain, both in the person with the disability and in his associates. An estrangement between himself and persons who matter to him may eventuate, for when feelings are not shared, when much is not said but is guessed at and misinterpreted, the distance grows and the relationship suffers. Equally disturbing in the persistent "as if" behavior is the feeling that the person with a disability is only seemingly accepted—i.e., that he is not really accepted at all. Realization of the impracticability of ignoring the disability and of the negative consequences of attempting to do so removes a large barrier to communicating about the disability.

The conditions that underlie the person's evaluation of curiosity and talking about his disability affect, of course, the manner in which he actually meets the reality of such communication. It is the management that guides the social interaction and therefore may serve to reduce or augment interpersonal tensions.

Management by the Recipient

A person with a disability, meeting time and again the questioning and staring of others, gradually develops ways of coping with such situations. His manner of approach will partly depend on his general evaluation of the situation and partly on the social skills he has developed in the course of trying out different techniques. Some tactics appear satisfying; he feels comfortable in their use and they seem to be effective in their results. Other tactics leave him disturbed; he continues to brood about the incident and to chastise himself for his awkward management of it. The following scenes, demonstrating commonly used coping techniques, have been taken in most cases from autobiographical accounts. They have been grouped according to three general evaluations of the situation in which the other person is felt to be an intruder. In the first, attacking the offender, the person with the disability regards the intruder as a fatuous boor and wants above all to retaliate, if necessary by utilizing his disability in the attack. In the second, excluding the disability from the situation, the recipient is dominated by an imperative need to eradicate the disability as a socially real fact. And in the third, minimizing the disability and preserving the relationship, the recipient wishes to maintain at a congenial level the course of communication about the disability as well as the social relationship. There are other psychological situations and ways of handling them, but these will suffice to give an appreciation of ways of coping with the situation and their effectiveness in social situations with some potential threat.

ATTACKING THE OFFENDER.   The agent, usually a stranger, is seen as being idly or morbidly curious and therefore really interested not in the recipient personally but only in his disability. Sometimes the recipient senses (correctly or not) that the agent pries in the hope of savoring a lurid tale and thereby aggrandizing himself at the expense of the recipient. In any event, the reaction to the intruder is a deeply negative one; the recipient regards him with derision or hatred and wishes to retaliate in a cutting manner that will make the agent appear foolish. This is accomplished with the techniques, deftly maneuvered, of biting sarcasm and dramatic prevarication.

BITING SARCASM.   Louise is a young college graduate who lost a leg in childhood and uses crutches to get about. She recalls the following interchange inaugurated by a "snoopy old biddy":

"My poor girl, I see you've lost your leg."
That's the opportunity for the *touche,* "How careless of me!" [Baker, *1946*:97].[1]

Friends, too, can "ask for it." In the following sample, the recipient is the mother of Noreen, a young lady convalescing from polio:

[1] Reprinted by permission from *Out on a Limb* by Louise Baker, published by McGraw-Hill Book Company. Copyright 1946 by Louise Baker.

One day one of mother's friends telephoned to inquire about me.

"How is she?" he asked.

"Why, she is just fine," Mother said. "She is getting stronger, and we think she will be coming home soon [from the hospital]."

"Yes," he insisted, "but how *is* she? I mean is she really all right?"

"Why, of course," Mother said. "She will be just fine!"

"You don't understand me," he urged. "I mean, well, has she slipped a little? Does she think clearly? Does she remember everything?"

"Oh!" my mother said, and when she recovered, "Oh no—she has dreams! And she doesn't remember everything either, she can't remember where she put her red printed scarf that she wore last summer!" [Linduska, *1947:*189].[2]

DRAMATIC PREVARICATION.   This plan of attack is also exploited by Louise, above. Eventually she became quite cavalier about satisfying the curiosity of intruders by imaginatively exciting tales, as the following:

One of my choicest little epics was the heroic account of a swooping venture on skis. Down a precipitous mountainside I *slalomed,* a sick baby in my arms, only to collapse at the doctor's door, the infant saved, but my poor right leg frozen stiff as a poker. It was so completely refrigerated, in fact, that the doctor, without administering so much as a whiff of anesthetic, chipped it off with an ice pick.

Even unrehearsed repartee came easily. The flapping-eared recipient of the latter fancy cheerfully swallowed the hook, and was all agape for the line and sinker. How did it happen that my left leg was so providentially spared, she wanted to know, not satisfied with what I already regarded as a very generous slice of my imagination.

"Well, I've been educated about weather," I said. "Me, I'm a Norska from Oslo. I was smart enough to anticipate chilblains. I decided I'd preserve at least one leg. Owed it to myself, I figured. I skied on only one foot, after pinning up my spare in a blanket."

"Well, I do declare!" The hypnotized listener didn't bat an eyelash [Baker, *1946:*92–93].

EXCLUDING THE DISABILITY FROM THE SITUATION.   In this psychological situation, the person wants above all to avoid reference to the disability. He may resent the intruder, but he cuts him short—not by attacking, but by excluding the disability from the situation. This is accomplished by what we have called the ostrich reaction and redirecting the interaction course.

OSTRICH REACTION.   The most direct expression of the need to exclude the disability is to escape from the situation. Such literal behavior is more characteristic of children; not infrequently the child runs out of the room

[2] Noreen Linduska, *My Polio Past,* copyright 1947 by Noreen Linduska. Used by permission of the publishers, Farrar, Straus and Cudahy, Inc.

or buries his face in the mother's lap. Henry Viscardi, dwarfed through congenital deformity of his legs, offers the following example:

. . . My mother took me home on a street car. It was open on the sides and had high steps. She had to lift me up onto the straw seat, then she got in. I sat with my boots straight out in front of me but they did not reach the edge of the seat. Across the aisle a woman in an orange coat nudged the woman next to her and pointed at me. I held my mother's hand tight. Then I saw that everybody on the street car was looking. My mother put her arm around me and I hid my face next to her coat. I wanted to run away from all those people [Viscardi, 1952:10].[3]

This direct blocking out of the disagreeable is less readily open to an adult. It appears too childish and exposes too blatantly the personal hurt that an adult generally also wishes to keep private. The adult's efforts to escape the situation, therefore, take more subtle form.

He may return an icy stare that freezes the atmosphere. Viscardi, as a college student less than four feet tall, describes his more adult management of staring, staring that he encountered day after day after day:

There were the thick-skinned ones, who stared like hill people come down to see a traveling show. There were the paper-peekers, the furtive kind who would withdraw blushing if you caught them at it. There were the pitying ones, whose tongue clickings could almost be heard after they had passed you. But even worse, there were the chatterers, whose every remark might as well have been "How do you do, poor boy?" They said it with their eyes and their manners and their tone of voice.

I had a standard defense—a cold stare. Thus anesthetized against my fellow man, I could contend with the basic problem—getting in and out of the subway alive [Viscardi, 1952:70].

The person with a disability may lower his eyes and look past the intruder and hate the source of his anguish. Goldman, lame from polio, recalls an incident in his adolescence:

I stand in the doorway to a restaurant, as yet unnoticed, my heart sinking, my body filling with a great tumor of anguish. The sensation is akin to both swelling and shrinking. I wish that I would shrivel away to nothing, like a paper curling to ashes in the grate, or that I would burst with the swelling.

People! Eyes! Eyes!

Something in the back of my mind moans, O God, O God, O God! I lash my courage: *Enter! Get it done and over with! What the hell? What's the dif-*

---

[3] Henry Viscardi, Jr., *A Man's Stature.* Copyright, 1952, by Henry Viscardi, Jr. Used with permission of The John Day Company.

ference? The hell with 'em! I want to be bitter, get mad, put the blame on them
—those people sitting there with eyes. I want to hate them so that I won't care
what they think.

I press my teeth together. I clench my fists. Every muscle of my body
tightens and I enter with my head up. I walk down the aisle between the rows
of tables, looking neither to left nor right.

But you need not see eyes; you can feel them. Even when you know that you
are past them and they are behind you, they reach out with something that
touches you.

The aisle is miles and miles in length but at last I reach my table and seat
myself. I relax. There is a light dew of sweat on my fact. I'll be all right in a
minute. The tablecloth is long, my legs are under the table. Now to order, eat,
and enjoy a hard-earned meal. I don't want to look too far ahead. After a
while I must get up and walk out again [Goldman, *1947*:65–66].[4]

REDIRECTING THE INTERACTION COURSE.   One can sometimes escape
the unpleasantly intrusive question by stopping it before it is uttered and
then taking control of the conversation. Louise, with one leg amputated,
was a frequent target of the curiosity of others. She developed a manner
that said in effect, "I know what you're thinking, but keep it there" [Baker,
1946:91].

And when an intruder has already made some headway, the recipient
is sometimes able to collect himself sufficiently to ignore it with a matter-
of-fact, otherwise empty comment that reveals nothing of the self but
serves to rechannel the interaction to nondisturbing areas. This is seen
in the following interchange between Frances, a college girl with impaired
hearing who is frightened of deafness, and Victorine, a casual acquaintance:

"Why don't you try a chiropractor?" she [Victorine] asked me, chewing
corned beef, giving no slightest indication that she was about to knock the
bottom out of my world. "Dr. Fletcher told me he's curing one of his patients
of deafness."

My heart skittered, in panic, against my ribs. What did she mean?

"My dad's deaf," she revealed. "I can spot a deaf person anywhere. That
soft voice of yours. And that trick of letting your sentences trail off—not
finishing them. Dad does that all the time."

The bottom fell out of my world. What was she saying? That she spotted
me for a deaf person? That it was perfectly plain to anyone that I didn't hear
well? That wasn't so. It couldn't be so. Nobody could possibly guess I didn't
hear well; I had everybody bluffed. Besides, I could hear all right. Nobody
could call me a deaf person. Nobody with long spindle legs and a bad complexion and fuzzy yellow hair that looked as if she never brushed it.

---

4 Selection from Raymond Goldman: Even the Night. Copyright 1947, The
Macmillan Company, and used with the permission of the publisher.

My head spun with fury. Did I trail my sentences? I did, often. Often I'd see, from the expression on another person's face, that I was talking on the wrong track, that I'd misheard something. . . .

"Dad's wonderful," Victorine was saying. "He can't hear thunder without an earphone and not very much even with an earphone, but he keeps trying. He's got our dining-room table and his favorite chair in the living-room all wired up for sound; you can't move without tripping over electric wires and storage batteries. Just lately one of the hearing-aid companies came out with a portable model that he can carry around in a black box. It weighs . . . [Victorine continued to ramble on in this fashion, oblivious of the panic she had created. Finally, Frances, with a forced indifference, interrupts.]

"Really? We'd better be getting back for the Math exam," I said freezingly [Warfield, *1948*:44–45].[5]

MINIMIZING THE DISABILITY AND PRESERVING THE RELATIONSHIP.   There is also the situation in which the recipient accepts his disability as a social fact but wishes to moderate the intensity of involvement with it. Instead of a serious concern centering around his disability, he wishes to keep the discussion at a superficial level. At the same time, not feeling any ill will toward the intruder, he desires to maintain a congenial relationship. This may be accomplished through the techniques of good-natured levity and superficial discourse.

GOOD-NATURED LEVITY.   Some persons build up a repertoire of light remarks that they can use in appropriate settings. Russell (*1949*) found that strangers more quickly took him and his hooks for granted after some such icebreaker. He might make a crack about how the one thing he could not do with his hooks was to pick up a check at a restaurant, for example. In providing a light touch, such remarks set the social climate. They say, in effect, "I am not disturbed by my disability. So you may feel comfortable about it too, and we can go on to other things from here."

SUPERFICIAL DISCOURSE.   The following conversation is between two young teen-agers, Criddle who recently lost his sight in a childhood accident, and Red, his friend:

"What's it like to be blind?" Red asked.
"How do I know?" I said, still irritated by the word. "I ain't blind. I just got bad eyes, that's all."
"That's what I mean," he placated. "What's it like?"
"It ain't like nothing. You just can't see, that's all."
"Does it hurt?"
"Nah, you bump your shins sometimes, and that hurts, that's all."
"Is everything dark?"

[5] F. Warfield, *Cotton in My Ears,* New York, Viking Press, Inc. Copyright 1948 by Frances Warfield. Used with permission of Viking Press, Inc.

Knowing Red was fascinated by my blindness, I exploited the opportunity, and drew on what mother had said: "It's like looking through a frosted glass, like we have in our bathroom only not so frosted. Your ears, smell, and touch make up for your eyes."

"You mean you can see with your ears?"

"No, of course not. You just hear better, that's all."

"And smell better?"

"Sure" [Criddle, *1953*:25–26].[6]

Criddle avoided talking about the deeper and more personal meanings of blindness by brushing off any insinuation that he is seriously handicapped. He effectively guided the conversation to moderate inconveniences and at the same time maintained a comfortable relationship with his friend.

SITUATIONS NOT REQUIRING SOCIAL TACTICS.   Thus far we have analyzed situations in which the questioner is felt to intrude, actually or potentially, into the privacy of the recipient. Some communication about the disability, however, does not threaten privacy. Sometimes the attitude toward the disability is so matter-of-fact on both sides that the discussion can arise very naturally. This occurred during Karen's first day at kindergarten. Around the sandbox, Lucy, a schoolmate, asked Karen if her braces were broken at her knees. "Karen explained that her braces had joints where her legs had joints so she could move right, and then added very matter-of-factly, 'I have cerebral palsy, you know. I'm a spastic. Are you hungry? I am'" (Killilea, *1952*:114).[7]

Also, as discussed earlier (p. 211), there are times when the person needs and wishes to talk about his disability. Sometimes the person himself may introduce the topic to someone close to him, to a therapist, or, more rarely, to a stranger. Sometimes it is the situation that brings up the disability. When the person wishes to talk and his listener is sympathetic and understanding, discussion about the disability may continue without special maneuvering on the part of the recipient. Russell Criddle offers an example of this. He had been in a "fight to the death" at his high school with Mike, a boy who had been taunting him relentlessly about his blindness (see pp. 245–246 for incident). The next day, certain that he would be expelled, Criddle was called into the principal's office. At first he was sullen and would not participate in the conversation. Then the principal said something that struck a sympathetic chord and Criddle poured out what had long been kept within him. The principal said:

[6] Reprinted from *Love Is Not Blind* by Russell Criddle by permission of W. W. Norton & Company, Inc. Copyright 1953 by Russell Criddle.

[7] Reprinted with permission of Prentice-Hall, Inc., from *Karen* by Marie Killilea. Copyright 1952 by Marie Lyons Killilea.

. . . "You have a good head, Russell, and you must learn to keep it. People like Mike and me can afford to lose theirs once in a while, but a man that is blind needs to keep his. Society will not tolerate normality from you; you will either have to be nearly perfect or completely bad."

"I know," I said. "I expected to be expelled."

He seemed surprised at this. There was real curiosity in his voice as he asked, "You did? Why?"

"People pity me," I answered, "and it hurts them. They want me to go away all the time. They're afraid of blindness," I went on, "and they think I feel afraid all the time, like they think they would be if they were like me. It's because they think I'm scared that they think I'm dumb. People are always dumb when they are scared, that's why people can't use their intelligence when they think about me, and want to help me. They're scared of blindness. That's why Mike kept hurting me, because he was afraid of me. People, most of them, hurt people they are afraid of" [Criddle: *1953*:104].

And the conversation that continued was good and full and central. Social tactics had no place, for in this situation Criddle had nothing to guard.

THE SPECIAL PROBLEM OF CURIOSITY IN CHILDREN.   Many social forms have emerged because they permit or even give rise to congenial interpersonal relationships. Children have to learn these social expressions of politeness and to regard them as logical, or natural, or helpful toward comfortable relationships among people. For example, the adult ordinarily greets a visitor. A child, however, may just as naturally merely glance at the guest and turn away to his immediate interests with nary a gesture of recognition or welcome. To the adult this behavior may appear so incongruous that it seems amusing, or it may be taken as downright rudeness or a sign of poor breeding. In any case, the child has to learn that greeting a visitor is the usual way of making him feel welcome. Similarly, there are social forms that regulate the manner of satisfying one's curiosity. Although, as we have seen, adults often overstep accepted propriety, children, albeit unwittingly, probably do so more frequently and more flagrantly. It is only gradually that they learn to refrain from asking a stranger directly and openly about his disability, to wait until a person is out of earshot before asking the mother questions about him, to keep from staring and pointing, etc.

To some persons the frank curiosity of children is not markedly disturbing. They feel that it is a natural expression of interest, void of malice, and therefore it should be responded to in a matter-of-fact and friendly way even though one may not have chosen to engage in the transaction. The story is told of an elderly woman whose chin trembled. When asked by a small child why her chin went up and down like that she simply replied, "Well, you know, I have something that makes my chin go like that." The child looked some more and then passed on to other things (Dembo, Leviton, Wright, *1956:*50). To other persons, children remain a constant threat. If the person believes or tries to believe that his disability is not very noticeable, it is all the more upsetting when a child innocently calls attention to it. Not only do young children barge in, but they are so preoccupied with their own curiosity that they can remain insensitive to the other person's reaction. Even though the recipient may appreciate that the curiosity of the child is natural, he may at the same time feel confused, embarrassed, and resentful.

It is well for the individual who inevitably will face the curiosity of children to think over how to meet it. In thinking it over, in talking with others about their reactions, he may become aware that his own feelings about his disability and how he regards himself are really among the more important factors in his general reaction (see Chap. 7).

INDICATED RESEARCH. Clearly, further research is needed to determine which of the variety of techniques discussed above are most appropriate to particular situations and to the needs of the recipient. Although there is no systematic research on this question, an investigation by Citron, Chein, and Harding (*1950*) of a related problem exemplifies one fruitful approach to problems of management of social tensions in general. The study dealt with the handling of antiminority prejudice through appropriate counteracting retorts. In setting up the experiment, the investigators decided that:

The study would concentrate on the behavior of the answerer rather than on the behavior of the bigot or the object of the bigot's attack.

An ideal answer should meet the following criteria: Its effect on the bigot should be to dissuade him from expressing his prejudice in public. It should raise the personal morale of the minority group member and of the answerer. It should minimize in the bystanders any increase in prejudice that might have resulted from the bigot's remarks, and should encourage potential answerers in the audience to become actual answerers in the future. Because of practical considerations, an answer must be made in a few words, simply expressed, suitable for a variety of incidents, and not demanding histrionic skill.

During the exploratory phases of the research, many types of answers that appeared promising with respect to the criteria above were tried out in a number of different situations. Two answers were selected for experimental study. These were the American Tradition argument, which stressed such values as fair play and the fact that this nation was built by all races and creeds, and the Individual Differences argument, which stressed that one should not generalize from one or two cases. In the main experiment, each answer was presented half the time with high emotion and half the time in a calm manner. This yielded four types of counterargument.

The incident selected for the experiment involved a public situation in which one of the characters in the scene managed unintentionally to offend one of the other characters, who in turn insulted the ethnic group to which the first person belonged. A bystander challenges this.

The incident was presented to the subjects as a dramatic skit. The script for the incident with the American Tradition counterargument follows:

The scene is an employment bureau in which several men are seated waiting to be interviewed, some filling out application forms, some smoking and chatting:

SECRETARY: "Who is next?"

(Two men stand up and exclaim simultaneously.)

GOLDSTEIN AND JONES: "I am."

SECRETARY: "Well, I don't know for sure who is next. It's hard to tell with so many fellows coming and going. Suppose this gentleman (pointing) comes in now, and another interviewer will be ready for you in a minute. May I have your name, please?"

GOLDSTEIN: "My name is Harry Goldstein."

SECRETARY: "This way, please, Mr. Goldstein."

(Goldstein exits with secretary. The other man turns to resume his seat and exclaims disgustedly so that the others cannot help hearing him.)

JONES: "He was not next! Goldstein, huh? Another Jew who can't wait his turn. These Jews are all alike. Who do they think they are anyway?" (Mutters.)

American Tradition counterargument:

BYSTANDER: "Take it easy, fellow. I wouldn't say that if I were you. We don't want that kind of talk in America."

JONES: "Ah-h . . . these Jews are always trying to get away with something. Pushing ahead. . . ."

BYSTANDER: "That's no way to talk. What kind of country would we have if we didn't stick together? We'd be easy suckers for someone to make trouble."

JONES: "What business is it of yours?"

BYSTANDER: "I'm telling you it's unfair to pick on the Jews, or any other group, for that matter. Everybody in America should get the same square deal."

JONES: "Why are you so worried about the Jews?"

BYSTANDER: "It's not just the Jews I'm worried about. It's the danger of that kind of talk to our democracy that worries me. This country is made up of all races and religions and it's up to us to see to it that they all get an even break."

(Secretary returns and speaks to Jones.)

SECRETARY: "It's your turn now—may I have your name?"

JONES: "My name is Jones, Edward Jones."

SECRETARY: "All right, Mr. Jones. Please follow me."

(Exit Secretary and Jones.)

Attitudes toward Jews measured after the play were compared with those expressed on the same questionnaire previous to the counterarguments.

Of the four types of answers presented in the dramatic skits two showed a significant net reduction in prejudice. These two were the American Tradition argument made in a calm, quiet manner, and the Individual Differences argument made in an excited, militant manner. Because audiences prefer a calm handling of the situation, the investigators recommend the former.

Note that the investigators had first to decide on the criteria for an ideal answer before they could select possible answers for experimentation and tests for their effectiveness. Likewise, in curiosity research one would have to make explicit what the recipient might strive to accomplish in a given interaction and the different techniques whereby this might be realized. Thus, as we have indicated, if the recipient is mainly geared to punish the intruder, certain behaviors will make sense; if he wishes above all to exclude the disability, other behavior will be more effective; if his main goal is to preserve the relationship another approach may be indicated; and if he wishes to affect positively the attitudes toward disability in the other person, still other means may be in order. Thus it is clear that social skills become the practical expression of the meaning of a social relationship as determined by events in the environment and events within the person.

Recommendations

To avoid being hurt by the other person and to make communication possible when desired, the subjects of the Dembo study gave recommendations to the nondisabled. In different ways they expressed the following rules (White, Wright, Dembo, *1948*):

1. Don't talk about it unless the person with the disability brings it up.
2. Don't talk about it unless he wants to.
3. Don't ask questions immediately.
4. Take into account the mood of the person.
5. Don't dwell on it.
6. Don't try to get him away from the subject.

A principle underlying these recommendations is that the person with a disability should determine when and how the discussion should *start* and the *course* it should take. However, the clues by which the nondisabled person may be guided are rarely clear-cut and definite. They are often subtle, elusive, and may even be covered up. When the communication is an outgrowth of a definite situational or personal context, the other person is better able to interpret the clues correctly, since the broader context helps to structure their meaning. By refraining from communication about the injury "until it comes up naturally," therefore, the other person can be more effectively guided by the wishes of the person with a disability.

The following example is an interesting case in point. It is taken from the life of Frances Warfield, the young woman with a hearing disability to whose reminiscences we have frequently referred. It may be recalled that her hearing impairment meant utter and complete degradation to her and that she tried at all costs to hide her disability. Finally, after secretly going from one doctor to another, after trying all the patent cures she came upon through newspaper and quack, she became resigned to wearing a hearing aid. Life was, she felt, over for her. Almost every facet of her being had been identified with her hearing disability, and now with the hearing aid that publicized it. In spite of her complete rejection of her disability, she was able, in the following episode, *for the first time* to mention her hearing loss, however falteringly, because it came up naturally with a person close to her—Phil, her suitor discovered the aid while rumpling her hair. Notice, too, that the topic is not dwelt on and that Frances in large part channels the direction it takes.

> When Phil came to take me to dinner that evening I was dead.
> He rumpled my hair, as he always did. Then—"What have we here, Junior?"
> "A gimmick," I told him. This was the end. He'd send me away now. "You wear it under your hair," I said. Then you don't need to be deaf . . . You don't need to be deaf . . . You just need to be dead. . . .
> He nodded at me approvingly. "Good girl. I've been wondering if you wouldn't get one of those, one of these days."
> "You know that I'm hard of hearing?"
> "Everybody who knows you knows that, Junior."
> "Well, I'll be a sonofabitch!"
> "And nobody gives a damn" [Warfield, *1948:*151].

We have drawn upon this example to show that adjustive communication about the disability is more effectively cued when the context of situation and personal relationships between agent and recipient are taken into account. The suitor, although not observing Rule 1 (i.e., Frances did not bring up the subject of her disability), recognized her covert desire to talk about it (Rule No. 2). Actually, one of the basic conflicts in a person with a disability—the conflict between wanting to be like a nondisabled person and wanting to accept himself with his disability— permits a person who is close to bring up the disability in a natural setting. Because of this conflict, the person with a disability may and may not wish to talk about his disability at the same time. Even a brief allusion to the disability may then have far-reaching positive effects, for the mere fact that it is brought up in an open, matter-of-fact way by a trusted friend may in itself help. One is silent or whispers about the terrible, but the mentionable has met the first criterion of the acceptable.

The problem of curiosity would be greatly eased if the nondisabled were familiar with such interesting aspects of disability as prosthetic devices and how they work, new ways to meet old situations, and success in spite of or because of a disability. Public education can well utilize the imaginative thinking and effort of those working in the field of rehabilitation. A report by Rusk and Taylor (*1946*) offers an example of meeting the problem of curiosity through public education:

> . . . when one of the authors was invited to speak to a group of eighth graders, . . . he took with him a number of prosthetic devices, crutches, artificial eyes, dentures, hooks, legs and hearing aids. Following a group session in which noted personalities who had severe disabilities were discussed, each of the devices was explained, and the children were invited to use them. They walked around the room on the crutches, put on the hearing aids, and tried to hold the artificial eyes in their eyes as though they were monocles. Two fourteen-year-olders got one of the artificial hands, and while one held it steady, the other tried to manipulate it to pick up objects like the bucket grab bags do at Coney Island. They had not only an instructive but an enjoyable time. Their inquisitiveness was brought out in the open and satisfied, rather than being fettered to the point that it might eventually become morbid curiosity [pp. 222–223].[8]

Information concerning the coping aspects of disability (see pp. 59–70) through knowledge of prosthetic devices, of persons with disabilities who have succeeded, of the fact that a disability is just one part of a person's life, does more than abate curiosity. It fosters that kind of understanding which will not only improve relations between those with disabilities and those without but will serve the latter well for the eventuality of needing to accept a disability on their own behalf.

THE PROBLEM OF HELP

The adult able-bodied person hardly gives a thought to the problem of help because it is not a problem to him. Help is a good thing; it expresses concern for another, a willingness to put oneself out for his well-being, all of which is sanctioned in our system of values as essential to the growth of man as a social being. Yet help may not simply be taken for granted by a person with a disability, for it connotes a variety of meanings and experiences, some of which threaten him. In the Dembo study, the sub-

---

[8] H. A. Rusk and E. J. Taylor, *New Hope for the Handicapped.* Harper & Brothers, 1946. By permission.

jects with disabilities evaluated help (bodily assistance) both positively
and negatively but emphasized the negative (Ladieu, Hanfmann, Dembo,
1947). Half of the subjects had more bad things than good things to say
about being helped, whereas in only about one fourth of the subjects was
this relationship reversed.

Help as a Social Relationship

The act of helping may be disturbing to the recipient because it is not
simply an act that may be more or less useful to him; it is primarily a
social relationship that expresses a variety of attitudes on the part of the
participants. As the study of the evaluation of help has stressed, the act
of helping represents a one-sided social relationship that easily leads to
status judgments. The person who is always the one to be helped is likely
to be considered as inferior.

Disparaging aspects of receiving help have a variety of contents. Sometimes the proffered help is interpreted by a person with a disability as
meaning that he is considered more helpless than he actually is, and
therefore not only is the help unnecessary but it also questions his status.
Sometimes the help is felt to be motivated by hypocritical self-aggrandizement; the helper, being intent on inflating his own ego, is completely
insensitive to the wishes of the recipient. Sometimes the act of helping is
resented because it calls attention to the person's disability or is felt to
set him apart against his wishes. Underlying this unwillingness to be
noticed is the fear of being devaluated as a disabled person. Not only
does he feel that his social standing is jeopardized, but also his defenses
against feelings of self-devaluation become threatened. Sometimes the
help is seen as oozing pity, in which event it is generally rejected with
bitter condemnation.

At the same time, the subjects in the help study did recognize the possible positive intentions of the helper. But what seems more striking is the
fact that such approval was generally half-hearted and qualified with
precautions against implications of inequality or threats to one's independence. It must, of course, be recognized that the subjects of the help study,
being men, might be expected to see in help evidence of personal inferiority and threat to independence more strongly than women. Whereas
helping a man might be taken as a threat to his manliness, helping a
woman is not as likely to endanger her sex role.

Help as an Expediting Act

Aside from social implications, the act of helping can either advance
the recipient toward his desired goals or actually impede his progress.

Unfortunately, even when a well-intentioned helper perceives the goal of the recipient correctly, he is not always able to help effectively. He may lack the necessary understanding of what the disability entails or the techniques of help that would be appropriate. The subjects in the help study registered an emphatic protest against what almost constitutes an unexpected attack by an awkward person who eagerly tries to help but succeeds only in getting in the way. "Help" of this kind menaces the physical security of the recipient, which may already be shaky.

The objection to help, however, is not limited to useless or interfering acts. Many of the subjects also objected because of an indomitable need for independence. Although assistance may expedite the achieving of an immediate goal, the long-range goal of learning-to-do-for-oneself is blocked. These subjects protested against being babied and spoke of the fear of becoming a burden and of being spoiled. Accepting help may lead to an anticipation of helplessness in the future, which creates uncertainty and fear. Rejecting help in order to learn to do things for oneself not only increases one's independence but also enhances feelings of personal worth.

Thus, with regard to expediting matters, many of the subjects restricted acceptance of help to *necessary* help; but because of the manifold meanings of help already pointed out, the concept of necessity tends to be more stringent than is commonly conceived. The degree of inconvenience tolerated by a person with a disability before he considers help necessary often far exceeds that ordinarily tolerated by a nondisabled person. The subjects in the help study tended to use the term "necessary help" in the strict sense of absolute necessity, i.e., without which a goal is excluded no matter how much effort one is willing to expend. Even then, the findings show, concern about help is due less to the question of its necessity than to the strong fear of social inferiority and dependency connoted by it.

This is not to say that help is never exploited. There is ample clinical evidence to show that certain individuals revel in their disability, demanding all kinds of unnecessary help, as a way of ruling the roost or satisfying their need for dependency or perversely reassuring themselves that they are loved. That these motivations for accepting help do not appear in the help study is not surprising, for they are personally unfavorable and tend to be kept private if not suppressed from consciousness.

Management by the Recipient

As in the case of curiosity, the recipient, for better or for worse, reacts in some way to situations involving help. In order to become more intimately in touch with the different meanings of being helped as well as to observe how the recipient does react and cope, we shall examine several scenes from real life experiences as reported in autobiographical accounts.

Henry, a young boy with dwarfed and deformed lower limbs, goes swimming with the neighborhood boys. The help he receives is so natural and situation-rooted that it is just as naturally accepted:

. . . one day some of the big boys came by and called up to ask Mamma if I could go for a walk—over by the river. Mamma finally said yes, but be careful.

I walked part of the way, and when I got tired they hoisted me up on their shoulders. Then I really was tall—taller than seven feet. We came to the railroad tracks. I had never been this far from home except with Mamma or Papa, and it was exciting.

"Look at that old cardboard," Marble Bags [the champion marbles player] said. It was a big piece. It must have been wrapped around a mattress or something.

"Let's build a shelter."

An empty freight car stood on a track and the boys put the cardboard under it and bent it like the sides of a house. Then we all crawled inside and they talked about baseball and girls. It started to rain, so we stayed. It was just like being in a clubhouse. One of the boys took out a cigarette butt and lit it.

"Give me a puff," somebody said.

"Look, the sun's out. Let's go swimming." Marble Bags ran across the tracks and down to the river where he peeled off his pants and shirt and dived off a big rock.

The other boys picked me up, and we ran after him.

I sat on the bank and watched them paddle around.

"Come on in," they yelled. "We'll hold you up."

Did I dare? Of course, they said. Hesitantly I took off all my clothes except my boots, and two of them let me down over the side of the rock.

"It's cold," I shrieked. But as soon as I had been in the water a minute it felt wonderful. I paddled with my short legs while they held onto my hands.

"I can swim! I can swim—almost," I gasped [Viscardi, *1952*:32–33].

However, the help situation is not always so comfortable. Sometimes it is hated but the recipient feels powerless to do anything but "grin and bear it." The following is an instance of boorish, self-aggrandizing help. Henry Viscardi, now a young man, is again the recipient:

The train disgorged a mass of us at a midtown station, and I glanced again at the address of the employment agency I would "visit" today, trying to memorize the address. . . . A dried-up-looking man came by and took my arm. Despite my unresponsiveness, he drew me up a flight of stairs and all the way out of the station where he deposited me with a sanctimonious smile on the wrong side of the street.

Mother of God, I thought, I bet he's the kind who goes to church and prays for those poor helpless cripples [Viscardi, *1952:*71].

In the following scene, Harold Russell, whose injury caused the loss of both hands, has no alternative but to submit. Though the help was necessary, it was unrelenting torture and continued to be as he mused over it. His pride is hurt deeply, for the help stirred again the desperate doubts about his manliness. The airline hostess has just instructed the passengers to unfasten their safety belts:

I started to pull my hooks out of my pockets, but they got stuck. I wrestled with them for a few seconds and finally I got them out after nearly ripping off my pants. Then I began fumbling with the belt. She had offered to close it before we took off, but I declined stiffly. Now she stood over me like a schoolteacher, watching me struggle with it. I just couldn't seem to get a grip on that slippery metal buckle. I could almost hear her saying, "See! What did I tell you? You can't do it by yourself." That only made me more nervous. Finally she reached down, flipped it open and walked off triumphantly into the cockpit.

I fell back against the seat. This was the ultimate humiliation. Only a few months before I had been the rough, tough paratrooper, boldly leaping out into the wild blue yonder. Now I had sunk so low I couldn't even open a simple safety belt without the help of a woman. I thought of what the boys in my old outfit would have said to that. I could hear them laughing [Russell, *1949:*128].

Though help may be humiliating, the recipient gradually learns how to make it more palatable in situations in which he cannot do without it. Russell Criddle, for example, while still a teen-ager, attempted to confine help to situations in which it was absolutely needed because of his poor vision; he then took the *initiative* as to where and how it should take place. The boys are planning a swimming outing down the river:

Someone grabbed my arm.

"Go get your suit, Russ. I'll lead you, and if anybody says you're blind, I'll push his face in."

It was Bud [leader of the gang]. He had humbled himself to such a degree just so I could go swimming. But I pictured him leading me, with the gang looking on in anguished pity, and the thought was intolerable.

"You won't have to lead me," I said. "Just let me put my hand on your arm down by the dump and across the tracks" [Criddle, *1953:*28].

Criddle also developed the policy of letting the most distinguished person in the group lead him through difficult places:

I found that it didn't seem to embarrass them so much as it did others, and it was easier for me to accept condescension from someone whom I admitted to be my superior [p. 42].

When help is not felt to be necessary, the reaction depends largely on whether the recipient is indignant or not. If an insult is presumed, it is met by an unfriendly counteraction. On that first furlough home after his injury, Harold Russell recalls:

> Fred [a sailor friend] was uncomfortable, too. We didn't know how to greet each other. Somehow, it seemed gruesome to extend my hook, so we just nodded stiffly and said hello. Then he reached out to take my bag, but I yanked it away quickly. I didn't need his help [Russell, *1949:*130–131].

If no offense is presumed the person is able to reject or accept the help in a matter-of-fact or good-natured way. In the following instance the help is naturally declined. Mr. Wilke, born without arms, visited the Bruckner family, whose child was similarly disabled. Mrs. Bruckner relates:

> It was almost eight o'clock when he arrived. My first reaction was sheer amazement at the size of the suitcase that he had strapped to his shoulders. Hy tried to help him remove it, but he quickly said, "Thank you, I am able to manage it by myself" [Bruckner, *1954:*175].[9]

Gracious acceptance of unnecessary help also becomes possible. Louise Baker, a young woman leg amputee, became convinced that this was by far the most agreeable reaction in most situations:

> Excess generosity is one of the problems a handicapped person faces. I have found that I am more likely to err in refusing than accepting. Seats offered me in crowded cars; special consideration in the queue at a theater; porters rushing through trains to open doors for me; shoppers giving me their turn at a busy counter in a store—and even cameos, presented by strangers. They all pose a problem.
>
> A handicapped person doesn't win any of these on his merit, and frequently he doesn't require any such thoughtfulness. In my childhood and teens, I am sure I was very rude in my constant huffy refusals of any kind of aid. I have grown more mellow, more sensible, and, I believe, more kindly.
>
> Frequently I accept proffered places in crowded buses or trolleys, from tired, elderly men who I know need the seats much more than I. But, according to faultless authority, "It is more blessed to give than to receive." For the most part, I am convinced it is up to the handicapped person graciously to let the giver be blessed [Baker, *1946:*117–118].

The person with a disability is sometimes in the position where he must ask for help. If receiving help is degrading to him, not only will he wait

---

[9] Leona S. Bruckner, *Triumph of Love,* New York, Simon and Schuster, Inc., 1954. By permission.

until it becomes absolutely necessary but his request will be made bitterly, or at best apologetically. When, however, the help situation does not connote any feelings of devaluation, but rather acceptance and good will, the request for help may come naturally and easily. Wilke, the armless visitor, sat down to eat. His hostess recalls:

> I tried to be casual as I placed his dinner plate on the table, explaining that I was serving him family style as it was quicker. I was determined not to offer to help him in any way unless he asked me to. I had thought that it might be embarrassing to him to have us all gathered around while he ate, but he very nonchalantly asked us to keep him company. He smiled at me as he said, "Oh, steak, this is a treat. But I am afraid I will need your assistance with this, Leona. This is one meat that I can't cut with a fork." I cut his steak into cubes while he continued talking. "I have a special combination knife and fork at home [which he uses with his foot], but since I try to travel light, I can't bring it along and must rely on the kindness of my hostess" [Bruckner, *1954:* 176].

The act of helping, as we have seen, can either lead to good will and firmer interpersonal relations or to ill will, personal hurt, and the disintegration of social relationships. What principles can be formulated whereby the act of helping will produce beneficial rather than negative results?

Recommendations

The investigators in the help study (Ladieu, Hanfmann, Dembo, *1947*) offer certain practical recommendations suggested by the findings.

The fact that rejection of help is both an expression of status anxieties and a realistic means for achieving self-reliance leads to two basic recommendations to the helper. First, the helper will be better prepared to meet the situation adequately if he keeps in mind that a person with a disability may want to limit his use of help to instances of absolute necessity. This mind-set should not be difficult to establish inasmuch as there is indication that the noninjured perceive cripples in general as being persistent and giving up only after definite proof of impossibility. In one study (Mussen and Barker, *1944*), the subjects rated cripples on 24 character traits; of these, self-reliance and persistence were rated nearest to their ideal. It would seem, then, that the effectiveness of this awareness may often be weakened by the helper's own needs, such as self-aggrandizement and pity, which lead him to insist on helping when help is not wanted. The helper must, therefore, become aware of his own feelings and needs so that these can be kept from obscuring the determination as to whether help should be offered.

Secondly, the helper can reduce the negative social implications of help by his own behavior. The subjects in the help study indicated two main principles for making the act of helping a more comfortable one:

To begin with, they stressed the importance of obtaining the consent of the person involved. The helper must realize that he is in a relatively poor position to know just when help is needed, and of what kind. For one thing, the helper as an outsider does not have knowledge of the actual behavior limitations and how best to meet them. In fact, the general tendency to overestimate the degree of disability frequently makes him see the person as more helpless than he actually is.

Who but the initiated or specifically informed would guess that Wilke, the armless visitor, could manage very adequately at the table, at personal grooming, and at being a man around the house? The following scenes are described by Mrs. Bruckner, the mother of the armless boy, whose home he was visiting.

At the table:

He pulled off his loafer, picked up the fork and started eating. I cannot describe how easy and graceful his motions were. He did not use his bare feet, as I had expected, but his left, black silk sock was specially made. It had been sewn like the first two fingers of a glove. He only needed the big toe, which he used like a thumb, and the first digit; an unusually large space had developed between them, like the space between a normal thumb and first finger. He did ask me to give him a cup instead of a glass, but aside from that he manipulated everything so easily and neatly that I couldn't help but compare him favorably with my own often clumsy movements. He selected a piece of bread from the bread tray and spread it with butter; everyone knows how slippery and difficult to manage hard butter is. But, unlike many of my able-bodied guests, he dropped no crumbs on my carpet and spilled no food on my tablecloth. When he had finished eating, his place at the table was orderly and clean, and I felt ungainly in comparison to his efficiency [Bruckner, *1954*:177].

At personal grooming:

. . . He bent down and wiggled out of his jacket. Then he picked it up with his toes and hung it on a hanger more neatly than my husband has ever been able to do. He wore suspenders, which he could slip off his shoulders with no trouble. His shirt had a full-length zipper, concealed in the front, instead of the usual buttons. . . . since he travels a lot on lecture tours and doesn't want to carry too much baggage, he wears only nylon or orlon shirts and underwear and washes them out each night [Bruckner, *1954*:179].

At being a man around the house:

He told us that he danced, but didn't care much for it. He owned and operated a car and had a regular driver's license. "I do everything that any other family man attends to around the house," he said. Then he grinned and looked down at his feet. We were sitting in the living room and he had not yet put on his socks. "You can see that I painted the baby's crib last week," he said. "I love to go around barefoot, and I haven't yet been able to get all the blue paint off my feet. I do all my own painting and repairing, take care of putting up the screens and storm windows and all that sort of thing" [Bruckner, 1954:181].

Can you imagine the same settings but differently enacted because a helper insisted on spoon-feeding Mr. Wilke, on removing his jacket and his shirt, on stirring the paint and painting the crib for him? Yet such annoying if not humiliating interference is precisely what occurred when the man escorted Viscardi across the street (see pp. 226–227) and is repeated countless times in the lives of many persons with disabilities.

Moreover, even if the helper correctly judges that the person needs help, he may lack the necessary experience as to just what to do to be most helpful. For instance, how could a sighted person realize without being told that it is better for the blind person to touch him lightly than to be held closely while crossing the street? Add to this the consideration that all too often the helper's own needs for a pat on the back or for reassurance that he is better off get in the way, and the advice *offer but don't persist* becomes obligatory.

Since the person with a disability may be too proud or otherwise restrained to ask for needed help, there is justification for sometimes offering help rather than waiting to be asked. However, only under special circumstances should continued efforts to help be made in the face of resistance by the recipient and generally in these instances the help should be offered again rather than administered without his consent. (See the case of Mary, p. 175.)

The second principle refers to the manner in which help is executed. The subjects strongly opposed all fuss and emotional display in helping. Ostentatious help conveys a feeling that the helper is enhancing his own self-satisfaction at the cost of one less fortunate. Rather, help should be offered matter-of-factly, in a way that is pointed to the demands of the situation rather than to the help relationship itself.

These precautions will minimize the danger that such experiences as the following will occur:

I went out with a teacher to a concert; we travelled by bus. I have enough vision to get on and off a bus without being told when to step and being clung to as if I would run away. Every time there was a step she would say "Step" in no quiet voice and I know everyone was looking me up and down. It made me feel like crying [Sommers, 1944:32].

Help offered matter-of-factly diminishes the possibility that help will be useless or hindering. It gives the person with a disability a chance to reject the help or to explain how it can best be performed. And most important of all, negative implications of subservience and inferior status will be minimized.

The authors of the help study also advance several penetrating recommendations to the person with a disability. They point out that the recipient could well take cognizance of the fact that the act of help in itself cannot be taken as a measure of how he is regarded, for refraining from helping may place more emphasis on the disability than casually offering assistance. They also point out that restricting help to situations of absolute necessity may foolishly eliminate much useful assistance. What is most important is a reinterpretation of the meaning of help—that is, of the reasons for which it is offered by the helper and accepted by the recipient. Just as help is offered to "normal" persons not because of their general state of helplessness but merely because a situation seems to call for help, so may a person with a disability realize that it can be offered to him *not* as to a *disabled person* but as to someone who is having difficulties in *particular situations*. This involves a reorganization of the self-image, for as we have seen (Chap. 7) the self-concept is central to the interpretation of social relationships.

Perhaps these points sound obvious if not platitudinous. If so, the obvious needs to be extricated from the dull and uninteresting. Consideration of help can no longer be neglected, for help *is* a problem. All too often the helper barges in and is so intent on letting the recipient or the wider group know of his solicitousness that what could have been welcomed help is resented. Likewise, the recipient all too often sees in the help relationship another indication of his inferiority whereas actually it is an expression of good will toward a person having difficulties in the particular situation.

Although the discussion of help referred explicitly to the narrower sense of bodily assistance, the reasons for approving and rejecting help as a social relationship or as an expediting act apply to nonphysical help situations as well. Criddle, for example, with vision poor enough to be classed as legally blind, could not accept the services of an agency for the blind, even though he was desperately in need of employment during the depression days. Sheltered employment meant to him dependency, helplessness, personal and social admission that he was inferior (Criddle, *1953:* Chap. 21). Likewise, emotional help as expressed in sympathy can be welcomed or distrusted, depending on the form it takes and the meanings conveyed to the recipient. It is to the emotional relationship of sympathy and pity that we shall now give our attention.

THE PROBLEM OF SYMPATHY

Sympathy, that basically human expression of warm concern of one person for another, does not always afford consolation. The same factors that were significant in the evaluation of curiosity and help apply to the evaluation of sympathy: self-regard, situational and personal context, wish for adjustment and desire to be understood, the behavior of the agent. Instead of detailing these factors again, we shall analyze the problem of sympathy in a somewhat different way. Unwanted sympathy will be examined first, followed by the kind of sympathy that is potentially acceptable. The latter will be examined in terms of the fundamental nature of the sympathy relationship. The discussion is based essentially on the work of Dembo and her associates (*1956*, Chap. 6).

Unwanted Sympathy

Sympathy may be rejected because of the *desire for privacy*. This occurs, most commonly, when the recipient wishes to hide his disability or at least to act as if it did not make any difference to him. It also occurs when the person wants to be left alone with his feelings because he needs to mourn (see pp. 109–115), because he does not wish to burden others with his troubles, or because he feels he must first get hold of himself.

Sympathy may also be rejected when the recipient senses *contaminating attitudes* in the other person, such as devaluation or insincerity. Pity as we shall use it presumes a status relationship in which the agent looks down upon the recipient; it involves devaluation even though the agent may wish to help the sufferer. Sympathy contaminated with pity is surprisingly easy to detect. The following examples show how difficult it is to camouflage the feeling of devaluating pity. In both cases the agent probably would have acknowledged only the most honorable motives, but the undercurrent of pity makes a travesty out of the seeming benevolence:

John, a spastic boy, related, "I went to the theater with my mother. A stranger walked up to her and said, 'I'm awfully sorry your son turned out this way' " [Foster, *1948*:9].

Nancy, a young girl, said, "I was sitting in the waiting room at a department store. A woman came up to me and offered me a quarter. She said it was because of my 'little crippled legs' " [Foster, *1948*:9].

Pity that produces the feeling of being devaluated and not worth much tends to cause additional suffering. Of all the attitudes of another person to the self, it is among the most hated.

Insincere sympathy may be expressed by the agent for the purpose of adhering to the ethical ideal of being a good person. Sometimes this implies self-aggrandizement, in which case it is resented. However, insincere sympathy may be evaluated as proper when seen as a formal expression of politeness. Here the agent conveys only a recognition of the seriousness of the event and his intention not to intrude further into the privacy of the recipient. Formal sympathy, therefore, bears no great dangers, but the investigators of the sympathy study caution that it should emphasize the event and not the man: To say, "I'm sorry it happened" conveys what is needed. "I'm sorry for you" may connote devaluation. Resentment may also be incurred when the recipient, mistaking the sympathetic overtures for genuine feelings, assumes a concern that does not exist. Should the recipient confide in the agent, he is left with a feeling of having been used, cheated, or shorn of his protective defenses.

Even when the recipient may be ready to accept sympathy, he may find the relationship a disturbing one because of certain *ineptitudes in the agent*. What, then, does characterize acceptable sympathy? How should sympathetic persons act? The specifications as to appropriate behavior can be seen as fitting into a human relationship that has a coherent underlying structure.

Nature of Potentially Acceptable Sympathy

The fundamental characteristics of sympathy, as delineated by the investigators of the sympathy study, are congruence, understanding, and readiness to help.

In a sympathy relationship, the feelings and perceptions of the agent and the recipient are not and cannot be identical because the content of their distress is different. The recipient is distressed over the loss itself, the agent because the recipient suffers. Their moods need not be similar. If someone is depressed, the sympathizer need not also become depressed. Instead of identity, what is required is a *congruence* of feeling and understanding of the participants. Congruence rather than identity, moreover, would seem to hold a better potential for diminishing the distress. Not only do different points of view introduce new angles, but the sympathizer can well remain free of the anxiety and fearfulness of the person in distress since these emotions act as barriers to realistic evaluation of the situation.

What makes for congruence in emotional relationships needs further study. We do know that gay attempts to divert a person suffering a loss will be felt as incongruous and "rub him the wrong way." The sympathy study also points out that expressions of concern that are immoderate may be very disturbing to the recipient. The reasons are several: The recipient may be emotionally so keyed up in regard to the whole disability situation that additional emotion is difficult to bear. Any strong emotional expression may also make the person feel that his situation is even more unfortunate than he thought it to be. It may arouse feelings of guilt in the person at having caused so much distress in others. It may lead to embarrassment because the person does not know how to act in the face of strong emotion. Furthermore, excessive emotionalism may lead the person to doubt the sincerity of the feeling and to sense self-aggrandizing motives. What is equally important, excessive emotion has the danger of making the agent imperceptive to the shifts in feelings and needs of the sufferer. Just as music may be cacophonic or harmonious, so may the array of emotions between two persons clash or be in tune.

The second essential to sympathy, *understanding,* requires first and foremost that the agent give sufficient weight to both sides of an underlying conflict in the sufferer, the conflict between wishing to remain preoccupied with the loss on the one hand and wishing to escape the negative character of the situation on the other. Thus, the agent must have sufficient respect for the distress itself (even if he is not aware of its cause or ramifications) and not try immediately to dissipate it. The investigators of the sympathy study provide the following example:

. . . a mother may be genuinely concerned over the unhappiness of her adolescent daughter, but if she tries to soothe her by saying, "It's only puppy love. You'll soon forget all about him," the daughter, even when recognizing her mother's concern, will feel that she doesn't understand and thus that she is not really sympathetic. Similarly, if someone tries to "cheer-up" an injured friend by saying, "Oh, you'll soon get a new leg," he may be felt to take lightly the feeling of loss which the injured man experiences. It is equivalent to saying to someone bereaved, "You'll soon get a new wife!" [Dembo, Leviton, Wright, *1956:*28].

At the same time, because the sympathizer wishes to help bring about emotional relief, he may with impunity try to emphasize certain positive aspects of the situation as long as his efforts are not taken as a defection from matters of great moment to the sufferer. In this way both sides of the conflict are respected.

The investigators point out that the word "understanding" does not imply only a conscious intellectual appreciation of the diverse meanings of the loss for the recipient. "It seems as though there is such a thing as emotional understanding—that is, grasping the emotions of the other person directly on the emotional level without the intermediate step of intellectual realization of these emotions" just as one may spontaneously catch a ball suddenly thrown to him without intellectually deciding on a course of action (p. 29). An excellent example of such emotional sensitivity is seen in the following example of a mother comforting her son. Ohnstad, when a young high school boy, knew he was going blind. He had not been able to go to school during the past year, and the fear of blindness was overwhelming. His mother emotionally understood. Ohnstad recalls:

I looked in the mirror many times daily to see if the redness in my eyes was going away. Sometimes they seemed clearer, and hope returned. When they looked redder than before, my heart sank. There was a strange tightness in my throat, a vague feeling of dread within me. The lids felt hot. When I awoke in the morning, matter had dried upon my lashes and sealed them together. I brooded over the fact that my classmates were going ahead in school while I sat at home doing nothing. I was being left behind.

Mother called me into her room one night.

"I thought you might like to have me read a little from the paper," she said as I stood in the doorway, blinking at the light. Her intention was, I knew, to try and cheer me up.

"There's a story here," she said. "I thought you might like to hear it." She read a few lines in her laborious broken English, then she stopped. "I wouldn't feel so badly about it if I were you," she said, apparently divining my thoughts. "Even if you have to stay out of school one year, that's nothing. You can catch up again easily."

I said nothing, but the tears welled into my eyes and trickled down my cheeks. Mother's voice faltered. She dabbed her eyes with her handkerchief. "I know it's hard," she said brokenly, "It's hard now, but some day—some day things will be better" [Ohnstad, *1942*:21–22].[10]

"I know it's hard, but some day things will be better" is the core of emotional understanding; it recognizes both the absorption with the difficulties and the need for eventual overcoming of the distress. Such emotional understanding can take place in young children. A child, without knowing the facts or understanding the implications, can sense distress in another and convey real sympathy.

The importance of emotional understanding by no means relegates intellectual understanding to second position. Intellectual understanding, by giving rise to useful suggestions that the recipient may be ready to accept, may increase the effectiveness of the help offered.

The third essential of sympathy is a *readiness to help* the recipient overcome his distress. Concern that does not carry with it a willingness to put oneself out for another is felt to be insincere or at best a formal expression of sympathy, otherwise empty.

[10] Karsten Ohnstad, *The World at My Fingertips,* Indianapolis, The Bobbs-Merrill Company, 1942. By permission.

But what can the sympathizer do to help? In a particular situation, concrete suggestions may be appropriate, as when the agent informs the person of rehabilitation facilities. What we are after, however, is not a listing of the concrete ways of sympathetically "saying and doing," for this is limitless, but rather some guides that can apply to the sympathetic relationship in general. Dembo and her associates (*1956*) propose one important guide—namely, that the agent should be *passive* or *active,* depending upon the recipient's wishes and upon the recipient's momentary tendency to remain absorbed with his suffering or to escape from it. They point out that a deep positive feeling on the part of the sympathizer can be conveyed without demonstrative manifestations. There are times, probably not infrequent, when the sympathizer can help best by just "standing by"; there is a mutual understanding that, as the situation warrants it, the agent is ready to participate more actively. This requires that the agent be sensitive to the occasions when he can strengthen the forces in the recipient to meet and overcome his suffering without provoking resistance from him. The authors of the sympathy study point out that the sympathizer must be ready to abandon any benevolent attempts at the first sign that he has proceeded beyond the ability of the recipient to follow him. Because the sympathizer wishes to help, he may proceed too quickly in his efforts to cheer the sufferer and even become impatient with the recipient's slow pace at overcoming his sorrow. The sympathetic person emotionally understands that "haste is made slowly" and thus his help is a readiness that ideally is transformed into more active participation as he receives cues from the recipient concerning the kind of help that will be most constructive. The actual adjustive value of the help will depend on the wisdom of both agent and recipient, though it is altogether likely that sympathy as an expression of we-group feelings, giving assurance that one is of worth to another person, always has some adjustive value.

Recommendations to the sympathizer as to how he may best serve the recipient have necessarily been woven into the discussion of the nature of acceptable sympathy. Management by the recipient of unwanted sympathy will not be described here, for sufficient material to understand the nature of such attempts has already been given in regard to the situations of curiosity and of help.

THE PROBLEM OF SOCIAL PARTICIPATION

"How can a blind guy be a member of the gang?" (Criddle, *1953*:20). In this way young Criddle was challenged when he returned to the club of which he had been a member until his accident had destroyed almost all his vision. And for the first time he feared blindness with a terror more blinding than his sightless eyes, for the consequences of blindness seemed irrevocably to include social ostracism. When a person with a disability fears his disability, he may above all fear that he will be left behind, that he will be out of the running, that he will stand alone, excluded from normal group activities.

"Treat Me Like Anyone Else"

In a desperate defense against threat to social acceptance and participation the person not uncommonly appeals to the world with the exhortation "Treat me like anyone else!" Underlying this may be the fervent wish to hide the disability, to act like a nondisabled person, and to be treated like a nondisabled person. This was true in young Ohnstad's case during his early adjustment to his blindness. At that time he needed the conviction that he was just as he was before, that blindness in fact made no real difference. To prove this illusion he had to maintain the standards of sighted behavior as his own:

I preferred the bruises, however, to walking around with my hands stretched out before me. It was too conspicuous. I did not want to be stared at and looked upon as helpless and *different from others*. And so I continued to bang into doors; and chairs out of their accustomed places continued to bruise and cut the flesh on the front of my legs with their sharp edges. At night my socks had grown fast to my skin, and I had to pull the scabs off with them [Ohnstad, *1942*:45, italics ours].

To maintain this illusion, Karsten Ohnstad had to insist on being treated like anyone else. He even wanted people to laugh at him when he fumbled and stumbled just because this reaction would have been elicited in the case of a nondisabled person (p. 45).

But had they indeed laughed, Ohnstad would have felt just as hurt; in either case, the silence or the laughter would have been seen as stimulated by the fact of his blindness. As long as he regarded this fact as a devaluating one, identity of treatment would remain impotent to effect a comfortable acceptance in social participation. Actually, identity of treatment in many instances may point up a difference that could remain quite unobtrusive with special treatment. Serving steak to an arm amputee because he should be treated like anyone else would more certainly call attention to his disability than had a more manageable main dish been planned. Identity of treatment may boomerang in yet another way, for unless one allows for modifications in the situation, the injunction resolves itself into an all-or-none rule: either one treats identically or one does not treat at all; that is, the person becomes excluded from the situation.

It is necessary to realize that special treatment in itself does not mean stigmatizing treatment. One does not debase a deaf person because one is careful to provide adequate light for lip reading. One does not debase an amputee because one gears the step to a more leisurely pace. Debasement does not depend upon how similar the treatment is to the usual pattern, but rather upon underlying attitudes.

Inclusion Through Accommodation

Instead of identity of treatment serving as the guide to social behavior, the person with a disability and those around him should think rather in terms of how the person can best participate. And with this thinking new and varied possibilities emerge. A lame boy plays baseball:

I played with the boys of the neighborhood, sharing in all their games and sports, even baseball. I was catcher, since that position required less getting around, and when it came my turn to bat, another boy ran the bases for me when I hit the ball [Goldman, 1947:53–54].

The following account of a party that Ohnstad as a blind college student attended is reported at some length because it demonstrates how a series of accommodating modifications evolved as a natural process:

At first those who invited me—and I myself—took it for granted that I could take no part in the fun-making. Parlor games were made for sighted persons, not for blind men. It was better for me to remain safely in one spot than to go galloping about the room crashing into furniture and knocking over the statuary. And so, while the others played games and had a good time, I sat in an easy chair like an old grandfather, smiling at the shouts and laughter of the youngsters and wistfully recalling the lost days of my youth. . . .

The girls who selected the games, however, were on the alert.

"You can play this one as well as the rest of us," Nan said. "All you've got to do is think about what the one who is thinking is supposed to be thinking, and—"

To everyone's surprise, there were more games that I could take part in than we had imagined.

"Bring your marked cards along," Chet reminded. "We're going to play five hundred or bridge or something."

Braille cards were a novelty to the others at the party.

"What are all these dots on here—flyspecks?" Joe asked, staring at the cards as I dealt them around.

Patty held a card out before me. "But how can you tell which is which?"

I explained the system of initials and numbers. "See these three dots? That's the letter J. And these two dots next to it? That's the letter C—the jack of clubs." . . .

Very soon I was taking almost as active a part in the fun-making as anyone else. . . . A delegation of four marched into the room.

"We are supposed to guess by their actions what book they are trying to represent," Clara said. "Two of them are sitting on the floor and another is— well, looks as if she's got a long stick and is trying to jab holes in the floor. Bob is waving his arms in a big circle as if he were turning wheels."

Bob moved slowly from one end of the room to the other uttering a dull, monotonous "hooo! hooo!" That was easy. He was a boat of some kind. Maybe a freighter. There was no book represented in all these indications of adolescence that I could make out, unless it could have been "Wynken, Blynken and Nod."

The two sailors on the floor began talking.

"Keep your head down until we get past!" The voice was piping and as boyish as a girl could make it.

"Yas sah! Dey nebbah see me whuh ah is!"

This was confusing. It might have been Robinson Crusoe and his man Friday, but where did the steamboat and the boy with the fishing pole come from!

"Ships in the Sky!" The audience was off to a catalogful of titles: "Showboat!" "Nigger of the Narcissus!" . . .

"Three Men in a Tub," I shouted. "Twenty Thousand Leagues Under the Sea."

Jack leaned toward me from the other end of the davenport.

"What would a steamboat be doing twenty thousand leagues under the sea?"

"That's right," I said, turning to my informant and back to the actors again. "The Wreck of the Hesperus!"

"I don't know what they'd be doing with that pole unless they were on a— I've got it!" Clara jumped up excitely. "Huckleberry Finn!"

"Right!" . . . [Ohnstad, 1942:208–211].

Participation was made possible at this party because Ohnstad was *not* treated like anybody else. Games were selected in which he could get along with little or no help; Clara described a little bit of the charades to him as they were being enacted; Alice helped him write down the geographic names; Ohnstad himself felt free to ask for some readily available equipment so that he could write on his own.

All this is special treatment, but when it is inaugurated and executed matter-of-factly according to the requirements of the situation as they arise and change, special treatment can have the *psychological feel of being treated like anyone else,* for it is then that the person is not set apart from but is made a part of the social group. The lame boy who played baseball by having someone else run the bases for him felt, "I won my battle for equality among my fellows. They perceived that I wanted no special consideration and they gave me none" (Goldman, 1947:54). The special treatment was not felt to be special at all. It was so natural a requirement of the situation that it led to a feeling of equality; in order to treat him *as a person* like anyone else, one had to allow special treatment for that part of his tool equipment which was inadequate to the situation.

The point is an important one and should not be glossed over with a glib acquiescence that merely pays token agreement to its substance. Participation is a preëminent requirement of group belongingness and acceptance. Without it the person all too often feels truly "different," abnormal, and not wanted. This is brought out by a young man both of whose legs were paralyzed when he was three years old; after learning to swim, he asked these questions:

Why did I have to wait until I was 21 to learn I could be like others? Why did I always have to go to study hall when the others went out to play? [Daniels, *1948*:20].

What this man is decrying is his *exclusion* from activities which he could have entered. When he learned to swim, he was struck by the remarkable thought that he could do things that others did even though the performance was styled to fit his own idiosyncrasies. It was then that he began to feel like others, in spite of the fact that the details of his performance were different. *New Fountains,* a provocative play about a 16-year-old girl who recently had polio, presents a clear demonstration of how participation in the social life of her high school helped her feel a part of the community of other young people (Gilmore, *1953*).

This is not to say that situations should always be accommodated to the needs and wishes of a person with a disability. There are occasions when the necessary modifications might place an undue strain on the group. For example, a deaf person, even though a proficient lip reader, has difficulty functioning in a large group discussion, and to require the other members always to face him and to watch for signs that he has lost the trend of the conversation would interfere not only with the free flow of discussion but also with the level of intensive thinking. In these circumstances, however, it should be left up to the person with the disability as to whether or not he wishes to join the group even though little special attention can be given to his individual needs. He may wish simply to get as much as he can from the occasion, or perhaps even to enjoy the presence of others. At the same time he may decline the invitation, and the danger that his absence will be ascribed to social rejection is less likely to occur.

As part of the Dembo study, serious thought was given to the problem of participation and social acceptance (Ladieu, Adler, Dembo, *1948*). The investigators point out that exclusion from certain activities because of the *realities* of a handicap is totally different from the exclusion that stems from social rejection. In the former case the person may miss the activity, but in the latter case he is also hurt by the affront, which says in effect, "You are not good enough to associate with us. Keep your distance." The person with a disability may feel socially rejected (even though objectively this may not be the case) when he is kept from participating in activities that he believes he could manage.

The Dembo study also points out that the problem of social participation is complicated by the discrepancy between what the person with a disability sees as his limitations and what others see (Ladieu, Adler, Dembo, 1948). Frequently, when others judge that certain physical characteristics preclude an activity, the person himself knows that he can manage. The phenomenon of *spread* (see pp. 118–119) is one important factor responsible for this discrepancy. The recommendation is made that since the nondisabled person in most situations involving social participation cannot readily acquire information as to the variable capacities of the person with the disability, a willingness to have him participate should be indicated, the judgment as to whether or not he will be able to do so being left up to the person himself.

THE PROBLEM OF RIDICULE AND TAUNTING

With civilized acceptance of the "Golden Rule" and the proprieties of good social form, outright ridicule and taunting of a person's physical imperfections are permitted only under special circumstances. Social sanction is given to ridiculing one's enemies; during wartime, cartoons fairly revel in caricaturing the physique of the opposing forces. In political campaigns remarks about vulnerable physical attributes of an opponent may be made. Where there is no evident reason for vindictiveness, however, ridicule may be permitted if the intention is to evoke some positive effect in the recipient. For example, an adult may belittle a child for spilling food over himself in order, presumably, to encourage more mature eating habits.

Requirement of Mourning

The requirement of mourning makes possible a deeper understanding of the motivations behind devaluating pity, ridicule, and taunting (Dembo, Leviton, Wright, 1956:21). This hypothesis states: When a person has a need to safeguard his values, he will either (1) insist that the person he considers unfortunate is suffering (even when he seems not to be suffering) or (2) devaluate the unfortunate person because he ought to suffer and does not. This implies that the devaluer wants the unfortunate person to suffer. He wants him to suffer as a sign that the values denied the unfortunate person are still worthy and important and good. Especially if his security depends upon maintaining these values will he insist that the unfortunate person admit his suffering. "Consider a woman to whom 'position is everything in life.' She must consider as unfortunate those who are omitted from the social register. If she does not it would mean that her position is not so valuable after all. If they do not accept the fact that they are unfortunate, she must consider them either too stupid to know better, or insensitive, or shamming; otherwise her own position is threatened" (Dembo, Leviton, Wright, *1956*:21).

This is why the bully is typically a person beset with inferiority feelings. By deriding another he gives himself a pat on his unsupporting back. This is also why some members of minority groups disdain other minority groups that they consider lower on the social scale.

In ridicule and taunting are found the most blatant expression of the requirement of mourning. The kind of ridicule undertaken solely for the purpose of seeking personal advantage in the suffering of another is ethically taboo. Because it is so untutored and open, it is more frequently the instrument of children, who have not learned the more sophisticated ways to express their needs. Unfortunately, it is also children who bear the brunt of ridicule, children who may be quite defenseless to cope with the unrelenting jeers. An indication of how common this form of self-aggrandizement is in children is given in a study of the nicknames of children living in an orphanage (Orgel and Tuckman, *1935*). Nicknames of both boys and of girls referred to physical defects in about one third of the cases. Virtually all such nicknames were derogatory and produced resentment and ill feeling.

Among adults ridicule generally occurs more covertly, though open ridicule is by no means nonexistent. A man whose face is paralyzed on the right side reports that on the job ". . . the fellows made my life miserable. They would tell jokes and make faces the way I do when I talk. Or they would say 'are you trying to be tough, talking out of the side of your face?' " (Macgregor, *1951*:634). Usually, however, the expression of ridicule by adults seems to be more subtle; it may assume the character of devaluating pity cloaked with sympathetic overtones. So-called playful teasing in some instances may be a more artful expression of underlying ridicule. On the basis of interviews with 200 male college students taking corrective physical education, it was concluded that experiences with adults were far more pleasant than experiences with children of the atypical child's own age or younger (Stafford, *1947*:80).

Management by the Recipient

What does a young child do who is the object of taunts and jeers? He may try to strike back, but when his uncertain attempts are of no avail, his desperation is given vent in crying that is full of anger and hurt. Henry Viscardi, markedly dwarfed as a result of congenitally deformed legs, presents a heart-breaking account of just such an experience. The scene is his first day at grade school:

Mamma and Papa had wisely chosen a flat in the same block as the school. It was on 101st street near Amsterdam Avenue. My sister Terry took me to school the first day. Clutching her hand I hoisted myself up the steps to the schoolyard. It was crowded with children, bouncing balls, playing hopscotch, and running up and down the steps. I had never seen so many children, not even at the hospital. And these were all so big. I tried to back away.

"What's the matter, Henry?" Terry patted my shoulder. "You'll be all right—soon as you get used to it."

Then I heard loud laughter. "Hey, Louie, looka the ape man."

Three big boys came toward me.

"I'll show you where your room is." Terry jerked my hand.

The laughs grew louder. "Come on, Henry," Terry urged. Her cheeks were red.

The crowd of jeering boys had grown. One of them, who had a thin face and dirty, light-colored hair, came over and shoved me. I shoved back, against his knee.

"Oh, you wanta fight, kid?"

"Cut it out, Mike," somebody yelled.

"You—you—leave my brother alone." Terry almost cried. But the circle of boys held us in.

"Hey, ape man, what you got tied to your feet, boxing gloves?"

I looked down at my mismatching boots. They weren't a bit like the shoes the other boys wore.

"I want to go home." I hung on Terry's arm, tears rolling down my cheeks.

"Sissy, sissy. . . ."

Another big boy shoved me. I lost my balance and sprawled on the cement. Terry helped me up and brushed the dirt off my clothes. I started swinging my arms. The crowd pressed in and I couldn't see my sister anywhere.

Then the bell rang, and the boys ran into the building. Terry came back. "Here," she said, "blow your nose." She gave me her handkerchief. "Your hand's bleeding." I thought I saw tears in her eyes.

"Come on," she said. "I'll take you to your teacher" [Viscardi, *1952:*13–14].

Henry Viscardi's first day at school—Raymond Goldman's first day at school (see pp. 145–146). How alike they were!

As such incidents recur, the recipient tries one way of reacting and then another, hoping to find some way which will be effective. Russell Criddle reviews his attempts to cope with ridicule as a young teen-ager with extremely poor vision.

There had been some teasing, some mimicry which I had already learned to tolerate during my first few years as a handicapped person. I knew that I must never retaliate to the various negative reactions which children usually had toward me. The best way, I had learned, was to pretend not to be hurt, and I sensed that in this way I eliminated the feeling of remorse that both I and others would suffer if I showed resistance, or retaliated. This submission, I think, balanced the distress caused others by my handicap.

There were a few boys of the little-bully type who wouldn't let me disregard their reactions. I tried a benevolent, understanding attitude toward them, an attitude which said to the rest of the class, "They don't hurt me. I know my eyes are funny, and it doesn't bother me if they laugh."

But what was, in truth, humility struck them as aloofness, and they were further irritated. In pretending not to be hurt or not to notice them I supplied sustenance for their stupidity and their insensible concepts of blindness.

I tried to make friends with the boys, to be one of them, entering into what they wanted to consider a game of wits—laughing with them when they "pulled a good one," covering up for them if they were caught by the teacher.

Once one of the boys, pretending to be engrossed in study, let his foot stick out into the aisle so that I would trip over it. The teacher hadn't seen his foot, but I know she suspected when she asked, "What happened, Russell?"

"I slipped," I said with a laugh. The teacher understood, as did the rest of the class, and I can understand how this added to the irritation of the boy who had tripped me. He was winning the scorn of everyone. Matters soon reached the stage of a running conflict. . . .

. . . It was in study hall. The teacher was out of the room, and I was reading a history book. I had not noticed Mike [a schoolmate] as he walked down the aisle toward my desk and was not aware of him until I felt the pain of a blow against my knuckles. He had struck them with the sharp edge of a foot rule, the kind which had a thick piece of metal imbedded along one edge.

I didn't flinch, I didn't move.

He hunched his buttocks upon the top of my desk so that he was half sitting there. I raised my head until I was looking into his face. I could see that he was smiling.

"Don't you have any feeling, Criddle?" he asked in a matter-of-fact tone. I stared at him, and he struck my knuckles again.

Someone said, "Aw, Mike, cut it out!"

"I'll stop when he asks me to," Mike said. He struck again. . . .

He was saying, in effect, Look, he isn't like us. He doesn't feel pain, and loneliness, and hunger. Blindness makes him different. It makes him defenseless. There is nothing he can do but let me hurt him until I get tired of the sport. This is fun, look at me smile.

I let my eyes fall to my knuckles. They were bloody.

Afterwards I was told that I just stared at my knuckles for a moment and then screamed and lunged at Mike with a force that knocked him across one row of desks into another aisle. I sprang after him, pounding his face with my bloody knuckles until he called for help. Then I started choking him. I remember Mr. Singleton pulling me away and leading me, hysterical, to the boys' washroom [Criddle, *1953*:98–99, 101–102].

The strategies attempted by Criddle over the years were:
Not to retaliate. To pretend not to be hurt.
To be benevolent and understanding, an attitude that says, "I know my eyes are funny, and it doesn't bother me if they laugh."
Not to notice the jeerers; to ignore them.
To join the jeerers by ridiculing himself and covering up for them.
To return the attack; to retaliate with physical force.

Actually, none of these tactics could be effective in all or even most situations, for as long as the attacker needs an inferior to sustain his own uncertain status, he will keep probing until the desired response of suffering is elicited. That is why ignoring the jeers, or showing understanding of them, or submitting to them only provokes more vigorous attacks. The bully must get the unfortunate person to agree that he is a lowly creature and to suffer.

The method of active retaliation is effective only when the person is fortunate enough to be stronger than the attacker. Then the bully does not dare provoke that person again, but will instead turn to an easier scapegoat. The bully seeks another scapegoat, because the defeat at the hands of the first has injured his vulnerable self-esteem still further, an insult he hopes to avenge by forcing inferiority on someone else through the requirement of mourning.

In the discussion of curiosity, it was seen how the recipient may actively retaliate in nonphysical ways; reciprocal jeering is parallel to biting sarcasm (see pp. 212–213). This again is effective only when the recipient is more masterful at this game than is the bully. Too often a child who is physically handicapped is so humiliated that the control required for effective sarcastic retort is denied him. Weak submission, pretense, and angry attack seem to be easier defense mechanisms.

Recommendations

What, then, is the answer, if there is no fully adequate way for children to cope with ridicule? It is our opinion that extraordinary care should be taken to cut down as far as possible exposure to ridicule. All too often the child "learns" to agree with the bully that he is indeed a pitiful object that ought to be scorned. Moreover, the power of ridicule to defeat the recipient is so great that even a single such attack in childhood can leave emotional scars.

The most general need is for the development of wholesome attitudes toward disability through education at all levels of community life. In accord with democratic principles, education against religious and racial discrimination has been encouraged, and only recently has serious attention been given in the schools to the necessity for education in the overcoming of prejudice toward persons with disabilities. We need good visual aids and other methods in the elementary and high schools to inform children that physical attributes and styles of life differ widely among individuals, that within this assortment of differences lies the common core of the human being, that differences per se need not make a difference in many important areas of living together. If these views were part of the broad teaching of community and school, the problem in the case of a single child would be vastly simpler.[11]

One of the most important arguments in support of integrating children with disabilities in the regular public schools is that it provides the opportunity for all children to become familiar with and accustomed to differences. However, just grouping children together does not necessarily provide good group experiences, either for the children with disabilities or for those without. This is an area that begs for serious investigation.

Below is a demonstration of how role playing can enlighten the able-bodied child toward more mature acceptance of physical deviation. In role playing, persons are assigned to various roles and act them out. The psychodramatic episode took place in a home, but its application to settings of groups of children is apparent:

Larry, a 5-year-old, talked about Kate, a child in his class who had some difficulty in walking owing to a birth injury. He remarked, "Guess I'm lucky to be all right and not be stiff in the legs like Kate." A few days later he made some remark to the effect that he and the other children thought Kate was a dope. She could not do the things they could do. Soon after his mother suggested "that they play a game and that he should get hurt by a car and that he would go to the hospital and then get better."

LARRY. "Here I am in the street, and a car comes whizzing along and clips the tail of my bicycle so that I am thrown off on the street. Then my friend

---

[11] There is available an excellent instruction booklet for elementary school teachers on how to introduce and discuss in the classroom the matter of living with a physical disability (*Understanding the Disabled, 1956*). The activities and techniques suggested are designed to stimulate reëvaluation on the part of the children, leading to the development of adjustive attitudes toward disability. The procedures outlined include role playing and the discussion of stories and incidents. For a brief description of these see pp. 268–269.

Jim (a much older and admired boy) comes along and trips over me so that I get hurt."

MOTHER. "Yes, he accidentally runs over your leg, perhaps."

Larry is delighted and lies kicking on the ground in supposed pain. Mother and nurse-sister come rushing along and put him in an ambulance and take him to the hospital.

MOTHER. "Now I am the doctor. Hello, little fellow. What happened to you? Oh, it is your leg. Say, it is pretty bad, and it will take a while to get well. You will have to walk stiff-legged for a few weeks."

LARRY. "You mean I can't run and jump any more?"

DOCTOR. "No, you must take care of it for a long while. I guess you can get up now and try to walk." He lifts Larry onto his feet. "Oh no, you cannot move like that. You must not bend your knee except by lifting it up by your hand. See, when you want to go upstairs, you must raise the leg with the hand like this."

LARRY. "Oh, that is difficult. It makes my back tired before I get up the first flight of stairs." He puts forth much effort and pulls each leg onto the next step. He gets to the landing and sits down. "Say, this is not fun. Why are we playing this? I want to get well soon."

The mother sits down a moment on the step too. "Well, Larry, did you ever think of what Kate has to do when she walks upstairs? She never complains but keeps right on trying. Don't you think she is brave and courageous like the soldiers were in the war?"

LARRY. "Say, she is. I never thought of that before."

MOTHER. "Do you know how you can make it easier for Kate and have more fun yourself?"

LARRY. "No. How?"

MOTHER. "It makes Kate happy to have the boys and girls nice to her and not impatient with her when she is slow about getting places. Perhaps you can help the other children to be nice to her too. You know they think a lot of you, and if you showed them that you like Kate and think she is brave, they will not talk about her being a dope. That must make her feel pretty bad like it would make a soldier feel bad if you said he was a dope because he lost a leg fighting in the war" [Lippitt, Rosemary, 1947:157].

For the first time Larry assumed the "inside position" with respect to disability problems (see pp. 63–64). This sensitized him to such values as effort rather than achievement (see pp. 116–117) and to the aspect of coping with the disability situation (see pp. 59–61). He was then able to accept the evaluation that Kate's behavior was courageous and not stupid.

To set up and direct a good role-playing episode takes more skill than one might imagine. Wisdom and skill are also required to lead a well-directed discussion or to organize a meaningful lecture. The leader utilizing any of the procedures above is on safe ground if the message is geared to the *person with a disability* rather than to the *disabled person,* to the coping aspects in the situation rather than to the succumbing aspects.

Thinking along these lines can go far in developing adjustive attitudes, not only for the benefit of someone else who is different but also for the person himself, since he cannot excel in everything.

In addition to general preparation in the schools on the matter of disability, it is sometimes helpful to pave the way specifically for a child markedly different who is about to enter school or any other group. This has the possibility, at least, of abating inordinate curiosity and of leading to some sympathetic understanding that this child who is different is for all that a child who is the same. Sometimes the principal may be the best person to lead the discussion, sometimes the individual teacher, sometimes an invited speaker, and sometimes the parent. Karen's mother relates how she went to speak to the kindergarten class the day before Karen was to start school:

"I have a little girl, just your size, named Karen," I began in a conversational tone. "She's nice and laughs a lot and has freckles and pigtails." I turned to a tot at the nearest table. "But her pigtails are not as long as yours." I had done enough public speaking to know when I had established "contact."

"Now God didn't make Karen's legs as strong as yours," I went on, "so we have to help them get strong, so she can walk. Some children wear braces to help their teeth and Karen wears braces to help her legs. There are some things she can't do and some games she can't play. Sister will let some of you help her once in a while. But don't spoil her!" I laughed as I stood up. I went over to the doll house, admired it properly and asked the little lass in blue to show me some of the furnishings. "We have a real bureau with drawers that go in and out that will just fit in the bedroom. Karen will bring it tomorrow. Good-by, Sister, good-by, kids," I waved [Killilea, *1952:*111].

The words were few and simple, but they struck just the right chord. They prepared the children to see a child who is really a child, so much like them, yet different in particular ways; a child who needs help, but only some of the time; a child who is managing her difficulties and can be part of the group.

Parents of children with disabilities may perhaps be heartened by the realization that with maturity their children will be better able to cope with ridicule and other difficult social situations and that among the adult population the rules have changed. Although pity is common, the public expression of ridicule tends to be more controlled. Viscardi was not taunted during his first day at college as he was upon entering first grade.

In the last analysis we need to develop emotional security so that the need to tear another person down in order to build oneself up will become an insignificant factor in the social relations among men. The bully, too, is a person with a handicap, and he too requires help and understanding in the effort toward better adjustment.

Curiosity, discussion of the disability, help, sympathy, devaluating pity, social participation, taunting and ridicule—these interpersonal relations are especially potent in the lives of persons with disabilities. Study of them not only shows that their significance is part of the broader problem of the meaning of disability to the agent and to the person himself but points the way toward more satisfying relationships. Such concepts as status value, coping, succumbing, and spread appear again and again in the analysis of everyday relationships and in the recommendations for improving them.

Yet a good deal of the burden in interpersonal relations will be borne by the person with the disability himself. Although the pathology may lie with the group, the person himself is the one who is annoyed or hurt most directly. It is he who has to "take it," who has to handle the ineptitudes of his associates in the ordinary affairs of getting along. Because so often his own management ameliorates or augments the difficulties, training in social skills on the part of the person with the disability is very much indicated. This topic is treated in Chapter 11.

Chapter 10

Sources of Attitudes Toward Persons
with Atypical Physique

THE MANY ASPECTS OF THE SOCIAL PSYCHOLOGY OF DISABILITY ALREADY explored in the preceding chapters have necessarily included discussion of factors contributing to negative and positive attitudes toward persons with unusual physiques. Among these may be mentioned the requirement of mourning, physique as a value loss, the coping-succumbing dimension, expectation discrepancy, and spread. These factors were selected as being particularly relevant to the problem under discussion, but they hardly cover the multifarious conditions that contribute to the development of attitudes.

Because attitudes and their sources are crucial to the understanding of man's reaction to disability, on both the behavioral and emotional levels, the present chapter is devoted to a review of several additional and widely diverse factors that could not readily be treated in other connections. They concern primeval predispositions as examined in terms of reactions to physical deviancy on the part of animals and in primitive societies. They deal with perceptual and cognitive aspects that influence the apprehension of cause-effect relations and the reaction to the different and strange. They bear upon environmental influences as revealed in childhood experiences and socioeconomic conditions. These topics were selected because of the availability of highly interesting research and observational material, because they indicate the range of considerations that enter the problem of reaction to physical disability, and because in some instances they challenge common preconceived notions.

REACTION TO PHYSICAL DEVIANCY AMONG LOWER ANIMALS

It is interesting that man sometimes explains his antipathy toward persons with unusual physiques by pointing to comparable instances in the animal world. Such similarity presumably implies that man's negative reaction is fundamental or even instinctual. The attempt to understand human behavior in terms of animal behavior has been referred to as the "principle of genetic reductionism," and questioned in some scientific circles (Scheerer, *1954:*124 ff.).

In any case, the facts of animal psychology clearly debunk the myth that animals *in general* ostracize the physically deviate of their kind. Maisel (*1953,* Chaps. 4–6) has collated many anecdotes and objective observations of research workers concerning the reaction of fish, birds, and mammals to physically exceptional members of their species. A sample will show the heterogeneity of reaction among various species:

Goldfish with amputated fins live "happily" among their fellows.

Sharks will converge on a wounded shark and eat it.

Some ants do kill their old and enfeebled. Higher ant forms do not.

Termites eat their injured, but notably where there is a shortage of nitrogenous food.

An albino penguin was observed to be loved by his family but received with hostility by strangers.

Among fish, unusual coloring is of no importance.

Baboons are ruthless toward their physical inferiors.

The wolf does not attack or avoid physically atypical wolves.

Among chimpanzees, taking the part of the underdog is not uncommon.

In the light of such variability, Yerkes, the psychobiologist who has worked for half a century in the field of animal psychology, has said, "I am quite unable to make with confidence any general statements" in regard to the reaction of animals to the disabled (Maisel, *1953:*538). Maisel, in his extensive review of this matter, has hazarded a bolder statement about icthyological ways: "If there is, indeed, a law of the deep, it might well be that anything goes, and all kinds of atypical bodies can survive" (*1953:*479).[1] Sometimes, of course, a weak member may not survive because of competition for food and shelter, but this is quite different from ostracism and rejection.

The fact that the fable of the ugly duckling and the metaphor of the black sheep live on as paradigms is again evidence of man's proclivity to perceive the facts that fit and to fit the facts that do not. To make this point more impressive, let us have a look at the ways of hens, the hen being a domestic fowl under common observation. Everyone "knows" that a hen is prone to peck, even unto death, another bird who has a raw spot showing. This fact is retained and disseminated because it fits with the preconceived notion—and, in some instances, the need—that physical deviation and injury are anathema to mankind and life in general. The

[1] Edward Maisel, *Meet a Body,* 1953, by permission of Institute for the Crippled and Disabled.

fact that fowls do not react in this way to other kinds of physical irregularities is not even noticed. A hen that is paralyzed, for example, will maintain her pecking order and will not be relegated to the bottom of the pile (Maisel, *1953:*516).

Another example that shows how "naturally" our preëxisting ideas and needs tend to perpetuate incorrect notions is provided by the legend of the shark. Although it is an indisputable fact that sharks do destroy the wounded members of their own species, the ready anthropomorphic inference that this is motivated because of an aversion to deviation or of fear of some kind is far from the truth. But typically one does not pursue the why of the behavior, for when something is "all figured out," the disturbance produced by new facts is not welcomed. It so happens, however, that sharks distinguish what is food and not food by olfactory cues; the juices of an injured shark set up a chemical stimulus that brings on feeding behavior in other sharks (Maisel, *1953:*470). If the dispersion into the water could be siphoned off, shark cannibalism would not occur. The shark, evidently, is indifferent to the atypicality or injury as such.

In a word, the belief that lower life forms defile their disabled cannot be accepted as even a rough approximation.

ATYPICAL PHYSIQUE IN PRIMITIVE AND NONOCCIDENTAL SOCIETIES

Just as there is a belief that "human nature" is basically "animal nature," so there is a feeling that what occurs among primitive societies is really the primeval and true nature of man, which is only repressed or camouflaged by the superficial niceties and hypocrisies of civilization. Though such reasoning is questionable, anthropological horizons certainly broaden perspective, especially in replacing an ethnocentric point of view by an awareness of the otherwise unimaginable variety in the ways of man.

That Spartan rule is by no means universal in primitive societies is clearly shown in Maisel's compilation of data on more than 50 tribes and societies drawn from the Human Relations Area Files at Yale University (*1953:* Appendix). This latter source is equivalent to an extensive survey of anthropological literature, for the material collected in the Files was culled from books, articles, and records of anthropologists and other observers, abstracted, and classified so that it could be expediently used in a variety of studies. A sampling of the material is provocative:

Among the Siriono Indians, sickness not infrequently leads to abandonment and death.

In the Azande tribe, infanticide is not practiced. "Abnormal children are never killed nor do they seem to lack the love of their parents."

"A supplementary fifth finger or first toe is surprisingly common amongst these [Azande] savages who are usually proud of the addition. . . ."

Among the Navajo Indians, the ideals proscribe sadistic humor against those with physical deviations but in practice "A great deal of enjoyment is derived from commenting verbally or through pantomime on the personal afflictions, infirmities, and peculiarities" of others. Uncomplimentary nicknames are not uncommon.

Among the Masai, misshapen and especially weakly children are killed immediately after birth.

Among the Dieri, a tribe of Australian aborigines, "infanticide is frequent, applying to the children of unmarried girls, and to deformed children."

Among the Chagga, an East African tribe, cripples were felt to satisfy evil spirits, thereby making possible normality in others. Hence, they did not dare to kill cripples (who included children with more or less than five fingers as well as the seriously deformed).

Among the Creek Indians, where "old age is revered to excess," the aged infirm were killed only out of humanitarian reasons, such as when they might otherwise fall into enemy hands.

Among the Truk peoples of the East Central Carolines, only the healthy and strong are esteemed. The deaf and dumb are called *umes* (crazy people). Old people and the disabled are considered to be superfluous.

Among the Wogeo, a New Guinea tribe, children with obvious deformities are buried alive at birth, but children crippled in later life are looked after with loving care.

Among the Dahomeans of Western Africa, it is a singular fact that the state constables are selected from deformed persons. Children born with anomalous physical characteristics are held to be under the guardianship of special supernatural agents. Some of these children are destined to bring good luck, and the fate of others must be determined by signs from the supernatural. They may even be "ordered" to be abandoned at the river bank.

Among the Ponape of the Eastern Carolines, crippled and insane children were treated like the normal children.

Among the Witoto Indians of the North West Amazons, the newborn infant is submerged in the nearest stream, for "if the child was not strong enough to survive it had better die." If the child becomes deformed later, the medicine man declares that it was caused by some evil spirit and may work ill to the tribe, making it necessary to dispose of the person.

Among the Jukun, a Sudanese Kingdom, deformed children are not allowed to live, but are left to perish in the bush or in a cave, for it is believed that such children are begotten by an evil spirit.

Among the Semang of the Malay Peninsula, the person looked upon as a sort of chief to settle disputes and admonish if necessary was a severely crippled man who could only move with the help of a long stick.

Among the Balinese, sexual relations with albinos, idiots, lepers, and in general the sick and the deformed, are tabooed.

Among the Palaung, an Eastern Clan, "it is lucky to have extra fingers or toes, and extremely lucky to be born with a hare-lip."

Among the Sema Nagas "the killing of idiots and similarly deficient persons, such as hunchbacks and deaf-mutes, is 'genna' (taboo)."

Among the Macri of New Zealand, deformed persons meet with little sympathy and often receive a castigating nickname.

If positive and negative attitudes toward persons with disabilities prevalent among the tribes and societies summarized by Maisel were to be tabulated, there is no doubt that negative attitudes would show a preponderance. But sheer frequency can have such diverse significance that we can do little more than note it. For example, just because infanticide is shocking even to the most objective occidental investigator, it is likely to be recorded as an impressive fact, whereas a benign attitude to the child with physical abnormalities is more likely to go unheeded.

Although the variety of ways in which deviant members of society are looked upon and handled in different cultures is in itself striking, it would be a mistake to conclude that "anything can happen." The role prescriptions for the aged among different societies provide an apt illustration. Though the diversity is great, a common principle emerges in the fact that all societies, as far as is known, differentiate between old age in general and the helpless state in which the individual is regarded as a sufferer and social burden (Simmons, *1952:*44).

Similarly, although attitudes toward physique vary among different groups, it is more than likely that all societies place a value on "body-beautiful" and "body-whole." We do know that what is defined as "body-beautiful" and "body-whole" varies, however. Scarification among the Dahomey and Ashanti and the artificially produced protruding lips of the Ubangi are looked upon with favor in these African tribes, whereas in our society such characteristics are regarded as deformities. Circumcision in our society does not destroy the intactness of the body nor does shaving the beard. Among sections of the Orient, on the other hand, "the total absence of it [the beard], or a sparse and stinted sprinkling of hair upon the chin is as great a deformity to the features as the want of a nose would appear to us; . . ." (Hentig, *1948a:*78).

Although one could add hundreds of examples showing differences among cultures in evaluation of physical characteristics, one wonders if there is not a core of physical attributes essential to the perception of "body-whole" and "body-beautiful" in all societies. Is there any culture, for example, in which the absence of legs at birth is considered beautiful or does not destroy the intactness of the body?

It is also conceivable that the psychological significance of certain physical functions is sufficiently uniform among the cultures of man to establish common attitudes. Thus, in explaining what he considers to be universal attitudes toward the blind, namely that the blind are both saints and sinners, pariahs and prophets, Blank calls attention to "the importance of vision in early psychosexual and ego development, and the existence in practically everyone of unresolved conflict over scoptophilia [pleasure from looking at] and exihibitionism" (Blank, *1957*:1).

Until there is more abundant anthropological research on the attitudes of different cultural groups toward physique and physical deviation, we can only hazard the guess that though the variation in attitudes is greater than we imagine, out of all the diversity will emerge psychological laws that will contribute to our understanding of the fundamental characteristics of attitudes toward physique. The following sections present several attempts to specify fundamental conditions that would or at least might have cross-cultural application in affecting attitudes toward disability.

REQUIREDNESS IN CAUSE-EFFECT RELATIONS

One might think that because attitudes toward physique vary considerably from culture to culture, they are simply absorbed by the person through repeated exposure to them without consideration of their sense. This is not the case. Attitudes and behavior toward physical deviation are tenaciously held and transmitted to the young as much because they are felt to fit with sound and comprehensible beliefs as because of less clear emotional prejudices.

In this section, we shall examine beliefs concerning physical disability from the point of view of the perception of causes and effects of physical disability. We shall try to explain certain characteristics of these a priori connections and to show how they relate to attitudes toward disability.[2]

Let us consider an example from the neighboring field of emotional disability. Until modern times the cause of derangement was viewed in terms of the occult. Such an association, foolish as it seems to us now, had a firm psychological basis. Where knowledge is lacking, primitive thinking connects the strange and inexplicable behavior of the insane with a strange and inexplicable cause, the occult.

In short, there is a similarity in the structure or quality of the effect and its perceived cause, just as the imprint in the sand (effect) fits the shape of the foot that formed it (Scheerer, *1954*:103–104). As has been amply demonstrated in the laboratory, similarity is one factor in perceiving visual stimuli as unified figures (Köhler, *1947*). Heider has extended this princi-

---

[2] Gestalt psychologists have emphasized the study of the perception of cause-effect connections and refer to it as the problem of phenomenal causality. See Duncker, *1945;* Heider, *1944;* Köhler, *1947;* Scheerer, *1954*).

ple by pointing out that "in general one may say that factors making for figural unit formation also make for causal integration" (*1944*:362).

Perceiving the cause of insanity in terms of witches and demons, society reacted accordingly. The beating and burning of emotionally disturbed persons were seen as neither unjust nor irrational. They were, rather, reactions that were appropriate to the perceived cause.

As science advanced the theory of mental *illness,* however, the former treatment became abhorrent because it clashed with the new understanding concerning cause of the disorder. At least certain attitudes and behavior toward disability, then, are not willy-nilly affairs that arise and change as fashion dictates. Rather, their underpinnings are solidly fastened to perceived cause-effect relationships.

Some enlightening aspects of perceived causal sequence especially significant in attitudes toward disability appear when we examine attitudes toward health as a value. In an experiment in which subjects were asked to make seven wishes for their fantasied new baby, four out of five subjects mentioned good health (Dembo, *1953a*). Good health is so prized that we spend untold millions of dollars in advertisements, education, and medical care, and even this is insufficient for the achievement of the optimal health of the nation. At an early age children are taught to brush their teeth and admonished to develop strong and healthy bodies. Surely not a day goes by for many children that health facts are not stressed in one form or another—at mealtime, at bedtime, at playtime.

At first the child may recognize the value of health as something unto itself, something to be guarded and cherished. This gradually receives the necessary support in the intelligible connection between health and positive consequences. He soon discovers that when he is healthy and can run and play he feels well, and when he is ill he suffers distress and must stay in bed. The endless assertions that make health the royal road to success strengthen the logic of this connection. Advertisements tell him that a certain dentifrice will make his breath kissing sweet and implies a blissful marriage. Parents and teachers tell him that his grades will improve with more adequate rest, and so on. (Ellis presents a lively account of the beatification of beauty, *1954:* Chap I.)

Not only does health become a highly valued goal and illness a disagreeable state, but the conditions that bring them about—i.e., their *causes*—become invested with befitting moral qualities. If the state is a negative one, its cause must be negative also. Thus, the child comes to feel that illness is a punishment for his transgressions. Two factors contributing to his perception may be distinguished. The first is his social and personal experience. He is often threatened with illness as the price for infringement of health rules. If he goes out without his rubbers, he is told that he will catch a cold. If he eats too much candy, he will get holes in his teeth. If he goes to bed too late, he will stop growing. Some of these rules are based on scientific fact, and others are myths and fancy. He also accumulates sufficient evidence to back up the connection between illness and punishment in his own eyes. He remembers, for example, the day he ate quantities of sweets and writhed in agony as a result.

Secondly, the felt appropriateness between illness and sin may well represent an *emotional syllogism,* a term first introduced by Franz Alexander to describe the elementary emotional sequences and connections in man (*1938*). That suffering is caused by evil appears to be grasped without additional argument. No elaboration is required for its comprehension. In the words of Heider, "a state of harmony or balance exists if entities which belong together are all positive, or if they are all negative" (*1958:* Chap. VII).

The person may ascribe the source of suffering to wrongdoing in himself or in someone else, but in any case the source is one of evil. We have seen how the person himself may feel he has sinned. In asking the seemingly naïve question that often besets a person who has suffered a disability or a deep loss: "Why did this have to happen *to me?*" is he not in some obscure way searching for a personal offense that might justify his hurt? A slight change in the question, to "Why did this happen?" represents a major change in the meaning of the disability, a change in which objective nonpersonal attribution is uppermost and guilt is less apparent. In other instances the source of the affliction may be attributed to the negligence of a second person, in which case it is often felt as willful negligence even though objective consideration may deny premeditation. Imputing an intention augments the sin to a level appropriate to the disastrous consequence.

Thus, hardly a parent of a child who has a disability can escape the conviction that in some way avoidable mismanagement was a contributing cause if not *the* cause of the disability. The mother may blame herself or her doctor for the sedation that might have caused the birth injury of her child. Someone has to be blamed, for disability is perceived as having its source in wrongdoing. This is brought out in a study of the attitudes of parents of blind children (Sommers, *1944*). On the basis of interviews with the mothers, the investigator distinguished four attitudes toward blindness:

Blindness as a symbol of punishment: "What have we done that God should wish this on us?"

Fear of being suspected of having a social disease: "I am sure the neighbors say this about me because they have mentioned it in reference to other handicapped children in the vicinity."

Feelings of guilt due to transgression of the moral or social code or to negligence: "I blame myself for not having had a doctor."

Blindness as a personal disgrace to the parents: "Our family felt it was a disgrace and were ashamed."

There is other evidence that disability and illness are linked to causes of a negative, evil signification. To the ancient Hebrews, illness and physical defect marked the person as a sinner. Twelve blemishes are enumerated in the Bible that disqualified a priest from officiating. Among those mentioned are "a blind man, or a lame, or he that hath a flat nose, or anything superfluous, or a man that is brokenfooted, or brokenhanded, or crookbackt, or a dwarf, or that hath a blemish in his eye, or be scurvy, or scabbed, or hath his bones broken . . ." (Hentig, *1948a:*16). Gradually other bodily imperfections were added, of which the later Talmudists mention no less than 142. A Roman priest also had to be free from physical infirmities, and the same rules apply to the Catholic priest to this day (Hentig, *1948a*). It was a strict commandment of the Old Testament that "The blind and the lame shall not come into the house." Illness was considered both a punishment and a means of atonement. Children in occidental cultures frequently regard their illness or disability as a punishment for personal sins and after frequent bouts with illness or continuing disablement may feel that "it is someone else's turn"; they have paid their debt.

In some societies, as among the Trobriand Islanders, the affliction is blamed on an enemy thought to have caused it through sorcery (Hanks and Hanks, *1948*). It has been noted that the term "ugly" in its aesthetic sense was preceded by a moral significance. It is derived from a root meaning "dreadful, fearful." In connection with weather, it means "threatening" (Hentig, *1948a:*64). We also note the equivocal meaning of such allusions as "his *bad* leg," "my *bum* arm," the child who is not "quite right." Hentig goes so far as to say that all peoples have had the idea that physical defect and punishment for some sort of wrong, committed perhaps by an ancestor, were somehow connected (*1948a:*17). This feeling is difficult to dislodge because of the cognitive limpidity with which it is grasped. It may be one reason why the theory of compensation as indemnity (see pp. 49–51) has so firm a hold on the minds of experts and laymen alike; the wrong is righted through compensation.

Moreover, it seems that human beings feel that suffering as such should be reserved as a punishment for evil. Our sense of justice requires this. We inveigh against events that bring suffering to the innocent. War becomes all the more reprehensible when we think of the children who become its innocent victims. In the same way we feel that we should deserve the rewards we get (Asch, *1952;* Heider, *1958*). Somehow virtue and reward go hand in hand as do evil and punishment or suffering.

The concept of suffering as rooted in virtue does not easily emerge as a self-understood connection. In order for it to become so, other purposes tend to be introduced. For example, one may conceive of suffering as a test for lofty future roles or as a means to attaining deep understanding (see pp. 78–82), or as a consequence of self-sacrifice in the interests of higher purposes. Thus, there are cripples among the gods; in the Nordic mythology, Wieland, god of smithery, was lame (Hentig, *1948a:*74). The Christian doctrine introduced the view that disease may be a means of purification and a way of grace. Where suffering stems from good, good must be its product. The suffering cannot be for naught. "That they shall not have died in vain" carries with it tremendous force just because the harmonious emotional sequence is threatened. On the other hand, where suffering stems from evil, it is sufficient unto itself. The matter can simply rest there. The a priori connections are complete. Evidently, the quality and nature of suffering and of evil are more compatible than those of suffering and virtue. Cross-cultural reference should, therefore, find frequent evidence of the former association, and of the latter only when elaboration leads to the necessary congruence.

Not only is the source of illness and disability seen to lie in evil and sin, but where there are further effects, the *consequences* often are also felt to be sinful. "A twisted mind in a twisted body" captures this devaluation of the total person. In Chapters 5 and 6 some of the conditions responsible for the negative spread from disability to other characteristics of the person have been discussed. Here it is sufficient to note that there appears to be a strong cognitive factor that makes for the seeming appropriateness between disability as an unwelcome state and its negative effects.

Illustrative are the following statements given by patients with facial disfigurements. They express fear of having negative character traits imputed to them because of their deformities (Macgregor, *et al.*, *1953:* 70–71). A patient with a grossly disfigured face resulting from war injuries recounted, "When I parked my car in front of a jewelry store, two cops came up and asked me for my identification card. They thought I was a gangster." A patient with harelip and cleft palate told how "children would make fun of the way I talked and looked and said I wasn't normal." That evil acts are associated with marked physical deviation has been shown in an experiment in which nondisfigured persons reacted to the photographs of persons with facial anomalies (Macgregor, *et al.*, *1953*). One photograph showed a 30-year-old man who had a low, narrow forehead, a prominent, convex nose, a receding, pointed chin, narrow, deep-set eyes, large buck teeth, and lop ears. The fact that he had superior intelligence and earned a good salary as a junior executive in a chemical corporation was not mentioned. The following conclusions were drawn about him: "He is mean and small—not bright. He might be a follower in a gang. He's a dope addict. Man seems to look like a maniac. Has desire to kill" (p. 77). The investigators conclude that "facial features which served as false clues led respondents not only to impute to these patients personality traits considered socially unacceptable but to assign them roles and statuses on an inferior social level" (p. 79).

Meng, a Freudian, has stated that the nondisabled unconsciously believe that the cripple has committed some evil act and is therefore dangerous; or, if he has not committed an evil act, that he will do something wrong in order to warrant his punishment (*1938*, reported in Barker, *et al.*, *1953*:87). Thus, with illness and disability both the perceived cause and the perceived effects often match the negative qualities of illness and disability. Moreover, the cause-effect relationships often have a moral reference. An Italian proverb records that "The squint-eyed are on all sides accursed" (Hentig, *1948a*:94).

Lest there be a too hasty overgeneralization, however, we should note again that a substantial number of people connect suffering or even tragedy with such positive effects as deeper understanding and higher values (see pp. 78–82). It seems likely that the connection in these instances is not made immediately but is rather built up through a complex of cause-effect relationships.

In conclusion, to affect attitudes toward disability in more positively adjustive directions, one must give substantial weight to factors determining phenomenal causality. It is in the nature of human beings to search for reasons and answers. We need to know, and where knowledge is lacking, we still try to make sense out of the course of events. And the sense that makes one kind of sense, in the absence of fact, is to link disability as a consequence and producer of error and evil. The sense that is both more adjustive and more scientific views disability as a physical fact which, being neutral, does not lend itself to concepts of evil, punishment, and sin. For example, the statement of former times that the cause of squint resides in an evil disposition immediately sounds absurd when one regards a squint as a physical condition of the musculature of the eye. Moreover, when one views physical disability as a physical fact, any psychological cause-effect relationships are not immediately perceived because of necessity but require psychosomatic and somatopsychological theory and investigation to establish them.

THE DIFFERENT AND STRANGE

"To be different" is to be "set apart," which, in the language of inter-personal relations, may signify rejection. During adolescence, for example, conformity in every respect to the ways of the peer group receives startling obeisance simply because "belonging" is highly valued. Many writers have also attributed the rejection of a person with a disability to the fact that he is *different*. "No one wants to be different" is accepted as an obvious law of man.

In his balance theory of sentiments, Heider (*1958*) gives firm support to man's negative reaction to the different and strange. Stated briefly, this theory posits an interdependence between a person's liking for another (sentiment relation) and the connection of belongingness (unit relation) he perceives with that person. There are many factors that give rise to the feeling that two persons form a unit—that is, that they belong together in some way. These are called unit-forming factors. For example, two persons may be associated together through kinship; through similarity of beliefs, nationality, and religion; through familiarity and interaction, etc. The idea is that when person p identifies with another person o because of any one of the unit-forming factors, a tendency for p to like o will be induced. The inverse relation also holds: if p likes o, a tendency to per-ceive similarities between them will arise. Parenthetically it may be noted that the concept of unit-forming factors had been systemically investigated by Gestalt psychologists who demonstrated their importance in percep-tion. Heider incorporated the concept within a theory of sentiments, adding such peculiarly human unit-forming factors as similarity of beliefs, the strong connection between a man and his deeds, and between a man and his property (ownership).

In Heider's work, many examples are given from research and every-day life of a relationship between liking and similarity between individuals. Thus it is noted that the point of many proverbs is that similar indi-viduals tend to associate and to like each other. In an experiment on social relationships, it was shown that the subjects perceived persons they liked best as more similar to themselves than those they liked least (Fiedler, Warrington, and Blaisdell, *1952*). Familiarity has also been demonstrated to give rise, at least under certain conditions, to a positive affinity of p for o.

The opposite cases of these factors—namely the effects of dissimilarity and unfamiliarity—have direct bearing upon attitudes toward disability. Heider's theory postulates that there will be a tendency for the dissimilar and strange to evoke a negative affection in p for o. An example presented is that of xenophobia, where the hesitancy in befriending a foreigner is accounted for by the dislike induced by the dissimilarity and perhaps also unfamiliarity of the alien member. Specifically dealing with attitudes toward crippling in the light of the different and strange is the work of Winkler (*1931*), reported earlier on p. 124. He accounts for the fact that negative reactions to children who were crippled but not consciously recognized as such occurred more frequently than toward healthy children by the hypothesis that there is little possibility that physically normal individuals can establish an empathic relationship with the crippled because of their unusual postures and movements.

Heider attributes the negative effects of unfamiliarity to at least two factors. The first has already been discussed in regard to uncertainty engendered by new situations (see pp. 99–104): that is, an unfamiliar situation is cognitively unstructured. It is full of possibilities that may be sufficiently threatening to an insecure person to make him withdraw from it. Conflict and unstable behavior result. The second factor is a more purely intellectual and aesthetic component of the resistance to the unfamiliar. "The strange is experienced as not fitting the structure of the matrix of the life space, as not fitting one's expectations. The adaptation or change in expectations which is required by meeting the unfamiliar demands energy. It is more comfortable to wear old clothes and to talk with old friends" (Heider, *1958:*194).

Actually, the evidence that similarity and familiarity induce liking is much more consistent than that dissimilarity and unfamiliarity induce disliking. Heider, on the basis of work stemming from his theory (Cartwright and Harary, *1956*), raises the possibility that whereas similarity and familiarity may lead to a real feeling of unity between *p* and *o,* dissimilarity and unfamiliarity may not necessarily lead to disunity, but rather to a mere absence of the unit relation in some cases. Resistance against being grouped together might be taken as one of the criteria for real disunity. The conditions underlying the two states of absence of a unit relation and its disjunction are not yet clear. Here research is sorely needed. We need to know much more about the nature of differences and unfamiliarities as well as the conditions surrounding them that evoke indifference on the one hand and withdrawal on the other. In any case, as applied to disability the distinction between absence of a unit relation and its disjunction means that a person with a disability need not necessarily be seen as separated from the able-bodied by an unbridgeable chasm. Moreover, Heider himself is careful to point out that there are many instances where the unfamiliar and the different have their own allure, and that under some conditions similarity and familiarity, instead of inducing liking, give rise to disinterest and disliking.

It is clear that the influence of similarity and familiarity on sentiment is not a simple one and, particularly in combination with other factors, may have diverse effects. Nevertheless, Heider's theory and the evidence in support of it do make it necessary to conclude that a person who is clearly set apart because of an atypical physique may by this very fact experience a certain emotional distance if not pronounced antipathy from others who regard him only in terms of this deviation.

The theoretical formulations of other investigators also can be drawn upon in the search for understanding of the negative reaction to the different and strange. In terms of the concept of body image as developed by Schilder (1935), for example, the other person's physical difference creates uneasiness because it does not fit with a well-ordered body image. Moreover, a person's unconscious body image of himself may be threatened by the appearance of a person with a missing part or deformity, inasmuch as he identifies to some extent with that person.

A neurophysiological theory to account for the fear response to the strange has been proposed by Hebb (1946), based upon observations that both man and chimpanzee show spontaneous fears of mutilated and unresponsive bodies (e.g., dead or anesthetized bodies). The statement of the theory that applies most particularly to reaction to disability is that "fear occurs when an object is seen which is like familiar objects in enough respects to arouse habitual processes of perception, but in other respects arouses incompatible processes" (p. 268). More broadly, the theory is one of disruption of the pattern of existing internal neurophysiological activity, especially that of cerebral events, which disruption may occur through different classifications of fear-invoking situations. Fears of mutilated and strange bodies are due to conflict, inasmuch as they arouse both usual and incompatible perceptions and intellections. Another source of fear is sensory deficit, as in darkness or loss of support, in which case the withdrawal of sensory stimulation disrupts the habitual modes of cerebral action.

The preceding discussion suggests certain measures in the interest of enhancing adjustive attitudes toward disability on the part of the community at large. It argues for the integration of children with disabilities into the regular schools wherever feasible, rather than the establishment of special schools, so that familiarity with physical deviation may take place in natural settings. It also calls attention to the proposition that it is less the physical deviation as such that creates a feeling of being different than the psychological characteristics imputed to the person through the phenomenon of spread (see pp. 118–128). This means that education to the effect that physical anomaly does not betray personality is of the first importance. All one knows about a person with a disability is that he has the disability. Until one knows more about him, one can hardly say more. Once spread has been held in check, physical dissimilarity may become a relatively minor feature among the welter of other characteristics that unite people. In short, rather than as a disabled person, he can be perceived as a person with a disability. The disability then makes less of a difference as far as unit formation is concerned, to use Heider's theoretical formulation. After all, the person with a disability is first of all a person, and as such already bears essential samenesses with the person observing or interacting with him. This point is one of the crucial elements of what is referred to as the "brotherhood of man."

CHILDHOOD EXPERIENCES

To the extent that attitudes are "made" and not inborn, their seeds may well be sown during the years of early childhood. But sown in what way? Direct plantings of attitudes toward disability and deviation are clearly significant.

As illustrative, the following account was selected for several reasons. It presents a naturally occurring incident in the life of an ordinary child in our own culture. It deals directly with the problem of individual differences in an aspect of physique not involving disability as such. It portrays positive influences on attitudes toward deviation, an emphasis we would like to underscore in the face of the variety of conditions underlying negative attitudes that have already been discussed.

Cathy is an 8-year-old child, somewhat above average in height, plump but not fat. She, however, feels that she is fat, and intermittently becomes somber and disturbed about this. The fact that she has beautiful, large blue eyes that have very often been commented upon may have overstressed the value of appearance to her, leading to an oversensitivity about body proportions and other physical characteristics.

SCENE I: Cathy has just returned from visiting Mary, an 8-year-old friend who is very slim.

CATHY (*somberly*): Mommy, why am I so wide?

MOTHER: You are not *so* wide. But some people are wider and some people are narrower.

CATHY: But why don't Mary's clothes fit me?

MOTHER: Well, people are different sizes. Mary is a very slim girl.

CATHY (*explosively*): But I don't want to be fat!

MOTHER: I don't think you are *too* fat. Isn't it interesting that every child seems to find something about himself that he doesn't like? Either he is too thin or too fat, or his hair is too straight or too curly, or he thinks he can't run fast enough, or his eyes are too small, or something.

CATHY (*with a somewhat lighter heart*): Well, I have two things about myself that I don't like. I am too fat and I wish I didn't have these freckles on my face.

MOTHER: Those freckles can't come off, Cathy, so don't keep rubbing at them. Those freckles are a part of you, and I love them because you're my little girl. Why, if you came down without those freckles, I'd say, "Where is my little girl?"

CATHY (*laughing with relief*):   What about yourself don't you like, Mommy?

MOTHER: Oh, now I'm not really bothered about anything like that.

CATHY: But what about yourself don't you like now?

MOTHER: Now I'm not bothered about anything like that. But when I was a little girl I used to think that my teeth were too crooked and my legs were too bow-legged.

CATHY: But your teeth aren't too crooked.

MOTHER: I know, but I sure thought they were. I used to mope about being bothered. But now I just know that these things don't really matter. Why, this world has room for all kinds of people—for big people, and little people, for fat people and thin people, for people who are very pretty, and for people who are not.

CATHY (*pausing*):   For people with different colored skin and different kinds of eyes.

MOTHER: Right. For loads and loads of different kinds of differences. (*Brother enters and conversation shifts.*)

SCENE II: The next morning at breakfast Cathy has filled a bowl of cereal.

CATHY: Mother, may I have this banana?

MOTHER: You already have one.

CATHY: I only have half in my cereal because I ate the other half.

MOTHER: O.K.

CATHY: I don't care if I'm fat as long as I'm your little girl (*rather gaily*).

SCENE III: Several days later at dinner (*Edward is Cathy's brother*).

CATHY: Why am I getting wider over here? (*pointing to her hips, somewhat furtively*)

MOTHER: You're not getting too wide. But you're growing up and that's why you're getting wider in the hips.

EDWARD: Boys get wide hips too.

CATHY (*matter-of-factly*):   But not as wide as girls.

EDWARD (*challengingly*):   Oh, yes they do.

MOTHER: As boys and girls grow older, they get wider and taller all over. But girls have wider hips because they need more room there when they become mommies.

CATHY (*seriously, but not solemnly*):   Rita's grandmother has *very* wide hips. They stick out like that (*extending her arms broadly on each side*). But that doesn't matter, because she is a very kind woman. (*On previous occasions, the mother reports that whenever discussions arose concerning race differences or physical deviation, she stressed that the kind of person you are is what counts, rather than such surface characteristics as color of skin, or whether you limped, which told nothing at all about the person himself.*)

SCENE IV: One month later. Cathy is getting ready for a birthday party.
CATHY (*firmly*):   I don't want to wear this dress because it makes me look too fat.
MOTHER: You are not too fat. You only think you are.
CATHY (*crying*):   Oh, yes I am. You only say that to make me feel good. I won't wear it! (*angrily throwing the dress on the floor*)
MOTHER: That's all right. You can wear another dress that you like better.

SCENE V: Several months later.
CATHY: Oh, I wish I didn't like to eat so much.
MOTHER: Why?
CATHY (*good-naturedly*):   Because then I wouldn't be so fat, silly.
MOTHER: The trouble is that food tastes so good.
CATHY: They should have made it so it didn't.
MOTHER: Convenient, eh?
CATHY (*laughing*):   Yeah. Ch well (*takes another bun*).

There is much in this sequence that would seem to influence more or less directly Cathy's attitudes toward disability. The general observation that Cathy's feelings about obesity fluctuated is interesting. This is often true of the process of attitude change. Adjustment seesaws because the required reorganization of one's system of values does not occur as a smooth, unidirectional pattern. For example, in situations evoking intellectual discourse, one might reach out toward adjustive understanding, but unless emotional acceptance supports these realizations, one may well slip back in situations that arouse feelings uncontrolled by conscious consideration. Thus, in the first three scenes Cathy was able to go rather far in viewing physique as a difference but not all the difference, whereas in the fourth scene, when she was all keyed up toward matters of appearance in anticipation of a party, she again became disturbed. Nevertheless, intellectual change is important, not only because it is conducive to adequate behavior in more rational situations but also because the intellectual and emotional levels are interdependent. Intellectual understanding may encourage emotional acceptance by helping shape events conducive to alteration of feelings; conversely, emotional changes affect intellectual conclusions (see Chap. 7).

Although Cathy will continue to struggle with her evaluation of obesity and the acceptance of herself, the new understandings that she already had begun to grasp will serve her well. Note how in the first scene Cathy at first substituted the less appropriate word "wide" for "fat." At that time obesity seemed to pervade her entire psychological world; it was ubiquitous and crucial. She was helped when she learned that she did not stand alone in her disturbing feelings, that other children also were dissatisfied with something about themselves. She needed the further support of believing that her mother too had lacks. Perhaps her mother would have been wiser to have given the child this reassurance instead of denying that anything bothered her now. Had she acknowledged some imperfection —a double chin or anything else—in a free and easy way, she would have conveyed the understanding that one can feel all right about a defect without denying or concealing it. Again in the fourth scene the mother tried to deny the cause of Cathy's concern: "You are not too fat. You only think you are." Though objectively the mother was right, this approach could not give Cathy a comfortable feeling about herself as long as she was convinced of the contrary.

An important realization grew out of the interchange in Scene I when the mother told the child in effect that she loved her because of herself and that having certain physical characteristics did not detract from that love. The mother sensitively imbedded Cathy's anxiety in a somewhat more lighthearted and easily manageable emotional framework when she said, "Why, if you came down without those freckles I'd say, 'Where is my little girl?'" Further basic understandings pinpointed in these scenes are that there are "loads of different kinds of differences," that the world has room for most of them, and that other things matter more than physique—"her hips stick out like that but that doesn't matter because she is a very kind woman."[3]

A direct attempt to influence attitudes toward persons with disabilities, an attempt on the wide scale of public school education, is provided in a discussion and set of instructions for classroom teachers as to how they might help boys and girls at the fourth-, fifth-, and sixth-grade levels reëvaluate their feelings toward children with various kinds of disabilities (*Understanding the disabled, 1956*). Briefly, the instructions include:

1. Use of a social distance scale technique to indicate the feelings of the children about boys and girls with various kinds of disabilities as portrayed in pictures.
2. Discussion of the children's ratings on the social distance scale.
3. Discussion with the children of stereotyped statements about people with disabilities, such as "I feel I should be especially friendly to people like that" or "A person like that can't do the things other people do."
4. Seeking further information by arranging discussion with local physicians and nurses, and if possible with an employer who welcomes employees with handicaps, contacting national and local disability organizations, and reviewing the lives of individuals who coped successfully with their disabilities.
5. Completion of a picture story involving a boy with a disability in order that the children may apply the knowledge and constructive attitudes which it is

[3] An enlightening account of effecting adjustive attitudes toward disability through role playing in the home appears in a paper by Rosemary Lippitt (*1947*) and is reported on pp. 247–248 of the present volume.

hoped have been accrued in some measure through the preceding activities. The stories are then acted out.

6. Discussion of an incident involving a girl with a disability in order to give the class an opportunity to evaluate the attitudes of someone else toward a person with a disability.

The lesson plans, based on sound psychological principles, provide a clear and encouraging guide for the teacher but allow her flexibility in taking into account her own feelings and judgments about her specific classroom situation. Moreover, the instruction booklet can be used to excellent advantage with other groups as well, notably parents of children with or without disabilities, and children with disabilities themselves for modifications of procedure to fit special conditions and purposes can readily be made.

Many experiences that influence attitudes toward disability need not involve the verbal expression of attitudes. Feelings and beliefs are transmitted—sometimes vaguely, sometimes precisely—by actions as well as words. When a child sees someone condescendingly toss a dime into the cap of a beggar, he is learning something. When the child sees a child with a disabled foot participating in the classroom, he is learning something. Such experiences, whether verbal or behavioral, can be crucial in the development of attitudes toward disability.

There is some evidence that attitudes toward disability are also conditioned by child-rearing practices seemingly unconnected with disability as such. This has been most clearly shown in the work of Whiting and Child (1953), who investigated the effects of socialization methods in child training by analyzing material in the aforementioned Human Relations Area Files.

Particularly relevant to our interest are the findings concerning the relation between theories held in the culture to account for illness and the severity of socialization practices devised to teach children to conform to adult standards. Since the results deal with attitudes toward illness, they may be presumed to be applicable to attitudes toward disability as well. Beliefs about illness were selected as potential reflectors of child-rearing practices inasmuch as most primitive cultures lack the scientific knowledge for basing their beliefs on reality. The particular areas of child development that were rated for severity of socialization promised to be of special significance according to psychoanalytic theory and included the following areas: oral, anal, genital, aggressive, and dependent.

One of the hypotheses borne out by the study was that those areas of child development which are severely socialized would create anxiety and therefore would be expected to be incorporated in the theories of illness in the society. For example, there were 23 societies with an oral theory of illness (e.g., illness is caused by eating something) and 16 societies without such an explanation. The average severity of weaning in the first group was 12.22 on a scale from 0 to 20, and in the second only 8.94, a difference that is highly significant statistically. In our society, middle-class practices concerning oral training are rated by Whiting and Child toward the severe end, a rating consistent with the prevalence of all sorts of oral theories of illness among this group. The results for the other areas of behavior are not as clear, but they are in the same direction.

It is worthy of note that these findings are consistent with the theory of requiredness in cause-effect relations discussed earlier (pp. 256–261). That is, illness is a negative state. As such its cause is sought in factors that also are negative—in the case at hand by virtue of their anxiety-laden character.

With respect to overcoming illness, Whiting and Child had expected that the therapeutic practices would show some connection with behavior that in childhood had been satisfying through a long period of indulgence on the part of adults. The findings were generally negative except for the sexual area of development. In only two cultures were sexual practices believed to have a specific therapeutic value; in these two societies there is a very high indulgence of childhood sexuality.

Another aspect of theories of illness studied was that of guilt. Guilt was indicated by the belief that the patient is responsible for his illness, as contrasted with attribution to accident or some outside agent. The hypothesis that societies with the severest socialization practices would create the most anxiety and guilt, and therefore would tend to impute responsibility for illness to the patient, was supported. Since the overall severity of socialization as evidenced in the middle class of our society was rated close to the top of the 51 cultures examined by Whiting and Child, it is not surprising that in this culture we commonly find attitudes of guilt associated with disability, specifically that disability is meted out as punishment.

A second hypothesis involving guilt was also supported, namely, that societies using loss of love as a threat to induce conforming behavior in the child should tend to have higher ratings on the acceptance of patient responsibility for illness. This hypothesis was based on a theory that guilt is due to anxiety over the loss of love of the person on whom the child is dependent.

The most general conclusion of the Whiting and Child study relevant to disability is that beliefs about illness are indirectly influenced by those significant early relations between child and parent that have to do with the child's conformity to adult standards of behavior. The study provides a good example of how theory—in this case a theory of the important phases in child development and the conditions of learning that surround them—can produce new knowledge and understanding.

In any discussion of the significance of childhood experiences, psychoanalytic theory has an important place. Because many good accounts of the psychoanalytic viewpoint are available (e.g., Thompson, 1950), we shall not review the theoretical framework here. Of the many facets of psychoanalysis, however, castration theory is directly related to emotional disturbance occasioned by the sight or thought of disability. A summary of it follows:

In brief, the castration complex comes about as a result of childhood experience. The child soon discovers the meaning of his genital organs and, in his earliest fantasies revolving about the love of the mother, unconsciously "posits" his penis as a rival to his father's. Fearing revenge from the father, however, the child imagines that retribution will take the form of depriving him of his male organ. Such a drastic procedure would, in his fantasy, be the only appropriate punishment from the father for taboo Oedipal desires in which the mother becomes an incestuous love object. Throughout his childhood, the child may extend these vague fears to encompass the notion that his father will, in one way or another, punish him for his sexual activities in general. Thus his remorse or anxieties about masturbation may be reflecting castratory fears.

The castration complex could, according to psychoanalytic thought, be symbolically brought into play by any remotely analogous equivalent of castration. Thus the loss of a leg, or seeing another person who has lost a leg, may stir up archaic castratory fears. Indeed, the loss of any part of the body, or the sight of such a loss, is said to be symbolically capable of recalling the Oedipal taboo and the father's potential revenge—that of cutting off or mutilating the phallus.

But could such a theoretical explanation offer a possible reason for women's reactions to disability as well? Yes, according to Freudian theory, even though women have no phallus to fear losing. For while the little boy is going through the Oedipal phase, with its taboo complications, phallus fantasies and fears, and rivalry with the father, the little girl is also experiencing incestuous desires. Indeed, she goes through two phases. Unlike her brother, who experiences only a mother fixation, and is never sexually attracted to his father, the girl child may first have a mother attachment, a survival of the oral (breast-feeding) phases of her existence. This leads her to an identification with the father, just as the boy identifies himself with his father as a rival for his mother's affections. The girl, however, discovers the difference between the sexes at an early age, and her own absence of a penis gives her a castration complex—she feels that she has been deprived of the male organ, and suffers a deep sense of loss. No longer able to rival her father, she then identifies with her mother, and makes a fantasy bid for the father's love. As opposed to the boy child's Oedipal-castratory development, the girl child passes through a phase in which the Electra complex (fixation on the father) and the castration complex are major experiences [Maisel, *1953*:551–553].

Whether or not castration anxiety is universal, and whether or not it necessarily has such ubiquitous effects where it does exist, are matters for conjecture and research. In any case, the clinical evidence is strong that castration anxiety does occur and can ramify to attitudes toward disability. The psychoanalytic viewpoint, insofar as it posits universal and far-reaching castration anxieties, leads to the conclusion that negative attitudes toward persons with disabilities are inevitable though, to be sure, they may be ameliorated through education and certainly through psychotherapy. The essential therapeutic process would seem to require either an elimination of castration fears or a separation of body deviations from meanings linked with the family triangle (the child's love for one of the parents in competition with the other).

Although early childhood experiences that have no direct connection with attitudes toward disability have a great deal of potency in determining those attitudes, it is undoubtedly also true that experiences directly involving deviancy of all sorts, illness and disability, leave their mark. Attitudes to which the child is exposed in viewing minority groups, the slow learner, his own shortcomings, and countless other differences cannot be underrated.

SOCIOECONOMIC FACTORS

The conditions that give rise to and support cultural attitudes toward physical disability have also been sought in the economic features of society. Hanks and Hanks (*1948*) note that among the Greenland Eskimos, where economic surplus is maintained at a very narrow margin, the congenitally defective are often killed in infancy and those with acquired handicaps are taken care of by the family until they are deemed an economic liability, in which event they commit suicide or are abandoned. In contrast is the different treatment of the handicapped by the Northern Blackfoot of the North American plains and by certain tribes in Melanesia, where the economy for the most part is adequate and the society democratic. Here, the protective obligation of the family toward the person afflicted is increased. Hanks and Hanks tentatively offer the following propositions: Protection of the physically handicapped and social participation for them are increased in societies in which (1) the level of productivity is higher in proportion to the population and its distribution more nearly equal, (2) competitive factors in individual or group achievement are minimized, (3) the criteria of achievement are less formally absolute, as in hierarchical social structures, and more weighted with concern for individual capacity, as in democratic social structures.

The role of economic factors in attitudes toward physique, an area barren of research, promises to yield important data and insights. Knowledge of these factors, however, is only part of the knowledge needed for understanding the full significance of physique and physical deviation, for otherwise greater consistency according to economic status should be expected than does in fact exist. The Hankses note, for example, that although the Paiute of the Great Basin of North America had a margin of existence almost as precarious as that of the Greenland Eskimos, infanticide was not practiced and their disabled were not abandoned.

In addition to economic conditions, cultural theories as to the source of disablement and its effects on the person doubtless play a role in the treatment accorded to persons with disabilities. The Hindu theological concept of *Dharma*, for example, explains an existing personal condition as the inevitable result of past behavior in previous incarnations (Hanks and Hanks, *1948*). It is consequently reasonable that sympathy for persons with defects is lacking since they have brought their affliction upon themselves. Or, to take an example closer to home, though shaving of the beard is the fashion, so much so that the bewhiskered male is subject to ridicule, the adult male must show that he has a beard though it be shaven; that is, his countenance must not be as smooth and fair as a woman's. Should it be, he is disparaged for ambiguous sex identification. It is this meaning that is necessary for the understanding of the emotional rejection of a truly beardless face, and is probably more immediately responsible for such rejection than economic conditions. Of course, one can propose that the reaction to possible sex ambiguity is in itself a product of the economic structure. Economic factors may indeed play a role, but the diverse meanings associated with physical attributes that exist in the present, whatever their historical origins, must still be identified.

Where the discussion of attitudes and their determinants suggested implications for child rearing and public education, these were made explicit. Undoubtedly, further consideration of implications will yield additional leads for developing wholesome attitudes toward disability. Understanding underlying conditions within a framework of ideological and ethical prescriptions provide the soundest guides for desired change. An essential problem remains, however: an understanding of the process of change itself. Though by no means the whole story, some notions on this matter have already been presented in the discussion of value changes in acceptance of disability, Chapter 5.

The following four chapters deal mainly with rehabilitation procedures as such. The first of these presents a variety of training approaches that are promising in helping the person with a disability to manage more comfortably and effectively the everyday interpersonal relations described at length in Chapter 9.

Training in Social Skills

IT BEARS REPEATING THAT A PERSON'S REACTION TO SOCIAL INCIDENTS IS conditioned by how he perceives himself and his disability—i.e., by his self-concept (see Chap. 7). Nevertheless, the form his reaction takes may in itself go a long way in worsening the disturbing relationship, or in controlling it, or even in shifting it to a congenial interchange. More than that, it may have some consequence for his own self-regard, for both behavior and the self-concept are reciprocally interdependent—they are both cause and effect of each other.

The individual himself experiments with different coping techniques, and on the basis of "trial and check" (an expression credited to Robert S. Woodworth) adopts those that seem appropriate to him. However, there is reason to believe that special training in social techniques can prevent painful ineptitudes and lead to a deeper realization of constructive social relationships.

ROLE PLAYING

Role playing is a method in which problem situations are acted out by various members of the training group who have been assigned to certain roles. It stems from psychodramatic methods of therapy used by Moreno (*1937*). The method will be described here, but it must be used judiciously and by persons who have the background of training and outlook to channel the experience constructively, for role playing, like any professional tool, can be harmfully misused.

The form of the role playing can vary widely, depending on the purposes of the session. "The problem situation and the roles to be played may be defined so strictly as to constitute . . . a demonstration; or they may be set so loosely that the 'play' is highly spontaneous and the outcome all but unpredictable. The play may deal with a single incident, or it may contain a series of incidents each growing out of the preceding one. Various individuals playing parts may be instructed as to how to react if certain events take place, or they may be told to react 'naturally'" (Bavelas, *1947*:184).

To teach social skills, it is Bavelas' experienced judgment that effective role playing requires (1) the use of carefully planned "stereotype" situations as basic training material, and (2) rather close controls of all roles being played, with the exception of the role primarily under consideration—that one being left entirely free to be played as the individual sees fit (Bavelas, *1947*:187).

The following is an adaptation to disability problems of an outline by Bavelas describing the succession of events in a typical role playing session (Bavelas, *1947*:187–189). Let us imagine a group of ten persons with orthopedic disabilities gathered together:

1. The session is begun with a short discussion of the general area in which lie the problems to be taken up. In our example, it is the ordinary social experiences encountered daily by a person with a disability. The group may be encouraged to tell about cases or personal experiences that illustrate the various aspects of the problem.

2. If this is the first time role playing has been attempted, a few minutes should be spent explaining what role playing is all about. It might be pointed out that often a person thinks he knows how he should behave, but when he attempts it in actuality it doesn't work out; that research has shown that living the situation by acting it out allows for direct observation of the pitfalls and positive consequences of different behaviors and for discussion on the basis of a common and real experience.

3. Two of the participants are then selected to go out of the room. Particularly if role playing is new to the group, individuals should be selected who are expected to have least trouble in entering into the spirit of the thing.

4. The problem situation to be enacted is then described. This might be developed from an earlier discussion on problems of everyday relationships, but often the situation has greater teaching value if it has been carefully planned by the leader in advance of the meeting. It might be a situation in which a person with an obvious disability realizes that two strangers are staring at him and talking about him. Enough background material should be given so that not only will the problem come alive but also the persons who are to play the auxiliary roles (in this case the two strangers), should have a fairly clear notion of how they are to feel and act. For example, the details might be:

(a) The two strangers, a husband and wife who are seated in a bus, watch a man with crutches and leg braces laboriously enter and find a seat. (b) The husband and wife have a son who a few years ago suffered severe crippling in an accident. (c) They watch the man intently because they are very much interested in his Canadian type crutches (short crutches which are held by the hands). Their own son uses the long arm crutches. (d) They comment about this together in a low tone. They wonder if their son could be fitted with short crutches. (e) They smile in a friendly way at the man when he glances in their direction.

5. Two members of the group are selected or volunteer to play the roles of husband and wife. In initial sessions, the trainer himself may play one of these roles. If the group is very small, one person may play the husband or wife with an imaginary partner.

6. It is pointed out that the individuals out of the room who will play the man with the crutches and braces (the primary player) will not be told anything about the strangers. The primary player will simply be informed that the scene is a bus which he is to enter with some effort and find a seat. He notices two people staring at him and talking about him.

7. Enough simple "props" are set up to bring the situation to life. In this case, chairs may be used to indicate the seats of the bus. Their arrangement is important for it should allow for varied behavior on the part of the main actor in interacting with the strangers and choice of a seat. The accompanying illustration presents one possibility. The strangers occupy two adjacent front chairs.

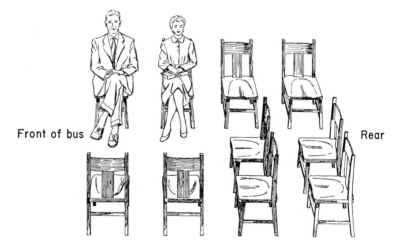

Front of bus   Rear

8. The group is asked if the setting is clear. It is well for some discussion to take place which will orient the group as to what they are to look for. Questions may be raised briefly, such as "What might the man on crutches do? Will he feel self-conscious? Will he feel angry? Hurt? Annoyed? Undisturbed? How will these feelings manifest themselves? Why did he choose the seat he did? What was he thinking?"

9. One of the persons waiting outside is then called in. The setting is

explained to him, and the action may be started: "The problem is clear? Very well. You are entering the bus here. It takes quite a little effort. You notice these two people watching you. You are to find a seat and behave as many people would in such a situation." Because the primary player is asked to act the role of someone in general with his disability rather than of himself, he is protected from the threat of too great personal exposure. In later sessions, when the group has reached the security of competent guidance, personal roles labeled as such may more safely be enacted. Discussion of the behavior in either case is productive of real insights.

10. This kind of situation may end by itself with the man finding his seat and, for example, gazing out the window. Sometimes the situation does not come to an end naturally if left alone. The trainer must then decide when the play has gone on long enough for the purposes he has in mind and arbitrarily end it.

11. The primary player is then asked to take his place with the group. Those parts of the problem of which he is not aware are explained to him, such as the fact that the strangers had a son with a disability, so that he can watch the second player on a par with the rest of the group. The trainer briefly sums up the action that took place in the first play without giving any interpretations. Sometimes it is helpful to outline the events briefly on a blackboard and cover it up before the second play starts. Discussion does not take place at this point. Rather the group is primed to look for differences between what they have seen and the next play.

12. The second player is called in and the procedure is repeated. The persons taking the role of husband and wife essentially repeat their previous behavior.

13. When the second play has ended, the leader sums up the action of the play and reviews what happened in the first one. The review is important because the second player must be brought up to date. If a blackboard is used, there will now be two outlines, each describing the action in one of the plays.

14. Before general discussion begins, it is usually best to ask all the actors for their reactions. This gives the players a chance to point out the errors that they have made and serves to give the group additional information.

15. The meeting is then opened to general discussion. It is sometimes helpful to get a third outline on the board indicating what the group now feels would be the preferred behavior of the man with the disability. The preferred behavior should be examined in terms of principles since there is generally no one best way of doing things.

16. A member of the group who has not yet played a role is selected to act out the main role along the lines indicated by the group. The group

is instructed to watch carefully for flaws in what they have set up as "preferred" behavior.

17. There is considerable value in making a tape recording of the role playing. This permits checking remembered events against the actuality and listening again to the nuances of verbal expression and tone.

Modifications of this type of role playing session to fit specific conditions and purposes readily suggest themselves. A white cane and dark glasses can be substituted for the crutches and braces. The group can consist of persons with diverse disabilities or similar disabilities and even, in special instances, of persons with disabilities and those without. The sex and age of the characters can vary. Problem situations involving help, sympathy, pity, ridicule, curiosity, nonparticipation can be tried. The primary character need not always be a person with a disability; it may be enlightening to the person and the group to center on the role of an able-bodied person.

Bavelas (1947) points up the following advantages of role playing, which are here illustrated in terms of disability problems (pp. 184–85):

1. Playing a role before an "audience" makes an individual self-conscious. This self-consciousness is desirable because it makes the individual aware of his actions in a new way. Commonly the person makes the same mistakes he has been observed to make unconsciously in real settings, but because he has become "sensitized" to himself, he is able to point out some of these errors himself as soon as the play is over.

2. Since the secondary roles are also played by members of the group, it is possible to get direct expression of the effects caused by the actions of the primary actor. For example, the persons playing the role of the curious strangers can report how it made them feel when the man on crutches acted the way he did. This helps the trainees to get a better insight into the effects of their actions on others.

3. Sometimes the individual who has just played the role of the person with a disability assumes the role of the able-bodied in the very next play. This offers the stimulating experience of "feeling the difference" between the two positions.

4. The fact that sooner or later everyone takes a turn at playing a role alerts the audience to the positive and negative features of the current play.

5. Role playing has the advantage of emphasizing *showing* how one would do something rather than *telling* how one would do it. Many individuals who "talk a good game" are woefully inadequate when it comes to performing the actions.

6. Role playing is conducive to experimentation in ways of behaving. The mistakes made do not have negative consequences for real-life situa-

tions. Moreover, the atmosphere in role playing sessions is (or ideally should be) warm and sympathetic rather than blaming.

Role playing can be used in any setting in which a group of persons with disabilities can be brought together—the hospital, rehabilitation center, or school, for example. The importance of a good leader cannot be overestimated. He must be a person who understands disability problems, is sensitive to the feelings of the group, and if possible has had training in role playing as well.

Several experiments have demonstrated the positive changes that can be initiated in role playing sessions. As part of the series of experiments already referred to (pp. 219–221) on answering antiminority remarks, subjects were given training with respect to the manner and content of the most effective answers (Citron and Harding, *1950*). The basic training method was role playing and discussion. In the role playing sessions, the subjects assumed the role of the answerer to the bigot's remark. Discussion of the incident followed. Five sessions of about two hours each produced marked improvement in ability to answer according to principles based on general psychological knowledge, on experience with incident situations, and on the results of previous experiments. Role playing and discussion have also been used as effective methods in the training of leaders (Bavelas, *1942;* French, *1944;* Lippitt, *1943;* Zander, *1947*), management (Bavelas, *1947*), foremen (French, *1945*), interviewers (Barron, *1947*), etc.

It is Lippitt's conviction that "a training process which aims to effect changes in the behavior style of a person cannot efficiently depend upon lectures or other patterns of verbalization such as discussion. Actual experimentation in the desired ways 'ways of behaving' must be provided, in situations where intensive guidance and encouragement is possible, and where the pressures against making mistakes are removed" (Lippitt, *1943:* 291–293). Role playing is a widely accepted approach for effecting change both in behavior and attitudes.

REAL-LIFE SITUATIONS WITH A PERSON WHO "KNOWS"

A second promising teaching procedure is to deal directly with real-life experiences by having the person who is faced with a disability accompany someone well adjusted to his disability on various social excursions. Russell (*1949*), the veteran who lost both hands in World War II, was fortunate enough to have such an experience while still in the hospital. Charley McGonegal, whose hand amputations antedated Russell's by one World War, took a drive with Russell and Tony, a hospital mate:

. . . At first we thought he was joking. How could anyone with hooks, even if he was Charley McGonegal, handle a car? We soon found out. Charley didn't have any special gadgets or gimmicks on the steering wheel or gear-shift, but he was a smooth, capable driver. After we'd driven awhile, he stopped the car and let Tony and me try it. To my surprise, I discovered it wasn't very difficult at all. I just grabbed hold of the wheel with my hooks and off we went.

But the incident that left an even deeper impression on me took place that afternoon. Charley drove us into town and we stopped off for a soda. He steered us to the most conspicuous table in the place and ordered sodas and a package of cigarets. When the waitress brought the cigarets he made quite a show of opening the package, pulling out the cigarets, passing them around and lighting them for us. Everyone in the store watched him as if it were some kind of theatrical performance which, as it turned out, it was. Charley wasn't the least bit disconcerted by their fascinated stares. He acted as cool, as unconcerned as though we were all alone.

On the way back to Reed I noticed something odd. He pulled out a silver case filled with cigarets, lit one. Then I got the point of that little performance back in the soda parlor. He purposely ordered the pack of cigarets, which he didn't really need, just to show us, in his own quiet, indirect way, how to behave with strangers gawking at you [pp. 108–109].[1]

The effectiveness of such an experience can be partly attributed to the following dynamics. McGonegal gave meaning to the situation by his behavior. Instead of indicating that the situation was threatening, by his nonchalance he produced a totally different interpretation. Strangers gawking could gawk without ruffling the object of their curiosity. In the same way does parental teaching often proceed. The child may not be afraid to be left in the nursery school until the oversolicitous behavior and concerned look of the parent tells him that this is and should be a dangerous situation. Situations often become fearful, embarrassing, friendly, or comfortable, depending on the meaning defined by the behavior and reaction of others.

It should not be assumed that one such experience as Russell had, however impressive it was, is enough to ensure smooth social relationships in the future. Russell had yet to suffer much bitterness in his encounters with others, for until he began to accept his disability, the experience with McGonegal could be only potentially helpful. But it was there, as part of his reservoir of meaningful recollections, to aid him when he was ready to utilize it.

Again, modifications of this procedure may be introduced. The size of the group venturing forth can be varied, as well as the situations to be experienced. Discussion of the experience may follow, or its impact may

[1] Harold Russell with Victor Rosen, *Victory in My Hands,* copyright 1949. Used by permission of the publishers, Farrar, Straus and Cudahy, Inc.

well be left to be digested alone. A second expedition to the same setting may take place so that the person can observe change in his own reactions. He may be encouraged to take a lead in the ongoing social events, or he may be allowed to assume a back-seat position from which he can still observe and experience. In any case, observing the behavior of an experienced person in a situation which is of great moment to the subject is apt to leave him with an impression so potent as to produce changes in feelings and behavior.

It would be well for administrators of rehabilitation programs to reflect upon this matter. Just as provision is made for the employment of physical therapists, so ought provision be made for the employment of persons with disabilities whose adjustment and experience have taught them wisely. Opportunity could then be provided for patients to be exposed to a variety of real-life situations with a person who "knows."

REAL-LIFE SITUATIONS WITH OTHER NOVICES

Real-life situations are also experienced to advantage by groups of persons with similar disabilities, all of whom are "learners." The fact that there is likely to be a variety of reactions and interpretations of the situation tends to stimulate reappraisal of the disability and events connected with it. In an early experience, during his first pass to town from the hospital, Russell (*1949*) became bitterly upset when a stranger offered drinks and made reference to his hands (see pp. 162–163). He defiantly ended the episode by ordering the man away and shaking his hooks at him, threatening, "Before I give you these." The following conversation then took place among the buddies:

"I guess maybe we better get used to have people pester us like that," one of the boys said.

"Why the hell should we?" I said. "It's none of their damn business. Would any of us go up to somebody and ask him if he was wearing a toupee or had store teeth?"

"Maybe they just figure we're heroes and belong to them, our great, adoring public—"

"Nuts!"

"Or maybe they think it's patriotic to be interested in us—"

"Or maybe," one of the others said, "they feel kind of guilty because they're not in there pitching and so they want to make up for it by slobberin' all over us" [p. 123].

Russell learned much as a result of this experience, even though he could put it into practice only gradually. He learned that people like himself, other amputees, could see some acceptable motives in the stranger. His buddies implied another way of handling the situation predicated on the proposition that they ought to get used to the behavior of strangers. Such suggestions are more apt to be taken seriously by the person when they come from someone who also has a disability, for otherwise it is natural to discredit the advice with the indictment that a nondisabled person "just couldn't understand."

Rehabilitation and hospital centers might well consider the feasibility of arranging excursions into the outside world by small groups of patients. There the patients will be exposed to the staring and curiosity of strangers, the offers to help and expressions of sympathy and devaluating pity, but they will experience these situations together, and together they will be able to discuss them. In so doing they may discover new meanings and more effective ways of managing. Variations, of course, may be introduced. An experienced person, for example, with or without a disability, may be called in to join the discussion. Eventually the patient may be encouraged to venture forth alone. For this short period he is on his own, but when he returns to the temporary refuge of the hospital or rehabilitation center, he will then be able to unburden himself of the questions and irritations to others who understand.

BRINGING THE OUTSIDE INSIDE

There are other simple and inexpensive methods by which the patient can gradually be introduced to the uncertain outside within the more protective environment of the hospital. For example, after the initial medical phases of treatment, it may be feasible to transfer the patient to a mixed convalescent ward instead of keeping him on a ward for amputees, or cardiacs, or for persons with visual ailments. In this way he comes into contact with persons different from himself. They will stare and ask questions and offer advice, but they are sick too; he will be exposed to "ordinary social relations" in an atmosphere in which status differences are leveled and sympathetic understanding is more easily sensed.

It may also be possible to provide temporary jobs in the hospital where the patient can come into daily contact with persons from the outside but feels that he is not the only deviate. Thinking along these lines opens up other possibilities. In England, for example, hostels for paraplegics have been established near light industries. The patients take regular jobs at the factories while living under medical supervision (Rusk and Taylor, 1946:170). In this country there is a growing development of "member employee programs" in hospitals. Although remuneration and physical conditioning are certainly among the major purposes of these programs, not to be ignored is the advantage of being placed in real-life situations early in one's adjustment to disability under living arrangements that are somewhat protected. This kind of step-wise preparation is not, of course, necessary in all cases of disability.

SHARING LIFE EXPERIENCES THROUGH GROUP DISCUSSION

Free discussion of common problems in facing other people can lead to ideas never before entertained, ideas which may effect basic changes within the value system of the person and in his behavior. The following is a transcript of a discussion by a group of children with cerebral palsy, ages 11 to 14 years, about their experiences in being with other people. The discussion is led by their friend and teacher (Sutter, *1954*). Joe's speech is hardly intelligible, Eddy's is moderately involved, and Bobby's, Carol's, and Lily's is very clear:

EDDY: Sometimes wise guys just come along and decide to pick on you. I mean sometimes I sat just there and watched these kids the way they talk about you and the way they look at you and stare at you. I don't know. I just come to the conclusion that they just have to get used to you.

TEACHER: Good enough, Eddy.

BOBBY: Well, they kid you about your condition and some of the younger kids kid you and some of the older kids they kid you saying, "Oh, you can't run as fast, Oh, you keep falling down. Why can't you run fast and why can't you talk so good?"

TEACHER: Any of the rest of you have any experiences? Like Bobby's? Carol?

CAROL: Well, Mrs. Sutter, you know I went to Juilliard School of Music two summers ago in New York and I spent six weeks in the city and once or twice when my companion went shopping or when we were even coming out of our apartment children, I mean, children, would stop me on the street and say, "Hey, what's the matter with you" . . . because children stop me more so than adults actually and just saying "What's the matter? What's wrong with you?" And I'd say, "I have cerebral palsy." And I'd say, "I wouldn't care," and my companion would try to pull me away from it but I would just be willing to tell them."

TEACHER: It's a good thing to face these things if we have to. Yes, Joe. Joe is very anxious to say something. All right, Joe.

JOE: When you walk down the street people look at you.

TEACHER: [Repeating in order to make his remarks understandable.] People look at you.

JOE: And stare.

TEACHER: And stare. How do you feel when that happens, Joe? All right, tell us.

JOE: [Unintelligibly]

TEACHER: The best thing is to ignore them, said Joe.

ONE OF THE

CHILDREN: Yes, that's what I said.

TEACHER: Yes, it is, but how about what you're going to do about the way you're feeling inside? Yes, Bobby, what?

BOBBY: After I tell 'em I say well, take one of the kids who is about five, you know. And he said, "What's the matter with you? Can't you walk?" I said, "I've got cerebral palsy." He said, "What's that? Is it like polio?" and I said, "Something like that. If you have it, you have it and you go on."

[1 minute of discussion omitted.]

TEACHER: Eddy has wanted to say something over here. Now have you forgotten? I hope not, Eddy. You had your hand up.

EDDY: Well, I'm trying to say that many times I walk down the street and people who are a good twenty or thirty years old and they just stand there and look at you most of the time. It burns me up, the way they look at you. It doesn't even bother you if a small child looks at you but you get these grownup people. I don't know; most of the time I don't say nothing to 'em.

TEACHER: No you can't.

EDDY [continuing]:   The idea is mostly ignore them but sometimes you can't. You know. As how you have to tell them something.

TEACHER: Yes, Bobby?

BOBBY: It isn't the way the grownups look at you, but I remember one time I was at the theater you know. I couldn't hold still you know. I tried to keep stiff because people were watching you know. But I just couldn't and one of them says, "Hey kid, don't you mind your manners or something."

TEACHER: Oh, yes. There could be that kind of misunderstanding.

BOBBY [Continuing]:   But I couldn't keep them stiff any longer because it had been a long time.

TEACHER: Sometimes adult C.P.'s who are out in public and maybe they walk with sort of a staggering gait with which we are all sort of familiar with, aren't we?

CHILDREN: Yes, we know.

TEACHER: And other people, what do they think? [The children say something]. Yes, they think they are intoxicated. There is that sort of misunderstanding, too.

JOE [With very belabored speech]:   I think sympathy people. . . .

TEACHER [Helping him out]:   Oh, I'm glad you mentioned that. Sympathy people, people who are too full of sympathy.

ONE OF THE

CHILDREN: Oh you poor boy! That sort of people.

TEACHER: Tell me about it.

BOBBY: One time I met an old lady and I was sorta, I couldn't walk so good and she says, "Oh you poor little boy!" [Children laugh with amusement.]

TEACHER: And what's the answer to that? I don't know. I don't know. Do you?

BOBBY [Continuing]:   She said, "You poor little boy. What's the matter with you, you drink too much soda or something?" [Children laugh.] That kind of stuff makes me sick!

TEACHER: Eddy?

EDDY: Well, last night I was in the movies and along comes someone in the town, a noseybody I should say, and he says, "Oh, leave him alone, he's a—" [Eddy then interjects] you know, I don't like to use this word "cripple," and well I just get up and I tell 'em that right off, I tell 'em, "What's it to you?" I mean, I don't know I just like to tell them so they don't bother me no more 'cause I just *hate* that word.

BOBBY: And I just hate that word. Because there's a kid up my block who's always. . . . One time I was walking down the street and this kid was with me, you know, and an old lady comes along and she almost tripped over me and she says, "Oh, he's crippled, don't touch him." [said with scorn].

TEACHER: There's that word again Eddy said he didn't like to use. Let's face that word very squarely. It's a label, isn't it, that word "crippled," it's a label and you don't like it, do you?

CHILDREN: No.

TEACHER: No. Are there any other ways of being crippled than in your legs or in your hands?

CHILDREN [Answering in unison]: Yes!

TEACHER: Yes. And in an even more important way, you know?

JOE: Inside.

TEACHER: Joe said inside and he meant?

CAROL: To be crippled in your feelings!

EDDY: About that, uh, I don't want to go back to that word, . . . about that idea of people sympathizing with you, and stuff like that. Well, there are two kinds and don't forget. There are the guys who don't look at your handicap who look at . . . uh, well, I can give you an example. A number of times when Allen a couple of years ago here would pick on me and someone would come up and say, "Lay off. He's smaller than you," or "He can't fight back as good as you" or . . . I mean they don't mention that, they don't make you understand that you are, as I said before, crippled or handicapped.

TEACHER: Yes. That is in other words, excuse me, Eddy, there may be occasions when you really do need help from somebody else but there are ways and ways of giving help. And now the other kind?

EDDY: The other kind I don't care much for.

TEACHER: I know you don't.

EDDY: I just don't like it, that's all.

TEACHER: Yes. Because one has real understanding and the other has none.

BOBBY [Excitedly]: Oh, boy! This was an experience. This was yesterday, as a matter of fact. This guy, he was walking along, you know, and he thought that I kept falling down when I was walking down the street. And he said to me, he said, "How do you feel?" and I said, "I feel fine." And he said, "What's the matter?" I said, "Well, I'm handicapped, that's all." [The rest of the children laugh.] He said, "Oh, you better see a doctor." Oh boy, that kills me.

TEACHER: Well, this is good for us to talk about. Yes, Lily.

LILY: I also find it very hard to accept the fact when people sometimes see that you can walk, let's say, all right with one cane, that you're capable. Maybe they don't see it but when you feel that you can walk perfectly well, but maybe another person doesn't see it, and they try and help you. You know they try very hard.

TEACHER: That is pretty natural. It's awfully hard not to, Lily. You know, after all these years I still have to catch myself. I want to help you. I have to remember not to. Diane, how do you feel about this?[2]

What did the children gain from this discussion? How did it affect their reactions to the difficulties of ordinary living? We do not know. And what we can guess at is based partly on clinical observations that talking can bring about change in outlook and partly on faith. How could it be otherwise than helpful to hear one among the group say, when affronted, "I've got cerebral palsy. . . . If you have it, you have it and you go on"? How could it be otherwise than helpful to have the children distinguish between two kinds of "sympathy," the understanding kind and the pitying kind? The fact that the children could hear each other complain about some of the annoyances on the outside, the fact that they could laugh about some of the misunderstandings, undoubtedly serves to relieve some of the burden. When this is bolstered by new understandings of one's own feelings and the feelings of others, important preparation for subsequent changes in the management of social relations has taken place.

We do know, however, that discussion is likely to be more effective in producing change when combined with actually *trying out* new ways of behaving than when it stands alone. French (*1944*) reports a study of retraining an autocratic leader. In spite of the fact that full discussion had taken place in the group concerning the advantages of democratic procedures in leading a discussion, one of the trainees completely regressed to his usual autocratic style when he was asked to lead. The children with cerebral palsy could well capitalize on their discussion by some form of reality practice where the new learnings are brought to life and thus more firmly set by behavioral experience.

DISCUSSION OF A STORY

Stories to prepare a person for experiences that might be painful have proved useful. It has been reported (Dinkel, *1947*) that a Negro father had considerable success in softening the shock of race prejudice upon his children through the use of stories that he began telling before they had had encounters with white hostility. The fictitious Negro children who

---

[2] From a tape recording.

were the principal characters in these stories went through a series of incidents of the kind that the father anticipated that his children would experience. By means of doll play he also rehearsed with his children techniques that could be used to avoid or lessen the social difficulties that might befall them. When they later encountered racial antagonism, they were not disturbed greatly and were able to adjust to it more skillfully than neighboring children who had not had such careful training.

Stories are also helpful in the case of adults who find difficulty in referring to their own personal experiences and feelings. By discussing the behavior and attitudes of a character in a story, direct exposure of oneself is avoided. Favorable use of stories with adult amputees has been reported (Dembo, Leviton, Wright, *1956*). Insofar as the intention is to promote behavioral skills as well as adjustive attitudes, it is worth-while to use some form of reality practice in addition to the verbal exchange. Note that the Negro father also had his children *act out* in play with dolls the techniques demonstrated in the stories. This is a form of role playing.

Each of the training procedures we have considered stimulates serious consideration of new possibilities of behaving. This is a first step in the development of more appropriate social skills. When, in addition, these possibilities can be tried out in reality practice, the opportunity is provided for testing the new learnings and improving the skill with which they are executed. The behavior, it must be emphasized, is not alone altered. Underlying attitudes and meanings concomitantly are affected, and it is such changes that make possible the well-managed social interaction; otherwise the "skill" would be only an awkward imitation of the training model.

Chapter 12

The Parent as a Key Participant

THE PSYCHOANALYTIC MOVEMENT, AS IS WELL KNOWN, DID MUCH TO emphasize the importance of the early childhood years for personality development. As a corollary to this emphasis, it is recognized that parents or their surrogates are the pivotal figures who determine in large measure the eventual psychological fate of their children.

Research is being accumulated to show that, although love is not enough, genuine love, warmth, and acceptance by the parent for his child will carry the child far toward developing a healthy personality. "Love, to be worthy of the name in any human relationship, consists of a sincere desire for the other individual's best good rather than mere self-indulgence of the one who gives the affection" (Laycock and Stevenson, *1950:*120). Sommers' study (*1944*) on adolescent blind children, for example, brought out that "the lack of satisfying parental love . . . produced a feeling of loss which seemed to be more injurious to the personality of the blind child than his lack of sight" (p. 103). The important review by Orlansky (*1949*) on such child-rearing practices as breast versus bottle feeding, age of weaning and toilet training, showed that these factors as such had little psychological significance for the child's development whereas the attitude of the parent in carrying out the procedures was crucial. Langdon and Stout (*1951*), looking into the lives of more than 250 well-adjusted children, point out that the background information about the parents (such as their age, religion, etc.) gives little help in accounting for the good adjustment of their children. What does stand out from the many diagnostically insignificent variations is the parents' statement of the "most important of all"—namely, conveying to the children in behavior and words that they are loved, respected, and wanted.

Because of the influence of parents on their children, because the realization of the best that is known concerning the health, education, and welfare of children with disabilities requires coöperation between parents and rehabilitation workers, rehabilitation agencies working on behalf of children must perforce work through and with the parents of these children.

QUALITATIVE ASPECTS OF A SOUND RELATIONSHIP

The terms "rehabilitation worker" and "counselor" are used in the generic sense of anyone working in an official capacity on behalf of a person needing help—e.g., the doctor, physical therapist, school teacher, etc. The following are guideposts in building toward a good relationship with the parent:

1. The parent must feel that the rehabilitation worker is not working against him, that together they are seeking solutions to problems.
2. The parent must feel that the rehabilitation worker likes his child, sees him as an individual, a personality.
3. The parent must feel that the rehabilitation worker appreciates his strengths, his struggle to do the best he can for his child, that though the parent may have shortcomings, neither are they "picked on" nor do they lead to rejection of him.

Further analysis of these points, so obvious that they may appear as truisms, reveals the complexity of feelings with which they are invested on both sides of the relationship.

Interfering Parental Attitudes

Of great significance is the likelihood that the parent carries to the relationship certain attitudes which, unless modified, act against the most productive use of the time together. Considering the rehabilitation worker as a person in authority, the parent may look upon him with fear on the one hand and with awe on the other, emotions reminiscent of his childish reactions to his own parents and to such other authority figures as his teachers and doctors.

In addition to these diffuse feelings that alert his defenses, the parent often enters the relationship with a number of well-defined fears. He may expect, for example, to be blamed for any and all of the difficulties that beset his child and fear that his guilt as a parent will be exposed. He may be worried that demands that he is unable to meet will be made on his financial resources, on his time, strength, and emotional involvement. He may fear that the expert will shatter his strands of hope that his child can be cured or at least appreciably helped. He may believe that the specialist will not understand him as a parent and will become impatient with his desperate wish that all will be well. He may also fear that the worst aspects of the reality will be kept from him. Finally, he may be anxious lest the child become "too attached" to the therapist, this being no small threat to a parent already uncertain of his relations to his child.

Whatever the complex of fears, we can be sure that the parent enters the situation full of apprehension, hopes, and doubts that often set him apart from the rehabilitation worker, aligning them at opposite poles until constructive forces enter with sufficient strength to bring the two together in a real coöperative endeavor.

Of the constructive forces, those moving in the direction of points 2 and 3 above carry considerable weight. In short, the parent must come to feel that the rehabilitation worker likes and respects him and likes and respects his child. That this is not always simple will be seen below.

Interfering Counselor Attitudes

The following are some attitudes which, if carried to the relationship by the rehabilitation worker, militate against a constructive relationship with the parent:

"The trouble with children is their parents." This attitude in professional circles is more common and more resistant to change than we like to think, for it rests upon many supporting experiences of an emotional as well as rational nature. To begin with, there is the resentment against one's own parents which the rehabilitation worker, like other adults, may feel. The rehabilitation worker has added proof in his own practice of the lack of wisdom of some, if not many, parents when they fail to carry through the recommended plan or openly defy it. Moreover, he has the edict of the theorists who have laid on the parental doorstep the tremendous responsibility for maladjustments in children.

The rehabilitation worker himself, therefore, has to examine and reexamine his own feelings in regard to parents as a group. Stereotypes about parents must give way to the reality of the individual parent. The counselor has to reach the point where, though recognizing parental shortcomings, he can still respect the positives which are there if one looks for them. Of course the rehabilitation worker cannot ignore the destructive influences. He must take them into account in planning with the parent, in working through troublesome issues. He must appreciate that the shortcomings of the parent have their own origins, and the effort to understand and cope with them must supplant derision of them.

Whether the rehabilitation worker will be positively or negatively inclined toward the parent largely depends upon the parental characteristics extracted as the main lines of striving. For example, if the rehabilitation worker sees a particular parent primarily as rejecting his child, even hating him and wanting to absolve himself of all responsibility, then, to say the least, a real liking and respect for the parent is precluded. If, however, the rehabilitation worker sees that parent as torn by conflict, as being bothered by guilt, as running away from his responsibilities because he is already overburdened with stresses of various sorts, then the emphasis is on the parent's struggle to come to terms with his problems. Such an emphasis, being directed toward the growth potential of the parent in the wake of emmeshing, undermining factors, is one of the best guarantees that the counselor will look with an attitude of acceptance essential in constructive counselor-client relationships.

This point is another example of the principle of positive identification referred to on page 148. There it was pointed out that, by highlighting and identifying with the aspects of coping with disability, the person himself is able to relegate devaluating aspects of his physique to positions of little influence on the self-concept. Similarly, the rehabilitation worker can truly respect the positive strivings of the parent, for even the most disreputable person is not lacking them, and he can look upon the destructive forces as unfortunate interferences which, in some cases, may require therapeutic handling and in others managing in spite of them.

The professional person must orient himself to parents by the principle that generalizations about parents (and about any group for that matter) have to be made with caution, that he is far better prepared to see the parent as he is if he remembers that "parents love and hate . . . [handicapped] children just as parents love and hate children who are not physically impaired. Parents protect, guide wisely, pamper, neglect, and even abandon children whether or not they are handicapped. Some children were unwanted, but are loved and have the security of a healthy relationship with their parents. Some children were wanted, but are unloved and insecure, whether or not they are sound of mind and body" (White, *1955:*470).[1]

"My job is to provide the answers." The key to the psychological issue involved in this deleterious attitude is revealed with the metamorphosis produced by the grammatical substitution of "our" for "my." The parent as a member of the rehabilitation team has answers too. His set of answers is no less important than that of the professionally trained person, and the best solutions can result only from a dovetailing of both. The audiologist, to take a concrete example, knows far more about audiograms and hearing aids than does the parent, but the parent, after all, knows far more about himself and his child than the audiologist. Even if a social worker, psychiatrist, or psychologist is part of the team, the knowledge, insights, and lack of insights on the part of the parent are just as essential and worthy as are the knowledge, insights, and lack of insights on the part of the professional worker.

---

[1] G. White, Social casework in relation to cerebral palsy, in W. M. Cruickshank and G. M. Raus (Eds.), *Cerebral palsy: its individual and community problems,* Syracuse University Press, 1955. By permission.

Furthermore, since the parent in most cases must assume the ultimate responsibility for his child, it is necessary that he actively participate in the rehabilitation process from the beginning. He will be ill prepared for the many independent judgments he will have to make if, during his contact with the rehabilitation situation, his primary role was that of passive listener to the wisdom of the diagnosticians.

It should also be anticipated that the parent's admixture of awe and fear, of gratitude and resentment, of pride and guilt, of self-respect and self-pity will tend to keep him in a turmoil and lead him to expect and accept his role as second-class listener. This means that the rehabilitation worker must actively encourage questions and opinions on the part of the parent. It means that the parent needs time to disentangle his feelings and thoughts and to absorb the new information presented to him. Opportunity should be given for more than one contact with the professional person, because questions and formulatable opinions often come *after* the parent leaves the counselor's office. He should be asked to write these down for the next occasion, an occasion that will still open the dam to the flood of fears and anxieties.

We even venture to propose that systematic research be done on how and when the parent can well serve during case conferences as an integral and equal part of the team planning for the child. To be sure, the parent sometimes does work through the problems of his child in more or less equal partnership with a single therapist—the social worker or teacher, for example. But in the usual team approach, the parent is typically excluded. Traditionally, the team approach describes case management in which at best the several therapists (e.g., orthopedist, speech correctionist, psychologist, pediatrician, social worker, occupational therapist, physical therapist, etc.) gather together, each reporting his findings and as a group arriving at conclusions, but *without* the parent. One of the experts then conveys certain of this information to the parent. In support of this, it is assumed that the presence of the parent would interfere with the frank presentation of facts that would be disturbing to him.

However true this may be, it is well to weigh these considerations against such negative effects as the following: (1) The parent gets the feeling that much is being said and done behind his back. (2) Decisions and conclusions are made, albeit in the form of recommendations, without his active participation. This always carries the danger that the parent will be unable or unwilling to carry them out. (3) It places the parent in the position of a child who has to be told what to do without having a real say in the telling or doing.

Even though one may want to spare the parent who is just beginning to face the realities of the struggle ahead, surely in follow-up conferences, for those parents who are adjusting to the realities at hand, the possibility of full participation on the team should be explored.

The findings of systematic research may surprise us on several counts. They may show that nothing is lost if things that would unduly hurt the parent are not said. They may show parents to be abler than we think to withstand an honest discussion of their child's problems, especially if matters are discussed realistically and hopefully at the same time and with full respect for the parent. They may establish clearer criteria as to which parents are and are not ready for such participation, as to which parents are emotionally still so involved that a presentation of the problems from many points of view would be so overwhelming as to interfere with problem solving. They may make evident that nothing is basically lost if even the indifferent parent or the parent with borderline mentality is present at the conference and that something valuable may be gained. It may show that the time required for explanation of technical terms is time saved in the end, for the participation of the parent at the conference makes possible the introduction of further facts and a point of view essential to a sound consideration of the total problem.

If one seriously respects the parent, if one is confident that he can win out in his striving to work through the problems that face him and his child, then the conviction emerges that more often than not the parent, in the long run, will be an asset as a full and equal member of the rehabilitation team. The parent is, after all, generally the only person who has lived with the child for 24 hours a day over the years of the child's life. Few professional persons, in fact, can claim such intensive experience with children as part of their formal training. Does one dare to say that the parent knows and understands his child less well than an outsider? Only in some instances, and in regard to certain problems. It is more correct to consider him an expert, just as the professional worker is an expert, each bringing to the discussion an important point of view and special understandings of the child.

Of course, the successful realization of such parent participation also requires certain mature attitudes on the part of the specialists, particularly that of liking and respect for the parent and child as well as a readiness to admit to their cloisters a fifth estate, the parent, who also is an expert in his own endeavor. Certainly, too, we need to know a good deal more about types of conferences, including their structure and procedures, so that that approach can be selected that is most constructive for particular purposes. This is a problem of group dynamics and requires the aid of research. Thoughtful, systematic observation of current practice and research on untried procedures holds promise of making better use of the parent as a key participant in the rehabilitation process. This issue is also applicable to participation of the adult client in case conferences and is raised later in that connection (Chap. 14).

"I do not feel comfortable with disabled people." This is another attitude on the part of the specialist that interferes with a productive and close relationship with the parent. Particularly interfering are such emotional attitudes toward disability as aversion, devaluating pity, and dislike. Such feelings countermand one of the cardinal criteria of a constructive rehabilitation relationship—namely, that the parent believe that the counselor likes and respects his child. Confidence in the specialist cannot easily be developed when his belief in the child as an important and to-be-loved individual is doubted. Moreover, the opportunity for the parent's own attitudes toward disability to be positively affected is lost. In a sound relationship the specialist, by his own wholesome attitudes toward disability, conveys to the parent that a person is not his disability, that the child can have a full measure of life's happiness though he will have his share of its sorrows. Next to eradicating the disability itself, the parent's supreme wish is that this be true. This attitude of the professional person can be so comforting that the parent begins to view the disability not as an overwhelming tragedy but as a reality which can be lived with. Finally, of course, the child's own responses and behavior will be affected by the attitudes of the rehabilitation personnel with whom he comes in contact.

The main antidote to emotionally negative attitudes on the part of the rehabilitation worker toward persons with disabilities lies in self-understanding, in making a real effort to come to grips with what one basically feels and why. It is hoped that a volume such as this, in exploring some of the social-psychological factors important in adjustment to disability, in considering attitudes as fundamentally involving value issues, will provide some of the directions that such a self-analysis can take.

The proposed self-analysis takes place under favorable conditions when the specialist is actually working with persons who have physical disabilities, for then emotionally he begins to see *people* and not simply diseased and deformed structures. As one teacher reports: "I remember my first visit to the hospital—my feelings of revulsion at the disfiguring conditions of the children. Gradually I came to grips with myself and began to understand some of the reasons for my feelings. By the fourth clinic session, I was completely at ease. These were children who needed help. I hardly noticed the disfiguring conditions which had first repelled me. I know now, that what counts is not the handicap, but what is done with it and about it. Teaching these children is a challenge and a charge— but most of all a richly rewarding experience" (*Helping the physically limited child, 1952–1953*).

Although the underlying attitudes of liking and respect for the child and the parent are so fundamental that one wants to underscore it as all-important, there are some rules in the order of techniques for interacting with the parent that aid in conveying it. The desirability of stressing or referring to the assets of the child before his liabilities has been mentioned (Laycock and Stevenson, *1950:*133). Even if the counselor knows that the parent wants to find out just what the situation is with respect to the disability and would be impatient with any excursions about other characteristics of his child, however laudable, a brief transitional phrase pointing to a positive attribute can be an important cue to the parent that the counselor stands behind his child. What one says—and how one says it, of course—will depend upon the personality and convictions of the rehabilitation worker. As illustrations, the following remarks of a psychologist in opening the conference with parents concerning their deaf children are presented: "Mary was awfully good during the examination. . . ." "Do you know that David has developed exceptional skill in speech reading? . . ." "Such a smile! Even the children around him sense that he is friendly." Needless to say, the rule to start with the positive will fail completely unless the words also silently convey "I like your child. He matters. Our search together will be rewarding. . . ."

Certainly one doesn't have to wax maudlin. On the contrary, the emotional relationship should be restricted to warm but not demonstrative acceptance and support for the efforts of the parent and his child. The parent often is already so deeply involved that he can well do without additional emotionalism which feeds into self-pity or the tragedy of the situation. Doubtless, mere reference to disability-connected matters will cause some parents to spill over, to become overwhelmed with their uncertain hopes and still more uncertain fears. The counselor then needs to stand by, sometimes putting into words the feeling that can also be silently conveyed—namely, "I understand. Things will get better. Both you and your child will manage."

The following rule is mentioned only because it is so often violated: The rehabilitation worker should make a conscious decision each time as to whether the child ought to be in the conference room. Sometimes the child's presence does not matter or can be helpful. When the physical therapist is explaining the exercises that will have to be done daily at home, the child is needed for demonstration. Besides, this is a matter-of-fact area where, by listening, the child is learning what to expect and what is expected of him. But, when the therapist is discussing with the parent the difficulties at home that are upsetting to the child, or when the surgeon is describing the nature of the operation soon to be performed on the child, etc., etc., what then? The answer is obvious, but evidently children are so easily regarded as unknowing entities that even professional people fail to consider the effects of their presence. It means that the rehabilitation setting has to provide facilities for the care and occupation of the child while the parent is in conference.

TOPICS AND UNDERSTANDINGS COMPRISING A BROAD REHABILITATION PROGRAM

In addition to the significance of the underlying emotional relationship between counselor and parent, there are many specific topics and insights that should find a place in a total rehabilitation program. The following summary draws heavily upon a thoughtful account by Laycock and Stevenson (*1950*) of parents' problems with exceptional children.

• Parents must be helped to realize that handicaps in children are part of the general problem of human imperfections, which all must face in themselves and in all other human beings. The problem of parents of exceptional children is therefore not unique but applies to all parents. These are not mere palliative words, for all parents must learn to accept the limitations of their children.

• Parents make a tremendous step forward when they realize that any course other than acceptance adds to the child's handicaps and increases their own difficulties.

• Parents can be helped to see that frequently it is not the handicap that hinders a child's adjustment, but how he himself feels about his handicap.

• One of the best helps that can be given parents comes from understanding the potentialities of their children. Instead of concentrating on the fact that the child will never walk, for example, the parent can be helped to lay emphasis on the fact that the child can be taught to use his hands and to talk. In this way the coping rather than the succumbing aspects of the situation guide the emotional and practical life of the person (see pp. 59–61). The important point is that every parent must adjust to what his child *can* do.

• Parents need to understand that their exceptional child is fundamentally like all children, that "all children need an adequate and balanced diet, sufficient rest and sleep, a comfortable temperature, and activity when well rested, that all need to be loved and wanted, to have a reasonable independence in running their own lives and in making their own decisions, to feel a sense of achievement that comes from making things and doing jobs, to win the approval of others for what they are and do, and to feel that they are worthwhile individuals who reasonably come up to their own standards" (Laycock and Stevenson, *1950:*123).

• At the same time, the parent needs to recognize the special problems brought about by the disability of his child. But such recognition must be coupled with precautions against the natural tendency to view all or most of the child's growing-up problems as disability-connected. (See spread, pp. 118–119.)

- The parent needs to understand the different means that may have to be used in the education of his child.

- The parent may have to be helped to face early separation from his child in hospital and school.

- The parent will have questions about medical aspects—cause, course, and treatment—of the disability. There will be anxious questions about hereditary implications regarding the matter of further children and grandchildren. Here is a place where the all too common feelings of guilt can be brought to the surface and, with proper handling, to some extent if not largely dissipated.

- Parents need to reach some understanding of the relative roles of maturation and learning in the child's development and to realize that the child has to be ready for the next step in his progress before he can take it.

- The dangers of comparison with other children need to be realized, and the child's own progress needs to be accepted as the primary basis for evaluation.

- Instructions as to how the parent can best help the child at home in the development of specific skills should be given. But the therapist must be careful not to make too great a demand on the parent's time and energy (or on the child's, of course), appreciating that the parent has many other responsibilities in regard to maintaining the family.

- The parent needs to appreciate that progress in the child may require a great deal of regular practice and much encouragement as well as untold patience on the part of the parents themselves.

- Parents should become aware of the threats to the emotional security of their children caused by continuous quarreling in the home, major disagreements between the parents in regard to child-rearing practices, inconsistent or baseless discipline, dominance or coddling of the child, the playing of favorites by the parents, and the feeling on the part of the child that he is a burden.

- Parents need to understand important practical principles of child guidance. The usual areas of concern should be explored, such as toilet training, sleeping, eating, thumbsucking, nailbiting, bed-wetting, temper tantrums, etc. Parents also need understanding with respect to sibling relations, sexual development and sex education, the development of constructive social patterns of behavior, shyness and aggression, problems of discipline and, later on, the considerations involved in vocational choice.

- At the same time it must be recognized that, though rules are helpful, they are far less so than we might imagine. In no case can they take the place of love for the child, of sensitivity to the child's reactions to the learning experiences to which he is exposed. The parent needs to grasp not only the "letter" of the rules and principles but also their spirit.

• Parents, too, need to be prepared for the ordinary frustrations and gratifications aroused by their child's disability. Help in meeting the curiosity, rejecting attitudes, sympathy, and devaluating pity of neighbors and friends should be part of the rehabilitation effort.

These are some of the areas that should be tapped in a broad rehabilitation program involving the parents of children with disabilities. There are others. The rehabilitation team can decide which of the topics above belong to whose domain. Actually, many of them cut across specialties and in one way or another are related to the work of all. The importance of the rehabilitation worker as a counselor and as a person cannot be overestimated. Training and skills are essential but so are wisdom and maturity.

Fortunately, there is a growing body of excellent reading material to which parents can be directed for sound information concerning child development in general and matters revolving around disability in particular. Spock's classic book on baby and child care can unquestionably be recommended, and its brief review dealing with the handicapped child contains basic wisdom of benefit to any parent (*1946*). Lowenfeld's book (*1956*) written especially for parents of blind children is first rate. Myklebust's book (*1950*) written for parents of deaf children, to say nothing of the many pamphlets and articles distributed by national and private organizations concerned with problems of disability, all offer enlightening and encouraging material which can be a real source of help and comfort to parents. They provide technical information concerning questions of etiology, treatment, and home management; they convey basic attitudes of realistic yet hopeful acceptance. Suitable autobiographical accounts can also extend the horizons of parents. Of books written by parents, the one by Henderson (*1954*) dealing with the blindness of her child and the one by Bruckner (*1954*), which reveals so well the passion in first rejecting and then meeting the challenge imposed by her son's crippling, are examples. The amount of autobiographical material written by persons with disabilities is vast, and almost any of it can help a parent toward fulfilling the insatiable demands of understanding.

The world-famous library of the National Society of Crippled Children and Adults, in Chicago, Ill., will provide the parent (and the professional worker) with sources of bibliographical material covering many areas of child development. Other national organizations, such as the Volta Bureau in Washington, D.C. concerned with problems of deafness, and the American Foundation for the Blind, Inc., in New York City, also maintain reference and lending libraries. Guidance materials distributed by state departments of education or social welfare and the Department of Health, Education, and Welfare of the federal government are also available.

If they are to be used to best advantage in the relations between parent and child, the knowledge and insights must be emotionally accepted as well as intellectually understood. In this connection the sustaining power of certain religious precepts which posit in disability a purposefulness divinely ordained may be mentioned. Karen's mother, for example, strengthened by her religious beliefs, conveyed a comforting outlook to her child crippled with cerebral palsy:

. . . She [Karen] had been singing contentedly and broke off in the middle of a bar. Looking at me squarely, she asked, "Mom Pom, why did God make me a cripple?"

"Here it is," I thought, "and I'm not ready after all." I breathed a swift prayer for guidance. I fully realized how much depended on my answer. I dried my hands and sat at the table beside her.

"I think, Karen, because God loved you better than most people," I answered slowly. "He didn't pick Gloria or Marie or Rory [Karen's siblings] to be C.P.; He picked you. You have suffered already and you will suffer more. Not only will your body be hurt at times, but your mind and your heart. It takes a very special person to handle hurt." I moved closer to her. "Karen, whom do you think God loved more than anyone else in the world?"

She pondered. "His mother, I guess."

"You're right, darling, He loved His mother more than anyone else, and yet he allowed her to suffer more than anyone else. Suffering, sweetheart, is a sign of God's special love. That's why you're crippled and we are not. He just loves you more, that's all."

"It's hard, but I'm really lucky. It's all right now I know" [Killilea, *1952*:212].[2]

And Karen's mother feels that she is privileged to care for Karen:

I had never thought that "capable" hands (the tactful way of referring to large hands) would be a source of gratitude. Nor that the years spent on tennis court and in fencing would produce anything but the problem of covering bulging biceps, summer or winter. That both would one day be a source of facility and strength in teaching my child to walk, could never have occurred to me. God works in mysterious ways. In giving me a passion for sports and an aptitude thereat, He had been equipping me since childhood for a task not entrusted to the average parent [pp. 81–82].

Mrs. Bruckner, the mother of Billy who was born without arms,

[2] Reprinted with permission of Prentice-Hall, Inc., from *Karen* by Marie Killilea. Copyright 1952 by Marie Lyons Killilea.

became convinced when he survived a nearly fatal illness that he was born for a purpose, and as the months progressed increasingly saw the positive intent of God's work with respect to Billy (Bruckner, *1954*).

Religious beliefs serve to organize one's feeling and thinking about illness and disability through value judgments of right and wrong, of purpose and ultimate meanings. But it should be clear that values enter into the scientific approach also. As a matter of fact, as the discussion of acceptance of disability well testifies (Chap. 5), it assigns to values a central position. Instead of considering supernatural forces to be a factor in the causality and meaning of disabling diseases and accidents, however, science attributes these events to amoral, natural conditions. Human values, nevertheless, may loom high, and it is the process of reëvaluation that can carry the parent far in giving his child the love, support, and acceptance needed to face constructively the reality of his disability.

In the account below, a father was able to achieve an emotional and intellectual acceptance of his son's disability without specifically calling upon divine judgment. The son, Bill, had lost both arms in a car accident. The father, in service during the war, wrote his son a letter on the eve of Bill's discharge from the rehabilitation center:

. . . He told him, in words as simple and plain as those he used in making his reconnaissance reports, about a man's rights. He said he was fighting in Korea for those rights, for his own, for Bill's, for Marty's [mother]. "For everybody's rights, Son, no matter where they live. But sometimes a guy gets mixed up. You hear so much about rights these days you begin to think you have a right to everything. Even to a body with two legs and two arms and sight and hearing and so on. But you don't. No one has a right to that kind of body. It's a gift. God gives it to you or nature gives it, or you can call it the evolutionary process, or however you want to speak of it. In big words or little words, it is a gift. And not everybody is given it. For accidents happen before birth, as well as afterward. I know a great chap who was born without arms and legs. . . .

"And sometimes," he said in this letter, "even when we have a gift to begin with, it gets messed up. You know about that. And I know too, out here, because it has happened to some of the bravest men I've flown with. It's funny how a guy can get mixed up about things. He loses a leg, say; or his arms, or his sight; he begins to feel he hasn't had a fair deal; things are raw; he's been gypped; somebody's taken his right to a whole body away from him. He's all wet, Bill.

"But there is a right that you do have; everybody has; and that is the right to a whole life, whether you have legs and arms, or not; no matter how different you may be. And I mean by a whole life, a life full of fun and interesting experiences (along with the hard things), and people you love, and a girl some day, and a job you like to do, and sports, and making things better for others. We are going to do our best, Bill, to help you hold on to that right. To see that nobody takes it away from you. But you have to walk to it, boy, like Guillaumet [a pilot who had suffered untold hardships and whom Bill admired]. All your mother and I can do is stand by, and help when we can" [Smith, *1954*:178–179].[3]

THE PROBLEM OF HOPE VERSUS STARK REALITY

The presence of a disability brings a special salience to certain psychological problems common to human adjustment in general. Among these is the problem of hope versus stark reality, a problem first stressed by Dembo (*1955*). The problem will be examined here from the point of view of the parent; its applicability to the process of adjustment in the person who has the disability will readily be seen.

On the basis of interviews with parents of children with cerebral palsy, Dembo has concluded that rather than emphasizing the permanence of a child's severe handicap, those working with the parent should support his hopes for improvement. The argument rests on two main points. First, the harsh, realistic view in the early stage of adjusting to severe disability leads to despair and the severest suffering. Secondly, hope, however unrealistic in terms of probability of its actualization, does not necessarily interfere with the practical and sensible care of the child. On the contrary, it provides the needed encouragement to continue with the interminable demands of rehabilitation whereas the recognition of stark reality can so deplete one's emotional resources as to make one ineffectual in the job ahead. An important theoretical analysis of the difference between realistic and wishful expectations in terms of (1) the assumption concerning lawfulness of nature and (2) the focus given to probabilities versus possibilities in the future, is also made in that study.

In regard to the practical working relationship between specialist and parent, however, the issue of hope and stark reality does not always provide a ready-made guide. On the one hand a parent may need to hope, but on the other hand a certain degree of realism is necessary for the parent to take steps and make plans toward constructive coping. Moreover, hope built upon evasion is hardly reassuring. As indicated in the study by Davis (*1958*) of the process of recovery from polio as this takes place in the interaction of child, hospital, and family, the parent often needs both more facts and greater support for hope than he gets.

We therefore propose two guiding principles: First, the realistic state of affairs as it relates to the *current welfare and planning of the child* must be discussed with the parent, but even then hope can cast its glow

---

[3] By permission from L. E. Smith, *The Journey,* copyright 1944, World Publishing Company.

on the problem. For example, it may be important to convince the parent that the child *is* deaf in order that the necessary speech training program be instituted as soon as possible. The parent may have to be convinced many times over that current knowledge of surgery and other medical treatment will be of no avail, but this does not mean that the parent must discard all hope for medical advance and that the child may eventually hear.

Secondly, the emphasis given to the reality of the future can be guided by whether the parent gives indication that he needs and is ready to know it. In spite of his wishful thinking, the parent does gradually absorb the reality before him, at first unconsciously, and then with conscious acknowledgment. Time psychologically prepares the parent. It makes it unnecessary that he be shocked into reality by the callous words of the professional person.

The readiness of the parent to face the facts can be paced with less risk if the parent is given an opportunity to "see for himself." For example, Cruickshank (*1955*) has suggested that parents of children who are mentally retarded as well as cerebral palsied be given the chance to see their child's progress in a nursery school with other children with disabilities but who have normal mentality, since "clinical findings fail to convince parents, who cannot be expected to understand the ultimate implications of a slow rate of development; untold mental anguish and feelings of guilt of parents can be alleviated if the parents . . . convince themselves of the failure of their child to respond to educational opportunities. . . . Realistic planning should ideally allow for this phase of parent-enlightenment before further planning is undertaken" (p. 347). If a parent of a deaf child visits a school for the deaf, he may be upset by the fact that the voices of the graduating seniors are monotonous and far from what he had hoped could be accomplished, but his reaction remains one of disappointment and not despair when gradually he has been learning about deafness.

In short, instead of informing parents of everything at once, it is proposed that they be taught at a pace determined by their readiness to assimilate the facts. This does not mean fooling the parents. But it does mean dealing primarily with the present reality in an atmosphere of hopeful expectation, allowing the bleak probabilities of the future to fall into place as the parent seeks and is ready to face such clarification.

Some will disagree with this advice. It may be held that a wound, however deep, is better when it is clean-cut. The Dembo point of view, on the other hand, maintains that for the wound to be clean-cut, the area must first be prepared by the proper presurgical care. If one is grateful for the bitter truth, it is because one already has been prepared; one already "knows" and needs the voice of authority to give certainty to that knowledge, a certainty that provides relief only after floundering amid the unknown and being exhausted by it. Even then hope is not precluded.

There is one more important point. Not infrequently misconception and prejudice masquerade in the name of reality. When Karen's doctor told her mother, "I don't believe that cerebral palsy children have any mentality" (Killilea, *1952:*29), he thought he was being realistic and that she ought to know. When another doctor advised the parents to take Karen to an institution and leave her and forget they ever had her (p. 34), he also thought he was being realistic. The judgment of reality depends partly on whose eyes are perceiving. By and large the eyes of the parent become very good perceivers when he is given time and opportunity to see and to feel as well as to hope, which gives to that reality a promise for the future.

Coating reality with hope does not mean living in a world of unreality. Accepting a disability does not mean banishing hope. Even when one has reached the most wholesome adjustment to disability—namely, that of viewing physical normalcy as an asset value—hope is not ruled out. Secondly, as a general principle, shocking a parent into reality has doubtful value. As he struggles to adjust to the loss, reality takes shape before him. But he needs time and experience with the disability to face it. Although he cannot or ought not live by hope alone, in proper proportions it can be a leavening agent that lightens one's burdens.

These are assertions. Research is needed not only to provide more substantial support for them but also to shed further light on the balance between "hope" and "fact" most conducive to ultimate adjustment at different stages in the process of accepting a disability.

THE PROBLEM OF OVERPROTECTION, DEPENDENCE, AND INDEPENDENCE

In any study of the attitudes and behavior of parents toward their children who have some disability, overprotectiveness is likely to appear as one of the main categories. Research involving children with cerebral palsy (Shere, *1954*), other crippling conditions (Kammerer, *1940*), the blind (Sommers, *1944*), etc., well illustrates this. Moreover, the generalization can probably be made that parents tend more frequently to be overprotective toward their children who have a disability than toward those who do not. A study of thirty pairs of twins, one twin of each pair being cerebral palsied (Shere, *1954*), revealed that of these, thirteen children with cerebral palsy were judged to be overprotected, whereas none of the nondisabled twins was so judged. An enlightening account of three families differing in their degree of acceptance and overprotectiveness toward the cerebral palsied child and his twin is also presented (pp. 129 ff.).

The person who has a disability often rejects the overprotection to which he believes he is subjected. In the Heiders' study of the attitudes of deaf persons toward those with normal hearing (*1941*), for example, it is reported that former pupils of schools for the deaf spontaneously mentioned, among other negative interpersonal relations, that deaf people are overprotected by and lose their freedom to those with normal hearing. The following excerpt from a tape recording of a discussion between a teacher and several young adolescent cerebral palsied children shows how strongly these subjects feel about the need for independence (Sutter, *1954*).

BOBBY: They [my parents] don't understand that you *have* to go out and buy something.

TEACHER: I like that, Bobby, they don't understand that you *have* to get out. Curtis, you had something to say and I want to hear it.

CURTIS: My family babies me too much.

TEACHER: Your family babies you too much. . . .

BOBBY: My mother won't let me take my own bath.

TEACHER: How old are you Bobby?

BOBBY: Twelve.

TEACHER: And you can walk around pretty well. All right . . . we can't leave this subject without finding out why parents feel this way. Why?

BOBBY: They're afraid for you.

TEACHER: They're afraid for you. Joe, does your family protect you too much, take too good care of you sometimes, do you think, or do they let you do anything that is reasonable, going out to the store and so on?

JOE: She won't let me go to the store because a lot of my streets are dangerous and she don't trust me too much.

TEACHER: I don't think it's that your mother doesn't trust you. I think she may not trust your ability to see very clearly or well enough. Well, that's not distrusting you. Sometimes there are very good reasons for these things. Yes, Joe?

JOE: Look for a car.

TEACHER: Sometimes there are ways and means to get around these things like taking a bath or going down to the village. If we can work closely enough with your parents, the teachers and you, we all get together, maybe some of these problems can be solved. . . .

DIANE: After all, you're going to have to do it eventually. You're going to have to do it when you really are more or less on your own, when you don't have anybody to look after you you're going to have to do it and if you can't do it now while your parents are still with you, why then when something happens to them and you try to do it something terrific is liable to happen to you.[4]

Now our problem first begins. We have to think through what over-protection signifies before we dare condemn or commend the "nurturant" relations of one person toward another. The following are some important considerations, helpful in the understanding of this concept.

Overprotection Negative by Definition

By its very syntax the term "overprotection" has a negative connotation, for too much of anything is undesirable. A certain amount of protection is good; deviation from that optimal amount is not good.

The following behavior patterns have been ascribed to overprotective parents:

1. They are highly child-centered; they are eager to sacrifice themselves (and the rest of the family) for the "good" of one particular child.
2. They are continually helping the child, even when he is fully capable and willing to help himself; they bathe, dress, and undress him; they feed him.
3. Their discipline is inconsistent. There are occasions when they meticulously adhere to regulations and mete out punishment for the slightest infringement; at other times, they are overindulgent and lax.
4. They are dictatorial and arbitrary; they make decisions which involve the child without considering his wishes. Among overprotective parents, those who are acceptant give lavish toys and tell the child how to play with them; those who are rejectant withhold gifts and privileges or withdraw them on the slightest pretext.
5. They hover over him; they offer suggestions; the rejectant parents nag and criticize; the acceptant parents call attention to the child's every activity and bestow more praise than is deserved.
6. They protect him from every imaginable discomfort or difficulty, the acceptant parents because they cannot bear to see the child suffer; the rejectant parents because their anxiety serves to disguise their rejection of him.
7. They restrict his play, the acceptant parents because they fear he may get hurt; the rejectant ones because by their restriction they frustrate and punish him.
8. They deny him opportunities for growing up; they thwart his curiosity; the acceptant parents because they want to keep him a baby; the rejectant parents because they do not want to take the trouble to teach him.
9. They do not understand his capabilities and limitations; they set goals which are too high for him, or they are content with goals which are too low.

[4] From a tape recording.

10. They monopolize his time; they sleep with him; they allow him few friends of his own choosing; they take him to parties and call for him; they persuade him to stay at home with them [Shere, *1954*:48–49].

A notion of the equally unfortunate effects imputed to the child who is overprotected is given by the following manifestations:

1. He is overdesirous of petting and cuddling. He likes to sleep in the same room with his parents or even in the same bed with one of them. He is afraid to sleep alone.
2. With younger children he is bossy and aggressive but with older children or adults he is oversubmissive and docile. He is usually very well behaved in school.
3. He is cheerful when he is with his parents or anyone with whom he feels secure but is inclined to cry or be unhappy when he is separated from them.
4. He is overconforming; he obeys implicitly.
5. He is usually apathetic, but in the presence of strong stimuli he may become highly emotional. He may have temper tantrums.
6. He has little or no curiosity. He is interested only in matters of which his parents approve. He shows behavior indicative of insecurity when he is with children of his own age who are more mature than he is.
7. He is shy and unfriendly to strangers. He does not know how to play with other children, yet does not like to play alone; he may prefer to be with his parents; he may like to read rather than to play.
8. He is jealous of anyone who appears to threaten his position with loved ones.
9. He is afraid in many situations, even where there is no real danger.
10. He is pleased by flattery and depressed by adverse criticism. He constantly asks for assurance of parental favor; he often asks for approval of what he is doing.
11. He prefers to have help in all his activities and is inclined to reject responsibility. He does not dress himself or get to school on time without help.
12. His feeling of insecurity is manifested by nervous habits, which may serve as emotional releases or as attention-getting devices [Shere, *1954*:51–52].

It might appear that, with such explicit criteria as given above, identification of the overprotective parent would not be difficult. The judgment as to whether the child is being overprotected, however, depends upon who is doing the evaluating. The second criterion, for example, states that the overprotective parent is continually helping the child, even when he is fully capable. The parent himself, however, generally does not agree that this is the case. Instead, he is usually convinced that the child is not in fact fully capable of self-help in the particular instance. As he sees it, it is the realities of the situation that require his help and protection.

That the label "overprotective" involves a point of view is also seen in other comparisons. The independence given children today would have been considered excessive by the Victorian parent or schoolmaster. Socioeconomic level also influences standards of protectiveness. The developmental stage of the child is especially important in dictating what does and what does not constitute overprotectiveness. Not allowing a three-year-old child to cross a street unaided is sensible, whereas in the case of an ordinary twelve-year-old it is unduly restrictive. The adolescent tends to regard any parental guidance as overprotective. Finally, diversity in appraisal is presented by neighbors who may feel that the parent is *under*-protecting his child when he allows his blind or deaf child to cross city streets, though both the expert and parent may believe that they are building toward independence.

Glorification of Independence

The problem of overprotection is part and parcel of the cultural value placed on dependence and independence. A notion of how American middle-class society compares in this respect with other societies is provided in the important study of child-rearing practices by Whiting and Child (*1953:* Chap. 4).

1. Initial nurturance. Among the 38 primitive societies rated, indulgence of the infant's tendencies to be dependent is generally rather high. This is also true of American middle-class society, though 30 of the societies allowed their babies to be more dependent than ours.

2. Age at beginning of training in independence (self-reliance, responsibility). The median age at which serious efforts at independence training are begun for the 38 societies is a little above 3.5 years, American middle-class society being placed at 2.5 years. However, independence training among the American group is completed at a very late age in comparison with the societies rated.

3. Severity of independence training. American middle-class practice is placed at the median of all the societies surveyed, a high rating being given, however, for that aspect of independence concerned with the responsibility of the child for taking an adult role in the household economy (e.g., self-help in dressing, chores) and a low rating for fending for oneself without adult surveillance. The evidence further indicates that in regard to overall indulgence and severity of training as applied to a variety of behaviors (nursing and weaning, toileting, sex behavior, dependency, aggression), American middle-class society is comparatively not only extremely low in average indulgence but is also rather extreme in the severity of its socialization practices.

A major study by Sears, Maccoby, and Levin (*1957:* Chap. 5) contributes additional data on dependency in American children. Almost 400 mothers of kindergarten children were asked how much attention her child seemed to want, whether he followed her around, whether he objected when she left him for a while, and whether he asked for unnecessary help. On the basis of these indications of dependency, it was found that by the time the children were five years of age, a preponderance showed little of the dependency behavior rated; only about 20 percent showed a considerable amount (Table D:13, p. 524). There was, however, a wide variability in the attitudes of the parents toward the kind of dependent behavior investigated. About one-third showed little tolerance for such dependency; the middle third was moderately permissive, and the remaining third was lenient.

Taking the various lines of evidence into account leads to the conclusion that independence as a global, emotional ideal is highly valued in our society. It goes along with strength, masculinity, leadership, rugged individualism. Dependence, on the other hand, is often disvalued. It is associated with weakness, femininity, indecision, selfishness, and helplessness. No one would be startled to find a book or a chapter entitled "Growing toward Independence" but one would be rather surprised to find the heading "Growing toward Dependence." The shock might be tempered by the assumption of a typographical error, or that the chapter dealt with all the bad things which lead children to grow in the wrong direction. If the author argued that children and adults need to grow toward *de*pendence, would the reader take him seriously?

This hypothetical situation indicates how deeply rooted is the conviction that independence as a goal has the weight of an axiom. Add to this the fact that disability may threaten independence and we have a combination of circumstances that makes understandable, if not completely justifiable, the tremendous emphasis placed on independence in work with persons who have a disability.

As long as dependence is arbitrarily disvalued and neglected in interpersonal relations, independence becomes distorted as a goal. What happens, for example, to the warmth and friendliness between parent and child when the parent is imbued with one mission—namely, to get his child to eat alone, dress alone, walk alone? There is no doubt that these are important goals, but when independence becomes virtually the dominating guide for parental behavior, the cost in emotional security is unjustifiably great. This is seen in the following example of a mother who insisted on self-reliant behavior in her five-year-old child:

I[NTERVIEWER]: How did you feel about it when she wanted to be with you all the time?

M[OTHER]: Well, I had to teach her she had to be alone at times and not have me around.

I. How do you generally react if she demands attention when you're busy?

M. I don't pay attention to her.

I. How about if she asks you to help her with something you think she could probably do by herself?

M. I tell her she's supposed to do it herself, and I'm not going to help her.

I. And then does she do it?

M. Oh, yes, if she feels like it.

I. Otherwise, what do you do?

M. Otherwise, I just let her alone, let her have one of her stubborn streaks, or just take things away, tell her she can't play any more if she's going to be like that [Sears, Maccoby and Levin, *1957*:164].[5]

This is the kind of overriding pressure that independence as a dominating goal can exert. It is the kind that destroys the essentially human quality of a relationship.

Several research findings are pertinent here. In the study of children with cerebral palsy mentioned earlier (Shere, *1954*), the children who were *both* loved and overprotected, but not those whose overprotection stemmed from rejection, appeared to be friendly, cheerful, with a good sense of humor, and free from aggressive behavior. In the study of patterns of child rearing by Sears, Maccoby, and Levin (*1957*) it was found that:

Punishment for dependency only made children more dependent than ever.

Withdrawal of love as a disciplinary technique and severity of punishment for aggression toward parents were significantly related to degree of child dependency.

Those mothers who had an accepting tolerant attitude toward the child's dependent behavior tended also to be affectionately warm toward the child, gentle about toilet training, low in their use of physical punishment, high in sex permissiveness, low in punishment for aggression toward parents, and high in esteem for both self and husband.

The findings of these two studies alone suggest caution in decrying dependency (or for that matter overprotection) without considering the broader relationship between parent and child, the emotional needs of the child, and the ways of achieving a satisfactory dependence-independence balance.

A great step forward was made when psychoanalytic and other theories stressed that the early period of dependence of the child on his parents

[5] R. R. Sears, E. E. Maccoby, and H. Levin, *Patterns of Child Rearing*, copyright 1957. By permission of Row, Peterson & Company.

is important and that the need for nurturance in its broadest sense must be satisfied. Emotional support for this emphasis was given by the strong cultural and human value placed on love and acceptance and by the anxiety about social rejection, which is especially strong in our culture. Nevertheless, dependency as such is usually not posited as a desirable end in itself. Instead, it is seen as a means to emotional security or to ultimately greater independence.

We should like to extend the emphasis on dependency by submitting that dependence in itself is a value, that it is essential in many important kinds of interpersonal relations. A person should be able to rely on others, to ask for and accept help, to delegate responsibility, but these relations occur naturally only when the person has "learned" how to become dependent or, what may sound better, has learned that there are many occasions when dependence is indeed laudable. Dependence becomes then not a second-best alternative but a valuable end in itself. The physical realities of life as well as the needs of psychological man require that he be dependent on others as well as independent of them. And this holds true for the adult as well as for the infant.

But, it may be protested, independence guarantees future security; to the extent that one can do things by oneself, one becomes independent of what, after all, are but transient relations among men. The counterargument is that independence is also but a transient state. One does become sick, disabled, and old, states that do require interpersonal dependence. Even in the optimal state of health, family members, citizens of a community, mankind as a whole, are interdependent. An important lesson can be learned from the realization that if, instead of heightened nationalism and the struggle of each country toward complete independence, a one world of coöperative nations would emerge, the gains to humankind as a whole would be unfathomable. But this presupposes that dependence and interdependence are respectable facts. So it is with individual man. Independence cannot be upheld as a value without the framework of sound dependency needs.

And just as people may be excessively dependent on others, they may also be excessively independent of others. In both instances the person is denying to himself and others certain values that could accrue through a healthier balance between dependence and independence. Excessive dependence denies the obvious value of freedom and ability to do for oneself. Excessive independence denies the less accepted value of emotional sharing and a readiness to rely on others and to delegate responsibility. It also may wear a person out. Being goaded by independence, he may insist on doing for himself only to be depleted of energy and emotional resources that might well have been spent more usefully. Glorification of independence must give way to an appreciation that independence and interdependence go hand in hand.

This principle suggests a new look at parent-child relations. It suggests that parents, through the pressure of their own principles and those of the specialist, may be pushing children too fast and too soon toward the vague and abstract goal of independence. It suggests that the priceless quality of warmth in interpersonal relations may be usurped by the calculated zeal to teach the child independence. It suggests that ratings of overprotectiveness, which appear as central findings in research reports, may be unduly weighted by the high cultural premium placed on independence. It suggests the need for investigation of the kinds of dependence that should be fostered during the various phases of the entire life span of a person's development.

There are numerous specific guides as to what we may expect in the way of independence at various age levels. The Vineland Social Maturity Scale itemizes the kinds of activities that the average child can be expected to accomplish independently at various ages—e.g., goes to bed unassisted, makes minor purchases. There are some items that deal with dependency relations, but very few of them. If a child has the capability for independent activity but has not achieved this, we know where help may be applied. Thus: "Cerebral palsied children are seen who have reached ages of one and one-half to two years who are capable of learning to sit and are not sitting except to be propped in the corner of a heavily upholstered chair or divan" (Snell, 1955:289). But we do not have a scale listing the kinds of maturing dependency relations at various age levels. And we do not often find statements to the effect that a child needs help along specific lines to enable him to become more dependent on another. The "do-it-yourself craze" may apply just as aptly to interpersonal relations as it does to material constructions.

Specific Aids in Achieving the Dependence-Independence Balance

It has already been pointed out that the judgment of overprotectiveness varies not only with the person making the judgment but also with the signs of the times. Although this implies that there are no universal criteria as to how much is too much and not enough, there are some aids to the parent in arriving at what is for him a satisfactory course to take in the specific teachings of his children.

The opportunity for parents to *observe other children* with the same disability as that of his child, so that he can learn what various children are able to do and what they are allowed to do, opens up new possibilities to the parent. Where children with particular disabilities gather together, as in a special preschool, special school, or special class within a school, this opportunity is easily provided.

Extended awareness of what can be realistically expected of the child also emerges through participation in *parent discussion groups.*[6] More and more "Institutes for Parents" are being organized on a statewide basis; here parents facing some of the same problems involved in the disability of their children gather for several days to learn, with the aid of specialists and through each other, how best to help their children. The point cannot be overemphasized that parents frequently hold their children back, overprotect, and indulge them, because they simply are not aware of the possibilities for doing otherwise. In observing other children and in exchanging ideas with parents and specialists, such reorienting notions may emerge as: "I think my [blind] child will be able to ride a trike too." "He [cerebral palsied] could lace his own shoes if I'd give him enough time." "I will let my [deaf] child go to the store. The grocer will be able to understand him." And on the side of accepting or developing dependent needs: "My child is too aloof from others. He needs to play more with other children." "My child always wants to be the leader. He should play a little with older children so that he can enjoy following." "My child is afraid to ask for help. I wonder why." "My child is such a mama's boy. Maybe it's because I didn't have enough time for him, what with the new baby and all. . . ."

Because comparisons are often somewhat dangerous, we should like once again to interject a word of caution. Although the gains from parental interchange and observation of other children are many, they may be offset by the ill-considered adoption for one's own child of standards based on what another can do. Even though another child has a similar disability and is of the same age, the principle of individual differences, of course, still holds. But because parents seek the fulfillment of the highest aspirations for their children, there is a strong tendency to take over as a standard the performance of the superior child in the group. Here the parent can use the guidance of the specialist. He needs help in understanding the abilities and limitations of his child as an individual.

The parent also needs to be informed of *special techniques* that can aid in the development of his child. Many of these require very little in the way of mechanical equipment. As Lowenfeld (*1956*) points out to parents of blind children: "Your child, if he is totally blind, may not be familiar with the way in which legs must be moved in walking since he cannot see it done. You can help him easily in this situation. Let him stand on your

---

[6] General principles for organizing and leading such groups appear in Bice (*1955*). A study of parent groups for children with handicaps is reported by Levy (*1952*).

shoes while you hold him by the hands. Thus he will be able to observe with his own body your movements when you walk. This should be done in such a way that your child faces the same direction as you do in walking. If you do this frequently enough while he is gaining control in standing up, he will one day step off your shoes and go through the actions of walking himself" (p. 53).[7] The suggestions outlined by Snell (*1955*) are simple and beneficial: "Parents [of cerebral palsy children] complain that their children do not like to sit in a high chair or that they slide down in the chair, and after a few attempts . . . the high chair is discarded. Adjustments can be made in high chairs, such as reducing the length of the back legs slightly, so that the front of the chair is higher than the back. A piece of wood two inches wide and four inches high may be attached to the center front rim of the seat on the high chair, this padded and covered with a plastic material, so that it can be easily cleaned. The child is placed in the chair with a leg on either side of the bar so that it is not possible for him to slide out . . ." (p. 289). The importance of informing parents of "know how" would hardly require mention if it were not for the fact that simple solutions and aids are often overlooked in rehabilitation requiring such complex procedures as bracing and special education.

The idea of *creating opportunities* for specific kinds of experiences should also be raised with parents. Although this is obvious as a principle, parents need help in applying it concretely. Again an example from Lowenfeld (*1956*) is apt. We do not have to think very much about opportunities for moving and exploring for the ordinary child, for on his own he will expand his horizons beyond his own body, from his crib to his play pen, his room, house, yard, and neighborhood. But in regard to the blind child, or the child with marked physical incapacity, indifference on this score will markedly impede growth and development. "The blind child will often remain unaware of his environment and of interesting objects in it because he cannot see them, and his other senses do not make him conscious of them. Therefore, he will often need to be taken to things, or from one place to the other before he will venture out on his own. But he is just as eager to move and explore as any other child if he is stimulated and encouraged in ways which are suitable for him" (p. 17).

The creation of opportunities applies, of course, not only to locomotion. A common-sense through fallacious notion regarding deaf children, for example, is that since the child cannot hear it is futile to talk to him; instead, one must gesture. The parent's realization that the child must be spoken to so that he may develop speech-reading skills represents a major

---

[7] From B. Lowenfeld, *Our Blind Children*, 1956. Courtesy of Charles C Thomas, Publisher, Springfield, Ill.

step forward. Not only must the parent talk to his child when interacting with him, but it is also desirable that the opportunity be created for persons not of the family to communicate with him.

Invoking situations in which the child can assume responsibility commensurate with his abilities will also aid his growth toward mature independence. It hardly needs mentioning that independence unbridled by responsibility lacks the necessary guidelines for effective use. A child may learn to cut his meat with his knife, but if he has to be watched every moment lest he also cut up the tablecloth, his level of independent functioning will be seriously restricted. On the other hand, a child who does a trustworthy job of feeding his pets or of planning a birthday party is at the same time building up feelings of responsibility, self-esteem, and confidence, all of which count in the progress toward a mature dependence-independence balance.

Opportunities for increasing responsibility must be thought about and planned for all children, and particularly for children with major handicaps. One has to guard against two insidious tendencies—namely, the tendency to see a child who has a severe disability as severely disabled in all his functioning (see pp. 118–119) and the tendency to yield to the fact that it is often much easier—from the short-range point of view, at least—to limit his scope of activities than to enlarge it to include real responsibility. In an important ecological study by Barker and H. Wright (1955) in which an institution for cerebral palsied children was compared with a nearby rural community, one of the sharpest differences found was that the institutionalized children entered far fewer positions of responsibility and status than did the rural children. Relatively rarely were they leaders, joint leaders, or responsible functionaries in a particular setting. More typically were they onlookers or participants with little power in the situation. Children need to become the main actors in some of the home, school, and community settings, and not serve only as auxiliary players. Parents (and schools) need help in recognizing those naturally occurring situations that are well within the child's command, and in devising others where they do not exist.

The creation of opportunities is not always easy to effect, even though awareness of the child's needs often does suggest simple solutions. The parent may realize how important it is for his cerebral palsied child to have experience with a variety of adults and may look for a baby sitter to provide this opportunity, only to have considerable trouble in finding a person who is willing to undertake this duty. Or the parent may be aware that his child needs the companionship of other children, but, in spite of his efforts to provide interesting play situations for invited children, he may sense a reluctance on the part of neighbors to encourage this. The children themselves may prefer other outlets for their play time. The rehabilitation worker must be aware that even with the best of intentions solutions sometimes are "easier said than done." Follow-up is necessary to correct the false leads and seek solutions in other directions.

Finally, the judicious use of *reading material* (see pp. 298–299) can be invaluable in imparting to the parent constructive attitudes and factual information, the background necessary toward realizing a healthy balance between striving for independence and striving for dependence.

Parental Attitudes Underlying Overprotection

Because all of us are eager to attach specific causes to specific behaviors, the counselor needs to remind himself that overprotection is an ambiguous symptom. It can stand for such different underlying emotional relations between the parent and his child that by itself it offers no clues to the innermost thoughts and feelings of the parent. A good deal more information about the parent's attitudes is required before the overprotection can be understood and most effectively modified. Some of the more common underlying feelings that can find expression in overprotection are discussed below.

Genuine Love and Concern for the Child. Love and concern for the child do not necessarily constitute the most important or the most likely basis of overprotection, but all too often they are entirely disregarded. Reasons for this disregard may be found in the strong current tendency to perceive only negative relations between parents and children; in the fact that unhealthful relations trouble us, not healthful ones; and in the cognitive principle that it is easier to relate a negative effect (overprotection) to a negative cause (rejection) (Heider, *1944*). Nevertheless, a parent may enjoy doing for his child and want to do as much as he can, not realizing that the "doing for" may in the long run be "doing against." Add to this a real concern about the child within a complex emotional setting and we have a relationship, albeit warm and loving, which is conducive to overstepping the optimal range of protectiveness.

Guilt. Guilt provokes compensatory behavior—i.e., a person atones by making up for the presumed wrongdoing to the other. If a parent feels guilty, therefore, it is understandable that he may indulge his child and continuously protect him from real and imagined dangers. The parent may feel guilty because he basically rejects the child, dislikes and even hates him, and would rather be rid of responsibility for his care. He may feel guilty because of a belief or unconscious feeling that he is responsible for the child's disability. His guilt about the child may be a displaced guilt, the experiences originally instigating it being far removed from consciousness and the current scene.

Need for a Dependent Child.   To feel needed and wanted may so dominate the pursuits of some parents that only by keeping the child in an infantile relation to him is the parent guaranteed security. Such a parent will tend to magnify the disabling aspects of his child's disability and the dangers of the world. Every time he does something for his child he is reassured that he matters to someone. Every time the child makes a step forward toward independent management, a twinge if not a pang of regret is the conscious symptom of fear that he himself is being left unneeded by the wayside.

Impatience.   Not to be overlooked is the fact that during the beginning stages of learning it often requires a good deal more patience on the part of the parent to stand by and let the child do for himself in his own inefficient and sometimes work-producing way than for the parent to take over. This point has been stressed and realistically exemplified by White (*1955*): "More time and patience is needed to allow a child to dress himself who has difficulty using his hands and poor standing ability. The mother must be around to do the one or two things he cannot do, such as put on the trousers or fasten the buttons, and she may have poor tolerance for waiting around. Cleaning up after a child who eats his meals in a messy way is more work to a mother than feeding him, so she may procrastinate in letting him feed himself. . . . A great deal of resourcefulness, imagination, patience, and self-discipline is required to maintain a happy medium" (p. 479). Sometimes impatience is an expression of rejection of the child. Sometimes the parent is simply not aware that progress is made slowly. And sometimes the parent is already overburdened with emotional problems or with the time and energy demands of homemaking.

Some specific aids toward achieving a "happy medium" between independence and dependence have been discussed above. It would seem that these would have the best chance of being effectively utilized where love is the prevailing underlying feeling, for then the predominant effort of the parent, consciously and subconsciously, is geared toward the child's needs, not the parent's. Guilt and a need to keep a child dependent, on the other hand, instigate behavior that is basically parent-centered, not child-centered. If the parent is driven by these feelings, the kind of emotional reëvaluation necessary before a comfortable relation between the child and the parent can be reached may require the services of a psychotherapist. Parent discussion groups can, however, do much to help the parent become aware of his feelings. Hearing a disquieting attitude talked about in a socially permissive atmosphere makes it easier to see it in oneself. As one father participating in a discussion group said, "If anyone had asked me before it was mentioned here if I ever felt guilty about our boy, I would have denied it; I realize now that I did" (Bice,

1950). Not to be overlooked is the fact that good feelings also may come through to consciousness as a result of sympathetic discussion. Some parents may be so bothered by their shame and guilt or by problems extraneous to the child that they have no idea of the real affection and closeness they feel toward the child.

As for the problem of impatience, all parents, some more, some less, experience this. The specific aids again can be a real help, for in observing other children, in sharing attitudes with other parents, in learning specific techniques of management, the parent also achieves a better perspective as to what really counts. The unmade beds may become less of a threat to the mother's status as a housekeeper and more of a sign that she is taking time with her children. "Make haste slowly" may become a meaningful guide in her relations with her children. Impatience, after all, flourishes when the person feels he *must* be on to other things.

At the same time it must be realized that a parent can do only so much, beyond which excessive impatience and other signs of psychological stress become inevitable. By the time one carries out the specific procedures recommended in the home rehabilitation plan, one sometimes has consumed the better part of the waking day. Especially where the parent is counseled in assembly-line fashion by the speech therapist, the physical therapist, the occupational therapist and orthopedist, the psychologist, and social worker is there a great likelihood that the total program will be unrealistic in terms of the time and energy demands on the parent, to say nothing of the child. A desirable balance is more readily assured when the several aspects of the rehabilitation plan are integrated by all parties concerned, including the parent.

One should note that no matter what the parent does he will be criticized by some people. Parents need to be prepared for this. There will be neighbors and friends who will view necessary care and concern as signs of oversolicitude. More frequently there will be those who will interpret as neglect and rejection the efforts of the parent to emancipate his child by encouraging him to do and learn by himself. Even well-meaning friends will not be able to understand the mature calmness of a parent toward his child's disability. In not understanding, they are prone to be accusing.

Chapter 13

Motivating Children in the Rehabilitation Program

HOW TO GET A PERSON TO DO WHAT HE IS SUPPOSED TO DO AND LEARN what he is supposed to learn? This is the problem of motivation and deals with incentives, rewards and punishments, goals and subgoals, success and failure, values and meanings and much more. Although our discussion will be focused on children in "rehabilitation situations," the principles extracted apply to learning in general and to older age levels as well.

REHABILITATION EXHIBITS

Below are presented three records of minute-by-minute observations of children involved in some phase of rehabilitation. These were gathered by trained observers in the ecological research on child development by Barker and H. Wright in the years 1948–1951 (*1955*). Because of the unusual opportunity to study "on the scene" problems of motivation, they are presented here fully. The first is an 8-minute record in which Wally's mother attempted to get Wally to put on his braces. The second reports a 35-minute session between Ben and his physical therapist. The third is a 10-minute account of Lila participating in a speech therapy class. It is suggested that the factors in the situation which interfere with the learning process and those which are conducive to it be noted as the records are read. Later these records will be drawn upon to exemplify principles that make a difference in the readiness and willingness with which a person undertakes the task of learning.

Wally, His Mother, and His Braces

Wally is a 4-year-old boy who is unable to walk as a result of poliomyelitis which occurred some two years earlier. The scene opens at eight o'clock in the morning with Wally sitting on a big chair in the corner of the living room, hunched over, with his face on his hands:

1'[1]   Wally's mother went directly to stand in front of Wally's chair. She said gently, "Let's get dressed, Wally." Wally made no move to change his position. He sat with his head down on his arms. His mother picked up a T-shirt and said pleasantly, "Put your arms up, Buddy. Don't you want to get dressed?" Again Wally made no response; he just sat there, hunched up. His mother, encouraging him, said, "Hurry," as she pulled off his pajama upper quickly with no coöperation from him. His mother, with a little more urgency in her voice, said, "Put your arms up," as she held out the T-shirt. Rather reluctantly and in response not only to her words but also to her hands, because his mother put her hands on him and helped to lift up his arms, he put his arms up. At first he was languid and then he stretched, as if he rather enjoyed the stretch. His expression as he lifted his face a little was disgruntled and sleepy. His mother slipped the T-shirt over his head quickly, and gave it kind of a firm pull over his head. Wally said, "I don't like this," in rather a whiny voice. (He seemed to refer to the tight T-shirt being pulled over his head.) His mother admonished mildly, "Wally," and obtained his coöperation. When he had his T-shirt on, his mother held him under the arms, and stood him on his feet. She suggested as she did so, "Hold onto me." He held on, but weakly, so that he wobbled. She quickly and quite efficiently pulled his pajama pants down over his seat as he was standing.

2'   She admonished him again for his general limp behavior and lack of coöperation by just saying, "Wally," in a mildly reproving voice. As soon as the pajama pants were slipped over his seat, she picked him up by the arms and put him back on the chair with his feet sticking straight out. Then she pulled off his pajamas over his feet. He already had on his shorts; they were under his pajamas. (Whether he regularly wears them under his pajamas or whether he had been partly dressed before I arrived, I don't know.) She picked up his socks and quite hastily put first one sock on and then the other. Wally braced his back as she put on his socks, but was still very limp in his head and shoulders.

3'   His mother picked up from the floor a high shoe with the brace attached and started to put it on Wally's left foot and leg. The brace extends the full length of his leg with a curved part just under the buttocks. Wally immediately responded to this by saying vehemently, "I don't want to wear that damned old brace," in a very negative voice. His mother ignored this and went on putting on the shoe and the brace. He said, "I ain't gonna wear this old brace," with more vehemence and some defiance. His mother said mildly, "You don't have to wear them long," then explained, "I have to clean your shoes first, and then I'll put your shoes on." Argumentatively Wally said, "You *did* clean my shoes the other day." His mother smiled at that, partly to me, implying that cleaning them the other day would not mean that they were clean now, but she didn't argue about it with Wally.

4'   His mother continued to lace up the shoe and fasten the brace. Wally said, whining now, more than belligerent, "I hate that brace," though still

---

[1] Time notation, the first minute.

somewhat defiant. As she fastened the brace up high, he put his hand around and rubbed his hip at the place where the brace hit and said crossly, "I hate you." (This referred to his mother for insisting he wear the braces rather than to the braces, I felt.) And then he said, equally unhappy about everything, "I don't like that lady," meaning me. (I felt that I was included in his general unhappiness rather than being the cause of it.) His mother responded in quite a joking way, "You're in a bad mood, ain't ya?" trying to get him a little bit out of it.

5′   She continued, saying, "You wouldn't let your daddy see you in such a bad mood, would you?" a little bit jocular, still trying to get him out of it. Then she added, "Where did your daddy go this morning?" (I think she was trying to engage him in conversation to get him out of his negative mood.) Wally said very negatively, "I won't tell you." Then his mother said something about going where there was a big red barn. Stubbornly, Wally said, "I won't tell her where my daddy went." (I think he sensed that his mother was trying to get him to talk partly for my benefit and he was not going to coöperate. He sounded as though he were hanging onto his bad humor and not that he was really very upset.) His mother remarked that his daddy would be home for lunch. As she was talking, she put on his right shoe and brace and fastened it. Wally whined in a very complaining voice, "These hurt me." His mother continued to fasten them without responding.

6′   Wally more belligerently said, "And I ain't gonna wear them." He turned and looked at me for the first time, scowling. (The paper boy opened the door and laid the morning paper on the chair near the door.) Wally did not appear to notice him. He again whined at his mother, this time a little more as though he were pleading with her, as though he could make some progress, "Mamma, I don't want them on." His mother said conciliatorily, "I'll take them off after a while, after you've had breakfast and play a while." He responded quite argumentatively, "No, you won't." She put his feet in overall legs. His mother took his hand and pulled him to his feet. Now, with the braces on, he could stand with very little support. He held on to the chair or his mother all the time. She pulled his overalls over the braces and took out some suspenders. She sat in the chair and he stood in front of her as she fastened his overalls. She started to fasten the suspenders onto the overalls. (He was completely passive in all this dressing procedure and he didn't offer any assistance at any time.)

7′   As he stood, he whined, "These braces are too heavy, I don't want them." His mother, a little reproving said, "Wally," meaning probably that he shouldn't fuss so much. Wally responded by exclaiming, "God, I don't want them." Then again more belligerently, "I'm gonna throw them in the river." Wally alternated between pleading with his mother and denouncing his braces. His mother responded, "I don't like them either. All right, when shall we do it?" meaning when shall we throw them in the river. (Her voice was joking; I don't believe he could have believed seriously that she would let him throw them in the river. It was more an effort to go along with his mood.) She added, "Next time we go across the big old river, shall we throw them in?" Wally made no response to this.

Mrs. Wolfson continued with an attempt to change the topic of conversation, "Did you see Jack bring the paper?" Wally did not answer. As he stood in front of his mother looking sleepy and disgruntled, she turned him around so that she could fasten the suspenders in the back. Then with that she was finished dressing him and said, "Okay," indicating that she was through.

She stood up and came around in front of him and took hold of one hand. He took half a dozen steps toward the kitchen as she held the one hand and walked backward toward the kitchen. She held out her other hand, possibly so that she could take both his hands and give him more help. When his mother put her hand out for his other hand, he made no response. But he stood there limply with his shoulders bowed and his head down. It seemed as though, except for the braces, he would crumple in the middle, too. Then she let go of the hand she held and held out both hands to him as one does to a baby to lure a baby that's walking, to come to you. At that he smiled for the first time, a sweet smile, at his mother. He leaned forward and fell into her arms.

8′ She picked him up with a swish and carried him halfway across the room. She put him in the chair at the east end of the dining table in the kitchen. He sat with his legs straight out, his back against the back of the chair. The chair was well pushed in to the table. The table had a cloth on it and a clear, plastic cover over the cloth.

Maud, the two-year-old sister, was in the kitchen now, waiting for her breakfast. Maud said, "That's what I want," concerning some food. Wally immediately answered in a cross, grumpy voice, "I'm going to eat them all up." Maud whined, "Buddy's going to eat them all up." His mother said, placating Maud, "Oh, no, he won't." And Wally said, "Yes, I will," teasing Maud. Maud continued to whine about how Buddy was going to eat them all up.

Wally continued to be irritable and uncoöperative for several minutes more until dabbles of sugar and a hearty breakfast made him considerably more cheerful. The braces remained on for about an hour and a half, during which time Wally ate breakfast and then played actively and happily outdoors with his wagon and two cousins. At 9:20, 17 minutes before the braces were finally removed, Wally for the first time asked his mother to take them off. His mother replied warmly from the kitchen, "Well, just a minute, baby." At 9:28 Wally repeated his request, more imperiously this time, and his mother responded promptly, "Okay, just a minute." At 9:37, a final pleading from Wally brought his mother out of the house with a pair of shoes without braces.

A Physical Therapy Session with Ben

Ben is a 6-year-old child with cerebral palsy who has been a resident in a school for cerebral palsied children for two years. He speaks with difficulty and is not yet able to crawl or to stand alone. "In the characteristic picture of Ben he is seen strapped in a chair with his arms hanging at his sides, his head tilted to one side, his mouth open, and his tongue hanging out and drooling spittle on his chin" (Barker and H. Wright, *1948–1951*). It is early afternoon. Ben had just been brought into the physical therapy room: Mr. T. is the physical therapist, Miss O. the occupational therapist, and Celestia an older child with cerebral palsy:

1′   Mr. T. came over from working with Celestia to Ben. As he did so, he said in a very cheerful, pleasant, yet business-like way, "O.K. Brother Benrod." Ben made no response that I could see. Then Mr. T. unstrapped Ben from his chair, picked him up and laid him down on the floor. Ben seemed to accept this as just what he had expected; he displayed no particular feeling about it.

Noticing that Ben's shoelaces were unfastened, Mr. T. commented gaily and in a slightly teasing way, "How come your shoelaces are all undone?" Ben mumbled quite happily, "I didn't do it." Mr. T. replied in a gay, joking and nonchalant way, "Oh, I know, I know. You didn't do it. You *never* do it." Then Ben said happily, really enjoying himself, "Elmer did it." Mr. T. laughed restrainedly and said knowingly, "Oh, Elmer did it, huh? Yeah, Elmer always does it."

2′   Mr. T. continued working with Ben's shoelaces. Benjamin talked gaily away to Mr. T. who seemed to be paying very little, if any, attention. Since he was not looking at me it was impossible for me to understand what he said. Apparently Mr. T. didn't understand either, for at one point he said questioningly, "Huh?" Ben mumbled something else still quite gaily, but I couldn't understand what he said.

3′   Celestia came over and said something to Mr. T. and Mr. T. replied to her question. Benjamin made no response nor took any notice of this interaction. Mr. T. continued lacing Ben's shoes. Then Benjamin said something else to Mr. T. I didn't understand what it was but I felt sure that it was just pleasant conversation.

Mr. T. said somewhat more seriously but still in a pleasant way, "How far are you going to crawl today?" Benjamin mumbled something which I couldn't understand. I couldn't tell for sure whether he was responding to Mr. T.'s question or not.

4′   Mr. T. finished with Ben's shoes and said gaily, "There you go!" Then Mr. T. picked Benjamin up from the floor. He stood him up for just a moment and then placed him on the floor on his hands and knees. Mr. T. had a little trouble getting Ben settled in this position. He moved Ben's hands close together and straight out in front of him. He moved Ben's legs so that he sat in a froglike position on the calves of his legs and his feet.

5′   Miss O. walked in from the Occupational Therapy room and made a few gay, happy, cheerful remarks about the fact that Ben was going to be six very soon. Ben looked up at her but made no other response. Then Mr. T. said somewhat seriously, "Well, any little boy who's going to be six is going to have to learn to crawl." With this Miss O. and Mr. T. walked to the far end of the room. Ben did not try to say anything in response to the comments by Mr. T. and Miss O. but I'm sure he understood what they said. He sat on his hands and knees, jerking somewhat rhythmically, wiggling slightly, apparently trying to keep his balance. Ben had been placed on the floor just about in line with the doorway into the kitchen. It was a distance of nine or ten feet to the north end of the room which was established as Ben's goal in his crawling. Ben continued to sit on his hands and knees in this froglike fashion and seemed to be trying to balance himself. (Miss O. returned to the Occupational Therapy room without further comment and Mr. T. began talking with Celestia. Ben paid no attention to them.)

6′   Ben continued sitting in this froglike position. He continued balancing, wiggling slightly as though he might be trying to crawl, although it wasn't clear that this was what he was trying to do. Mr. T. looked over from where he was working with Celestia and said pleasantly, with no irritation or impatience, "Come on, Ben. Let's go." Ben made no response. He continued his rhythmical jerking and wiggling.

7′   Ben's face assumed a very serious look. He began jerking harder and wiggling more rhythmically as though he were trying earnestly to crawl. (Mr. T. continued talking with Celestia. Ben paid no attention to them at all.)

Then Mr. T. looked over at Benjamin and said with more insistence in his voice, "Come on, Ben. Crawl. Lift those knees way up. Now, your left knee, then your right." Benjamin made no verbal response but it seemed that he tried a little harder, shifting his weight so that he could slip a knee a fraction of an inch forward. So far Ben had not moved more than one or two inches from where he began.

8′   Celestia, taking up Mr. T.'s previous comment, said, "O.K. Benny. One, two," meaning that Ben should move his legs in a steady, rhythmic fashion. Her comment was very pleasant and cheerful and was not a demand of any kind. Ben, as far as I could tell, made no response to Celestia's remark. He continued his efforts to crawl. Again Celestia said quite pleasantly, "Come on. One, two." This time Ben looked over at Celestia and mocked her saying, "One, two," imitating Celestia's tone of voice. Then Ben grunted and whined just a little and tried to push himself forward along the floor.

9′   Ben wiggled and bounced quite hard again. His face screwed up into a deep frown. He whimpered as though he were almost ready to cry. Celestia chattered gaily something about Ben's sixth birthday. Ben did not respond to this but continued wiggling and trying to crawl.

At this point, Ben had moved some six or seven inches. Then Mr. T. looked over and said somewhat insistently, "Come on, Ben. Crawl." Ben did not look at Mr. T. but he half-said and half-cried, "I can't do it." But Ben continued bouncing and wiggling. As he strained very hard, he screwed up his face and his breathing was quite jerky. He shifted his weight from side to side and jerked his hands around as he endeavored to crawl along the floor.

10′   Ben made more noise of a whimpering kind, almost crying. He continued trying very hard, struggling with his movements. Ben bounced up and down on the calves of his legs, apparently using the momentum of the bouncing to inch himself forward. Ben whimpered again, and it sounded almost like crying. He kept struggling, wiggling and bouncing, trying to inch along on the floor. (Celestia walked up and down the Physical Therapy room, passing quite close to Benjamin. Ben didn't look up and made no response to her at all.)

11′ Mr. T. went over close to Benjamin. He reached down, moved Ben's hands apart and said, "Now, get your hands apart. Keep pushing with your legs. You'll go. Pull with your hands. Come on, pull." This was said in a didactic way; it was business-like instruction given in a not very pleasant way—a type of very demanding encouragement.

12′ In response to Mr. T.'s urging, Ben intensified his efforts. He fussed louder, making a crying noise. His face was very sober. Mr. T. put his hand on Benjamin's back to be of some slight assistance although not very much. Benjamin continued to try very hard. Mr. T. said rather critically, "Ben, you're not working. You're just not working at all. Let's go. You're just getting lazier and lazier." There was no warmth or friendliness in this comment; it was straight criticism.

13′ Ben put forth even more effort. He screwed up his face, bounced and wiggled, apparently straining very hard. He managed to move forward a little. Then Mr. T. said more pleasantly, "Now, you're making headway. Just keep going." Without responding directly to Mr. T.'s comment, Benjamin continued his wiggling and bouncing. He managed to move another inch or so.

14′ Mr. T., still standing right behind Ben with his hands on Ben's back, said, "Come on, now. Quit fussing and work. Let's keep going." This was said almost bitterly. Ben continued his vigorous bouncing. He made crying noises and whimpered with the exertion. At this point Ben's noises and whimpering came very near to crying, but still Ben did not open up and bawl unrestrainedly.

15′ Perhaps in response to Ben's intensified whimpering Mr. T. stepped around behind him and lifted some of the weight from Ben's legs by pulling up the belt straps in Benjamin's jeans. This apparently helped considerably for Benjamin's fussing and crying noises diminished sharply.

16′ Ben continued his efforts to crawl, struggling along the floor. At this point he had traveled three or four feet from the initial starting place.

Marilyn [an aide] walked past and said cheerfully, "How are you doing, Benrod?" Benjamin made no response.

Then Mr. T. released his support and stepped away from Benjamin. He said insistently, "Come on, Ben. Pull 'em up. Pull 'em up." Benjamin continued bouncing although not as earnestly as he had been just before.

17′ Mr. T. said, "That's the way. Come on, now. You're moving." This was said somewhat hopefully but still demanding that Ben continue his efforts.

Ben looked up almost tearfully at Mr. T. and asked, "How far?" Mr. T. responded as though somewhat surprised that Ben should ask such a question, "How far? Just as far as you can go, that's how far." Then Ben mumbled something else which I couldn't understand. He continued to bounce and wiggle, trying to inch along the floor.

Miss O. came through from the Physical Therapy room on her way to the kitchen. She looked down at Ben and said jokingly and good-naturedly, "Aw, dry up and blow away." Ben made no response but continued wiggling and pushing. Miss O. continued on her way without saying anything further.

18′ As Benjamin wiggled and bounced, he continued making whimpering, almost crying sounds.

Celestia, who was walking back and forth under Mr. T.'s supervision, called to Ben pleasantly, "Ben, are you laughing or crying?" She repeated the same question. Ben responded, "Laughing," but it was said as though he didn't really believe it. Then Celestia replied in a pleasant, joking way, "What are you laughing at? Yourself?" Ben said, "Yes," as though he knew this weren't really true but he had to put on a good front.

Ben continued bouncing and wiggling as he struggled along. He continued making the very same sounds, however, which to me were clearly much more like crying than laughing.

19′ Mr. T., standing behind Benjamin, said, "Come on, Ben. Keep working. You're laying down. Get your knees way up." This was said insistently, with no pleasantness even attempted. Ben made no response but continued wiggling and bouncing.

Miss O., returning from the kitchen, said pleasantly, "Come on. Come on. You're not even moving." Then she walked into the Occupational Therapy room and stopped in the doorway. She turned around and looked down at Ben on the floor.

20′ She said jokingly but with sincere affection, "Oh, look at the monkey. Look at the monkey." Ben looked at Miss O. A brief smile flitted over his face at the joking comment. He quickly resumed his sober expression and continued his efforts.

At this point Ben had moved about six feet from the starting place. Mr. T., who still was standing just behind Benjamin, said pleasantly, "Can you see yourself in the mirror?" Ben replied, "No," matter-of-factly. Mr. T. said, "Well turn so that you can," in a businesslike way. The mirror was directly in front of Benjamin at the north end of the room. It was about five feet away from him.

21′ Benjamin continued struggling. He made whimpering sounds as he struggled along. Mr. T., still standing behind him, said insistently, "All right. Let's go. Let's go. Keep moving." Ben continued bouncing and wiggling as he struggled along. He was roughly seven feet from his starting point. Mr. T. turned away from Ben and walked toward the south end of the room where Celestia was standing.

22′ Apparently in response to Mr. T.'s leaving him, Ben began fussing a little more. He made more and more noise until he was almost crying aloud. He kept trying, however, bouncing on his haunches and pulling with his hands. The more he tried, the louder he fussed.

23′ Ben kept fussing and wiggling. His efforts were in vain, however; he had made no progress since Mr. T. went to the other end of the room. Ben continued struggling.

24′ He stopped, turned his head around and peered back at Mr. T. at the opposite end of the room. (This was the first time since he started that Ben apparently was not trying to crawl.) Mr. T., who was just standing quietly with his arms folded, patted his foot on the floor with impatience, indicating that Ben should get busy. Then Ben promptly turned around and began trying again very hard. Again Ben whimpered very intensively, just on the verge of crying.

25′   Ben wiggled and bounced. He fussed loudly. Then he turned around again and looked at Mr. T. Since Mr. T. left, Ben had managed only to turn himself around so that instead of facing north he was almost facing east. But still he continued wiggling.

At this point Miss O. stepped into the doorway of the Occupational Therapy room and said teasingly but pleasantly, "Come on. Come over here and I'll give you a bite. Come on." She was talking about an apple which she was eating. Ben looked up at Miss O. and smiled momentarily. Then he resumed his efforts.

26′   Mr. T. said more pleasantly, "See how far you've gone Ben. Quit fussing and go up to the mirror." The mirror was three to four feet away. Benjamin made no response to Mr. T.'s insisting.

Miss O. did something with reference to the waste can which was right by the door, and she laughed very hard at whatever she had done. Ben looked up and joined momentarily in Miss O.'s hilarity. Miss O. commented gaily, "I knew that would make him laugh." Then she sat down on the edge of the trash can.

Ben resumed his wiggling and bouncing as he struggled to crawl.

27′   Miss O. stepped around behind the mirror and playfully peeped out around the other side, trying to boost Ben's spirits. Ben apparently made no response but just continued his wiggling and bouncing.

Ben intensified his efforts. As he did so his whimpers became louder and louder until they amounted to a virtual cry. From the south end of the room, Mr. T. called in a very threatening, not-to-be-questioned tone of voice, "Ben, do you want to go to the bathroom with me?" [This means a spanking.] Then Mr. T. continued, "All right then, settle down and get busy." Miss O. went into the Occupational Therapy room.

28′   Ben made no observable response to Mr. T.'s severe orders but continued with his whimpering, fussing and wiggling as he tried to crawl. Then Ben looked up into the mirror and continued with his efforts. Celestia talked glibly with Mr. T. about something that would take place on Saturday. Then she cheerfully asked Ben if he could see his face in the mirror. Ben made no response; he simply acted as though he hadn't heard Celestia's comment.

29′   Ben looked over at me briefly with no meaning in his look. Still Ben continued trying. He fussed and wiggled. Ben had moved not more than a foot or a foot and a half since Mr. T. went to the other end of the room. (Otto and Verne [children] passed through the Physical Therapy room on their way into Occupational Therapy. Ben apparently did not notice them.)

30′   Mr. T. came to the north end of the room and moved the mirror out of the way. Then Mr. T. pointed with his toe to a line on the floor and said seriously, "All right, Ben, get up to this line and then I'll put you in your chair. Let's go, now." This was said somewhat hopefully and with real promise in his voice.

31′   Ben tried with renewed effort, it seemed. He bounced, wiggled vigorously and cried with a little restraint. (Ben was extremely involved in this and his efforts had been continuous from the very beginning except for the one point which I mentioned.) He continued now, wiggling, fussing, and crying as he tried to reach the point which Mr. T. designated. With all the exertion Ben began coughing a little. As he coughed he relaxed his efforts somewhat. The line to which Mr. T. had pointed was about two feet away from Ben.

32′   Miss S. [school teacher] stepped into the doorway between the Physical Therapy room and the classroom and made a very bitter comment about a little boy who insisted on acting like a baby, saying that she was so tired of it she'd like to throw him in the lake. She was obviously talking about Benjamin. Ben, however, made no response. I'm not even sure that he heard her. He continued his wiggling and bouncing, trying to get to the line.

33′   Miss O. and Hilda came slowly through, going from Occupational Therapy into the classroom. As Miss O. neared Benjamin, she jumped over him, put one foot on each side and came down very hard making quite a noise. This she did in a very joking, good-natured way. Benjamin made no response to this but kept trying earnestly to get to the line. (Miss O. went on into the classroom.)

Ben had managed by this time to cover about half the distance.

34′   He reached his hand out as far as he could, pointed to the line and looked up questioningly at Mr. T. Mr. T., who was standing just on the other side of the line, looked down and said, "No, no. Now cut that out. That's fudging. You've got to get all the way up to the line. You've got to get your arms across and get your knees almost up there, about halfway across." This was said in a more kindly, explanatory way. Benjamin resumed his struggling, wiggling and bouncing as he tried to reach the required goal. After just a little more effort, Mr. T. said, "O.K.," with finality. Then Mr. T. went to the other end of the room and brought Ben's chair back. Ben relaxed visibly and just sat waiting quietly. Mr. T. rolled the chair up to Benjamin.

35′   Mr. T. picked Benjamin up and set him down rather forcefully in his chair. Then as Mr. T. began strapping Ben in his chair, he gave Ben a lecture about what was going to happen tomorrow if Ben insisted on continuing with his fussing and crying while he was in Physical Therapy. He told Ben that he just wasn't going to have any more of this whimpering and fussing and that if he came in tomorrow and started whimpering and fussing they would go to the bathroom and Ben knew what would happen then. ("Going to the bathroom" means a spanking.) He told Ben that he was just getting lazier and lazier and he was going to have to snap out of it. Mr. T. was quite critical and very serious. There was no attempt to be good-natured or to gloss over the criticism. It was straightforward and almost bitter. Ben made no observable response to this lecture. I'm sure, however, that he understood everything Mr. T. said.

Then Mr. T., having finished strapping Ben in the chair, took hold of the back of the chair and shoved Ben out of the room with haste and dispatch. He rolled him quickly up the ramp and took him into the classroom where he left him.

Lila Participates in the Speech Class

Lila is an 8½-year-old child who has lived at a school for cerebral palsied children for nine months. She has both the athetoid and spastic type of palsy. In walking, she extends her arms for balance, but falls quite frequently. Her speech is very difficult to understand. Ben, Jimmy, and Newton are three other children in the speech class, Ben being our little friend who had such a hard time in the physical therapy session. Miss B. is the speech teacher. It is the first class in the morning:

1′ Lila watched with mild interest as Miss B. moved Ben's chair over so that the three were sitting in a line. Lila looked up as Jimmy, a new boy in the speech class, came in bringing a chair and set it next to Ben's.

2′ Lila watched Miss B. who asked if "we should take our blow first." Miss B. was referring to the exercise of blowing toy horns. Lila smiled a little as if she liked the idea. All the children seemed to.

Miss B. gave each of the children a toy horn, telling them to blow long and hard. Lila routinely took the horn Miss B. offered her. Lila held her horn with her right hand, which she supported with her left hand. She put the horn in her mouth. She had a little difficulty getting the horn to her mouth because of the mild athetoid movements of her head.

Lila looked at Miss B. who said, "That's a good one," to Ben, who was blowing his horn rather loudly. Lila continued to blow her horn. She took the horn out of her mouth to take a breath. She put it back in the mouth to blow again. She watched Miss B. who went from one child to another, encouraging them in a friendly way.

Miss B. seemed to be trying to impart more enthusiasm to the children. Miss B. encouraged the children by displaying her own enthusiasm. She said to the group, "Come on, let's blow real hard." As she talked she directed her attention first to one child, then another.

Lila still held her horn with both hands. She blew it for all she was worth. She worked so hard at blowing her horn that when she took the horn out of her mouth to take a deep breath, her feet came up off the floor. The activity of trying to blow hard seemed to be such an all-over activity that when she gave out with a blast as loud as she could, her feet came up off the floor again.

Miss B. indicated this activity was over by holding out her hands and asking for the horns. Lila routinely handed her horn to Miss B.

4′ Then Miss B. said, "Now we'll do blowing sounds." The sounds they were using were "f" sounds. Miss B. said, "Good, Newton." Lila watched as she complimented Newton on his blowing sound. Speaking with warm enthusiasm, Miss B. asked Lila, "Let's hear yours." Lila made an "f" sound vigorously. Miss B. spontaneously complimented her on it but helped her to do it more smoothly. She encouraged Lila to do it again. She said to Lila helpfully, "Let's do it again and this time do it all through your mouth." This time Miss B. held Lila's nose for her to help show her how to make the sound all through her mouth. Lila watched intently as Miss B. demonstrated and seemed to put herself wholly into this activity, trying to do it just the way Miss B. wanted it.

Lila watched intently as Miss B. asked Newton with friendly anticipation, "What do we have when we go to a picnic?"

5′   Miss B. asked Lila to give the answer to the question, "What do we have when we go on a picnic?" and Lila said, "Fun." Miss B. said, "Fine," explosively as if she were really happy with the sound Lila had made. Lila had done a good job.

The teacher went down through the rest of the children, Ben and Jimmy, with questions requiring "f" sound answers. Lila turned to watch as each of the children performed. Ben was asked a question, "What is this?" as Miss B. wrote a "4" on the blackboard. Lila watched intently and smiled at Miss B. Then Lila turned to look at the blackboard where Miss B. was writing a letter, "S". Miss B. asked Jimmy to make this sound. Jimmy made the sound.

6′   Miss B. exclaimed, "Good." Lila smiled. Lila watched with quiet interest as Miss B. indicated Ben and asked him what he had eaten his breakfast with. Ben failed to put the "s" on "spoon" and said, "poon." Miss B. in a friendly way seemed quite disappointed as she said Ben had done just what they were talking about. He had left off the "s" sound and she asked him to say "spoon." Ben did. Lila smiled as Ben got it correctly.

Lila cocked her head to the left, to watch Miss B. intently as she went back to the blackboard.

7′   Lila watched Miss B. who said, "What do we do with our eyes?" Lila said, "See," and Miss B. said, "Fine, let's clap for Lila." Then all of the children clapped and smiled. Lila smiled bashfully; apparently she enjoyed the recognition she was getting for having said the word so well. Then Lila looked over to me and smiled. I smiled back at her. It seemed that she was still happy to have done such a good job with this word.

Lila turned back to look at Miss B. She rubbed her upper lip with her hand just under her nose as if she were still a little sleepy. In rubbing her upper lip, she turned her hand over, bent it sharply at the wrist, and rubbed with the top of her wrist.

8′   Lila dropped her head to her chest. (It wasn't quite clear to me if Lila had dropped her head to her chest because she was tired or if it was just an uncontrolled athetoid movement.) She let her chin rest on her chest for just a moment. Then she raised her head and pulled it clear back; that is, she rested the back of her head on the back of her chair so that she was looking up at the ceiling.

9′   Lila pulled her head back up to look at Miss B. She watched as Miss B. said, "Now, let's make our singing sounds." Lila pursed her lips; she seemed to be doing this as thoroughly as she could, really intent upon her job. She tried to make the sounds that were indicated. She stopped and looked up as Miss B. said, "Whose name begins with an 'm' sound?" She made the sound for "m," the "m-m-m" sound rather than saying the letter "m." Lila said spontaneously, "Mattie." Lila watched Miss B. who asked next, "Whose name begins with an 'l' sound?"

10′   Miss B. asked questioningly, "Does your name begin with an 'l' sound?"

Lila shook her head negatively, saying, "No." Miss B. acted very surprised and indicated to her that it did. Then Lila laughed as if she recognized her mistake. Newton, who was sitting next to Lila, laughed, too, in a friendly way at Lila's mistake.

QUESTIONS TOWARD IMPROVING MOTIVATION

These three records represent a range of "techniques," of attempts on the part of the adult to motivate the child. Some of them bear promise of sound learning; others seem to impede learning, and even to lead to wrong learning. In discussing them we do so with the recognition that it is one thing to display wisdom under conditions of relaxed and objective appraisal and quite another thing when one is involved in the day-to-day difficult and time-demanding therapy with a child.

The problem of motivation would be vastly simpler if desirable activities were satisfying in themselves. The natural pleasure of a child when he eats an ice cream cone, romps, solves a problem which he has set up, is enough to ensure the "positive valence" of these activities. All too frequently, however, as we well know, the task at hand is at best a bother, at worst intolerably disagreeable, unless incentives are provided. There is no fun, in and of itself, in wearing braces as did Wally, in laboriously crawling as did Ben, in making "f" and "s" sounds as did Lila.

The number of incentives used to motivate intrinsically neutral or negative tasks is endless: the adult may promise the child a penny, a piece of candy, a toy; the adult may threaten to spank the child, scold him, report his poor progress; the adult may pat the child on the head, tell him how well he is doing, give him an A or a gold star; the adult may make a game of it or ignore the child, etc. Let us examine this variety in the light of the following key questions:

Can the Task Be Recast so That It Becomes Part of an Activity That the Child Likes to Do Anyway?

This principle can be applied to the difference between body building through calisthenics and athletic games, or between learning to play the piano through exercises and musical pieces. It simply takes advantage of the natural interest of the person. Its application is seen in the speech therapy class with Lila in the teacher's use of toy horns in developing blowing skills and her use of a question-and-answer game for drill on particular sounds. In Ben's case, some effort was made to enliven the task at hand by playful teasing and by reminding Ben of the mirror (20′),[2] but

---

[2] Time notations in parentheses refer to specific portions of the records.

no real embedding of the crawling within an enjoyable activity was attempted. Wally did not have to do anything with his braces except wear them; after his initial resistance the braces were forgotten for a long while in the excitement of the outdoor play and in this way they became an unobtrusive part of an activity that Wally enjoyed. Occupational therapists have devised many activities based on the principle of embedding, as when children become involved in unbuttoning exercises in anticipation of the surprise picture hidden beneath the buttoned cloth. In physical therapy there is the use of weighted doll buggies in developing the child's balance in early walking. Here is an area that could well be explored further by all therapists: How can skills in sitting, standing, crawling, walking, eating, dressing, talking, and so on be developed by submerging the necessary drill within a framework that makes a pleasurable activity of it?

Although the principle of embedding also applies to adult motivation, it is far more vital in the case of children who have greater difficulty in keeping before them the significance of hard, dull, and sometimes painful exercises for ultimate goals that are often indefinitely far into the future. The child is much more bound by the immediate situation, and he may well be unimpressed by the promise that crawling for a half hour on the floor will eventually help him to stand with crutches, or that wearing his braces will some day enable him to walk.

The principle of embedding need not, of course, be applied at every turn. Sometimes repetitive drill is a happy relief from fun and frolic. Also, the experience of doing something just because it should be done is valuable even though it is tedious, as long as the child realizes the significance of the task and is not overburdened by it. The danger arises when the latter two conditions are ignored. We doubt, for instance, that either Wally or Ben had much notion as to why he had to carry through the adult directives. It is certain, in any case, that the task for Ben involved excessive strain. Furthermore certain kinds of drill may be necessary or desirable simply because they accomplish far more than could be achieved through a playful activity. Finally, there are other motivating factors that also elicit the coöperation of children with respect to the job at hand, factors that may be more easily applied in a particular instance. Some of these are discussed below.

Is the Child's Overall Experience in the Rehabilitation Session One of Success or Failure?

"Nothing succeeds like success" is a psychological truth of everyday life. Experimental investigation has discovered at least three important reasons for this. To begin with, success often enhances the attractiveness of a task, whereas failure often acts contrariwise, turning an otherwise acceptable task into a disagreeable one (Cartwright, *1942;* Gebhard, *1948*). Comparable effects hold for anticipated success and anticipated failure. Secondly, success normally increases the level of aspiration—i.e., the goal one sets for oneself with respect to the task—whereas failure tends to decrease it (Lewin *et al., 1944*). Finally, it has been shown that persons with a background of success in the particular area of concern differ significantly from those with a background of failure, with respect to how realistic their goal-setting is. The academically successful children in Sears' study (*1940*), for example, expected improvement well in line with their current performance whereas those with a background of failure tended either to expect no improvement at all or to expect completely unrealizable gains.

Whether or not success has occurred can be indicated to the person primarily in two ways. First, there is the performance as such. In the usual level-of-aspiration experiments, as well as in many situations of everyday life, the person can readily tell whether he has achieved his goal or not. If his goal is eight bull's-eye hits out of ten, for example, a score of two or nine speaks for itself. There are many situations in real life, however, when success is indicated not so much by the performance itself as by how that performance is judged by others. Social evaluation, then, becomes a second indicator of success. When the goal itself is not too clear, or when the performance is not easily ranked with respect to the goal, then praise and reproof become, for the person, the main signs as to how well he is doing. Lila, for instance, knew that she was improving her "f" sound not as a result of the raw data presented by the sound itself but by the complimentary remarks of her teacher (4').

Whatever the indicator, however, the experience of success and failure is a psychological experience, the essence of which is either satisfaction and pride in accomplishment or dissatisfaction and, more extremely, blame on the self for the failure. As a psychological experience, the feeling of success usually requires that the person achieve by his own efforts goals important to him and near the top of his ability level. If he is engaged in tasks that are very easy for him, or if the task itself is repugnant to him, or if it is accomplished largely through the efforts of others, then any success is likely to be a peripheral experience, lacking the pride in accomplishment that provides the strongest bolster to one's ego and encouragement to go on. This means that the child's abilities need careful assessment so that realistic goals requiring some effort on his part can be established. It means that the goals themselves must become sufficiently important to the child, so that *he* upholds and strives toward them.

Some words of caution are in order. First, although the task must assume some importance for the child if success is to be experienced, one must be careful lest it become too heavily invested with a do-or-die significance. Praise, if overdone, can bring about just this kind of emotional intensification. It can also make the child too heavily dependent on flattery and commendation, too sensitive to possible failure, too much concerned about his status rather than about the task as such.

Secondly, not every occasion must be designed so as to elicit a success experience. As the work of Barker and H. Wright showed (*1955*), most of our waking hours by far are neutral with respect to success and failure (see pp. 90–91). Likewise, in rehabilitation programs, the stimulation of success can become an overstimulation if the person is geared to it in every activity he undertakes. One needs the temperance afforded by activities that are indifferent to success and failure, though it still remains true that the overall program should be marked by well-paced success experiences.

That success is a potent motivating factor, leading to heightened goals and making the task at hand more pleasant, is not to be taken lightly, and yet the motivator often neglects to take this factor into account. Sometimes it even seems that he is determined to ensure repeated failure. Let us see how the principle of well-paced success fared in the experiences of Wally, Ben, and Lila. The analysis will concern both the relation between performance and goal as an indicator of success and the reaction of the adults as social evaluators.

Wally may not have experienced failure, but he certainly did not feel any pride in accomplishment, the main criterion of a success experience. Moreover, the situation did not provide any of the indicators that could reveal to him that he was succeeding in anything worth-while. Not once did his mother praise him during the hour and a half that he wore his braces. If anything, her acknowledgment that she did not like the braces either (7′) provided social confirmation that the whole affair was disagreeable and to be avoided. As for Wally's performance as an indicator of achievement, the necessary goal structure was lacking. Moreover, the vague goal as imposed by his mother—to wear the braces until he had breakfast and played a while (6′)—became vaguer still because he doubted her intentions. His mistrust evidently had some basis, for an hour and 15 minutes later he was still wearing them, and it took three imperious reminders on Wally's part before his mother removed them. A vague and unacceptable goal, with no encouragement along the way, provides little support for striving.

To be sure, Wally was generally in an uncoöperative mood (some of the reasons for which are suggested in the following sections) and at the time nothing might have worked, but certain suggestions do come to mind as to what Wally's mother could have tried. She could have commented, after putting on his braces, that now he was standing nicely (6′), for without them he could do nothing but slump. At least this would have reminded him that he was accomplishing something worth-while. She could have counted the seconds that he could stand alone, or the steps that he could walk holding on with one hand or unaided, as well as kept a record of his progress. At least this would have established a concrete and realistic standard, a goal that gave meaning to his performance here and now.

The importance of establishing well-structured goals that are attainable within a relatively short time and are guided by past performance warrants further comment. One difficulty is that we are often unable to establish long-term goals because we do not know them. We cannot say with assurance, for example, that this three-year-old child with cerebral palsy who is just beginning to learn to sit tailor fashion will eventually be able to walk, with or without crutches. Fortunately, long-term goals are not necessarily the most desirable from the point of view of the immediate task at hand or of motivating potential. Doubtless, it might be most helpful for purposes of educational planning to know whether a child will remain bedridden or be able to get about in a wheelchair, but for getting him to sit alone this need not play a role. Actually, immediate goals may more fruitfully be established in terms of recent performance rather than future, hoped-for accomplishment, for one's gains become successes. In the following account, a young woman in the rehabilitative phases of polio recalls:

. . . "Come now," the therapist would lie beautifully, "you stood for twenty seconds longer yesterday," and I almost collapsed as I remembered standing for almost three hours talking to a boy who had carried my books home for me from high school. Twenty seconds! I felt as though I had been there twenty years! But in this manner my therapist increased my standing time, my confidence, and my strength. And I seriously realized that unless I tried harder, tomorrow would be no different from today, and I tried to do just a little better than I was asked to do [Linduska, 1947, p. 116].[3]

In Ben's case, unmitigated failure pervaded almost the entire session, being capitalized at the end by undisguised chastisement and threats of punishment. Also the goal was apparently both unclear and unattainable for Ben.

Perhaps the therapeutic procedures from day to day were so similar that the therapist did not see the need to orient Ben explicitly toward the goal. If so, one of course would call this into question, since it would seem desirable to establish and make clear each day just what the objectives are

[3] Noreen Linduska, *My Polio Past*, copyright 1947 by Noreen Linduska. Used by permission of the publishers, Farrar, Straus and Cudahy, Inc.

and, equally important, something of the why of them. The therapist did ask during the third minute, "How far are you going to crawl today?" but the interaction was so brief that it could hardly have been a serious exploration of the task ahead. And though in the fifth minute the goal, crawling about 10 feet, was mentioned, 12 minutes later Ben whimperingly asked, "How far?" The therapist missed this excellent opportunity to clarify the situation, and instead made the goal uncertain and hopelessly out of reach by replying, "How far? Just as far as you can go, that's how far."

Early in the lesson Ben was convinced that the goal, whatever it was, was beyond his capabilities. If Ben had been soundly motivated, crawling 10 feet might have been well within his capability. But as it was, after about four minutes of trying to crawl, Ben was very discouraged, saying, "I can't do it." (9') The therapist, busy with another child, ignored Ben until two minutes later, when he did instruct Ben on just how to crawl: "Now, get your hands apart. Keep pushing with your legs. You'll go. Pull with your hands. Come on, pull" (11'). But this businesslike instruction, demanding and unsympathetic, hardly served to convince Ben that he really could accomplish the task if he tried. The therapist could have pointed out that Ben already had crawled seven inches, that yesterday he did such and such. The goal could also have been structured anew and even modified to make it more in line with what Ben could accomplish.

This point has frequent application in teaching situations: When a task appears to be too overwhelming, breaking it down into *subgoals* can make it seem far more manageable. Suppose that Ben's therapist was convinced that Ben could and ought to crawl 10 feet that day. But observing that this appeared to be a Herculean task for Ben, Mr. T. should have altered the situation. The first lap of the journey across the floor could be set at five feet or two feet if necessary. These substations could even be different towns or stores on the way to the circus, the ultimate goal 10 feet away. Appropriate rewards, all in the spirit of the play, could provide further incentive at each of the subgoals. The task as recast has been turned into a game consisting of parts that should be felt as attainable *by the child* with reasonable expenditure of time and energy. It must be remembered that Ben was just 6 years old, and surely for so young a child immediate goals should be within reach in less than the 30 minutes during which Ben labored.

As it was, Ben strained and whimpered, almost as if he wished to prove that the task was in fact beyond him. It is noteworthy that 20 minutes after Ben started to crawl, he was not even facing the mirror, though at that time he was about four feet from it (25').

One suspects that the interpersonal relations between Ben and his therapist led to a turn-about-face in Ben's motivation, so that instead of wanting to reach the goal, however vague, he wanted *not* to reach it. Certainly for Ben crawling was a difficult job, but apparently he made more ado about it than was warranted. This annoyed the therapist, who did not realize that by it Ben was trying to say, "See how I am trying. See how miserable I am. Give me credit for my straining and pain."

Throughout the session Ben was chastised so that even if he had finally reached the goal, there would have been but small joy in its achievement. Toward the end of the session (30') the goal was lowered but certainly not in a way that would give Ben a feeling that he had done an adequate job. Four minutes later (34'), when Ben had virtually reached the new goal by stretching out his hand, he was in effect slapped down for "fudging." Finally, at the end of the session (35'), Ben was reprimanded and threatened in no uncertain terms. He was told that his performance was fussing, crying, whimpering, lazy. One can hardly imagine greater defeat, for not only did he fail the goal of the therapist, but Ben's own goal of proving his effort was totally unrealized. The change in Ben's mood, which was quite cheerful at the outset, is striking. The session is an excellent example of the effects of persistent failure: the goal is lowered; the task becomes more disagreeable.

Lila's experience was very different from that of either Wally or Ben. She started out being pleased (as was Ben, but not Wally) and ended being pleased (as neither of the boys was). Satisfaction with her performance, even when she was given help in bettering it, pervaded the session. The feeling of success primarily grew out of the teacher's encouragement and praise of the children's efforts and accomplishments. Satisfaction spread to the group as a whole so that success was further underscored by the smiling and hand-clapping of peers. Notice that when Lila was corrected it was in a positive, noncritical, certainly nondisparaging way (4', 10'). Furthermore, the goals were sufficiently immediate and clear for the children to appreciate what it was they were trying to do. To blow a horn, make certain sounds, answer certain questions, provided definite guides for their efforts. Though success was heavily determined by the teacher's evaluation, it was not bandied about irrespective of the child's efforts and performance.

In none of the records did the children have much to do with determining their goals. It is not proposed here that the child must always be "the architect in his own betterment" but participating actively in the setting up of goals not only provides needed experience in this important area but also is an excellent means for eliciting the child's coöperation. Active participation and enthusiasm are not unrelated. Helping to determine a goal is one of the best ways for the person to become motivated to achieve it. One could imagine that even Wally, who wanted to have nothing to do with the braces, could have been maneuvered into specifying how many counts he could stand alone while wearing them. Certainly Ben would have been eager to help decide how far he could try to crawl that day.

If the children make their task too easy, or too difficult, in time their judgment can be expected to become more in keeping with their real ability since success and failure usually act as a sound gauge for the level of aspiration. Besides, the guidance of the adult in these matters is certainly not precluded. The level of aspiration is usually set near the top of the person's ability when the person has been free to raise and lower it in accordance with his experience of success and failure. Of course the sensitive teacher also raises and lowers the child's goals in accordance with this evidence. In any case, sound goals insure an adequate amount of success, which in turn acts as a stimulant to motivation and leads to the establishment of new challenging goals.

Unfortunately the interaction of success, failure, and the level of aspiration does not always act as such a happy regulator of optimum experience (Barker and Wright, 1952:29).

1. If aspirations are placed well below the level of a person's highest ability, he will not experience success. He will, in effect, be a deprived, frustrated person because his central needs for self-esteem and social appreciation are not satisfied. This may occur when the person, for complex reasons, is afraid to risk even momentary failure, or when rigid goals are superimposed from the outside.

2. Dissatisfaction is also the lot of the person who, though placing his goals sufficiently high, does not attain them by his own efforts. We have all known children, and adults too, who have been *given* "everything" yet who are supremely unhappy and often insatiable in their demands for more things, more attention, more experiences.

3. Finally, there are those who consistently place their aspirations above their ability to achieve. They are then regularly confronted with failure and deprived of self-esteem and social satisfaction. In the case of disability, this frequently occurs when "normal" physique and ability become the idolized standard so that the goals he sets for rehabilitation remain far out of line with even the best that can be realistically hoped for.

In each of these three situations, something is interfering with the feedback between success and failure on the one hand and the level of aspiration on the other. Sometimes the disruption is due to the imposition of rigid and unrealistic goals from the outside. Sometimes the anxieties of the person himself prevent him from raising and lowering his goals in accordance with the realistic evidence of success and failure. Since goal behavior is not an incidental aspect of a person's adjustment but determines much of the person's overall feelings of satisfaction and failure, it is well for the adult to keep on the alert for opportunities in the rehabilitation situation where the child can feasibly be drawn into this important process.

To sum up, the following can be asked in evaluating whether well-paced success characterizes the child's experience:

Is the goal within the child's reach?

Is it flexibly gauged in terms of actual performance?

Has the child had a part in establishing it?

Are subgoals necessary to encourage striving?

Has praise been given to indicate success?

Has praise had the balance of matter-of-fact and task oriented appraisal?

Is the child able to determine accomplishment in terms of the performance itself?

Are there sufficient interludes where success and failure are not at stake and the activity carries itself, either because it is accepted as a job to be done or because it is enjoyable?

Success as presented here may seem overemphasized. Some may argue that particularly in the American culture the success story is already excessively highlighted. The issue here, however, does not identify success with unusually high standards but rather with individually reachable ones. Moreover, as Hilgard and Russell (1950) point out, the child does not have to be taught to accept failure by providing him with repeated failure experiences. "A better preparation for failure is to have a sufficient backlog of success experiences so that failure is not devastating" (p. 52). They remind us that it is possible to teach toleration of failure, as shown in the study by Keister (1937), by drawing upon success, not failure, as the regulator of conduct. In that study the children were taught to accept failure by linking temporary failure with ultimate success. They were taught not to be impatient but to keep striving until success was achieved. When failure indicates "how to do what better," it can stimulate learning, but certainly the children in the Keister study were not taught to endure lasting failure.

This point fits in well with one of the main themes of this book—namely, that maintaining the standard of the nondisabled as the guide and evaluator of the behavior of the person with a disability has the probable outcome of relegating him to a life of failure, the acceptance of which is equivalent to resignation. On the other hand, according to the theoretical position held in this volume, acceptance of a disability requires basic changes in values so that new and *reachable* goals become meaningful.

Is There a Place for Extraneous Incentives?

The attractiveness of an activity and the satisfaction of goal achievement provide what may be considered to be intrinsic incentives. There are other sources of motivation, however, that are external to the activity itself. These are commonly referred to as rewards and punishments.

Experimental investigation supports the common belief that rewards and punishments can serve as powerful motivators of learning. They can do so in at least two ways. First, they can provide important information to the person as to what constitutes incorrect and correct responses. If the subject is reprimanded (or, as is the *modus operandi* with experimental animals, shocked with an electric current) every time he makes a wrong move, and praised (or fed a pellet) every time he makes the right response, then he may be able to correct his behavior and learn accordingly. If a child is excluded from the game because of misbehavior, he may become impressed by the necessity of abiding by the rules on the next occasion. Secondly, rewards and punishments can serve to mobilize the person's energy and attention toward the learning task. In a well-known experiment by Hurlock (*1925*), for example, it was shown that school arithmetic improved most when the children were praised, next when they were reproved, and least when they were ignored. Because the praise and reproof were administered to the children as a group, no information was gained as to specific errors and correct responses.

Although punishment can stimulate learning, psychologists are generally agreed that, unless it is carefully considered, it is easily misused. In the words of Hilgard and Russell (*1950*), "The interpersonal aspects of the punishment situation are fraught with more hazards than those in reward. As a teacher or parent becomes emotionally upset, it is an easy matter to take out aggression on children through punishment. The children may be provocative, but the danger of injustice in punishment is great, and children are extremely sensitive to injustice. The meaning to the child of being punished by a powerful adult is complex, and regardless of the effect on immediate behavior there may arise concealed attitudes of resentment, of dislike of the work for which punishment was imposed as well as of the punishing teacher" (p. 49).

What Else Is the Child Learning?

One of the most important questions we can ask in evaluating incentives is: What else is the child learning? In the case of intrinsic incentives, the verdict is positive, for to know the pleasure of an enjoyable activity and the satisfaction of goal achievement leads to a feeling of well-being and enhances striving still further. But in the case of extrinsic incentives, the end result is not as pure.

If castigation predominates in the person's life, his self-concept is in danger of becoming an abject apology. In just the single session, Ben heard (and learned?) that he was lazy, fudging, a cry-baby, and in fact a total failure. More than that, he was learning that effort did not count for much (he had really worked hard for more than half an hour); it was achievement, and an unattainable one, that mattered. He also learned to dread the next session.

Even so-called playful teasing on the part of the adult may easily be misconstrued by the child. When Miss O. jokingly said to Ben, "Oh, look at the monkey. Look at the monkey" (20'), was this a delightful jest to him? When Wally's mother agreed with him in disliking his braces and that they would be tossed in the river at the first opportunity (7'), was this taken merely as sympathetic understanding? Or did this interplay also reinforce Wally's emphasis on the succumbing aspects of his disability—that the braces signified pain and trouble and his inability to walk—rather than the aspect of coping?

As for rewards, one can well ask whether the child is learning to rely on adult adulation or bribes in one form or another as a necessary accompaniment to striving. When used judiciously, however, the child may not only become motivated, but also may learn that effort, coöperation, progress, etc. are indeed important.

In Chapter 5, in the discussion of acceptance, it was pointed out that one of the helpful value changes is that of subordinating physique. At the same time, the very purpose of rehabilitation—to improve physique—serves to emphasize it. This contradiction makes it even more necessary to free the rehabilitation setting of emotionalism, which makes physical achievement all-important, a goal upon which one's destiny rests.

These examples are sufficient to bring out that in the rehabilitation situation the child learns far more than the immediate task at hand. He learns about himself and others, what is valued and what is not, basic attitudes that become an influential part of his orientation to life in general and to his disability in particular. By questioning what else the child is learning, one is often able to spotlight the strengths and weakness of one's methods.

Are Background Factors (Time, Place, and Social Conditions) Optimal for Learning?

Especially because all of us hold preconceived notions as to the background conditions most conducive to learning, these must be consciously checked by the evidence presented in actual practice. The following is a good example of how a parent's reasonable notions turned out not to fit the facts:

> During this summer, I experimented with giving Karen her physiotherapy on the beach. It didn't work.
>
> I found that the cold water increased her spasticity, making already stiff muscles that much stiffer (temporarily). I found that more than twenty minutes of sun had much the same (temporary) effect.
>
> I then tried doing her therapy immediately after her nap and so learned something interesting, and today still inexplicable. Instead of being relaxed and "soft" immediately after sleep, as one might reasonably expect, our daughter is more spastic and it is necessary to allow one full hour to elapse from the time of waking to the start of any therapy [Killilea, 1952, p. 149].[4]

To question the background conditions of the case at hand is also necessary because individual differences in diurnal rhythms pertaining to alertness, moods, and energy are great. Wally's general mood, as the scene opened at eight o'clock in the morning, was resistant and fretful. Although this could be attributed to the possibility that he was reacting to the prospect of his hated braces, it is to be observed that he became cheerful during breakfast. One wonders if Wally needed time to wake up after rising, if he is not generally disgruntled until breakfast sets him right with the world. If this is the case, one would certainly recommend postponing bracing until then.

The factor of social facilitation, as we well know, can have a tremendous impact on the person's readiness to undertake a task. Lila's therapeutic situation made the most of this background condition. There, other children were doing the things she was asked to do. They were praised and she was praised. They were pleased with her success and she was pleased with theirs. Ben, on the other hand, had to become involved in a task very much apart from any supporting group. To be sure there were people around, but they were engaged primarily in other pursuits, their contact with Ben being more or less capricious and sometimes only adding to his misery. His therapist was also preoccupied with working with another child. In fact, he remained with Ben for only one minute after he placed Ben on the floor (4′). Intermittently he did direct Ben from afar, but without the necessary positive emotional involvement for generating a genuine "we feeling." Several minutes later the therapist rejoined Ben and remained with him for about 10 minutes (11′–21′). It is to be observed that when the therapist left again, Ben's fussing increased as though he were fairly crying out for someone to be "together with" him in his ordeal. During the next eight minutes the therapist was across

---

[4] Reprinted with permission of Prentice-Hall, Inc., from *Karen* by Marie Killilea. Copyright 1952 by Marie Lyons Killilea.

the room and Ben made little progress (22'–30'). In spite of the steady stream of people in and out of his orbit, Ben apparently felt very much alone.

Not always, of course, does a child need the stimulation of other children. And it is not always easy to provide that stimulation. Wally was not in an institutional setting where there were other children who needed similar treatment. In such circumstances, the child may resist the therapy just because none of his playmates has to be bothered with it. It sets him apart, makes him feel different and lonely. Being aware of this, the parent may be able to draw the child's friends into certain phases of the rehabilitation program. An older child could keep score as Wally stands alone and all could rejoice in his progress. Karen's mother called the neighbors in to watch Karen for the first time as she walked with her new crutches (Killilea, 1952:217–219). The important point is that care should be taken to keep the child from feeling that no other children have any interest in the rehabilitation task before him.

What Are Some of the Basic Attitudes That the Child Has Toward His Disability and the Rehabilitation Procedures That Surround It?

A child's readiness to participate in the rehabilitation program depends not only on specific conditions surrounding the task that promote enthusiasm or not but also on the whole personality of the child, on his general attitudes toward himself and the disability. Why did Wally hate his braces so? It may have been because the situation was poorly constructed from the point of view of specific motivating factors, but it may also have been because the braces represented for Wally "nothing but trouble." They may point to the succumbing aspects to the exclusion of their significance for coping with the problems imposed by the disability. In Ben's case, the predominant attitude was "I can't." Again, this may have been a consequence of the unfortunate way in which the task was planned but it also may reflect Ben's pervasive feeling about himself—that he is helpless, pitiable, and unable.

In other words, the child comes into the situation with important needs and attitudes that will affect his reaction to it. Needless to say, what happens in the rehabilitation setting can influence for better or worse the child's attitudes toward himself and his disability.

Sometimes our best efforts to motivate a child fail just because we remain unaware of what the total situation means to him. Although such awareness often requires a sensitive orientation to the child, it is surprising how often we overlook even the most direct cues. Neither Wally nor Ben was asked why he felt as he did. What might Wally have said? What might Ben have said? We need not necessarily probe for unconscious motivation. Our handling of manifest attitudes can also lead to sympathetic understanding of underlying feelings. Even a superficial rationalization on the child's part needs to be taken into account. A child's ability to contribute knowledge and understanding to his situation must always be respected. This may be an obvious truth, but it is all too often violated just because of the devalued status of children.

Does the Motivator Feel Friendly to the Child and the Task at Hand?

Human motivators are human beings and as such they, too, come into the situation with needs and attitudes toward the child and his disability that profoundly influence the proceedings. The enthusiasm and friendly encouragement contributed by Lila's therapist to the situation is clearly not something divorceable from her personality and warmth toward her pupils. On the other hand, if the adult dislikes the child, easily becomes angered and impatient, is discouraged about the rehabilitation possibilities, or is basically uninterested, then no matter how many motivating devices are introduced, they cannot be fired with the necessary spark for effective and sound learning. Perhaps the most important question of all concerns the adult's underlying feelings toward the child and toward disability.

Aside from these additional factors determining so much of the adult's performance in the rehabilitation situation, there is the practical problem of repetitive therapy. The question concerns motivating the motivator: How can therapy that must be carried out day in and day out continue to be of sufficient interest and challenge to the therapist so that he enters at least most of the sessions with that enthusiasm necessary to encourage and motivate his charges? This problem, of course, applies to all teachers, including parents. Part of the answer lies in the selection of personnel, and part in the arrangements of the working situation.

We know that in teaching institutions, rehabilitation workers see added challenge in the daily routines because what they are doing is shared with students in training and other members of the staff. There is something new in everyday events when they are analyzed and thought about, when they have to be justified and evaluated. Other instances of the kind of social involvement that tends to keep alive one's work and interest result when visitors frequent therapy sessions and when the rehabilitation worker participates in planning and evaluating the rehabilitation program. One must add, of course, that heavy case loads, long hours, and insufficient respect for the functions of the rehabilitation worker are unfavorable conditions for the kind of keen awareness we are seeking.

Parents seldom have sufficient opportunity for that sharing with other adults which does so much to strengthen understanding and determination to persevere in spite of boredom and difficulties. Parent discussion groups and more frequent contacts with visiting nurses and other therapists are indicated. Of course, the genuine motivation of most parents for whom the welfare of their children is uppermost will carry them a long way.

Little has been said in the foregoing discussion of motivation that has not been said before or that is difficult to grasp. But because the key questions often find little reflection in actual practice, they need to be raised again and again as checks that highlight the psychological significance of the learning situation.

One might wonder why "theory" and "practice" are frequently far apart. Perhaps it is because the questions raised here are obvious only after they have been raised and because the principles that provide some of the answers are not such truisms as one might think. After all, though the motivators in the three rehabilitation records which provided our "living" material tried to be on their best behavior, being under observation as they were, they were nevertheless unable to avoid glaring errors. Sometimes, of course, one's best intentions become deflected by conflicting feelings. Wisdom helps, but only succeeds when it is sustained by feelings that support it.

Chapter 14

The Client as Comanager in His Rehabilitation

THE EFFECTIVENESS OF REHABILITATION, WHETHER IT INVOLVES PHYSICAL, vocational, or emotional adjustment, depends largely upon the degree to which the client has made the plan his own. Barring special circumstances, this support on the part of the client in the long run is enhanced when he takes an active part in decision-making; it is often weakened when he feels that his life is being manipulated behind the scenes, even when it is by the experts who know best "where he is to go and how he is to get there."

Few counselors would deny the importance of active participation on the part of the client. But it should be emphasized that active participation as it is used here is not, as is often assumed in practice, synonymous with "coöperative attitude." Of course it is pleasing to the counselor to find that the client willingly submits to all manner of test procedures, that he responds to questions fully and with enthusiasm, and above all that he follows the counselor's recommendations. This is the "good" client. But this is not the active participant.

The specifications of active participation become clarified when the client is thought of as part of management. Then it is that he not only answers questions but raises them; that he not only contributes data to his case but helps evaluate them and works through to their solution; and finally that he claims the veto power as well as voting privileges (except in special circumstances; see pp. 357–358). The "principle of comanagement" is an apt designation for the kind of relationship advocated. It connotes active participation by *both* client and specialist. This principle, or even philosophy, also underlies a good deal of the discussion of the parent as a key participant and of motivation in the rehabilitation situation (Chaps. 12 and 13).

BASIS FOR ENCOURAGING COMANAGEMENT
ON THE PART OF THE CLIENT

The reasons why the adult in particular and the child as he grows older should participate in the management of his rehabilitation are important. The first of these concerns the matter of self-esteem.

. . . the worker-client relationship tends to be an asymmetrical one in which the professional person has the higher status position. Just as in the case of doctor and patient, lawyer and client, or teacher and pupil the disabled person may easily feel [himself to be] in a dependent position in which it is hoped that the wisdom of the worker will guide him through his difficulties. But it is just such an atmosphere of a wise and powerful one, on the one hand, and a dependent, suppliant one on the other hand, that so easily can nourish the feelings of inadequacy and personal inferiority that true rehabilitation seeks to avoid. The inner strength and self-respect which we wish to build in the client grows in a relationship in which the disabled person feels that he has an important role in planning his life and that what he says and what he feels is respected. . . . Even a disabled child needs to have a feeling that he knows what is happening to him and why, that he has a choice in the decisions. How much more true this is of the person who has reached adulthood with all the independence of judgment and self-determination that this implies [Barker and Wright, *1952*:20–21].[1]

To repeat: Inner strength and self-respect grow in a relationship in which the person feels that he has an important role in planning his life and that what he says and what he feels are regarded as important.

Motivation to make the plan work is the second important reason for stressing the participation of the adult in the evolving as well as the executing of the rehabilitation program. As one pamphlet addressed to patients put it: ". . . the final result depends on you and how much you put into it. Their [staff] job is important, but yours is more important" (Rusk and Taylor, *1946*:85).[2] When the client feels that he had little to do with the plan in the first place, it is all too easy for him to dissipate his energies in minor complaints. He is less apt to be ready to make personal adjustments as required by new and sometimes disagreeable circumstances than when he has been a participant in mapping out the

---

[1] R. G. Barker and B. A. Wright, The social psychology of adjustment to physical disability, in J. F. Garrett (Ed.), *Psychological aspects of physical disability,* Department of Health, Education, and Welfare, Rehabilitation Service Series, No. 210.

[2] H. A. Rusk and E. J. Taylor, *New hope for the handicapped,* Harper & Brothers, 1946. By permission.

rehabilitation course. How often does a person, presumably vocationally rehabilitated, leave the job after six months as a result of relatively unimportant sources of irritation just because, not having had a crucial say in the vocational alternatives, he has readily placed in the counselor's lap the responsibility of getting him the perfect but nonexistent job! Experience with psychotherapy has well established the proposition that successful outcome is generally favored when the patient assumes some responsibility during the planning phase of his rehabilitation. Patient responsibility forms the cornerstone of what is known as "nondirective" therapy (Rogers, *1951*) and is certainly an essential building block of the more directive types of psychotherapy (Fromm-Reichmann and Moreno, *1956*).

A third consideration is the fact that our fund of knowledge is often not sufficiently exact to enable the counselor to know which course of action is best for the client. On these grounds alone it would seem desirable to allow for the views and intentions of the client.

As a concrete illustration of this point, let us examine the controversial issue as to whether people of good intelligence should be provided higher education irrespective of the degree of physical disability. Cruickshank (*1955*) has spoken out strongly in the negative, arguing that "the 'overtrained' physically handicapped person is one of the real tragedies of our time" and that such persons "will be happier if adjusted in a less skilled job than when they are frustrated in an attempt to adjust and compete in professional fields where the possibility of real achievement is seriously limited if not impossible" (p. 360).[3] In support of his argument, he presents the following case:

A quadriplegic athetoid young woman graduated in psychology from a college, *summa cum laude*. She was admitted to a graduate school of another university for her master's degree which she completed in the upper tenth of a class of 225 students. Parental requests were made to the university to continue the girl on to the doctorate, which on the basis of innate ability could easily have been achieved. The girl was hopelessly handicapped and crippled. Her speech was more than poor. She needed a companion to assist her in all basic self-help skills. She could not independently walk. Her accomplishments, great as they were, were laboriously achieved through the use of an electric typewriter. Permission was denied for further graduate study in clinical psychology where her opportunity for employment was seen to be nil. A currently unhappy person with more unusable professional training than she ever should have been permitted, this girl should initially have been admitted—at

[3] W. M. Cruickshank, Educational planning for the cerebral palsied, in W. M. Cruickshank and G. M. Raus (Eds.), *Cerebral palsy: its individual and community problems,* Syracuse University Press, 1955. By permission.

most—to a culturally oriented liberal arts program geared primarily to self-enrichment and no more. Inadequate guidance failed this student and her parents [pp. 360–361].

Although this point of view cannot be ignored, the following issue is crucial to its final evaluation: Isn't a judgment of employability at best an estimate of probability and isn't an unwarranted wisdom assumed on the part of even the most expert vocational counselor when he feels able to say with assurance that a particular individual will be unable to put his training to productive use? The remarks of Lowenfeld (1956) with respect to the vocational pursuits of blind persons have wide generality. He reminds us that any list of occupations must remain incomplete because "a singularly gifted blind man or woman can be found doing work which others—even those experienced in work with the blind—would consider impossible for a blind person. Thus we know of a highly successful blind scientist in atomic research, an equally successful blind chemist, and a physicist, and I know myself of a totally blind man who owned and ran the largest bookstore in a city with almost half a million population—and he really did run it successfully" (Lowenfeld, 1956:12).[4] The fact that even those experienced in work with the blind would consider these occupations impossible for a blind person should have sobering implications.

It must also be remembered that employability is not related in a simple way to degree of disability, that many unforeseen social as well as personal forces may combine to open up opportunities for even the most severely disabled. There is the enlightening fact, uncovered in Glick's study of adults with cerebral palsy (1953), that of those whose disabilities were categorized as mild, 7 percent were employed as compared with 22 percent of the moderately and 24 percent of the severely disabled.

The question can even be raised as to whether employability should be the only criterion for deciding whether a person should enter a given program. It is entirely possible, for example, that the aforementioned graduate student with cerebral palsy would have made productive use of her training though not gainfully employed in the usual sense. If she could laboriously use an electric typewriter to be graduated *summa cum laude* and achieve a master's degree, surely her psychological knowledge could find some outlet useful to community life. The possibility of volunteer work and of self-employment enormously extends the avenues toward productive use of professional training and need not be denied because of emphasis on competitive employment.

[4] From B. Lowenfeld, *Our blind children,* 1956. Courtesy of Charles C Thomas, Publisher, Springfield, Ill.

This point of view does not, of course, decry vocational counseling for persons with physical disabilities. But the vocational and educational counselor cannot with impunity make the decision as to whether or not the client should enter one or another program because of his physical limitation. Instead, the counselor should *assist* the client in deciding the course of his destiny by making available necessary information and by helping him come to terms with basic issues involved in the choices. A good example of such mutual sharing in the process of vocational counseling appears on page 351. To be sure, there will be instances where hindsight will prove the client's errors, but there will also be instances where the counselor's misgivings will not have been borne out.

Seidenfeld has made a special plea for the point of view supported here, commenting that "unfortunately a number of psychologists working in medical programs are called upon not infrequently to make 'psychological diagnoses,' job suitability predictions, appraise personality characteristics, etc. These requests are generally made in good faith and are based upon the assumption of the physician and others, that such information at hand should make it possible to decide for the patient what his whole future should be like. Such an idea is obviously in error for it fails to take cognizance of the fact that the most important element in the entire matter is what the patient can and will do to make his own future" (*1948b:*247).

Whether or not one agrees with the particular conclusion concerning vocational guidance, the general point should be taken seriously by all rehabilitation workers—namely, that the lack of omniscience on the part of the counselor gives additional support to the principle that the adult client should be a key planner in his rehabilitation. The point could have been illustrated by many other areas, as, for example, choice of a prosthesis or even selection of surgical methods where there is something to be said for several alternatives.

Finally, there is the important question as to which issues belong rightfully within the inviolable domain of the adults directly involved. This is clearly a matter of values, of prerogatives, of rights that should be interfered with only in the most particular and dire circumstances. An example, the question of institutionalization, will illuminate this point. The professional person needs seriously to consider whether he is ever justified in insisting that institutionalization of a child is the only reasonable course of action. If the answer is in the affirmative, he should try to become clear as to conditions, in principle, which warrant such a drastic decision. He must remind himself that at best it is difficult for an outsider to judge when the care of a child, however feebleminded or physically incapacitated, is too much for a family, for their love and concern may so lighten the burden that what to others may be an unwise expenditure of family resources may to the parents be simply taken as a matter of course. To be sure, the parents should be kept informed of the possibility of institutionalization, and any misinformation should be corrected. In time they may agree that institutionalization is the only alternative, but then it is their decision and not that of anyone else. Sometimes, of course, the parent fairly pleads for the recommendation of institutionalization, fearing to take the responsibility for such a course of action upon himself. Certainly recommendation in such cases is not necessarily contraindicated. But the right of the professional person to recommend institutionalization when the parent is opposed to it should be seriously questioned. The following situation is not uncommon and can well be pondered from the point of view of "rights":

Mrs. Brown is completely unable to accept the recommendation of placing Susan, age five, in an institution for the feebleminded. She can admit only that Susan is retarded in physical functioning and speech. She now refuses to believe that the doctors at the center have been interested in her child and that they tried to help her the past three years. . . . [White, 1955:487].

Some persons may regard many areas as falling within the "inalienable rights" of the individual. Choice as to having more children, even defective ones, may be so regarded, as may choice concerning living conditions, vocational endeavors, and medical care. The principle of self-determination may be so highly prized as a value by some rehabilitation workers that only in the most unusual circumstances would they feel compelled to defy the wishes of the client. Other specialists see a much narrower zone for decisions that are inviolably the client's. In any case, every professional person must face the issue as to whether he has a right in the particular situation to make decisions or even in some cases to offer recommendations. On p. 357 we shall consider circumstances in which the client cannot or should not be a key planner in his rehabilitation.

CLIENT AND COUNSELOR AS PART
OF MANAGEMENT ILLUSTRATED

The specific approach used to encourage comanagement will depend on the setting, the character of the problem, and personality factors in the counselor and in the client. Moreover, because of strong resistances to its actualization on the part of either the counselor or the client (see pp. 361–363), the active participation of the client generally does not come about naturally but rather has to be developed.

The following approach, used successfully by Garrett (1955) for vocational guidance with cerebral palsied adults, is exemplary:

In this method a large sheet of paper is used, divided down the middle with "Assets" on the left column first and "Liabilities" on the right. Jointly counselor and counselee explore whatever both know about the client, carefully listing them in the appropriate column. Suitable items for listing are . . . ability for self-care, physical capacities, mental abilities, emotional status, vocational opportunities, hopes, ideals, aspirations, preferences, and similar data. The listings are made in terms comprehensible to the client and he may even be encouraged to do the writing. Care should be exercised lest the "Liabilities" column be greater than the "Assets" although a realistic appraisal of client strengths and weaknesses will almost always reveal more ability than disability, especially with those to whom this technique would be applicable.

When the listing has been completed, occupations under consideration are then compared in detail with each asset and liability and an informal "score" of so many assets and so many liabilities is obtained. When all of the occupational groups have been completed, a rough scale of values in terms of suitability of the occupations is ready. Usually the client is ready after such a process to choose wisely, realistically, and with satisfaction to himself since he has been an active partner in the process.

In this procedure, the . . . individual analyzes himself, determines those elements which have vocational significance, evaluates their specific importance to a given job, sorts and shifts the results of the process into a particular occupational pattern and determines that which suits him better than others. This process is dynamic and thus a guard against the . . . client remaining, dependent, detached and avoiding reality whether of disability or of work. . . . In this process the counselor makes it clear that he does not have the answers and emphasizes this by the mutual working through of the problem [pp. 452–453].

One could hardly accuse the counselor in the account above of having been passive. Guidance was given, but a guidance which allowed the client, even encouraged him, to explore those aspects about himself which had vocational significance, to examine the total situation with respect to particular occupations, and to determine which plan suited him better than others. The conclusion that "usually the client is ready after such a process to choose wisely, realistically, and with satisfaction to himself" is not to be taken lightly.

As a corollary to the principle of comanagement is the suggestion that the client, whenever it is feasible, be involved in staff conferences on his own case. This proposition has been suggested as a problem for research with respect to the parent's participation (see pp. 292–293). The points made in that connection apply also to the client himself as a participant and need not be repeated here. It is notable that efforts to include the person in such an important matter as a conference about himself are appearing on the rehabilitation scene. In one large rehabilitation center, it is reported that after preliminary interviews and examinations by various specialists, the patient, early in his stay at the center, attends a staff conference at which all members of the professional visiting and consulting staffs are present: "Each person presents such of his findings as are pertinent and nonconfidential in the presence of the patient. These are discussed with the patient participating, and feasibility and length and type of rehabilitation training are estimated" [Rusk and Taylor, *1946:95*].

Eventually, after more experience and research on this problem have been accumulated, students will be schooled in how to participate in and conduct conferences in the presence of the client. Until the nature of such conferences is better understood, we are in a poor position to instruct others as to what variations are appropriate to different purposes and circumstances.

Another example of involving the client as part of management may help give meaning to the fact that this principle has general application. A prosthetics specialist tells his patients:

We cannot recommend a limb until we get to know you. There is no such thing as a "best" limb. The limb that is best-suited to the needs of one individual may be entirely unsatisfactory for another. The type of work you do, your personality and temperament, and the accessibility of a satisfactory limb fitter to make necessary adjustments are but a few of the factors which must be considered. *It is also important from a psychological standpoint that you yourself make the final selection. It's your limb, and you are going to wear it* [Rusk and Taylor, *1946:142*, italics added].

Of course, enormous variability in just what is done and said is possible within the comanagement role of counselor and client.

The belief that the principle of comanagement has general applicability helps to reveal instances where the principle is violated to the detriment of the goals of rehabilitation. Such instances also make us appreciate how much easier it is for the counselor to direct, determine, and decide than to share mutually these management functions, for in spite of best intentions, one often slips into the role of "boss."

The following remarks addressed to a group of professional persons represent the thinking and practice in many rehabilitation facilities. They have to do specifically with vocational counseling, but the objectionable principle, implied by the italicized phrases, underlies all too often the procedures in the various branches of rehabilitation:

Through a preliminary interview with the client and by studying reports from other agencies, *the counselor learns* of the disabled individual's desires, needs, and problems. This is followed by a general medical examination and any specialty examinations which may be necessary. The next step is for the *counselor to arrive* at a vocational diagnosis. This is based upon a review of medical data and the case study, and an appraisal of the client's aptitudes, abilities, interests, and background including social, economic, and psychological factors. The plan may include one or more of such services as surgery or other medical care, artificial limbs or other appliances, training for a job, occupational tools, placement, and follow-up to effect adjustment [Italics added].

Our main point is that *both* the counselor and the client should learn of the client's desires, needs, and problems and that *both* should arrive at a vocational diagnosis. The plan evolved should be the product of the joint thinking of the rehabilitation team, of which the client himself is a key member not only as the object of study but also as the one who casts the deciding vote (see pp. 357–361 for exceptions).

To take another example, let us examine the following statement:

Preferably prior to an operation, or at least as soon after as possible, the surgeon, the medical social worker, and any other members of the rehabilitation team who are involved should start to build insight and understanding on the part of the patient into the problems he faces.

This advice seems to be most commendable, but how much more commendable it would be if these specialists were advised to ". . . start *to help* build insight and understanding on the part of the patient." After all, who works at the job of coming to grips with the patient's problems, of trying to understand them? Who lies awake at night thinking of the "ups and downs," the "ins and outs" and where it all will lead? The specialist may, at times, but we can be sure that the patient does so far more persistently. We must not forget that insight is built up by the person himself with the help of outsiders if he is fortunate, but only with their help. The process goes on within the client, and without his active participation it becomes dissipated for lack of stimulation. "To help build insight" reflects the emphasis that is necessary. When the specialist is said "to build insight," there is a displacement of the primary causal agent to the outsider.

The last sentence in the following quotation from a booklet addressed to amputees in the hospital shows clearly how one-sided direction by the professional person often unnecessarily and perhaps unwittingly creeps in: "If you are going to turn misfortune into a valuable asset the time to start thinking about your future is while you are still in the hospital. Do not wait until you are ready to leave the hospital. The doctor, the social worker in the hospital, the rehabilitation counselor in your district are ready to answer your question, 'where do I go from here?' " Surely, the question of "where the patient goes from here" can be worked through only with the patient's full participation. Why not, therefore, state the matter in some such fashion? To assert that the doctor, the social worker, and the rehabilitation counselor are ready to answer this question is to place the reins in their hands, with the patient at best becoming a back seat driver.

Endless examples of the spoken and written word addressed to patients or to the professional person, to say nothing of hospital and other procedures, could be presented to demonstrate the easy error of subordinating the client to the position of one who should comply with directions and advice. This error is so "natural" (see p. 362) that it is essential to take specific measures to discover and thereby correct it. Just as any experienced writer corrects his first draft extensively, examining every paragraph and sentence from the point of view of grammar, readability, coherence, etc., so the rehabilitation counselor must conduct an ongoing examination of his words and deeds to check whether they imply in any way that he is the knower of all things or that he is the main actor, with the client acting as the supporting cast. The counselor must always be on guard lest he become so absorbed with procedural rules and principles that the reaction of the client is ignored. After all, the real test of effectiveness is what is happening to the client.

FURTHER IMPLICATIONS OF THE PRINCIPLE OF COMANAGEMENT

Terminology as a Problem of Communication

If the client is to be encouraged to assume a leadership role in the management of his disability, it is important that the counselor use language that is comprehensible to the client. Too often the specialist is unnecessarily obscure. A study by Stratton (*1957*) recognizes this problem and points up certain precautions as a guide for the professional person. It measured, by means of a vocabulary test, knowledge of tuberculosis concepts by patients hospitalized with this disease. More than three-quarters of the patients had no understanding of the following words: *lesion, function, study, thoracoplasty, resection.* Less than half the sample had a good understanding of these words: *germ, spot, fluid.* Words comprehended by four fifths of the group were: *sputum, negative sputum, positive sputum, clearing, gastrics, fluoroscopy, bronchoscopy.* More than half the patients knew the meaning of the terms: *belly gas, pneumoperitoneum.*

The main conclusions were: (1) The professional person should use words that are as concrete as possible, relate directly to situations which the patient experiences, and are more common and less technical. In accounting for the fact that some of the most widely known words were long and technical whereas some of the least-known words were short, the investigator concludes that direct, personal, concrete experience with a word appears to be a more important factor for the patient's understanding than the length or technicality of a word. (2) Care must be exercised in simplifying technical terms, for although the specialist knows what he means when he uses, for example, the figurative term "bug" for "germ," many patients take this literally and visualize a many-legged creature chewing on their lungs. (3) Anxiety may easily be created in a patient when the specialist uses terms that are misunderstood. For example, "imagine the feelings of a patient who is told that he has a *spread of disease* if he believes, like one patient, that spread of disease means 'cancer,' or if, like another patient, he thinks that *spread of disease* means 'the lungs are about ate up'" (p. 42). (4) Finally, the results strongly indicate that one cannot assume that the more intelligent and better educated patient has a much better understanding of medical vocabulary or that the patient hospitalized for a protracted period is a great deal more sophisticated in terminology than the new patient. In fact, nothing should be taken for granted about the patient's knowledge of the disease and words used to describe it.

Communication and understanding are also facilitated if the patient himself is encouraged to learn some of the technical terms and concepts related to his disability. Once the patient's role as comanager is accepted, it becomes natural that, like a new foreman, he share in "on the job training." Simply written and well illustrated explanatory pamphlets can be of great value in this connection. Fortunately there is a growing collection of good materials which could be used for such purposes in hospitals, clinics, and schools.[5] Discussion of written material with the patient, if possible in groups, provides the opportunity for further clarification of misunderstandings and, what is of the highest value, for the development of adjustive attitudes toward disability.

It would be a mistake, of course, to place undue emphasis in the rehabilitation program on the acquisition of technical terminology and knowledge, for certainly such factors as underlying attitudes between counselor and client, hospital procedures, and family coöperation are also crucial. Nevertheless, the problem of communication as such does suggest not only that specialists must be made aware that what are obvious expressions to them may be unknowns to the client, but also that special

---

[5] For example, there is the pamphlet prepared in coöperation with the American Heart Association under the title *Know Your Heart* (Blakeslee, 1948). There is also the series of brochures dealing with selected disabilities under the title of *Patient Publication,* inaugurated by the Institute of Physical Medicine and Rehabilitation (1957). The first in the series is called a *Primer for Paraplegics and Quadriplegics.*

training is indicated in the use of language which does in fact communicate what is intended. Cantor (*1956*), in discussing specific ways in which the anxiety of the patient may be alleviated, mentions certain written materials designed for the patient that can be of great value and also offers concrete examples of "good" and "bad" descriptions by the physician of the illness and postoperative course. Such discussion is commendable and points up the need for specific training on matters of communication. The research recommendation made by Barker *et al.* (*1953*) should be heeded, namely, that increased knowledge is needed as to the kind of information useful to patients and the manner of presenting this information. "One can foresee the day when physicians [and other practitioners] will be schooled in ways of informing patients of conditions confronting them in terms adapted to the comprehension and emotional needs of the individual" (Barker *et al., 1953*:316).

The issue raised here also calls into question the common practice of making a mystery of a pharmacologic prescription by the use of Latin. It may be desirable in some cases to deceive the patient or to keep certain information from him, but the isolated case is never a justification for generalizing to the whole.

The Importance of Clarifying the Situation

Terminology is one aspect of the broader problem of clarifying the situation to the client. Barker *et al.* (*1953*:312–316) view the usual diagnostic and treatment situation as a new psychological situation for the patient, producing such behavior as conflict, caution, emotionalism, exploration, suggestibility, and vacillation. They point out that much can be done to remove the conditions causing this sort of behavior.

Among the more evident principles is "letting the patient know what will happen when." Except for considerations that may justify concealment (see p. 357), this principle can do much to dispel the anxiety that thrives on the unknown. Janis (*1958*) who studied patients undergoing surgery, presents several lines of evidence supporting the importance of authoritative information concerning the nature and course of treatment in warding off fear (Chap. 25).

The following memory of an incident that occurred in childhood unfortunately also has countless parallels in the experience of adults in treatment situations. How much needless anxiety could have been averted if time had been taken to inform Raymond, age 8, of the nature of the examination:

. . . [the doctor] replaced me on the table and measured me. So far nothing bad had happened to me, but I was still afraid. Each time he lifted me to change my position I was sure that he was going to use on me that terrible contraption that hung from the ceiling. I wanted to beg him not to, but I thought that I had better be quiet and not remind him of it. At last, while I was still unharmed, he turned to Mother and said: "Dress him, please" [Goldman, 1947:27].[6]

Certainly, adequate communication consumes time. And realistic pressures of time as well as energy limitations tend to minimize communication between practitioner and client. Nevertheless, even the harried counselor must regularly pause to remember that often simple and brief explanations can relieve anxiety. Davis (*1958*) presents a valuable discussion of the interplay of diagnostic, professional, and institutional constraints, which lead therapeutic personnel to erect barriers against the communication of relevant facts about the illness to the patient and family.

Barker *et al.* also call attention to office and hospital practices that serve to remove the unknown (*1953:*312–316). In certain dental clinics, children are allowed to familiarize themselves with dental equipment and procedures before they require dental treatment. Visits by expectant mothers to labor and delivery rooms are increasingly encouraged in medical practice. Even the space arrangements for medical equipment and procedures have a psychological impact. It makes psychological sense to raise such questions as: Should control panels in the radiologist's office be exposed or concealed? Should there be a common waiting room for patients as opposed to private rooms? "These questions are not related to the patient's comfort only. The possibility of beginning treatment early, when therapy is most effective, depends upon lowering resistance to securing treatment. Likewise, the therapeutic effect of many treatments is undoubtedly influenced by the emotional reactions of the patient" (Barker *et al., 1953:*314).

Conditions for Withholding Information and Imposing Decisions

The problem of communication leads ultimately to a specific and practical question: Are there not times when information ought to be withheld? So broad a question is bound to receive an affirmative answer, but in the critical consideration of its specifications insights can be found.

Certainly acute illness and trauma are states that preclude full participation on the part of the client. Physically and psychologically the client may be unable to attend even to the general circumstances of his condition, let alone the details concerning etiology, treatment, prognosis, and

---

[6] The selection from Raymond Goldman: *Even the Night,* Copyright 1947, The Macmillan Company, is used with the permission of the publisher.

future planning. His best medicine may be his conviction that he is in the hands of competent specialists interested in his welfare. This reassurance releases his already overtaxed adaptation resources for the main and immediate task of coping with the physiological trauma. Even in these circumstances, however, the patient needs to know more than is commonly assumed. He should be informed of what is happening—for example, that he is being taken to the hospital, that he is being prepared for a blood transfusion, that doctor so and so will operate. This can be done in a simple and reassuring manner without the opinion of the patient being solicited. A main value of such communication is that even if the facts presented are not really comprehended by the patient in his debilitated state, it conveys to him that he is, after all, a respected human being and not an object—a difference of such psychological import that it must not be passed over lightly.

If the condition has a poor prognosis, even ultimate death, should the patient be told? The experts are themselves divided on this question, with perhaps an increasing majority leaning toward the affirmative. But even then it is generally acknowledged that there is really no one answer, since it depends not only upon the type of person with whom one is dealing but also upon such factors as his age and family circumstances. In a panel discussion of this problem as related to cancer, the following pro and con points were made (Cantor and Foxe, *1956:*204–208).

Pro:

• Most patients who undergo radical surgery of the face, breast, or any visible part of the body know, or what may be worse, suspect, that they have cancer anyway. The large majority live well with this knowledge. Why, then, should one embark on the surreptitious approach in the case of an internal tumor?

• Besides, the patient must be informed of early symptoms of possible recurrence; he will be far wiser if he has knowledge of the original process.

• In the case of a fatal cancer, unless he understands the problem, the patient will be more inclined to seek the services of quacks as he goes downhill.

• The adult patient with a cancer of poor prognosis needs to know in order to arrange his affairs wisely.

• When the physician hesitates to speak out, he usually acts a little guilty, failing to look the patient in the eye and shifting his story. His whole manner is conducive to the worst fears of the patient and the poorest doctor-patient relations.

• Cancer, with all its publicity, is much on everyone's tongue nowadays, and with medical advances, hope can be maintained even in the worst cases.

• A patient has a right to know the truth when he asks a direct question.

Con:

• To most people, cancer means an inevitable and miserable end, and patients, even on their deathbed, should never be told they are dying.

• The issue is not a matter of telling the truth, for even those who advocate openness will not deny the importance of glossing over certain facts and stressing the more positive.

• It depends entirely on what you think the patient wants to know. Since most patients do not want the diagnosis presented to them flatly, the matter should be approached obliquely, in some such manner as "This could be a serious condition. I won't know until I have made my studies, but it needs surgery."

• There are a good many patients who have lived comfortably with the knowledge that they had some serious illness, but as soon as the diagnosis of cancer was given them, they did not fare well at all.

Of the six physicans on this panel, only two leaned toward the position that by and large knowledge of cancer should be shielded from the patient, and only a minority of the medical audience favored this belief. At the same time the panel members agreed that an unequivocal "always" or "never" to the original question was impossible, since special factors in the individual case may require special handling.

What does the patient himself think about the divulging or concealment of information? There are no data, as far as we know, concerning cancer, but there is a study reported by Harrower and Herrmann (*1953*) concerning multiple sclerosis, a disease that attacks the central nervous system, that is often progressively and seriously disabling, and that ultimately may lead to death. Of 300 patients with this disease, 90 percent believed that they should be told. Their reasons were: to be able to plan one's life, to be free from the strain of uncertainty, to avoid spending money uselessly, to be able to take better care of oneself physically, and to remove the fear that one might be neurotic. In effect these patients said, "If I am to guide my life satisfactorily, I need to know." Of 34 patients with multiple sclerosis who were not told their diagnosis only 9 percent were encouraged whereas 91 percent were discouraged.

Of course it would be helpful if there were some way to identify reliably those relatively few individuals who would fare better under the "bliss of ignorance." On the basis of the personality characteristics of patients with multiple sclerosis who wanted to be kept informed and of those who did not, it was concluded that the less differentiated, emotionally less mature persons are not concerned about medical details whereas those persons who are more intelligent and have more mature personalities become more apprehensive when information is withheld from them (Harrower and Herrmann, *1953*). On the basis of his work with surgical patients, Janis (*1958*) describes two types of patients requiring some form of quasi-therapeutic interview before information can be of benefit. The "overcontrolled neurotic," who tends to manifest low fear in generally threatening situations, needs help before information will activate the "work of worrying" and thereby motivate him to deal in his fantasy with the sources of danger and discomfort that he may encounter so that in a moment of crisis he will be better prepared. The "undercontrolled neurotic," who tends to show high fear in even mildly threatening situations, will need help before information and the work of worrying can effectively serve the function of psychological preparation.

The following conclusions, based on the preceding data and on certain hypotheses considered elsewhere in this volume, seem warranted:

1. In by far the majority of cases it is wiser to inform the patient of his condition than to conceal it.

2. Certainly where the patient is mature as a person, this course carries little risk.

3. Where the patient appears markedly immature and dependent, one may act more cautiously; but even in this case, if it is incumbent that the patient act realistically, sharing the state of affairs with him under the sustaining power of hope may be more efficacious.

4. Facing the situation realistically need not deny hope, for the two are psychologically not incompatible. Moreover, hope for a *possible* favorable turn of events may even sustain one's resources in acting realistically in terms of the *probable* turn of events.

5. Further research is needed to enable the practitioner more reliably to select those cases where concealment is desirable. We ought not rest content with speculation, for this is an area amenable to investigation. Concealing difficult facts from children, for example, may or may not have the consequences we assume. (Our prejudice, probably shared by most people, is that children should be shielded, but let us remember that this is a prejudice until put to more objective test.)

6. As in all matters of counselor-client relationships, the effects of different rules of behavior or procedure depend on the attributes of the counselor as well as of the client. If the counselor has an abhorrence of cancer, multiple sclerosis, or death, forces in him will resist mention of these facts. Or if the counselor devaluates the person who is ill or who has a disability, he will tend to overestimate the vulnerability of the patient to distressing information. These, by the way, are the kinds of hypotheses readily subject to experimental test.

The question concerning withholding of information can be paralleled by one concerning decision-making—namely: Are there not times when the client ought to be told what to do? The generality of this question again evokes a positive reply and again it is in the specification of circumstances that understanding is achieved. The situation of the acutely ill person, already considered in connection with the dissemination of information, applies equally to decision-making.

There are also times when the client, though not acutely ill, needs to be told what to do and welcomes such direction. The conclusion that the client needs surgery, for example, cannot be left up to him (unless there are at least reasonable alternatives). Such a decision presupposes a body of fact and experience which the patient cannot possibly hope to master in the time at hand. Moreover, although the patient or parent may have been dreading the verdict, he often feels relieved that positive action is being taken. In this situation the decision is made by the specialist and accepted by the patient.

But what about a client's refusal to accept the decision of the specialist? Certainly in instances involving life and death many physicians would justify the use of all sorts of efforts, even ruses, to achieve concurrence. Some physicians, however, would still reserve to the individual the right of self-determination. In less critical cases there is again variability of reaction, some withdrawing from the case when the patient refuses to accept the medical plan, and others continuing treatment with second-best procedures. Among the factors that contribute to this difference is the vital one concerning inalienable rights of the client (see pp. 349–350). It is therefore incumbent upon the specialist to reach an understanding of circumstances which, according to his values and standards, warrant his control over decision-making. This understanding cannot be achieved casually, for it presupposes not only a serious evaluation of the problem of comanagement in rehabilitation but also a coming to terms with one's own values.

FACTORS HINDERING THE MUTUAL SHARING OF THE MANAGEMENT ROLE

Conviction that active participation on the part of the client favors the ultimate goals of rehabilitation is, of course, essential for its effective application. Many factors, however, serve to make its application difficult. Chapter 12 discussed factors in the parent and in the counselor that impede a satisfactory relationship. These have application to the relationship between a counselor and the adult client with a disability as well. In the present context the discussion is recast to give prominence to particular points and to introduce others.

Perhaps the most important factor that hinders management participation on the part of the client is his social-psychological situation. The point has already been made that "help" in general frequently connotes an asymmetrical situation in which the one helped occupies a subservient, less powerful position. Rehabilitation services are special cases of a relationship involving help. Where a marked status differential exists, the counselor occupies the position of a benevolent and authoritative parent, protecting, guiding, and ordering, and the client occupies the position of a child, naïve, uninformed, and irresponsible, with negativistic and unrealistic tendencies.

In these circumstances the attitude that the expert has the answers, or at least should have the answers, is reinforced. The thought that the answers themselves may frequently require the judgments and decisions of the client is quite alien. Instead, it becomes natural for the counselor to take over and to receive the credit for successful rehabilitation, although in analyzing the conditions for such an outcome, the client should share the credit.

Not infrequently, of course, the client expects and wants the counselor to take charge of his case completely. And there are circumstances in which such action is definitely advisable. The acutely ill person often does not have the energy reserve, to say nothing of clarity of intellectual functioning, to become actively involved in alternatives and decisions. On the contrary, it may be important that he allow the therapist to take over with full confidence that he will manage wisely. But the client's readiness to shift responsibility to the therapist is also a second factor often interfering with the goals of rehabilitation. Especially when the success of the endeavor requires unsupervised and independent action on the part of the client is it essential that he be brought into a directorship role as soon as feasible. It is one thing if the patient while on the operating table yields to the wisdom of the surgeon, for both literally and figuratively the matter is out of his hands. But it is quite another thing if, during the patient's convalescence, the doctor, the vocational counselor, or the physical therapist lays out the course of action without genuine consultation with the client. Here the specialist cannot remain at the client's elbow to see that the plan works. Aside from the question of motivation, it is important to remember that the patient who is actively engaged in steering his rehabilitation course is able to take into account circumstances and facts which, if neglected, might lead to dead ends or at best to detours.

The needs of the specialist are also an important determinant of his role. If the specialist has a need to assert himself, to flaunt his knowledge, to buttress his status, then the authoritarian role not only is satisfying but is sought out. There is also the specialist who does not enjoy or who even may become anxious in a real give-and-take relationship. He prefers the more impersonal contact with his client that is possible in an authoritarian role.

One factor impeding comanagement in rehabilitation is so realistic that it is difficult to circumvent. It has to do with time shortage, with the need to spread rehabilitation services to as many people as possible. The unfortunate fact is that involving the client in a comanagement role takes more time than having the specialist accumulate the data and present the prescription. One can retort that time is saved in the end, but the immediate pressures in the light of severe personnel shortages and staggering numbers of clients in need make expedient the authoritative role of the expert. One of the solutions lies obviously in the training of more specialists. Another lies in the use of known techniques which, among other advantages, make possible more efficient use of the specialist's time. Group counseling and guided reading by the client are examples. The use of special personnel, such as social workers, who are able to pave the way for real participation on the part of the client and to act as a mediating link between the client and an overburdened specialist is another possibility.

Yet the point still needs to be underscored that, however pressured the specialist may be, belief in the principle of comanagement can go far in bringing it about. But just because it is easier to subscribe to the concept of comanagement in principle than in practice, the counselor must question at all stages in his relationship with the client whether in fact the client is at the helm helping to steer the course of rehabilitation or whether he is being paternalistically directed as a manipulatable charge who is to follow through but not wonder why.

Chapter 15

An Assessment of the Field of Somatopsychology

A LONG AND SOMEWHAT ARDUOUS PATH HAS BEEN TRAVERSED IN OUR search for understanding some of the psychological aspects of disability. Before some final statements are attempted, we shall review some of the precursors that heralded current efforts in the broad area of deciphering man by his physique. In the main they do not deal with somatopsychology as such. They are mentioned, however, so that somatopsychology can be seen within the perspective of the total effort to discover or impute physique-personality relationships.

THE HERITAGE OF SOMATOPSYCHOLOGY

Since time immemorial, men have held firm beliefs concerning the relationship between all sorts of physical attributes and personality. These have ranged from the revelatory signs of bumps on the head, physiognomic features, and body chemistry to the divinatory powers of the lines on the palms of the hands and soles of the feet. The widely divergent efforts have had the common goal of demonstrating that man's personality can, in fact, be read from physical constants. Here we can present only the barest highlights of some of the most relevant excursions dealing with this problem.[1]

Physiognomy, a method which attempts to discern character and temperament from the outward appearance of man, particularly from his facial features, is one of the oldest of all body-reading systems. Treatises on this first appeared in Aristotelian times and continue to appear today. The long historical line, however, is not a monotonous repetition of points

---

[1] Maisel (*1953*) has written a penetrating review of the various specific attempts to read personality from physical signs. Briefer historical accounts of "constitutional psychology" can also be found in Allport (*1937*) and Sheldon (*1940, 1944*).

laid down earlier, for modifications were introduced that reflected the beliefs as well as cultist trends of the times. Thus, when astrology was at its height, man's countenance was linked to the stars.

The effort to specify the facial signs that betrayed personality was often complex. Lavater, one of the most ardent eighteenth-century physiognomists, devised an inventory of hundreds of facial types with their corresponding personalities. Although primary emphasis was placed on facial features, other parts of the body were not excluded. For example, Lavater claimed that he could judge a person by the shape and movements of his hands, portending the modern emphasis on "expressive movements" (see p. 371).

Phrenology, historically one of the more important of the body arts, was devised by Franz Joseph Gall, an early nineteenth-century German anatomist. It was based on the assumption that man's faculties, over forty of which were eventually posited, were localized within the brain in such a way that the contours of the skull correctly mirrored their character. For example, one of the presumed faculties was acquisitiveness, and it was held that the corresponding external bump on the skull was prominent in pickpockets. Although these notions, in their specificity, hold no currency today, the study of the brain itself, stimulated by the work of Gall and his pupil Spurzheim, has led to important anatomical discoveries.

That body-reading systems had and continue to have interest far beyond the academic becomes clear when their implications for criminology are examined. As far as we know, the uglier of two suspects always tended to be considered the guilty one. The innovation of rigorous jurisdictional procedures to hold in check such bias attests to this. Lombroso, a nineteenth-century Italian physician who had a tremendous impact on criminology, anthropology, and constitutional psychology, made the most vocal and systematic attempt to prescribe a criminal physical type (1911). He tied together presumed physical stigmata by a principle of atavism which averred that the criminal was a throwback with degenerate mental and physical features. Darwin's theory of evolution as expressed in the then recently acclaimed *Origin of Species* provided the biological basis for Lombrosian notions. The criminal could, so it was avowed, be detected by physical features that pointed to his evolutionary inferior forebears, such as large jaws, receding or apelike chin, harelip, etc. Although during Lombroso's own lifetime the substantive content of his beliefs was discarded by many, the underlying notion that there are physical characteristics which, through one mechanism or another, are associated with asocial behavior has persisted to the present, as for example in the work of Sheldon (see pp. 367–369) and the less generally accepted work of Hooton (1939).

In addition to the visible and predominantly structural aspects of physique, events within the organism, notably the workings of the "humors," were also held accountable for man's character. The humoral doctrines were built upon the notions of Empedocles, the poet, philosopher, and statesman of the fifth century before Christ, who considered the universe to consist of four basic elements—air, fire, water, and earth —each of which had special properties definable by the dimensions "dryness" and "warmth." Air was warm and moist, whereas earth was cold and dry. Hippocrates, the "father of medicine," who lived during the same era, proposed that each of these four elements was represented in man's body by a humor, the relative prominence of which determined the individual's temperament. The theory evolved that men were sanguine, melancholic, choleric, or phlegmatic, depending upon their internal make-up, which in turn was related to the cosmic building blocks. For example, the person who flared with temper, the so-called choleric personality, owed his disposition to one particular humor, yellow bile, which corresponded to fire and its properties of warmth and dryness. Over the ages, particular humoral suppositions underwent change, and though modern thought has forsaken the four temperaments and their cosmological reference, our metaphoric language still reflects the humoral beliefs of the past. We still refer to damp spirits and dry humor, to individuals who have gall and who are cold-blooded, to the jaundiced eye and the splenetic personality.

Modern endocrinology, based on systematic test and observation, has accumulated considerable knowledge about the bodily secretions that stabilize functioning or create anomalies when there is imbalance. Cretinism, acromegaly, diabetes, hyperthyroidism, and many other conditions are due to faulty endocrine systems. Of this there can be little doubt. But again the temptation to draw far-reaching conclusions regarding consequent personality effects, conclusions based on supposition rather than on systematic observation, has been more than some could withstand. A person's readiness to anger, his state of depression or his happy-go-lucky outlook, has been attributed to particular combinations and lacks in the functioning of internal secretions.

Although serious research on the contribution of biochemical and physiological processes to personality appears promising, we can only agree with Maisel's (*1953*) conclusion: "Yet to reduce the phenomenon of personality to the interplay of body juices amounts to little more than a mechanical formulation of a human being—a complex entity whose dynamic brilliance gives the lie to segmental simplism at every turn" (pp. 196–197).[2] No matter how important a role glandular and other physio-

---

[2] Edward Maisel, *Meet a Body,* by permission of the Institute for the Crippled and Disabled.

logical phenomena play in personality formation, it is not likely that they can ever claim the whole matrix of determinants, for surely such psychological concepts as ideas about the self, beliefs concerning "oughts," expectations, and many, many others, as well as the sociopsychological conditions underlying them do not seem to be negligible.

In disputing the extravagant claims of body-reading systems, investigators took advantage of the newer methods of science, notably those which insisted upon adequate controls and the statistical treatment of sampling and other errors. The accumulated evidence has virtually discredited all the specific physical signs that had been used in times past as personality indexes. Nevertheless, in spite of refinements of measurement and perhaps greater appreciation of the human being as a complex whole, the underlying conviction that man reveals himself through visible aspects of his physique has not been shaken. Several lines of investigation that distinguish the modern trend are described below.

CURRENT APPROACHES LINKING PHYSIQUE AND PERSONALITY

Among the most prominent and systematic efforts on the modern scene is the work of Sheldon (*1940, 1942, 1949*) and his collaborators, generally referred to as "constitutional psychology." Sheldon's closest historical ancestor was Kretschmer (*1925*), who described physique in terms of four body types and related each to certain personality traits. For example, Kretschmer's classification "asthenic," designating the long-limbed, slender, narrow-chested person with underdeveloped musculature, was thought to indicate a tendency to be shy, sensitive, and cold and to become schizophrenic in the event of mental illness.

Sheldon's somatotype theory is far more complex than Kretschmer's and allows for a greater variety of individual differences.[3] Sheldon (*1940*) considers three types of body build corresponding to the embryonic layer that has shown predominant development: (1) The endoderm, or visceral layer, which predisposes the person to a soft, round physique, this component of physique being called *endomorphy;* (2) the mesoderm, or muscular layer, which gives rise to a strong muscular physique designated as *mesomorphy;* (3) the ectoderm, or layer involving the nerves and sense organs, which favors a slender, delicate physique termed *ectomorphy.* The variability in human nature is provided for by rating these dimensions along a seven-point scale with reference to five areas of the body and by rating several secondary components of physique such as

[3] For a relatively brief but clear and comprehensive review of Sheldon's work see Hall and Lindzey (*1957*).

"dysplasia" (a measure of the unevenness of the three primary components as they appear in different regions of the body). It has been possible to achieve adequate ratings of somatotype by the use of seventeen physical measurements derived from photographs and such additional data on the subject as age and weight.

The second aspect of Sheldon's task required a system of rating temperament that could then be correlated to the somatotype (*1942*). After a series of exacting studies, three components of temperament were isolated, each being defined by 20 traits that are related to one another and negatively correlated with the traits belonging to the other two temperament clusters. *Viscerotonia,* for example, is characterized by a love of comfort, relaxation, food, sociability, etc., *somatonia,* by a love of vigorous physical activity, adventure, risk taking, etc., and *cerebrotonia* by discomfort in social situations, secretiveness, inhibition, etc. Only after long acquaintance is the subject assigned ratings of 1 to 7 on each of the 60 traits that serve as criteria for the 3 components of temperament.

Studies concerning the degree of association between temperament and physique based on Sheldon's somatotyping and temperament scale have revealed substantial correlations between the two, although the findings of scholars not associated with Sheldon's laboratory have been less spectacular than those of Sheldon himself. Thus the person whose somatotype is high in mesomorphy is inclined to (though definitely not compelled to) display the temperamental characteristics of somatonia.

Sheldon has also applied his measurement instruments to the study of delinquents (*1949*) and is convinced that physique and the associated temperament do differentiate delinquents from normals and that they even differentiate subvarieties of delinquents. Thus Lombroso, whose theories of criminal physical type were cast aside by the sophisticates of modern science and methodology, is being somewhat vindicated by Sheldon's work, although the theory of atavism remains unsupported. Sheldon's complex indexes of basic physical components seem to show distributions according to one's asocial history, at least to some degree. Thus, among delinquents, Sheldon has found a much greater elevation of mesomorphy and a marked absence of ectomorphy.

Sheldon has also found a relationship between his components of physique and psychiatric diagnosis. In addition, the evidence that there is some relationship between constitutional type and propensity to certain kinds of organic disease, such as cancer, gall bladder disease, and duodenal ulcer appears to be accumulating. The evaluation of Sheldon's contributions by Hall and Lindzey is offered here as a concluding statement: ". . . an over-all appraisal of the many studies conducted since Sheldon began his work will lead the reader to accept the existence of a significant and interesting relation between physique and personality, but will leave him unconvinced that the relation is so close as Sheldon seems to imply" (*1957*:374).[4]

How Sheldon's findings bear upon the relation of physical disability to personality is still unclear. If it will be demonstrated that certain types of disability, congenital or acquired, are associated with particular somato-types, a relation between physical disability and personality via somato-typology would seem indicated, since somatotype and temperament are associated to some extent. As we have already noted, however, with the measurement instruments used in disability research to date, disability groups have not been distinguishable by personality criteria with any degree of consistency, and the overlap between groups studied appears to be the prominent finding. It has yet to be shown that physical disability groupings of the sorts we have been considering represent anything more than phenotypic classifications with little diagnostic significance for inferring temperament or personality.

Although Sheldon stresses biological determinants of behavior and personality, he by no means excludes other factors mediating physique and personality. This is especially important in the context of our problem, that of relating physical disability to personality. Sheldon also acknowl-edges the possibility that a person with a particular physique achieves success in certain activities and interactions with people, which behavior then becomes reinforced. Other people with similar physiques have similar experiences and therefore develop similar patterns of behavior and temperament. Sheldon also recognizes the fact that a given physique carries with it cultural expectations of how the person will feel and behave predisposing the individual to conform to that role.

A second attempt to discern personal traits from physical constants was initiated by the work of Brunswik and Reiter in the early 1930's. Instead of dealing with isolated physiognomic features, which have been shown to offer little, these investigators attempted to discover how the *interrelationship* between such factors as distance between eyes, length of nose, proportion of mouth to chin, and so on affected various observers. The subjects were asked to judge almost 200 schematized sketches on the 7 qualities: (1) Mood (gay-sad) (2) Age (young-old) (3) Beauty (beautiful-ugly) (4) Character (good-bad) (5) Likability (likable-un-likable) (6) Intelligence (intelligent-unintelligent) (7) Energy (energetic-unenergetic) (Brunswik and Reiter, *1937*). Judgments of physiognomic or personality qualities were shown to depend upon the geometric features varied in the sketches. For example, a high mouth produces the impres-sion of gayety and youth, whereas a low mouth yields judgments of sad-

[4] Reprinted with permission from C. S. Hall and G. Lindzey, *Theories of Personality,* 1957, John Wiley & Sons, Inc.

ness, age, and bad character. Eyes that are far apart and a short nose exert influences similar to those of a high mouth, though to a lesser extent. The longest noses generally produce unfavorable impressions.

This experiment was repeated with feature-patterns arranged in pairs and representing opposite extremes for each personality quality, as determined by the previous study. The subject had to indicate which of each of the pairs presented reflected the quality in question. The results clearly corroborated the earlier work (Samuels, *1939*). Moreover, in still another study the same judgments were elicited from subjects with brain disease and subjects with mental illness (Halstead, *1951*). Developmental and comparative data were also collected by Brunswik, using children and adolescents from predominantly white, predominantly Negro, Chinese, and Indian reservation schools, the results again being borne out (Brunswik, *1956:*113). Thus, the physiognomic impressions of the geometric features that were experimentally controlled appear to be highly generalizable across populations including persons with brain damage and psychosis as well as differences in developmental level. Brunswik has summarized additional studies in which the impression value of the eye region, the mouth area, the hairline, and of the grooming of hair, beard, and moustache were investigated by means of schematic faces (Brunswik, *1956:*114–115). A similar approach, with representations of the full human figure, has also been used (Brunswik, *1956:*116–119).

When photographs of real people with facial features of the proportions appearing in the schematized faces were judged, however, a marked drop in uniformity of judgment occurred (Samuels, *1939*). This result, together with divergencies of the impressions of different photographs all having the same facial measurements in terms of the variables studied, led the investigator to conclude that there is a "relative lack of influence of the Brunswik and Reiter cues in the real faces" (Samuels, *1939:*25).

It must be remembered that the concern of these studies has not been with the *validity* of the judgments but rather with the determination of factors that *influence* the judgments. Although application to real faces and people has still to be demonstrated, the approach appears promising. After all, the art of caricature by emphasizing certain features in relation to others seems to bring out the personality in the physical likeness.

Another direction of research interest is represented by the study of what has come to be described as "expressive movements." Instead of dealing with structural relations and body constants, the attempt here is to view the more active aspects in the belief that these more vividly mirror underlying personality dynamics. This belief is not without confirmation in everyday experience; gait, hand movements, and facial expressions are a language which we seem to understand whether it be solely relied on as in stage pantomime or elaborated verbally as in **drama and ordinary** interpersonal relations. A person whose jaw is set and who strides across the room with hands clenched behind him gives an aura to his feelings that is apparent without the aid of the deciphering measures of science.

Of the investigations that have contributed to the modern study of expressive movements, the work of Allport and his collaborators is indicative of both the general approach and the findings. (See especially Allport and Vernon, *1933* and Estes, *1938.*) In their series of studies the investigator recorded such indexes of behavior as strength of handshake, handwriting, voice, speed of walking, amount of movement during natural speech, and speed of reading. Two main problems were investigated: (1) In order to determine whether expressive movements of different parts of the body, however functionally disparate, do indeed bear some resemblance to one another, they were intercorrelated. (2) In order to determine whether there is a congruence between expressive movements and the attitudes, traits, values, and other dispositions of the "inner personality," some of the indexes were matched with independently derived personality sketches of the subject.

In regard to both these objectives, positive findings were obtained, though the consistency was not absolute and the accuracy of reflecting personality not strikingly great. (See also Wolff, *1943.*) The results do show that one's style of moving, his gestures, handwriting, voice, and personality are interrelated, but only to some extent. This, of course, is in line with the fact that all behavior is multidetermined. The style of behavior is not solely a matter of idiosyncratic traits, for there is also the role of sociocultural and biological determinants, which are more or less nonpersonal in character, as well as the fact that transitory states of moods and organic conditions, though affecting the immediate manner of a person, do not necessarily affect the more enduring aspects of personality. Besides, insofar as personality itself is not integrated in every aspect, expressive movements as reflectors of personality could be expected to show inconsistencies also.

Another approach in the never-ending search to find body correlates of personality is represented by the scope of this book—namely, the field of somatopsychology. In the following sections an attempt will be made to reduce the findings scattered among the somatopsychological problems already dealt with to the order of orienting principles and conclusions.

OVERALL FINDINGS OF RESEARCH IN SOMATOPSYCHOLOGY

Inconsistencies in Results and Their Usefulness

Inconsistency is fairly typical of the status of many of the findings in the field of somatopsychology. Indeed, it is an integral feature of the growth of all empirical sciences. As Feigl (*1953*) points out, "Factual knowledge cannot attain either the absolute precision or necessity of pure mathematics. The knowledge claimed in the natural and the social sciences is a matter of successive approximations and of increasing degrees of confirmation" (p. 9). Inconsistency of results, moreover, may be an important finding; it may challenge the investigator to reappraise both hypotheses and research techniques in an attempt to bring together the divergencies.

An example of inconsistent findings in somatopsychological research is the summary of 15 studies on blindness that have utilized personality inventories (Barker *et al.*, *1953*:282).

1. In 6 studies, both the subscale test scores and the total test scores are in the direction of greater maladjustment for the blind as compared with seeing groups.

2. In the other 9 studies, the visually handicapped did not consistently fall significantly below seeing controls on subscale and total test scores.

3. Studies using the same tests produce different results. Of two studies using the California Test of Personality, one showed that the blind scored lower than seeing controls on social adjustment, and the second showed the two groups equal in this respect. Of two studies using the introversion scale of the Bernreuter Personality Inventory, one found that the majority of blind subjects scored as introverts, whereas the other showed the blind to be no different from the controls. Moreover, the investigators of both studies note that test results and observational data were not in agreement.

Even the more sophisticated type of laboratory experiment, which avoids certain methodological weaknesses common to the use of personality inventories, shows diversity of results to be the rule. This is well illustrated by the review of studies on the goal-setting behavior or level of aspiration of persons with disabilities. Some of the studies indicate that the goal-setting behavior of the subjects who had a disability differed in some way from their normal controls (Rotter, *1943;* McAndrew, *1948;* Wenar, *1953;* Rutledge, *1954*). Others, however, found no differences (Arluck, *1941;* Heisler, *1951;* Johnson, *1954*).

Such inconsistency and diversity among findings force serious attention to the dangers of overgeneralization. With respect to subject overgeneralization, the matter can be put simply by the obvious although often ignored principle that because certain subjects with the same disability show certain reactions, it does not follow that all or most subjects with the disability behave similarly.

There is also overgeneralization of a different sort, *behavior* overgeneralization. Not infrequently, on the basis of one behavioral manifestation, conclusions are made as to the generality of that behavior; yet it is entirely possible that different situations would yield different results. An interesting example is found in an experiment on rigidity in the personality of deaf children (Johnson, *1954*). The investigator used not one but several different tests of rigidity. It was found that the relative rigidity of deaf children as compared with their hearing controls depended on the particular testing situation. The experimenter, therefore, was led to the conclusion that "deaf children are *not necessarily* more rigid than hearing children. . . . Deaf children may sometimes, in some situations, behave less rigidly than hearing children" (p. 71).

This conclusion is far-reaching because it directs thinking to additional situational and personal variables important for rigidity, which can then be pursued in continued investigation. For example, the experimenter, on the basis of the nature of the situations that produced "inconsistent" results in relative rigidity between deaf and hearing children, hypothesized that the deaf will be flexible in many situations that involve acute visual perception (p. 75). The necessity of including an adequate sampling of situations in research as well as an adequate sampling of subjects has been urged upon psychological science by Brunswik (*1947*) and is referred to as the problem of representative design.

Inconsistency and diversity among findings, in addition to alerting the investigator against overgeneralization and toward the formulation of new hypotheses, also force serious attention to one of the most important yet least accepted principles in somatopsychology, namely that *somatic abnormality as a physical fact is not linked in a direct or simple way to psychological behavior*. Heterogeneity of reaction to crippling is a necessary result. Possible underlying psychological factors, which might account for the differences in behavior, must become the main focus of investigation.

General Results

The following summary is not designed to list factual details that have been gathered in somatopsychological research. Rather we shall attempt generalizations of some of the broad areas that have commanded interest.

1. There is no substantial indication that persons with an impaired physique differ *as a group* in their *general or overall adjustment* (Barker and Wright, *1954*). (This statement does not apply to impairments of clearly psychosomatic origin, though even in such instances the evidence is far less consistent than might be expected.) Some studies show a somewhat greater number of persons with physical disabilities who have lower adjustment scores than their controls but in most of these cases the differences may well be experimental artifacts. At this time, it can be said

with considerable assurance that the great overlap in the level of adjustment of physically handicapped and nonhandicapped groups is at least as significant as the relatively small margin of difference found in some of the studies.

This is not to say, of course, that most persons with physical disabilities are well adjusted, any more than it is to say that most physically "normal" persons are well adjusted. Good adjustment can refer to a conceptual relationship between the person and the environment independently of how it is distributed in the population at large. But the findings do point strongly to the conclusion that most persons with physical limitations make about as good a personality adjustment as do the nonhandicapped.

2. There is also no clear evidence of an association between types of physical disability and particular personality characteristics (Barker and Wright, 1954). Such folklore as that of the euphoria and hypersexuality of the tuberculous and the paranoia of the deaf are not supported by available data. Even in disabilities involving gross neural lesions, as in cerebral palsy, individuals do not exhibit common characteristics of personality (Barker et al., 1953:64; Cruickshank and Bice, 1955).

The following statement by Johnson (1950) with reference to stutterers may be generalized with impunity at the present stage of our knowledge to other physical disability groups. The statement is based on over 100 scientific studies of stuttering in older children and adults, and 6 investigations involving more than 200 young children, stutterers and nonstutterers: "I believe any expert can safely be challenged to go into a room in which there are 100 adult men and women and pick out the ten stutterers whom we shall include in the group. He may use any tests whatever, except that he may not hear anyone speak, nor may he obtain any information about each individual's personality and mental ability so long as this information in any way relates to the question of how the person speaks or used to speak. I should be surprised if the expert could make significantly better selections with his test than he could by means of the eenie-meenie-minie-moe" (p. 7). The specific kinds of direct cues to be avoided, of course, will have to be specified for the particular disability in question.

The same point has been made in a study of whether emotional disturbance, when it occurs, assumes pathognomic patterns among children with cerebral palsy (Miller, 1958). The children with cerebral palsy and the physically normal children had been referred to a child guidance clinic because of severe learning and behavior problems. The conclusion reached was that if only test data on these groups were available, with no identifying data as to the physical handicap, one would be unable to select out the handicapped except as problems in perception and coördination existed. The test data gathered in the study included tests of intelligence and projective tests of personality.

It is not impossible, however, that better data will reveal general personality patterns associated with *more precisely defined* disability groupings. For example, in a broad and careful study of some personality characteristics of epileptics (Arluck, *1941*), it was found that the so-called "epileptic personality," characterized by such specific traits as irascibility, impulsiveness, and egocentricity, certainly does not apply to the nondeteriorated epileptic. And even should continued research show that they apply to deteriorated epileptics as a group (even on this point the results are unclear), *the individual variations are as important as the group trends* for at least two reasons. From the point of view of general scientific laws and principles it is these variations which suggest new leads for the discovery of "differences that make a difference." From the point of view of clinical practice, it is the person as an individual who must be treated.

An enlightening study by Levine (*1956*) also brings out the necessity of defining carefully the particular population that is being evaluated among the larger group of persons with the disability. She examined the productions on the Wechsler test of intelligence and the Rorschach test of personality of adolescent girls attending a residential school for the deaf. Although there was an absence of traditional Rorschach signs of emotional disturbance, the personality patterns of the deaf subjects were characterized by such features as mental and emotional impassiveness, strong egocentric affectivity, and personal inflexibility. Instead of generalizing to deafness as a whole, the crucial questions raised point to the fact that these children, who lost their hearing early in life, acquired language "fragment by fragment, slowly, painstakingly, in contrived situations, often out of context, and usually out of rhythm with the growing child's needs of the moment" (p. 164). The significance of isolation and protection of the children in many residential schools is also pointed out. The important end product of such an analysis is that thinking is directed to the particularization of conditions that predispose toward certain kinds of functioning (which then, of course, require further investigation as such) rather than to statements that blanket broad population groupings simply because they are alike on the surface in some way (see also Wittkower, *1949,* for psychologically differentiable subgroups among those with tuberculosis).

3. Although personality patterns have not been found consistently to distinguish disability groups as a whole, certain behaviors rather directly connected with the limitations have. An obvious example is the greater ease with which the able-bodied get about as compared with the paraplegic. An example one step removed is the fact that the blind are likely to be more adept at facial vision (obstacle perception through nonvisual cues) than the seeing, and even more so than the deaf (Meyerson, *1953*). But if we look for examples more remote from the direct limitations of

the disability itself, our search yields no highly generalizable facts. Even such an area as the level of independence from assistance and supervision by others attained by deaf children as compared with hearing children, for example, requires a good deal of specification of the findings. At the very least, the following must be mentioned: (1) no significant retardation in level of independence has been found in acoustically handicapped children of preschool ages (Avery, *1948*) and (2) as for school-age children, significant levels of retardation have been found among those attending residential schools for the deaf (Bradway, *1937*; Burchard and Myklebust, *1942*) but not among those attending day schools for the deaf (Streng and Kirk, *1938*).

But in these examples we are dealing with specific behaviors in specific situations. How these relate to differences in adjustment and personality is not clear. By the same token, the vastly different behavior of our pioneer forebears as compared with persons living in our own times by no means bespeaks *ipso facto* differences in personality and adjustment. Such differences may exist, but they need to be shown through systematic study, uncontaminated by folklore and biased expectation.

4. Although consistent group trends with respect to personality and adjustment have not been found, studies of individuals convincingly indicate that physical disability has a profound affect on the person's life, as our ample use of personal documents affirms. However, its effect is not of a direct, consistent kind. Of eight subjects with crippling conditions described in the literature, one is reported to be immature, nervous, unpopular, suspicious, and unhappy to the point of serious maladjustment; five are described as relatively more immature, socially withdrawn, or emotionally unexpressive than the control subjects, but well within the normal range; and two are said to be normal, integrated and socially outgoing individuals (Barker *et al.*, *1953*:62). In each of these cases, physique is credited with being a factor in the etiology of the reported adjustment. However, it is clear that if these eight cases were considered together as a group, their "average" behavior would not differ appreciably from that of their normal controls, and the correlation between disablement and level of adjustment would be close to zero.

5. Public, verbalized attitudes toward persons with disabilities are on the average mildly favorable. An appreciable minority openly express negative attitudes, though these are more frequently revealed indirectly (Barker and Wright, *1954*). Conditions giving rise to positive as well as negative attitudes can be seen in some instances primarily as products of the cultural milieu and in others as residing in the nature of social-psychological man.

6. The evidence is rather clear that the attitudes of parents toward their children who have a disability tend to the extreme more often than

toward their nondisabled children, centering about the following patterns: oversolicitude, rejection, pressing for accomplishments beyond the child's abilities, inconsistent attitudes (Barker and Wright, *1954*). Overprotection appears to occur more frequently than overt rejection. And genuinely positive attachments of parents to their disabled children are not infrequent.

7. What evidence there is on attitudes of persons toward their own disabilities suggests that these attitudes vary widely, have little relation to the degree of disability in massed data, are related to personality characteristics existing prior to the disability (Barker, *et al., 1953:*85), and are influenced in the direction of acceptance via change in the person's value system (Dembo, Leviton, Wright, *1956*).

Other generalizations could be enumerated here, such as those pertaining to the nature of the ordinary kinds of interaction between persons with disabilities and those without, which bring about gratification on the one hand and distress on the other. But the foregoing serves as a highly generalized picture of the findings of somatopsychological research in several important areas and leads to a consideration of one of the fundamental research principles, namely, the necessity for seeking underlying factors that will bring lawfulness into the relations between physique and personality or behavior.

NECESSITY FOR CONSIDERING THE UNDERLYING FACTORS

The failure to find basic personality differences between groups of persons with specific disabilities and nondisabled subjects undoubtedly has theoretical implications of such import that, indeed, these "negative" results are not negative at all. They indicate that persons with physical deviations are not a homogeneous group psychologically, that physical disability is a surface (phenotypic) classification. They point to the necessity of getting below the surface, of leaving the nonpsychological realm of physique and of seeking its underlying psychological significance. This is one of the main products of the great amount of investigation that has been carried on, and it is an important product.

The basic situation appears to be that the somatopsychological connection between physique and behavior is not direct but is mediated by what have come to be called *intervening variables*. The following example may clarify this. It is not the disabled physique as such that makes the person hide his deformed foot, but his attitudes toward it. These attitudes are the intervening variables that "logically" connect physique on the one hand with behavior on the other. Thus, where A's attitudes differ significantly from *B*'s—let us say that there is shame in the one case and acceptance in the other—their behavior may be expected to differ also. It is possible, then, to investigate the specific hypotheses connecting attitudes toward disability with behavioral consequences, or to interpret existing research findings in terms of these constructs. But, according to this orientation, if one were to group together all persons with a deformity of the foot, the observed behavior must show wide variations, depending on the heterogeneity of the intervening variables (attitudes in this case). And since intervening psychological variables are affected by many conditions, physique cannot be *the* factor determining them; hence the lack of one to one or strong relations between physique and behavior.

This point can be looked at in another way. The variability of psychological correlates of disability means that the same social situation is not linked mechanically to personality effects. For example, although a disability may subject a person to disparagement and discrimination, it does not mean that this lower status position, even if it occurs with upsetting frequency, *will* lead to these or those personality changes. It depends on what is happening within the person, and these adjustive or maladjustive changes in turn are affected by many variables in addition to those that inhere in the offending social situation.

In spite of whatever self-destructive tendencies, or even instincts, have been posited in man, the human being has a tremendous capacity for reëvaluating, for altering his aspirations, for changing the circumstances of his life, so that he can better cope with the social-psychological situations surrounding him. These adjustive changes have their source within the person. But adjustment is a continuing process that goes on at both loci of the person-environment interaction; changes that have their source outside the person also occur. Family, friends, and the larger society adapt to the person, for better or worse, just as the person adapts to them, and in so doing, these outsiders do change the psychological environment of the person. This interplay between events within the person and events from without, ever changing in the efforts of the person to manage more comfortably, wisely, happily, ever changing through outside influences, has the inevitable consequence that heterogeneity of effects on the person is to be expected.

This need not mean that lawfulness does not exist. It would suggest rather that one cannot predict psychological phenomena, particularly as they apply to the individual, from simple physical variables. In the words of Maisel, "neither the occult nor science has yet provided us with any sure-fire system for sizing up human beings from their physiques" (*1953*:233).

Much research has already been done in which physique as a *surface characteristic* has been taken as the basis for distinguishing the groups under study. And in most instances, as we have seen, the consequences have been an accumulation of helter-skelter findings. The time has come when we can look forward to more frequent groupings of subjects according to their psychological situations (intervening variables) which the investigator believes are significant for somatopsychological understanding. The problem becomes, then, one of determining the nature of the variables connecting physique and its effects.

The following list of some of the conditions and mechanisms (intervening variables) that have been proposed by various scholars to account for the psychological effects of physical disabilities is taken from Barker *et al.* (*1953*:92–93): (1) compensation for inferiorities, (2) easy narcissistic satisfactions deriving from pain and uniqueness, (3) lack of normal play and expressive actions, (4) easy cathexis to disabled part, (5) unrelated anxieties transferred to bodily handicap, (6) blame of parents, (7) feeling of guilt for hostility toward parents, (8) body image at variance with reality, (9) efforts to achieve social acceptance, (10) dependent, demanding, apathetic behavior deriving from oversolicitous protective situation, (11) variable, conflicting behavior in response to variable, inconsistent attitudes of others, (12) goals beyond achievement possibilities because of pressure from parents and physical, social, and economic restrictions, (13) conflict between withdrawal and compensatory tendencies, (14) acceptance of disability as a punishment for sin, (15) retaliatory behavior for "unjust" treatment by nature, (16) self-concept, (17) degree of acceptance of disability, (18) value systems, (19) cultural role of persons with disabilities, (20) intergroup dynamics.

To this list we could add other somatopsychological variables and such other mechanisms as covered by the terms "neural," "endocrine," "constitutional," and "psychosomatic." The list is long and varied. In the present stage of knowledge concerning somatopsychological effects of physical disability, it is advantageous to have a variety of theories of the sort that stimulate inquiry.

Some notion of the fruitfulness of intervening variables, we would like to think, is contained within the present volume. The emphasis here has been on such concepts as (1) values, (2) status position, (3) the need for social and personal acceptance, (4) the self-concept, (5) gradients connecting attributes with the self, (6) spread, (7) goals and standards of behavior, (8) acceptance of loss through change in values, (9) expectation discrepancy with its resolution in expectation revision, alteration of the apparent reality, and anormalization of the person, (10) the requirement of mourning, (11) the principle of positive identification, (12) overlapping situations, (13) new situations, (14) motivation, (15) coping and succumbing aspects of disability, (16) requirements in cause-effect relations, and others. There is much room for further conceptual clarification. Some of the explanatory concepts will prove expendable under the critical scrutiny of research. Others will take their place. Some will become more fruitful as the precision of their definitions is increased. In any case, it seems clear that henceforth, theoretical guidance, complemented by careful methodological checks in the testing program, will be essential in the effort to reach greater understanding of somatopsychological problems.

One final point ought to be made explicit. Progress does not wait upon research effort alone. Existing values, concepts, and factual information can go far in relieving suffering, in aiding social and psychological rehabilitation, if only they are applied more genuinely and generally in the ordinary affairs of life as well as among the many special enterprises that society as a whole needs to undertake. The present volume may have contributed to the appreciation of the far-reaching implications of the tetrad of values and concepts singled out by Linck as among the most important:

(1) the handicapped are a normal part of today's society and do not exist as a group apart with separate lives. Their needs and rights are the same as those of any other person; their problems are the problems of all people and should be considered as a part of the whole society; (2) the handicapped person should be regarded as a whole person, physically, mentally, socially, and emotionally, rather than within the narrow confines of his handicap; (3) plans should be made with and for the handicapped person on the basis of abilities, not disabilities, and of capabilities, not limitations, to most fully develop his assets; and (4) if these plans are to be reflected in care and treatment services for the handicapped, teamwork of the highest order is required of professional personnel in the medical, therapeutic, educational and social and vocational adjustment fields [and, we should like to stress, teamwork including the patient and family members] [Linck, 1954:8].

Bibliography

Adler, A. (*1917a*). *Study of organ inferiority and its psychical compensations.* New York: Nervous and Mental Disease Publishing Co.

Adler, A. (*1917b*). *The neurotic constitution.* New York: Moffat, Yard.

Adler, A. (*1924*). *The practice and theory of individual psychology.* New York: Harcourt, Brace.

Alexander, F. (*1938*). Remarks about the relation of inferiority feelings to guilt feelings. *Int. J. Psychoanal.,* **19,** 41–49.

Allan, W. S. (*1958*). Rehabilitation: a community challenge. New York: Wiley.

Allen, F. H., & Pearson, G. H. J. (*1928*). The emotional problems of the physically handicapped child. *British J. Med. Psychol.,* **8,** 212–236.

Allport, G. W. (*1937*). *Personality: a psychological interpretation.* New York: Holt.

Allport, G. W. (*1943*). The ego in contemporary psychology. *Psychol. Rev.,* **50,** 451–478.

Allport, G. W., & Kramer, B. M. (*1946*). Some roots of prejudice, *J. Psychol.,* **22,** 9–39.

Allport, G. W., & Vernon, P. E. (*1933*). *Studies in expressive movement.* New York: Macmillan.

Arluck, E. W. (*1941*). A study of some personality characteristics of epileptics. *Arch. Psychol.,* **37** (263).

Asch, S. E. (*1946*). Forming impressions of personality. *J. abnorm. soc. Psychol.,* **41,** 258–290.

Asch, S. E. (*1952*). *Social psychology.* Englewood Cliffs: Prentice-Hall.

Ausubel, D. P. (*1952*). *Ego development and the personality disorders.* New York: Grune & Stratton.

Avery, C. (*1948*). Social competence of pre-school, acoustically handicapped children. *J. except. Child.,* **15,** 71–73.

Baker, L. (*1946*). *Out on a limb.* New York, London: McGraw-Hill.

Baldwin, A. L. (*1955*). *Behavior and development in childhood.* New York: Dryden.

Bard, M. (*1952*). The sequence of emotional reactions in radical mastectomy patients. *Public Health Reports,* **67** (11), 1144–1148.

Barker, L. S., Schoggen, M., Schoggen, P., & Barker, R. G. (*1952*). The frequency of physical disability in children: a comparison of three sources of information, *Child Develpm.,* **23,** 216–226.

Barker, R. G. (*1938*). The effect of frustration upon cognitive ability. *Charact. & Pers.,* **7,** 145–150.

Barker, R. G. (*1948*). The social psychology of physical disability. *J. soc. Issues,* **4** (4), 28–38.

Barker, R., Dembo, T., & Lewin, K. (*1941*). Frustration and regression: an experiment with young children. *Univ. of Iowa Stud. Child Welf.,* **18** (1).

Barker, R. G., & Wright, B. A. (1952). The social psychology of adjustment to physical disability. In J. F. Garrett (Ed.), *Psychological aspects of physical disability*. Dept. of Health, Education, & Welf., Office of Vocational Rehabilit., Rehabilit. Service Series, No. 210, pp. 18–32.

Barker, R. G., & Wright, B. A. (1954). Disablement: the somatopsychological problem. In E. D. Wittkower & R. A. Cleghorn (Eds.), *Recent developments in psychosomatic medicine*. Philadelphia: Lippincott. Pp. 419–435.

Barker, R. G., Wright, B. A., & Gonick, H. R. (1946). *Adjustment to physical handicap and illness: a survey of the social psychology of physique and disability*. New York: Soc. Sci. Res. Council, Bull. 55.

Barker, R. G., Wright, B. A., Myerson, L., & Gonick, M. R. (1953). *Adjustment to physical handicap and illness: a survey of the social psychology of physique and disability*. 2d ed. New York: Soc. Sci. Res. Council, Bull. 55.

Barker, R. G., & Wright, H. F. (1948–1951). One of a series of records made in connection with the natural living conditions of children. See following reference.

Barker, R. G., & Wright, H. F. (1955). *Midwest and its children: the psychological ecology of an American town*. Evanston, Ill.: Row, Peterson.

Barron, M. E. (1947). Role practice in interview training. *Sociatry*, **1**, 198–208.

Bavelas, A. (1942). Morale and the training of leaders. In G. Watson (Ed.), *Civilian Morale*. New York: Reynal & Hitchcock. Pp. 143–165.

Bavelas, A. (1947). Role playing and management training. *Sociatry*, **1**, 183–191.

Berger, E. M. (1952). The relation between expressed acceptance of self and expressed acceptance of others. *J. abnorm. soc. Psychol.*, **4**, 778–783.

Berger, S. (1951). The role of sexual impotence in the concept of self in male paraplegics. Unpublished doctoral dissertation, New York Univ. Ann Arbor: University Microfilms, Publication No. 3606.

Bettelheim, B. (1943). Individual and mass behavior in extreme situations. *J. abnorm. soc. Psychol.*, **38**, 417–452.

Bice, H. V. (1950). Fathers participate in counseling series. *Cerebral Palsy Rev.*, **11**, 1–6.

Bice, H. V. (1955). Parent counseling and parent education. In W. M. Cruickshank & G. M. Raus (Eds.), *Cerebral palsy: its individual and community problems*. Syracuse Univ. Press. Pp. 411–428.

Blake, R. R., & Ramsey, G. V. (Eds.) (1951). *Perception—an approach to personality*. New York: Ronald Press.

Blakeslee, H. (1948). *Know your heart*. Public Affairs Pamphlet No. 137, New York.

Blank, H. R. (1957). Psychoanalysis and blindness. *Psychoanalytic Quart.*, **26**, 1–24.

Boorstein, S. W. (1935). *Orthopedics for the teachers of crippled children*. New York: Aiden.

Bradway, K. P. (1937). The social competence of deaf children. *Amer. Annals of the Deaf*, **82**, 122–140.

Brighouse, G. (1946). *The physically handicapped worker in industry*. Pasadena: California Institute of Technology, Bull. 13.

Bronfenbrenner, U. (*1951*). Toward an integrated theory of personality. In R. P. Blake & G. V. Ramsey (Eds.), *Perception—an approach to personality.* New York: Ronald Press, Pp. 206–257.

Brown, C. (*1955*). *My left foot.* New York: Simon & Schuster.

Bruckner, L. S. (*1954*). *Triumph of love.* New York: Simon & Schuster.

Bruner, J. S. (*1951*). Personality dynamics and the process of perceiving. In R. P. Blake & G. V. Ramsey (Eds.), *Perception—an approach to personality.* New York: Ronald Press. Pp. 121–147.

Bruner, J. S., & Postman, L. (*1948*). An approach to social perception. In W. Dennis (Ed.), *Current trends in social psychology.* Pittsburgh: Univ. of Pittsburgh Press. Pp. 71–118.

Bruner, J. S., & Postman, L. (*1949*). On the perception of incongruity: a paradigm. *J. Pers.,* **18,** 206–223.

Brunschwig, L. (*1936*). *A study of some personality aspects of deaf children.* New York: Teachers College, Columbia Univ.

Brunswik, E. (*1947*). *Systematic and representative design of psychological experiments.* Berkeley: Univ. of California Press.

Brunswik, E. (*1956*). *Perception and the representative design of psychological experiments.* 2nd ed. Berkeley: Univ. of California Press.

Brunswik, E., & Reiter, L. (*1937*). Eindrucks-Charaktere schematisierter Gesichter. *Zeitschrift f. Psychol.,* **142,** 67–134.

Buck, P. S. (*1950*). *The child who never grew.* New York: John Day.

Burchard, E. M. L., & Myklebust, H. R. (*1942*). A comparison of congenital and adventitious deafness with respect to its effect on intelligence, personality, and social maturity. Part II. Social Maturity. *Amer. Annals of the Deaf,* **87,** 241–251.

Cantor, A. J. (*1956*). General semantics of ambulatory proctology. In A. J. Cantor & A. N. Foxe (Eds.), *Psychosomatic aspects of surgery.* New York: Grune & Stratton. Pp. 78–88.

Cantor, A. J., & Foxe, A. N. (Eds.) (*1956*). *Psychosomatic aspects of surgery.* New York: Grune & Stratton.

Carlson, E. R. (*1941*). *Born that way.* New York: John Day.

Cartwright, D. (*1942*). The effect of interruption, completion, and failure upon the attractiveness of activities. *J. exp. Psychol.,* **31,** 1–16.

Cartwright, D., & Harary, F. (*1956*). Structural balance: a generalization of Heider's theory. *Psychol. Rev.,* **63,** 277–293.

Cattell, E., Dembo, T., Koppel, S., Tane-Baskin, E., & Weinstock, S. (*1949*). Social usefulness of the cosmetic glove. Unpublished, Research Division, College of Engineering, New York Univ. See Dembo & Tane-Baskin, 1955, for publication of part of the above.

Chevigny, H. (*1946*). *My eyes have a cold nose.* New Haven: Yale Univ. Press.

Cholden, L. (*1954*). Some psychiatric problems in the rehabilitation of the blind. *Bull., Menninger Clinic,* **18,** 107–112.

Citron, A. F., Chein, I., & Harding, J. (*1950*). Anti-minority remarks: a problem for action research, *J. abnorm. soc. Psychol.,* **45,** 99–126.

Citron, A. F., & Harding, J. (*1950*). An experiment in training volunteers to answer anti-minority remarks. *J. abnorm. soc. Psychol.,* **45,** 310–328.

Conference of Executives of Schools for the Deaf (1938). Report of the conference committee on nomenclature. *Amer. Annals of the Deaf,* **83,** 1–3.

Cowen, E. L., Underberg, R. P., & Verrillo, R. T. (1956). The development and testing of an attitudes to blindness scale. *J. soc. Psychol.,* in press.

Criddle, R. (1953). *Love is not blind.* New York: W. W. Norton.

Cruickshank, W. M. (1948). The impact of physical disability on social adjustment. *J. soc. Issues.,* **4** (4), 78–83.

Cruickshank, W. M. (1955). Educational planning for the cerebral palsied. In W. M. Cruickshank & G. M. Raus (Eds.), *Cerebral palsy: its individual and community problems.* Syracuse: Syracuse Univ. Press. Pp. 333–369.

Cruickshank, W. M., & Bice, H. V. (1955). Personality characteristics. In W. M. Cruickshank & G. M. Raus (Eds.), *Cerebral palsy: its individual and community problems.* Syracuse: Syracuse Univ. Press. Pp. 115–165.

Crutchfield, R. S. (1955). Conformity and character. *Amer. Psychologist,* **10,** 191–198.

Cutsforth, T. D. (1948). Personality crippling through physical disability. *J. soc. Issues.,* **4** (4), 62–67.

Daniels, A. S. (1948). I don't want to be different. *Crippled child,* **26** (4), 20.

Davis, F. (1958). *Polio in the family.* Unpublished doctoral dissertation, Univ. of Chicago.

Dembo, T. (1931). Der Ärger als dynamisches Problem. X. (Untersuchunger zur Handlungs—und Affektpsychologie. Ed. by Kurt Lewin.) *Psychol. Forsch.,* **15,** 1–144.

Dembo, T. (1953a). Investigation of concrete psychological value systems. Report submitted to the United States Public Health Services, Institute of Mental Health.

Dembo, T. (1953b). Devaluation of the physically handicapped person. Paper presented at Amer. Psychol. Ass., Cleveland.

Dembo, T. (1955). Suffering and its alleviation: a theoretical analysis. Report submitted to the Ass. for the Aid of Crippled Children, New York.

Dembo, T., Leviton, G. L., & Wright, B. A. (1956). Adjustment to misfortune —a problem of social psychological rehabilitation. *Artificial limbs,* **3,** 4–62.

Dembo, T., & Tane-Baskin, E. (1955). The noticeability of the cosmetic glove. *Artificial limbs,* **2,** 47–56.

Dinkel, R. M. (1947). The influence of nursery literature on child development. *Sociology and soc. Res.,* **31,** 285–290.

Dollard, J., Doob, L. W., Miller, N. E., Mowrer, O. H., & Sears, R. R. (1939). *Frustration and aggression.* New Haven: Yale Univ. Press.

Donofrio, A. F. (1948). A study of the intelligence, achievement and emotional adjustment of crippled children in an orthopedic hospital school. Doctoral dissertation, New York Univ.

Dunbar, F. (1954). *Emotions and bodily changes.* New York: Columbia Univ. Press.

Duncker, K. (1945). On problem solving, *Psychol. Monogr.,* **58,** 1–112.

Ellis, A. (1954). *The American sexual tragedy.* New York: Twayne Publishers.

Estes, S. G. (1938). Judging personality from expressive behavior. *J. abnorm. soc. Psychol.,* **33,** 217–236.

Faterson, H. F., as reported by Paterson, D. G. (*1930*). *Physique and Intellect.* New York: Century.

Faterson, H. F. (*1931*). Organic inferiority and the inferiority attitude. *J. soc. Psychol.,* **2,** 87–101.

Feigl, H. (*1953*). The scientific outlook: naturalism and humanism. In H. Feigl & M. Brodbeck (Eds.) *Readings in the philosophy of science.* New York: Appleton-Century-Crofts. Pp. 8–18. This article originally appeared in *Amer. Quart.,* **1,** 1949.

Fenichel, O. (*1945*). *The psychoanalytic theory of neurosis.* New York: Norton.

Festinger, L. (*1953*). Group attraction and membership. In D. Cartwright & A. Zander (Eds.), *Group dynamics: research and theory.* Evanston, Ill.: Row, Peterson. Pp. 92–101.

Festinger, L. (*1954*). A theory of social comparison processes. *Human Relations,* **7,** 117–140.

Fey, W. F. (*1955*). Acceptance by others and its relation to acceptance of self and others: a revaluation. *J. abnorm. soc. Psychol.,* **50,** 274–276.

Fiedler, F. E., Warrington, W. G., & Blaisdell, F. J. (*1952*). Unconscious attitudes as correlates of sociometric choice in a social group. *J. abnorm. soc. Psychol.,* **47,** 790–796.

Fielding, B. B. (*1950*). Attitudes and aspects of adjustment of the orthopedically handicapped woman. Unpublished doctoral dissertation, Columbia Univ.

Fisher, S., & Cleveland, S. E. (*1958*). *Body image and personality.* New York: Van Nostrand.

Fishman, S. (*1949*). Self-concept and adjustment to leg prosthesis. Unpublished doctoral dissertation, Columbia Univ.

Fitzgerald, D. C. (*1950*). Success-failure and T.A.T. reactions of orthopedically handicapped and physically normal adolescents. *J. Pers.,* **1,** 67–83.

Ford, H., in collaboration with S. Crowther (*1926*). *My life and work.* New York: Doubleday, Page.

Foster, I. A. (*1948*). How to cope with teen age problems. *Crippled child,* **27** (4), 9.

French, J. R. P., Jr. (*1944*). Retraining an autocratic leader. *J. abnorm. soc. Psychol.,* **39,** 224–237.

French, J. R. P., Jr. (*1945*). Role-playing as a method of training foremen. In J. L. Moreno (Ed.), *Group psychotherapy.* Beacon, N.Y.: Beacon House. Pp. 172–187.

Freud, S. (*1933*). *New introductory lectures on psychoanalysis.* New York: Norton.

Fromm, E. (*1939*). Selfishness and self-love. *Psychiatry,* **2,** 507–523.

Fromm-Reichmann, F., & Moreno, J. L. (Eds.) (*1956*). *Progress in psychotherapy.* New York: Grune & Stratton.

Garrett, J. F. (Ed.) (*1952*). *Psychological aspects of physical disability.* Washington, D.C.: U.S. Government Printing Office, Office of Vocational Rehabilitation, Rehabilitation Service Series 210.

Garrett, J. F. (*1955*). Realistic vocational guidance and placement. In W. M.

Cruickshank & G. M. Raus (Eds.), *Cerebral palsy: its individual and community problems.* Syracuse: Syracuse Univ. Press. Pp. 429–461.

Gebhard, M. E. (*1948*). The effect of success and failure upon the attractiveness of activities as a function of experience, expectation, and need. *J. exp. Psychol.,* **38,** 371–88.

Gesell, A., & Ilg, F. L. (*1943*). *Infant and child in the culture of today.* New York: Harper.

Gilmore, L. (*1953*). *New fountains* (An American Theatre Wing Community Play). New York: Nat'l Foundation for Infantile Paralysis.

Glick, S. J. (*1953*). *Vocational, educational, and recreational needs of the cerebral palsied adult.* New York: United Cerebral Palsy.

Goldman, R. L. (*1947*). *Even the night.* New York: Macmillan.

Goldstein, K. (*1939*). *The organism.* New York: American Book.

Goodwin, R. B. (*1953*). *It's good to be black.* Garden City, N.Y.: Doubleday.

Haire, M., & Grunes, W. F. (*1950*). Perceptual defenses: processes protecting an organized perception of another personality. *Human Relations,* **3,** 403–412.

Hall, C. S., & Lindzey, G. (*1957*). *Theories of personality.* New York: Wiley.

Halstead, W. C. (*1951*). Brain and intelligence. In L. A. Jeffress (Ed.), *Cerebral mechanisms in behavior: The Hixon Symposium.* New York: Wiley. Pp. 244–272.

Hamilton, K. W. (*1950*). *Counseling the handicapped in the rehabilitation process.* New York: Ronald.

Hanks, J. R., & Hanks, L. M., Jr. (*1948*). The physically handicapped in certain non-occidental societies. *J. soc. Issues,* **4** (4), 11–20.

Harrower, H. R., & Herrmann, R. (*1953*). *Psychological factors in the care of patients with multiple sclerosis for use of physicians.* New York: National Multiple Sclerosis Society.

Hathaway, K. B. (*1943*). *The little locksmith.* New York: Coward-McCann.

Hebb, D. O. (*1946*). On the nature of fear. *Psychol. Rev.,* **53,** 259–276.

Heider, F. (*1944*). Social perception and phenomenal causality. *Psychol. Rev.,* **51,** 358–374.

Heider, F. (*1958*). *The psychology of interpersonal relations.* New York: Wiley.

Heider, F., & Heider, G. M. (*1941*). Studies in the psychology of the deaf, No. 2. *Psychol. Monogr.,* **53** (5).

Heisler, V. T. (*1951*). Goal setting behavior of crippled and non-crippled children in situations of success and failure. Unpublished doctoral dissertation, Stanford Univ.

Helping the physically limited child (1952–1953). Board of Education, New York, N.Y., Curriculum Bull., Series No. 7.

Henderson, L. T. (*1954*). *The opening doors.* New York: John Day.

Hentig, H. von (*1948a*). *The criminal and his victim.* New Haven: Yale Univ. Press.

Hentig, H. von (*1948b*). Physical disability, mental conflict and social crisis. *J. soc. Issues,* **4** (4), 21–27.

Hilgard, E. R., & Russell, D. H. (*1950*). Motivation in school learning. *Yearb. nat. soc. Stud. Educ.,* **49** (Part I), 36–68.

Holst, J. C. (*1952*). The occurrence of blindness in Norway, *Am. J. Ophthalmology,* **35**, 1153–1166.

Hooton, E. A. (*1939*). *Crime and the man.* Cambridge: Harvard Univ. Press.

Horney, K. (*1937*). *The neurotic personality of our time.* New York: Norton.

Hughes, E. C. (*1945*). Dilemmas and contradictions of status. *Am. J. Sociology,* **50**, 353–359.

Hurlock, E. B. (*1925*). An evaluation of certain incentives used in school work. *J. educ. Psychol.,* **16**, 145–159.

Ichheiser, G. (*1949*). Misunderstandings in human relations. *Amer. J. Sociol.,* **55** (supplement to No. 2), 1–70.

Institute for Physical Medicine and Rehabilitation (*1957*). *Primer for paraplegics and quadriplegics.* Patient Publication No. 1, New York University, Bellevue Medical Center.

Interrelationships between perception and personality (*1949*). (Symposium.) *J. Pers.,* **18**, 1–266.

Janis, I. L. (*1958*). *Psychological stress: psychoanalytic and behavioral studies of surgical patients.* New York: Wiley.

Janis, I. L., & Feshbach, S. (*1953*). The effects of fear-arousing communications. *J. abnorm. soc. Psychol.,* **48**, 78–92.

Johnson, D. L. (*1954*). A study of rigidity in the personality of deaf children. Master's thesis, Univ. of Kansas.

Johnson, W. (*1946*). *People in quandaries.* New York: Harper.

Johnson, W. (*1950*). Open letter to the parent of a stuttering child. *Crippled child,* **28** (3), 7–9.

Kahn, H. (*1951*). A comparative investigation of the responses to frustration of normal-hearing and hypacousic children. Ann Arbor: University Microfilms, Publication No. 2766. Brief summary appears in *Microfilm Abstr.* (*1951*), **11**, 959–960.

Kammerer, R. C. (*1940*). An exploratory psychological study of crippled children. *Psychol. rec.,* **4**, 47–100.

Katz, D., & Braly, K. (*1933*). Racial stereotypes of one hundred college students. *J. abnorm. soc. Psychol.,* **28**, 280–290.

Keister, H. E. (*1937*). The behavior of young children in failure. *Univ. of Iowa Studies in Child Welfare,* **14**, 27–82.

Kelley, H. H. (*1950*). The warm-cold variable in first impressions of persons. *J. Pers.,* **18**, 431–439.

Kerby, C. E. (*1952*). A report on visual handicaps of partially seeing children. *J. except. Child.,* **18**, 137–142.

Kessler, H. H. (*1953*). *Rehabilitation of the physically handicapped.* Rev. ed. New York: Columbia Univ. Press.

Killilea, M. (*1952*). *Karen.* Englewood Cliffs: Prentice-Hall.

Klein, G. S. (*1951*). The personal world through perception. In R. R. Blake & G. V. Ramsey (Eds.) *Perception—an approach to personality.* New York: Ronald. Pp. 328–355.

Köhler, W. (*1947*). *Gestalt psychology.* 2nd ed. New York: Liveright.

Korzybski, A. (*1951*). The Role of Language in the perceptual processes. In R. R. Blake & G. V. Ramsey (Eds.), *Perception—an approach to personality.* New York: Ronald. Pp. 170–205.

Krech, D., & Crutchfield, R. S. (*1948*). *Theory and problems of social psychology.* New York: McGraw-Hill.

Kretschmer, E. (*1925*). *Physique and character.* New York: Harcourt, Brace. Translated by W. J. H. Sprott from *Körperbau und charakter.* Berlin: Springer, 1921.

Ladieu, G., Adler, D. L., & Dembo, T. (*1948*). Studies in adjustment to visible injuries: social acceptance of the injured. *J. soc. Issues,* **4** (4), 55–61.

Ladieu, G., Hanfmann, E., & Dembo, T. (*1947*). Studies in adjustment to visible injuries: evaluation of help by the injured. *J. abnorm. soc. Psychol.,* **42**, 169–192.

Landis, C., & Bolles, M. M. (*1942*). *Personality and sexuality of the physically handicapped woman.* New York, London: Paul B. Hoeber.

Langdon, G., & Stout, I. W. (*1951*). *These well-adjusted children.* New York: John Day.

Laycock, S. R., & Stevenson, G. S. (*1950*). Parents' problems with exceptional children. In the Education of exceptional children. *Yearb. nat. soc. Stud. Educ.,* **49** (Part II), 117–134.

Lecky, P. (*1945*). *Self-consistency: a theory of personality.* New York: Island Press.

Lee, D. D. (*1947*). A linguistic approach to a system of values. In T. M. Newcomb & E. L. Hartley (Eds.), *Readings in social psychology.* New York: Holt. Pp. 219–224.

Levine, E. S. (*1956*). *Youth in a soundless world: a search for personality.* New York: New York Univ. Press.

Levy, D. M. (*1932*). Body interest in children and hypochondriasis. *Amer. J. Psychiat.,* **12**, 295–315.

Levy, J. H. (*1952*). A study of parent groups for handicapped children. *Excep. Child.,* **19**, 19–26.

Lewin, G. W. (*1957*). Some characteristics of the socio-psychological life space of the epileptic patient. *Human relations,* **10**, 249–256.

Lewin, K. (*1935*). *A dynamic theory of personality.* New York: McGraw-Hill.

Lewin, K. (*1936*). *Principles of topological psychology.* New York: McGraw-Hill.

Lewin, K. (*1938*). The conceptual representation and measurement of psychological forces. *Contr. psychol. Theory.,* **1** (4).

Lewin, K. (*1939*). Field theory and experiment in social psychology: concepts and methods. *Amer. J. Sociol.,* **44**, 868–896.

Lewin, K. (*1948*). *Resolving social conflicts.* Lewin, G. W. (Ed.). New York: Harper.

Lewin, K., Dembo, T., Festinger, L., & Sears, P. S. (*1944*). Level of aspiration. In J. H. Hunt (Ed.), *Personality and the behavior disorders.* New York: Ronald. Pp. 333–378.

Linck, L. J. (*1954*). Cripples. (As written for publication in the *Encyclopaedia*

Britannica.) Chicago: The National Society for Crippled Children and Adults.

Linduska, N. (*1947*). *My polio past.* Chicago: Pellegrini & Cudahy.

Lindzey, G., & Rogolsky, S. (*1950*). Prejudice and identification of minority group membership. *J. abnorm. soc. Psychol.,* **45,** 37–53.

Lippitt, Ronald (*1940*). An experimental study of authoritarian and democratic group atmospheres. Studies in topological and vector psychology. *Univ. of Iowa Studies in Child Welfare,* **16** (3), 44–195.

Lippitt, Ronald (*1943*). The psychodrama in leadership training. *Sociometry,* **6,** 286–292.

Lippitt, Ronald (*1945*). To be or not to be—a Jew. *J. soc. Issues,* **1,** 18–27.

Lippitt, Rosemary (*1947*). Psychodrama in the home. *Sociatry,* **1,** 148–167.

Lombroso, C. (*1911*). *Crime, its causes and remedies.* (Translated by H. P. Horton.) Boston: Little, Brown.

Lowenfeld, B. (*1956*). *Our blind children.* Springfield, Ill.: Thomas.

Lubin, A. (*1957*). Replicability as a publication criterion. *Amer. Psychologist,* **12,** 519–520.

McAndrew, H. (*1948*). Rigidity and isolation: a study of the deaf and the blind. *J. abnorm. soc. Psychol.,* **43,** 476–494.

McDougall, W. (*1918*), *An introduction to social psychology.* 13th ed. Boston: Luce.

Macgregor, F. C. (*1951*). Some psycho-social problems associated with facial deformities. *Amer. soc. Rev.,* **16,** 629–638.

Macgregor, F. C., Abel, T. M., Bryt, A., Lauer, E., & Weissmann, S. (*1953*). *Facial deformities and plastic surgery.* Springfield, Ill.: Thomas.

McKenna, Sr. Helen V., S.S.J., Hofstaetter, P. R., & O'Connor, J. P. (*1956*). The concepts of the ideal self and of the friend. *J. Pers.,* **24,** 262–271.

Maisel, E. (*1953*). *Meet a body.* New York: Institute for the Crippled and Disabled. Manuscript.

Maslow, A. H. (*1939*). Dominance, personality, and social behavior in women. *J. soc. Psychol.,* **10,** 3–39.

Maslow, A. H., & Mittlemann, B. (*1951*). *Principles of abnormal psychology: the dynamics of psychic illness.* Rev. ed. New York: Harper.

Maslow, A. H. (*1954*). *Motivation and personality.* New York: Harper.

Mead, M. (*1949*). *Male and female, a study of the sexes in a changing world.* New York: Morrow.

Meng, H. (*1938*). Zur Sozialpsychologie der Körperbeschädigten: Ein Beitrag zum Problem der praktischen Psychohygiene. *Schweizer Archiv für Neurologie und Psychiatrie,* **40,** 328–344. (Reported in Barker *et al.,* 1953.)

Meyer, A. (*1948*). *The common sense psychiatry of Dr. Adolf Meyer: 52 selected papers.* Lief, A. (Ed.) New York: McGraw-Hill.

Meyerson, L. (*1948*). Physical disability as a social psychological problem. *J. soc. Issues,* **4** (4), 2–10.

Meyerson, L. (*1953*). The visually handicapped. *Rev. of Ed. Res.,* **23,** 476–491.

Meyerson, L. (*1955a*). A psychology of impaired hearing. In W. M. Cruickshank (Ed.), *Psychology of exceptional children and youth.* Englewood Cliffs, N.J.: Prentice-Hall. Pp. 120–183.

Meyerson, L. (*1955b*). Somatopsychology of physical disability. In W. M. Cruickshank (Ed.), *Psychology of exceptional children and youth.* Englewood Cliffs, N.J.: Prentice-Hall. Pp. 1–60.

Meyerson, L. (*1956*). Hearing for speech in children: a verbal audiometric test. *Acta Oto-Laryngologica,* Supplementum 128.

Meyerson, L. (*1957*). Special disabilities. In P. R. Farnsworth (Ed.), *Annual review of psychology,* Vol. 8. Palo Alto: Annual Reviews, Inc. Pp. 437–457.

Miers, E. S. (*1949*). Goals as we see them. Delivered in panel discussion at convention of National Society for Crippled Children and Adults, New York, N.Y. Speech printed as leaflet put out by NSCCA.

Miers, E. S. (*1953*). Gosh, I'm glad I'm handicapped. *The crippled child,* **31,** 4–7.

Miller, E. A. (*1958*). Cerebral-palsied children and their parents. *Exceptional child.,* **24,** 298–302, 305.

Monahan, F. (*1941*). *Women in crime.* New York: Ives Washburn.

Moreno, J. L. (*1937*). Inter-personal therapy and the psychopathology of interpersonal relations. *Sociometry,* **1,** 9–76.

Mowrer, O. H. (*1938*). Some research implications of the frustration concept as related to social and educational problems. *Charact. & Pers.,* **7,** 129–135.

Murphy, G. (*1947*). *Personality: a biosocial approach to origins and structure.* New York: Harper.

Murphy, L. (*1956*). *Personality in young children.* (With the collaboration of E. Beyer, A. Hartoch, E. Lerner, L. J. Stone, & T. Schmidl-Waehner.) New York: Basic Books.

Mussen, P. H., & Barker, R. G. (*1944*). Attitudes toward cripples. *J. abnorm. soc. Psychol.,* **39,** 351–355.

Myklebust, H. R. (*1950*). *Your deaf child: a guide for parents.* Springfield, Ill.: Thomas.

National Health Education Committee (*1955*). *Facts on the major killing and crippling diseases in the U.S. today.* New York: The National Health Education Committee.

Newcomb, T. (*1950*). *Social psychology.* New York: Dryden.

Ohnstad, K. (*1942*). *The world at my finger tips.* Indianapolis & New York: Bobbs-Merrill.

Orgel, S. Z., & Tuckman, J. (*1935*). Nicknames of institutional children. *Amer. J. Orthopsychiat.,* **5,** 276–285.

Orlansky, H. (*1949*). Infant care and personality. *Psychol. Bull.,* **46,** 1–48.

Piaget, J. (*1926*). *The language and thought of the child.* New York: Harcourt, Brace.

Piaget, J. (*1932*). *The moral judgment of the child.* New York: Harcourt, Brace.

Postman, L., & Bruner, J. S. (*1949*). Multiplicity of set as a determinant of perceptual behavior. *J. exp. Psychol.,* **39,** 369–377.

Randall, G. C., Ewalt, J. R., & Blair, H. (*1945*). Psychiatric reaction to amputation. *J. Amer. medical Ass.,* **128,** 645–652.

Ray, M. H. (*1946*). The effect of crippled appearance on personality judgment. Master's thesis, Stanford University.

Rogers, C. R. (*1951*). *Client-centered therapy, its current practice, implications, and theory.* New York: Houghton-Mifflin.

Rogers, C. R., & Dymond, R. F. (Eds.) (*1954*). *Psychotherapy and personality change: co-ordinated research studies in the client-centered approach.* Chicago: Univ. of Chicago Press.

Rosenzweig, S. (*1938*). A general outline of frustration. *Charact. & Pers.*, **7**, 151–160.

Rosenzweig, S., Fleming, E. E., & Rosenzweig, L. (*1948*). The children's form of the Rosenzweig picture frustration study. *J. Psychol.*, **26**, 141–191.

Rotter, J. B. (*1943*). Level of aspiration as a method of studying personality. III. Group validity studies. *Charact. & Pers.*, **11**, 255–274.

Rusk, H. A., & Taylor, E. J. (*1946*). *New hope for the handicapped.* New York: Harper.

Rusk, H. A., & Taylor, E. J. (*1948*). Employment for the disabled. *J. soc. Issues*, **4** (4), 101–106.

Rusk, H. A., & Taylor, E. J. (*1953*). *Living with a disability.* Garden City, N.Y.: Blakiston.

Russell, H., with Rosen, V. (*1949*). *Victory in my hands.* New York: Farrar, Straus, and Cudahy, Inc.

Rutledge, L. (*1954*). Aspiration levels of deaf children as compared with those of hearing children. *J. Speech & Hearing Disorders*, **19**, 375–380.

Samuels, M. R. (*1939*). Judgments of faces. *Charact. & Pers.*, **8**, 18–27.

Sapir, E. (*1931*). Conceptual categories in primitive languages. *Science*, **74**, 578. Abstract.

Saul, L. J. (*1947*). *Emotional maturity; the development and dynamics of personality.* Philadelphia: J. B. Lippincott.

Schachter, S. (*1951*). Deviation, rejection, and communication. *J. abnorm. soc. Psychol.*, **46**, 190–207.

Scheerer, M. (*1954*). Cognitive theory. In G. Lindzey (Ed.), *Handbook of social psychology.* Cambridge: Addison-Wesley. Pp. 91–142.

Schilder, P. (*1935*). *The image and appearance of the human body.* London: Kegan Paul, Trench, Trubner.

Schilder, P. (*1953*). *Medical psychology.* (Trans. & Ed., D. Rapaport.) New York: International Univ. Press.

Sears, P. S. (*1940*). Levels of aspiration in academically successful and unsuccessful children. *J. abnorm. soc. Psychol.*, **35**, 498–536.

Sears, R. R., Maccoby, E. E., & Levin, H. (*1957*). In collaboration with E. L. Lowell, P. S. Sears, & J. W. M. Whiting. *Patterns of child rearing.* Evanston, Ill.: Row, Peterson.

Seidenfeld, M. A. (*1948a*). The psychological sequelae of poliomyelitis in children. *Nerv. child*, **7**, 14–28.

Seidenfeld, M. A. (*1948b*). A clinical appraisal of the use of non-directive therapy in the care of the chronically ill. *J. clin. Psychol.*, **4**, 244–248.

Sheerer, E. T. (*1949*). An analysis of the relationship between acceptance of and respect for self and acceptance of and respect for others in ten counseling cases. *J. consult. Psychol.*, **13**, 169–175.

Sheldon, W. H. (*1940*). With the collaboration of S. S. Stevens & W. B.

Tucker. *The varieties of human physique, an introduction to constitutional psychology.* New York: Harper.

Sheldon, W. H. (*1942*). With the collaboration of S. S. Stevens. *The varieties of temperament; a psychology of constitutional differences.* New York: Harper.

Sheldon, W. H. (*1944*). Constitutional factors in personality. In J. M. Hunt (Ed.), *Personality and the behavior disorders.* New York: Ronald. Pp. 526–549.

Sheldon, W. H. (*1949*). With the collaboration of E. H. Hartl & E. McDermott. *Varieties of delinquent youth; an introduction to constitutional psychiatry.* New York: Harper.

Shelsky, I. (*1957*). The effect of disability on self-concept. Unpublished doctoral dissertation, Columbia Univ.

Shere, M. O. (*1954*). An evaluation of the social and emotional development of the cerebral palsied twin. Unpublished doctoral dissertation, Univ. of Illinois. Ann Arbor: Univ. Microfilms, Publication No. 9140.

Sherif, M., & Cantril, H. (*1947*). *The psychology of ego-involvements, social attitudes and identifications.* New York: Wiley.

Shortley, M. J. (*1948*). Introduction. In H. H. Kessler & D. Kerr, *Civilian amputees in action.* Washington, D.C.: U.S. Government Printing Office.

Simmons, L. W. (*1952*). Social participation of the aged in different cultures. *Ann. Amer. Acad. Pol. & Soc. Sci.,* **279,** 43–51.

Smith, L. E. (*1954*). *The journey.* New York: World.

Snell, E. E. (*1955*). Physical therapy. In W. M. Cruickshank & G. M. Raus (Eds.), *Cerebral palsy: its individual and community problems.* Syracuse: Syracuse Univ. Press. Pp. 257–293.

Sommers, V. S. (*1944*). *The influence of parental attitudes and social environment on the personality development of the adolescent blind.* New York: Amer. Found. for the Blind.

Spock, B. (*1946*). *The common sense book of baby and child care.* New York: Duell, Sloan and Pearce.

Springer, N. N. (*1938*). A comparative study of psychoneurotic responses of deaf and hearing children. *J. educ. Psychol.,* **29,** 459–466.

Stafford, G. T. (*1947*). *Sports for the handicapped.* 2d ed. Englewood Cliffs, N.J.: Prentice-Hall.

Steckle, L. C. (*1949*). *Problems of human adjustment.* New York: Harper.

Stern, E. M., with Castendyck, E. (*1950*). *The handicapped child, a guide for parents.* New York: Wyn.

Stolz, H. R., & Stolz, L. M. (*1944*). Adolescent problems related to somatic variations in adolescence. *Yearb. nat. Soc. Stud. Educ.,* **43** (Part I). Pp. 80–99.

Stratton, A. J. (*1957*). Patient's concepts of tuberculosis: observations and implications. Paper presented at the Nat. Tuberculosis Ass. Convention, Kansas City, 1957 as reported in *Newsletter for Psychologists in Tuberculosis,* **4,** 38–43.

Streng, A., & Kirk, S. A. (*1938*). The social competence of deaf and hard-of-hearing children in a public day school. *Amer. Ann. of the Deaf,* **83,** 244–254.

Strong, E. K., Jr. (*1931*). *Change of interests with age.* Stanford: Stanford Univ. Press.

Sullivan, H. S. (*1953*). H. S. Perry & M. L. Gawel, Eds. *The interpersonal theory of psychiatry.* New York: Norton.

Sutter, R. C. (*1954*). Acceptance and rejection. A tape recording of a discussion with cerebral palsied children presented at the International Council for Exceptional Children, Cincinnati, Ohio.

Thompson, C. (*1950*). With the collaboration of P. Mullahy. *Psychoanalysis: evolution and development.* New York: Hermitage.

Thorndike, E. L. (*1920*). A constant error in psychological ratings. *J. appl. Psychol.,* **4,** 25–29.

Tracht, V. A. (*1946*). A comparative study of personality factors among cerebral palsied and non-handicapped persons. Master's thesis, Univ. of Chicago.

Understanding the disabled (*1956*). Prepared by the National Foundation for Infantile Paralysis and the Citizen Education Project. New York: Columbia Univ. Citizen Education Project.

Viscardi, H., Jr. (*1952*). *A man's stature.* New York: John Day.

Volkart, E. H., & Michael, S. T. (*1957*). Bereavement and mental health. In A. H. Leighton, J. A. Clausen, & R. N. Wilson (Eds.), *Explorations in social psychiatry.* New York: Basic Books. Pp. 281–304.

Warfield, F. (*1948*). *Cotton in my ears.* New York: Viking.

Weiss, E., & English, O. S. (*1943*). *Psychosomatic medicine.* Philadelphia: Saunders.

Wenar, C. (*1953*). The effects of a motor handicap on personality: the effects on level of aspiration. *Child development,* **24,** 123–130.

White, G. (*1955*). Social casework in relation to cerebral palsy. In W. M. Cruickshank & G. M. Raus (Eds.), *Cerebral palsy: its individual and community problems.* Syracuse: Syracuse Univ. Press. Pp. 462–500.

White, R. K., Wright, B. A., & Dembo, T. (*1948*). Studies in adjustment to visible injuries: evaluation of curiosity by the injured. *J. abnorm. soc. Psychol.,* **43,** 13–28.

White, R. W. (*1948*). *The abnormal personality.* New York: Ronald.

Whiting, J. W. M., & Child, I. L. (*1953*). *Child training and personality.* New Haven: Yale Univ. Press.

Whorf, B. L. (*1947*). Science and linguistics. In T. M. Newcomb & E. L. Hartley (Eds.), *Readings in social psychology.* New York: Holt. Pp. 210–218.

Wilson, A. J. (*1950*). *The emotional life of the ill and injured; the psychology and mental hygiene of rehabilitation and guidance.* New York: Social Science Publishers.

Winkler, H. (*1931*). *Psychische Entwicklung und krüppeltum.* Leipzig: Leopold Voss. (Reported in Barker, *et al.,* 1953, *op. cit.*)

Witkin, H. A., Lewis, H. B., Hertzman, M., Machover, K., Meissner, P. B., &

Wapner, S. (*1954*). *Personality through perception: an experimental and clinical study.* New York: Harper.

Wittkower, E. D. (*1949*). *A psychiatrist looks at tuberculosis.* London: Nat. Ass. for the Prevention of Tuberculosis.

Wittkower, E. D., & Cleghorn, R. A. (Eds.) (*1954*). *Recent developments in psychosomatic medicine.* Philadelphia: Lippincott.

Wolff, W. (*1943*). *The Expression of personality: experimental depth psychology.* New York: Harper.

Woodworth, R. S., & Marquis, D. G. (*1947*). *Psychology.* 5th ed. New York: Holt.

Wright, B. A. (Ed.) (*1959*). *Psychology and rehabilitation.* Washington, D.C.: Amer. Psychol. Ass.

Yatsushiro, T. (*1953*). Political and socio-cultural issues at Poston and Manzanar relocation centers—a themal analysis. Unpublished doctoral dissertation, Cornell Univ.

Zander, A. (*1947*). Role playing: a technique for training the necessarily dominating leaders. *Sociatry,* **1,** 225–235.

Index of Names

Index of Subjects